AF847254

39,–

'17

Financial Stability Policy in the Euro Zone

Gundbert Scherf

Financial Stability Policy in the Euro Zone

The Political Economy of National Banking Regulation in an Integrating Monetary Union

Foreword by Prof. Dr. Henrik Enderlein

Springer Gabler

MÄNGELEXEMPLAR

Gundbert Scherf
Freie Universität Berlin
Berlin, Germany

Dissertation Freie Universität Berlin, 2012

ISBN 978-3-658-00982-3 ISBN 978-3-658-00983-0 (eBook)
DOI 10.1007/978-3-658-00983-0

The Deutsche Nationalbibliothek lists this publication in the Deutsche Nationalbibliografie; detailed bibliographic data are available in the Internet at http://dnb.d-nb.de.

Library of Congress Control Number: 2013941552

Springer Gabler
© Springer Fachmedien Wiesbaden 2014
This work is subject to copyright. All rights are reserved by the Publisher, whether the whole or part of the material is concerned, specifically the rights of translation, reprinting, reuse of illustrations, recitation, broadcasting, reproduction on microfilms or in any other physical way, and transmission or information storage and retrieval, electronic adaptation, computer software, or by similar or dissimilar methodology now known or hereafter developed. Exempted from this legal reservation are brief excerpts in connection with reviews or scholarly analysis or material supplied specifically for the purpose of being entered and executed on a computer system, for exclusive use by the purchaser of the work. Duplication of this publication or parts thereof is permitted only under the provisions of the Copyright Law of the Publisher's location, in its current version, and permission for use must always be obtained from Springer. Permissions for use may be obtained through RightsLink at the Copyright Clearance Center. Violations are liable to prosecution under the respective Copyright Law. The use of general descriptive names, registered names, trademarks, service marks, etc. in this publication does not imply, even in the absence of a specific statement, that such names are exempt from the relevant protective laws and regulations and therefore free for general use. While the advice and information in this book are believed to be true and accurate at the date of publication, neither the authors nor the editors nor the publisher can accept any legal responsibility for any errors or omissions that may be made. The publisher makes no warranty, express or implied, with respect to the material contained herein.

Printed on acid-free paper

Springer Gabler is a brand of Springer DE.
Springer DE is part of Springer Science+Business Media.
www.springer-gabler.de

For Emma

Foreword

Research on banking regulation has something of a Cinderella-like existence. On the one hand, the topic is clearly among the most salient, policy-relevant and thus clearly most attractive areas of study in political economy. But on the other hand, its high degree of complexity and technicality makes it one of the least researched topics in the field – some might say the field is boring. They are wrong. And this book tells them why. The choice over different types of banking regulation is not technical or technocratic. It reflects highly political considerations that reflect societal preferences. This books main contribution is to illustrate those choices and to explain why they have been approached differently in different countries.

The book thus provides a map to largely unchartered territory. Still several years ago, too few researchers seemed motivated to enter that field at the intersection of economics and political science. Only after the "great financial market crisis" this now seems to be changing. There is a quickly emerging interest in the understanding of different approaches to banking regulation, their institutional context, their underlying trade-offs, their strengths and weaknesses. Indeed, the international variety of banking regulation systems, approaches and practices is still very high – and this despite the considerable degree of international financial market integration and various regulatory attempts at harmonization (i.e., the Basel Accords). That paradox of banking regulation is particularly pronounced in the Economic and Monetary Union in Europe (EMU), where different national regulatory regimes coexist in the presence of a single currency. The variation in practices has led to the observed patterns of bank leverage and financial instability in Europe, which materialized over the financial crisis of 2007/8 and developed into continuous liabilities in the Euro crisis. Why?

Gundbert Scherf takes up this question. His book combines the economic analysis of the mechanics of the public good of financial stability with the politics that result from the multiplicity of economic interests and principals bargaining over the optimal use of a very limited set of instruments in this policy field. Through its rigorous analysis and understanding of these political economy interactions, this book provides original and relevant insights into the workings of financial stability policy in Europe.

The findings point to the importance of domestic institutions and political economy interests in explaining how regulators solve the trade-off between different objectives of regulation. Most centrally, this work identifies the key trade-offs in banking regulation as a new policy trilemma. This trilemma of regulation conceptually and empirically develops this three-way trade-off, arguing that the goals of (i) financial stability, (ii) international competitiveness of banks, and (iii) credit provision to the domestic economy cannot be pursued simultaneously. This trilemma, as is shown convincingly, has strong implications as it represents a limitation on purely stability-oriented regulatory and supervisory policy and ultimately can lead to excessive bank leverage – particularly in uncoordinated interaction with monetary policy. The trilemma is the most important analytical contribution of this work and constitutes also a key reference point that could inform further research as well as policy debate at large.

The book also shows that the incompatibility of the different objectives of the trilemma is particularly pronounced in the Euro area with its economically highly diverse but politically sovereign countries under the common umbrella of a shared currency. Not surprisingly, there have been large differences within EMU in terms on approaches to international regulatory standards. Breaking with prior accounts, which linked the stringency or laxity of regulatory policy along the Anglo-Saxon vs. Continental Europe divide, this book asks us to turn the focus towards the political economy make-up and in particular the degree of bank-reliance in European economies and relative strength of financial stakeholders to explain policy preferences of regulators.

We should take the approach of the book very seriously. It is impossible to think about a "Banking Union" in Europe or a "Single Supervisory Mechanism" without previously understanding the tension between the different policy goals as discussed in this book. In essence, the book argues that banking supervision as a national domain will make hawkish supervision politically unviable due to domestic political interests, thereby creating dynamic commitment or time consistency problems. This argument should be reflected with great care by those arguing a Single Supervisory Mechanism will be sufficient to prevent excessive boom-and-bust cycles in the euro area in the future. At the same time, the book clearly shows that there is a fundamental contradiction between a single, supranational currency and the continuation of nation-state-based economic policies. Scholars and policy-makers interested in finding ways to overcome this institutional asymmetry should read this book.

All in all, Gundbert Scherf presents an impressive piece of work that should become a reference point for further work in this field. I am confident the book will also contribute to ending the Cinderella-like existence of research on banking regulation.

Prof. Dr. Henrik Enderlein

Preface

This book is the product of my doctoral research, which I conducted at the Freie Universität Berlin and Sciences Po, Paris and completed in April 2012. As the title suggests, the external context of the great financial crisis of 2007/8 informed my intellectual curiosity and desire to make a contribution to our understanding of financial stability policy. When I set out on the vast and quickly growing field of financial stability research, my attention was quickly grabbed by national banking regulation as an economically powerful and politically very salient instrument of economic policy. After all, the crisis had derived from an over-leveraged banking system and had obviated the importance of banking regulation for the functioning of regulatory capitalism. This, however, had not been appreciated sufficiently in economic policy and political economy research.

In particular, the questions I found deserving of more attention were: Why do countries employ this important economic policy instrument of banking regulation and supervision so differently? What is the linkage of this instrument to the 'breed of capitalism', in which the financial system and banks are embedded? How does banking regulation interact with monetary policy in the context of an integrating monetary union, where control over monetary policy has been ceded to a common central bank? What explains the differing implementation of regulatory accords such as Basel as well as the largely varying levels of bank capitalization across countries?

In this book I shed some light on these questions, making two main contributions: Firstly, my research finds that national-level differences in financial systems and related institutions explain and drive variation in regulatory financial stability policy across countries through the regulatory utility function. Regulators face a complex *trilemma of policy objectives* that can be irreconcilable in the short to medium term, forcing them to make important trade offs with financial stability. The trilemma results from national regulators being exposed to various political and private pressures in their conduct of discretionary regulatory and supervisory policy. Secondly, examining these trade-offs in a dynamic context, I show that domestic banking supervision in a monetary union is subject to political *time consistency problems*. These derive from the uncoordinated conduct of monetary policy and national banking regulation. Good economics in an integrated monetary union requires supervisors *ex ante* to signal hawkishness; but *ex post,* when money is easy and the economy highly leveraged, democratic politics can create insurmountable resistance. As regulators have to decide over regulatory policy throughout their national cycles of boom and bust, they will become subject to specific pressures that constrain their optimal actions.

I am greatly indebted to a number of institutions, whose many forms of support have been instrumental in the completion of this book.

I have had the privilege of a scholarship for doctoral studies from the Friedrich-Naumann-Stiftung for Freedom. I am grateful for their financial and ideational support, which has given me the freedom to concentrate my efforts on my research. Amongst many other things this has allowed me to spend very valuable and precious time at the

Institut d'Études Politiques («Sciences Po») in Paris. I also want to thank the organizers and participants of the 4th Lindau Meeting in Economic Sciences for providing a 5-day-forum for inspirational discussion with fellow young economists as well as 19 Nobel Laureates. I thank regulators and monetary policymakers, particularly at the European Central Bank, for taking the time to exchange views on my research in background discussions and extending me an invitation to the 13th Conference of the ECB-CFS Research Network on macro-prudential regulation. Last, but certainly not least, I want to thank the Hertie School of Governance for giving me the institutional infrastructure and support for my research.

Most importantly I owe gratitude to a number of people, whose personal support and encouragement have also made this journey a fascinating and memorable one.

I want to thank Gabriele Brühl for her patience, kindness, and reliability that she extended to me throughout my research. I also thank my fellow research colleagues at the Hertie School of Governance and the Freie Universität for many constructive discussions on political economy and economics. I owe gratitude to Prof. Dr. Emiliano Grossman, Associate Professor at Sciences Po, who supervised my research during my time as 'Doctorante Invité' at Sciences Po, sharing his views on structural component analysis or the best places in the '18e arrondissement'. I also want to thank Sir Howard Davies for deeply insightful discussions on his experience as a regulator and central banker. I thank Bill Masterson for sharing his insights into the workings of the Irish boom and bust on many occasions. I am also very grateful to Prof. Dr. Susanne Lütz for sharing her expertise at critical junctures of my research.

Foremost, I want to thank Professor Dr. Henrik Enderlein for his outstanding support, encouragement, and mentorship. Doctoral research is subject to its very own and extreme 'boom-and-bust cycles' with the outcome highly uncertain. This makes taking on doctoral researchers a highly speculative investment. In Henrik Enderlein I found a 'Doktorvater' and personal mentor, who was not only willing to make this investment, but who also gave me the freedom to develop my own research style and academic profile and who knew, when and how to smoothen the ride through his experience, insight and 'anti-cyclical' guidance. This support has been an invaluable inspiration to my research as well as to me personally. I am very grateful for that.

I thank Barbara and Elisabeth for being the best sisters that I could ask for. I am deeply grateful to my parents for everything they have done for us. To my grandparents I owe gratitude for their support, which has made my journey towards completion of a doctoral dissertation so much easier than it was for them.

I dedicate my work to Emma for being everything, which she is to me.

Gundbert Scherf

Table of Contents

Foreword ..... **VII**
Preface ..... **IX**
List of Tables ..... **XV**
List of Figures ..... **XVII**
Abbreviations ..... **XIX**

Prelude: The financial crisis as a crisis of regulated capitalism **1**
Policy choices and regulation as root causes of the financial crisis 2
The de-regulated banking system as an accelerated contagion mechanism 7
Globalization of de-regulation and spread to European banking 10
Conclusion: The financial crisis 2007-9 as a crisis of regulated capitalism 12

1 Introduction **14**
1.1 Introduction of the research topic **14**
1.1.1 Financial stability: Why does it matter? 14
1.1.2 The regulation of financial stability 16
1.2 Research questions **17**
1.3 Status of the literature and the 'gap' to be filled **19**
1.3.1 The political economy approach to economic policy research 19
1.3.2 State of the art of the political science literature 20
1.3.3 State of the art of the economics literature 30
1.3.4 Conclusion: The need for an integrated political economy theory of banking regulation 37
1.4 Research design **38**
1.4.1 Theoretical framework 39
1.4.2 Research variables 40
1.5 The main argument **43**

2 Trading off financial stability: A political economy perspective on European banking regulation **47**
2.1 Financial stability **48**
2.1.1 Financial stability defined 48
2.1.2 Financial stability as a policy field 52
2.1.3 Conclusion 55
2.2 Regulatory policy objectives **56**
2.2.1 The public interest view: The regulator as delegated monitor for financial stability 57
2.2.2 The private interest view: The regulator as captured agent for credit and competitiveness 58

2.2.3 National regulatory mandates ... 59
2.3 Financial stability governance in the Euro Zone ... 61
2.3.1 The European Central Bank's limited role in financial stability ... 62
2.3.2 National regulators' strong role in financial stability policy ... 65
2.3.3 Comitology between the ECB and national regulators ... 67
2.4 Financial stability instruments ... 69
2.4.1 Monetary policy ... 69
2.4.2 Banking regulation and supervision ... 74
2.4.3 Macro-prudential regulation and supervision ... 77
2.4.4 Political economy implications ... 79
2.5 The regulatory ‚trilemma' ... 80

3 What drives the banking regulator? Varieties of financial systems and regulatory preferences ... 88
3.1 Regulatory preferences across financial systems ... 89
3.2 The varying organization and accountability of national regulators ... 92
3.2.1 Organizational design of the regulator ... 92
3.2.2 Political accountability/ independence of the regulator ... 97
3.2.3 Conclusion ... 99
3.3 Financial systems and the varying role of banks across countries ... 100
3.3.1 Financial systems: Varying financial stability configurations across countries ... 101
3.1.2 Legal institutions: The varying strength of depositors, creditors, and investors across countries ... 104
3.1.3 Conclusion ... 106
3.4. Empirical clustering analysis ... 107
3.4.1 Financial system clusters ... 107
3.4.2 Legal institution clusters ... 111
3.4.3 Joint cluster of financial systems and legal institutions ... 117
3.4.4 Conclusion and evaluation of findings against hypotheses ... 120
3.5 Regulating along a trilemma: Three stylized regimes ... 120
3.5.1 The 'arm's length'-finance regime ... 122
3.5.2 The 'competitive self-correcting'-finance regime ... 123
3.5.3 The 'relationship'-finance regime ... 126
3.5.4 Two varieties of relationship finance and regulatory orientation in the Euro Zone ... 127
3.5.5 Conclusion ... 130
3.6 Regulatory stringency outcomes ... 131
3.6.1 Regulation and supervision across regimes ... 131
3.6.2 Conclusion ... 137

4 International cooperation or race to the bottom? Banking regulation in an integrating financial market 139
4.1. Modeling international regulatory interaction 140
4.1.1 A simple open economy model of regulatory interaction 142
4.1.2 The role of international institutions in regulatory interaction 146
4.2 Financial integration in the Euro-Zone 148
4.2.1 Financialization 149
4.2.2 Financial integration 152
4.3 Institutional change 155
4.3.1 The asymmetric impact of integration on national competitiveness 156
4.3.2 Institutional change in capital stringency definitions 159
4.3.3 Institutional change in activities and conglomerate regulations 162
4.3.4 Conclusion 167

5 Committing to hawkishness? Time consistency problems in the interaction of banking supervision and monetary policy 169
5.1 Rules, discretionary regulation, and supervisory commitment 170
5.1.1 Defining time consistency problems 171
5.1.2 Sources of time consistency problems in banking regulation 172
5.1.3 Banking supervision as a dynamic strategic interaction game 177
5.1.4 Conclusion: Discretionary versus rules based supervision 182
5.2 Asymmetric leverage temptations in a non-optimum currency area 184
5.2.1 Asymmetric ECB monetary policy effects on credit growth 184
5.2.2 The institutional fitness of Euro Zone supervisory bodies 186
5.2.3 Conclusion: Predictions regarding the build-up of leverage due to time inconsistent supervision 190
5.3 Empirical analysis 190
5.3.1 Bank leverage buildup across countries 191
5.3.2 The case of Ireland 192
5.3.3 The case of Spain 194
5.3.4 Conclusion 197

6 Conclusion 199
6.1 Summary of findings 200
6.2 Theoretical implications 205
6.3 Policy implications: The Euro Zone as an optimal regulatory union? 208
6.4 Outlook 211

Appendix 215
Bibliography 239

List of Tables

TABLE 1: Comparison of price stability and financial stability concepts 16
TABLE 2: Focal point of this research to date vis-à-vis existing related literature 29
TABLE 3: Political economy approach to financial stability and banking regulation 39
TABLE 4: Regulatory mandates and objectives 60
TABLE 5: Euro Zone financial stability governance in comparative perspective 63
TABLE 6: Conventional view on monetary and regulatory policy instruments 70
TABLE 7: Impact of monetary policy on policy objectives in different financial systems 73
TABLE 8: Impact of banking regulation on policy objectives in different financial systems 76
TABLE 9: Macro-prudential policy and its impact on monetary policy and banking regulation 78
TABLE 10: Typology of institutional regulatory structure/ design 93
TABLE 11: Complementary configurations of financial systems and legal institutions 106
TABLE 12: Financial system features across countries 108
TABLE 13: Financial stakeholder rights across countries 112
TABLE 14: Financial system and legal institution variables and clustering results .. 116
TABLE 15: Aggregate financial system clustering and regulatory orientation 118
TABLE 16: Regulatory regimes and their 'resolution' of the trilemma 122
TABLE 17: Regulatory regimes and complementary institutional configurations 130
TABLE 18: Regulatory institutions for the Euro Zone, the UK, and the US in 2000 136
TABLE 19: Relative shock to competitiveness and predicted institutional change ... 160
TABLE 20: Regulatory reaction to shock to bank competitiveness 168
TABLE 21: Institutional credibility of the supervisory authorities 189
TABLE 22: Regulatory reaction to shock to credit availability 190
TABLE 23: Regulatory approaches to the trilemma across countries 200
TABLE 24: Exogenous shocks in the time period 2000-2007 203

List of Figures

FIGURE 1: ECB, Fed, and BoE's deviation from Taylor rule 2000-2008 4
FIGURE 2: Decoupling of home prices and household income 5
FIGURE 3: Leverage ratios of Euro Zone, U.K., and U.S. banking systems 8
FIGURE 4: Costs of the financial crisis in Euro Zone, U.K., and U.S. 15
FIGURE 5: Research design and chapter contents 41
FIGURE 6: Financial stability as a 'quiet'/ low political salience policy field 54
FIGURE 7: Private and public interests and resulting regulatory objectives 59
FIGURE 8: The regulatory 'trilemma' 80
FIGURE 9: Leverage and return on assets across financial systems in 2007 86
FIGURE 10: Development of aggregate Euro Zone balance sheet's asset side 86
FIGURE 11: Aggregation of regulatory preferences through institutional configurations 91
FIGURE 12: Organization of banking regulation and costs of financial crisis across countries 96
FIGURE 13: Independence/ accountability of banking regulation and costs of financial crisis 98
FIGURE 14: Dendogram of the financial system hierarchical clustering analysis 110
FIGURE 15: Dendogram of the legal institutions hierarchical clustering analysis ... 114
FIGURE 16: Dendogram of the joint financial system and legal institutions clustering analysis 117
FIGURE 17: Three regulatory regimes along the trilemma 121
FIGURE 18: Capital adequacy over time by regulatory regime cluster 135
FIGURE 19: Regulatory reaction curves and equilibrium leverage outcome 146
FIGURE 20: Potential equilibrium outcome in the presence of international institutions 147
FIGURE 21: Change in regulatory stringency as an outcome of international regulatory interaction 148
FIGURE 22: Development of capital markets across Euro Zone, UK, and US 150
FIGURE 23: Change in bank income composition in the Euro Zone in 2000 and 2007 151
FIGURE 24: Progress in financial integration in the Euro Zone by financial market segment 153
FIGURE 25: Origin of banks under supervision across Euro Zone countries 154
FIGURE 26: Relative capital stringency, profitability and financial system openness in 2000 158
FIGURE 27: Predicted and actual change in capital stringency 161
FIGURE 28: Predicted and actual change in activities regulation stringency 166
FIGURE 29: Predicted and actual change in activities regulation stringency 166
FIGURE 30: Time inconsistent supervision of banks over time along the trilemma. 175
FIGURE 31: Banking regulation and supervision as a dynamic commitment game . 177
FIGURE 32: Banking supervision as a dynamic commitment game with discretionary supervision 178
FIGURE 33: Banking supervision as a dynamic commitment game with .... rules-based supervision 183

FIGURE 34: Asymmetric monetary conditions in the Euro Zone 2000-2006 185
FIGURE 35: Supervisory corrective action capabilities and discretion as of 1999/2000 188
FIGURE 36: Increase in credit volume and leverage due to monetary shock 191
FIGURE 37: Macro-economic development and credit reliance of the Irish economy 195
FIGURE 38: Macro-economic development and credit reliance of the Spanish economy 195
FIGURE 39: Regulatory and supervisory choices and financial stability outcomes . 205

Abbreviations

ABCP	Asset-backed commercial paper
ARM	Adjustable rates mortgage
BIS	Bank of International Settlements
BOE	Bank of England
BSC	Banking Supervision Committee
CDO	Collateralized debt obligation
CEBS	Committee of European Banking Supervisors
CRA	Community Reinvestment Act
EBC	European Banking Committee
ECB	European Central Bank
EFCC	European Financial Conglomerates Committee
EMU	European Monetary Union
EP	European Parliament
ESCB	European System of Central Banks
EU	European Union
FDIC	Federal Deposit Insurance Corporation
FED	Federal Reserve System
FSA	Financial Supervision Authority
FSAP	Financial Services Action Plan
GSE	Government-sponsored entity
IMF	International Monetary Fund
IRB	Internal-ratings-based
LCFI	Large complex financial institution
LOLR	Lender of last resort
LTV	Loan-to-value ratio
MBS	Mortgage-backed security
NCBs	National central banks

OCC	Comptroller of the Currency
OTS	Office of Thrift Supervision
NRSROs	Nationally recognized statistical rating organization
PCA	Prompt corrective action
SEC	Securities Exchange Commission
SES	Systemic expected shortfall
SIV	Structured investment vehicle
QMV	Qualified majority voting
VAR	Value at risk

Prelude
The financial crisis as a crisis of regulated capitalism

"Bankers own the earth; take it away from them but leave them with the power to create credit; and, with a flick of a pen, they will create enough money to buy it back again... If you want to be slaves of bankers and pay the cost of your own slavery, then let the bankers control money and control credit."

Sir Josiah Stamp, Director, Bank of England, 1940

"The Great Depression, like most other periods of severe unemployment, was produced by government mismanagement rather than by any inherent instability of the private economy."

Milton Friedman

The debate about the key causes of financial and economic crisis is as old as the study of political economy. As the quotes show, this debate already in the aftermath of the Great Depression has been led between those pointing out the inherent instability of an excessively de-regulated economy and those pointing to the excessive intervention of government and badly designed regulation in the economy. The treatment of the most recent financial crisis of 2007/8 is no exception to this: There already is an abundance of literature in the economic literature, scientific and popular, examining both dynamics that turned it into global disaster with its well-known (real) consequences for most economies. Thus, this following analysis of the financial crisis as a prelude to my research is not for lack of good and comprehensive analysis of the causes of the financial crisis, but on the contrary to position the specific *focus* of my analysis in the context of the many analysis that do exist. I am interested in *the political economy drivers and policy choices made in relation to banking regulation* - in particular in the Euro Zone and the various forms of regulatory capitalism within it.[1] This interest rests on an analysis of the crisis, which finds that behind the confluence of market failures and misled individual business choices made, there were some key failures of politics and regulation that translated into highly influential policy choices contributing to the evolution and breakout of the financial crisis.

As such this analysis in spirit is close to both introductory quotes: The failure of Lehman Brothers and its consequences to a highly connected and over-leveraged financial system has obviated that when left to its own devices, financial systems are prone to riding the 'leverage cycle' and engaging in excessive maturity transformation that leaves entire banks such as Lehman Brothers highly reliant on short-term finance

[1] As such, the German research fields of 'Ordnungspolitik' and 'Wirtschaftspolitik' encapsulate my research interest in banking regulation as an economic policy field best understood from a comparative economic systems perspective.

on the interbank market. However, rather than stopping at this 'greed of bankers'-account as a root cause, I lay focus on the policy-decisions behind these business choices that enabled and facilitated the emergence of various risks which manifested in banks balance sheets. Regulation was the channel through which these policy choices materialized and distorted incentive structures in such a way, that the crisis could develop as an unintended consequence. Since unintended consequences should form the core of 'good social science' (J. Friedman, 2009), this narrative of the crisis establishes an important research agenda about the functioning of regulatory capitalism. Such analysis has once before triggered further research into the role of policy as a driver behind the Great Depression, which has enhanced our understanding of many areas of policymaking and has arguably influenced the response by policymakers in the recent crisis very positively.[2] It is this research agenda and its relevance to the events witnessed, that is my motivation for analyzing the political economy behind the crisis, that is the policy choices made, the political economy drivers and national preferences behind these choices, and the (unintended) consequences of these choices for financial stability. Particular focus lies on the role of financial stability in the Euro Zone countries, where a particular financial stability governance exists in the context of monetary union. The Euro Zone thus is a special 'beast' where an asymmetric monetary policy has tested regulators' ability to 'lean against the wind' in restraining bank leverage, when monetary conditions where (more than) tempting for banks to leverage up.

Policy choices and regulation as root causes of the financial crisis

There are many differences of opinion regarding the specific contribution or degree of impact of individual causes of the crisis, but in the rich literature available some consensus exists on what the destabilizing economic processes as such were and how they interacted (Brunnermeier, 2009; Buiter, 2007; J. Friedman, 2009; Geanakoplos, 2010a; Hanson, Kashyap, & Stein, 2010; Martin Hellwig, 2008; H.-W. Sinn, 2010; J. B. Taylor, 2008). On a macro-economic level it was the "macro-economic pathologies" (Buiter, 2007) of global capital flows, monetary policy and the supervisory environment, which made their relative contribution (Merrouche & Nier, 2010). On a micro-economic level excessive risk-taking were facilitated amongst others through the innovation of securitization, flaws in rating agencies' business model, procyclical mark-to-market accounting, the nature of Basel capital adequacy regulation, inefficient disintermediation, and general de-regulation on all fronts (Buiter, 2007). The interaction of macro-economic instabilities and conducive micro-economic incentives and structures created an excessive amount of 'systemic risk', which is generally considered to comprise the risk factors interconnectedness and/or exposure to a common shock on the asset side as well as interconnectedness, leverage and/or illiquidity on the liability side – of course the bigger the balance sheet, the bigger the systemic risk, ceteris paribus (Acharya, 2009).

---

[2] A prominent example is the work by Ben Bernanke on the Great Depression, which emphasized the lack of active intervention by the central bank in the Great Depression as a negative contributing factor to the depth of the crisis, which most certainly also informed the Fed's policy, over which he presided in this crisis, which has been generally assessed as very contructive.

Much less consensus exists on the role of politics and the nature of policy choices leading up to the crisis. The complexity inherent to the economic dynamics behind the financial crisis also extends to the policy sphere were fragmented accountability and blame games (Singer, 2010) on the domestic and international level have created a moral hazard problem of its own in the regulatory sphere. The following narrative therefore presents a rough sketch of this economic consensus and adds to it the policy dimension, i.e. the element of political choice that enabled many of these economic processes, which to a large extend were therefore 'unintended consequences' of policy. The analysis shows: Market failure followed policy failure and, as such, this crisis should be seen as "a crisis of politics, not economics" (J. Friedman, 2009).

The starting point of any root cause analysis of the 2007-2009 financial crisis must be the observation that this financial crisis quite closely followed the anatomy of all other financial crises and bubbles, going from 'mania' to 'panic' and then culminating in full-blown 'crisis'. In this specific instance, it was a U.S. housing bubble manifested in the subprime mortgage market bursting that spread internationally through the banking sector and then through a global 'credit crunch' affected the real economy (Diamond & Rajan, 2009; Hellwig, 2008). Regarding the build-up of the bubble, Diamond and Rajan (2008) identify the misallocation of investment into housing, the acquisition of these investments in the form of innovative securitized products by banks, and the short-term financing of these products as three proximate causes of the crisis. The misallocation of investment originated from the co-existence of a 'global savings glut' and the global liquidity creation: More specifically, as it has been shown that the term 'global savings glut' is somewhat misleading, as globally there was no real surplus of savings - on the contrary there was a shortage of it. It was more so the global imbalances and the excess spending in some countries vs. excess savings in others that produced instability. In the absence of real effective global governance for such imbalances integrated financial markets shifted large flows of capital from high-saving countries (China and commodity-exporters) to high-spending countries, notably the United States (Buiter, 2007).

A channel through which central banks certainly did affect the bubble creation process through liquidity provision and relatively 'loose-fitting' monetary policy, which manifested itself in long-term deviations from the 'Taylor Rule', i.e. interest rates that were too low, when considering inflationary tendencies and output gap deviations. Counterfactual analysis by Taylor himself suggests that the monetary policy choice of being on the more 'accomodative' side certainly contributed to the housing boom. This, he argues, is true not only for the Fed by also for the ECB, whose rate-setting seemed to follow the rates of the Fed quite closely (Taylor, 2008). Taylor's specific account of loose-fitting monetary policy as the ultimate driver of instability has of course been contested by other accounts. Here I do not want to adapt his particular focus on deviations from the 'Taylor rule' as *determining* financial stability outcomes. However, I do want to highlight the role of monetary policy *in interaction* with regulation and supervision as a crucial nexus in explaining financial stability outcomes, as recent IMF research has shown. This empirical work demonstrates that the interaction between monetary policy and global capital flows and the related 'imbalances' were the main channel through which monetary policy could and did lead to instability (Merrouche & Nier, 2010).

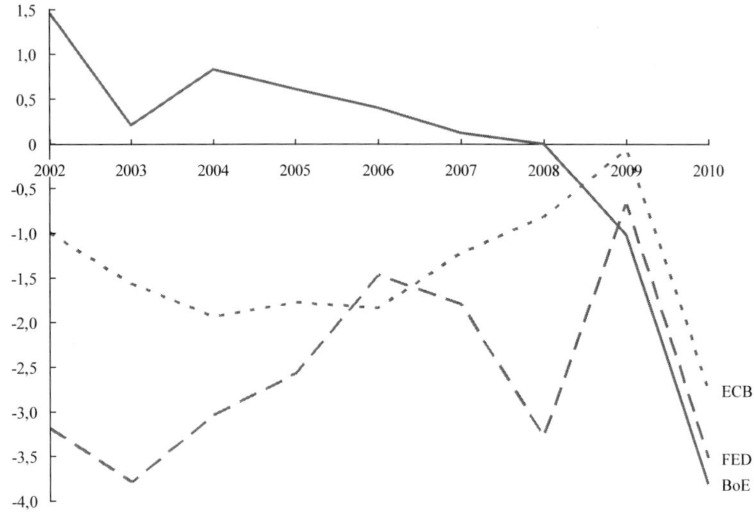

FIGURE 1: *ECB, Fed, and Bank of England's deviation from Taylor rule 2000-2008*

Source: Author's calculation based on a simple Taylor rule benchmark using OECD data for interest rates, inflation, and output gap and national central bank targets of 2%; for simplicity and comparability a 50% weighting on inflation and output gap is imputed for all three cases here; for a further theoretical discussion of different Taylor rules see for instance Orphanides (2007)

The impact of looser monetary policy *and* regulation in the case of the U.S. combined with home-prices on the rise for every single year between the mid-1990s and 2006, saw expectations adjust (Baily, Litan, & Johnson, 2008) and produced the irrational element or 'mania' that precedes all bubbles and is then followed by the panic associated with the bursting of the bubble (Kindleberger & Aliber, 2005). The lending to borrowers in the housing market, particularly the subprime housing market, was supported by the innovation in mortgage design, which seemingly 'dismantled' the constraints such as down-payment requirements or income guarantees. Adjustable rates mortgage (ARMs) forwarded much of the financial burden to a later date, by offering 'teaser rates', no-down-payments, and capitalization of initial interest payments to subprime borrowers, who were also cynically labeled in the financial world as NINJAs (short for No-Income-No-Job-No-Assets) (Baily et al., 2008). Such loosening of lending standards was of course politically supported by government policy developed in 1994 under the Clinton Administration in the form of the "National Homeownership Strategy", which was transposed into policy through an update of the Community Reinvestment Act (CRA) and the affordable-housing mission by the U.S. Congress. These policies encouraged home-ownership amongst the underprivileged by requiring mortgage lenders to make significant lending in that segment and made this political goal a responsibility of Fannie Mae and Freddie Mac – the both large government-sponsored entities (GSEs), that would therefore be heavily engaged in the subprime business. Wallison (2009) shows that government policy in the U.S. significantly shaped regulation and applied political pressure to ensure that banks would provide borrowers with mortgage financing. The tax deductibility of home-equity borrowing along with the lower capital requirements for banks on their mortgage assets and mortgage-backed securities (MBS) are expressions of this policy paradigm that supported the building of the bubble.

The dubious success of this policy was that housing demand did take off and saw home prices double between 1995 and 2007, decouple from real household income, setting off a self-reinforcing cycle of asset price rises. Despite lending standards dropping, evidenced by a drop of the share of conventional mortgage from 57 percent in 2001 to 33 percent in 2006 and a rise of subprime mortgages to 33 percent (Wallison, 2009), asset price rises were large enough and produced low foreclosure and default rates. This has been shown to be due to the presence of this policy-induced increase of leverage, as measured by the average loan-to-value ratio (LTV). Leverage increased due to the lower down-payments required, which for the period between 2000 and 2006 dropped from 7,7 percent all the way to 2,7 percent, a phenomenon Geneakoplos coins the "household leverage cycle" (Geanakoplos, 2010b). The distorting incentives due to regulation requiring the GSEs to acquire a large share of subprime (affordable housing) finance facilitated the resulting explosion in the subprime market by increasing demand and competition for these products and as a result suppressed the risk premiums for these products. Furthermore the financing of this housing bubble was eased by the innovation of securitization through the "originate-to-distribute"-model, which allowed originators of such mortgage loans to 'pass the buck' by selling off the mortgages to a third party, thereby reducing one's exposure to the various risks (interest rate, default, and pre-payment), which were associated with the loan.

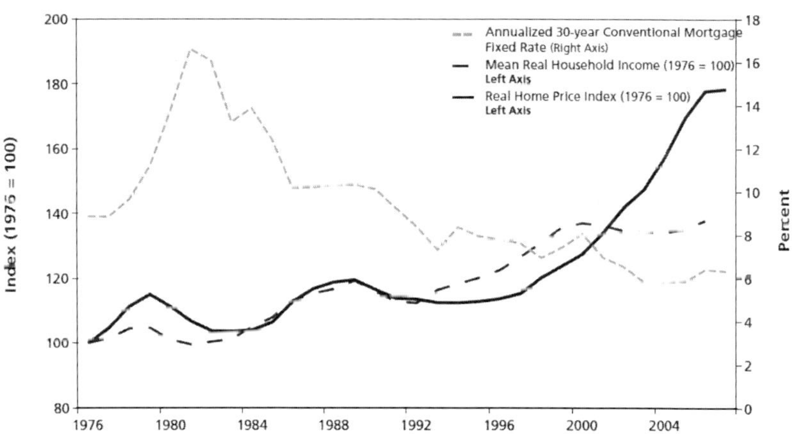

FIGURE 2: *Decoupling of home prices and household income (real home prices and real household income indexed to 1976 =100)*

Source: Baily, Litan, & Johnson (2008)

The GSEs took on the role of funding mortgage lending and bought most of the loans, kept the default and prepayment risk and sold the repackaged securities as MBSs, making a profit of the margin between their own cheap (implicitly) government-guaranteed funding and the returns on the assets. By 2008 they held staggering USD 5,4 trillion in mortgage debts on their books – essentially a very large bet on low default rates and ever-rising house prices (Baily et al., 2008). Other firms, mainly commercial and investment banks including Lehman Brothers and Bear Stearns, took on the remaining 60% of the market share of mortgages and participated in the securitization business. Thus, the policy-induced decoupling of originator's interest from the risk of the security, which would be sold in the market, increased the information asymmetry and moral hazard, i.e. conflict of interest, in the mortgage market and was the basis for the global participation in the U.S. housing bubble.

Rating agencies played a key role in this process, as they gave this process the crucial 'stamp of approval', providing ever larger shares of the subprime mortgages high ratings – in most cases the highest AAA-rating. Hellwig (2008) outlines the fundamental technical flaws in the approach of rating agencies to assessing risks. He finds that the mathematics of using historical time series insufficiently accounted for the tail risk of default and certainly with hindsight underestimated true risks in the market. Moreover these excessively mathematical assessments led to negligence in terms of judgment in assessing the real drivers of house prices and their likely development over the future, failing to comprehend that low interest rates, securitization, and correlation in price developments could all reverse simultaneously, leading to a fast, non-linear unwinding of the housing bubble. With respect to the motivation for such technical negligence, he notes the well-known conflicts of interests of rating agencies, who through their consulting arm were also involved in the design of securities and supported the separation of MBSs into various tranches from senior to non-investment grade. These relatively simple but nonetheless largely in-transparent tranched product in the majority of cases were then by the rating arm of the same company awarded the crucial AAA-rating, which enabled wide-spread market participation by highly regulated (state-owned) banks and insurance companies, who for regulatory reasons required such ratings to make the investment. While the tranching process as such does spread the risk and therefore justifies higher ratings for the more senior, less risky tranches, it led to a sheer proliferation of such ratings in this case. Sinn (2010) quotes IMF estimates that show that 80% of the collateralized debt obligations (CDOs) belonged to the AAA-category with only 2% belonging to the equity tranche, which bears the highest risk. Thus, additional revenue opportunities made the rating agencies less objective and corrupted their judgment, which many market participants relied on.

Again, it is important though to realize that also in the case of the rating agency, it was policy failure and misguided regulation that preceded the failure of risk assessment, by distorting competition in the rating market in such a way, that complacency and mis-judgment of risks became the 'rent' that the incumbents skimmed: White (2009) shows that the oligopoly in the rating market between Moody's, Standard & Poor's (S&Ps), and Fitch was based on U.S. regulation, which first gave them quasi-legal status as 'agencies' in 1936 and which effectively shielded them from competition ever since the 1975 and ensured that the technical mistakes made could be made without endangering their very existence or continuity of their business model. As nationally recognized statistical rating organizations (NRSROs) these agencies were the de facto authority or "force of law", as White puts it, regarding the risk of investments and determined which ratings would be awarded the important investment-grade or, even better, the much desired AAA-rating. Regulation regarding capital requirements stipulated the specific capital required to be held by institutional investors given the rating of the investment and thereby made the ratings officially legal. Barriers to entry were kept high through the Securities Exchange Commission's (SEC) limited designation of new rating agencies and through mergers with the incumbents the three players stayed amongst themselves until 2000. As more and more investment banks, who themselves commanded large shares of the rating agencies' revenues, moved into securitized CDOs and MBSs, the two oligopolistic markets 'colluded' and produced highly rated, fee-generating products that were designed for banks to serve the needs of institutional investors perfectly.

The de-regulated banking system as an accelerated contagion mechanism

The global spread of the housing bubble and its bursting in 2006 throughout the banking system, can, thus, be explained by the fact that these risks of excessive leverage in house-finance ended up in the balance sheets of highly leveraged commercial banks, through securitized assets, and in many cases off their balance sheets in certain types of 'conduits' (Acharya & Richardson, 2009). Investment banks but also commercial banks across the globe had participated in the securities-trading, because the Basel I rules allowed them to optimize their capital structure through these instruments, yielding higher returns through higher leverage ratios. The international regulatory framework for banks, Basel I, stipulated that mortgages in terms of riskiness were to fall in-between government bonds (zero-risk weighting) and commercial loans (100 percent risk weighting) and would receive a fifty-percent risk weighting. If originated by a government-sponsored entity (such as the two GSEs) or if awarded a AA-rating or better from an NSRSO, the risk-weight and the corresponding capital to be held would be reduced to 20 percent, thus, making the investment all the more attractive by allowing leverage to go up. Thus, the beneficial regulatory treatment of those assets that the U.S. government had wanted to be financed more, subprime mortgages opened a gap for regulatory arbitrage that was skillfully exploited by market actors across the world.

Availability of credit combined with regulatory arbitrage and a housing boom to kick off the 'leverage cycle' and increase banks' vulnerability to a common shock in U.S. housing markets. As Figure 3 shows, leverage was as much – if not more – a European phenomenon as it was an U.S. one, with leverage increasing throughout the period 2000-2006. Most striking is the disparity of leverage across countries with leverage factors ranging from around 10 (United States) to around 30 (Netherlands and Ireland). This illustrates the key point, that Basel regulations, whilst setting a minimum floor on regulatory capital, do not yet determine the actual equity held. Regulators and banks have some leeway in capital and risk definition, which jointly determine actual leverage as shown here.

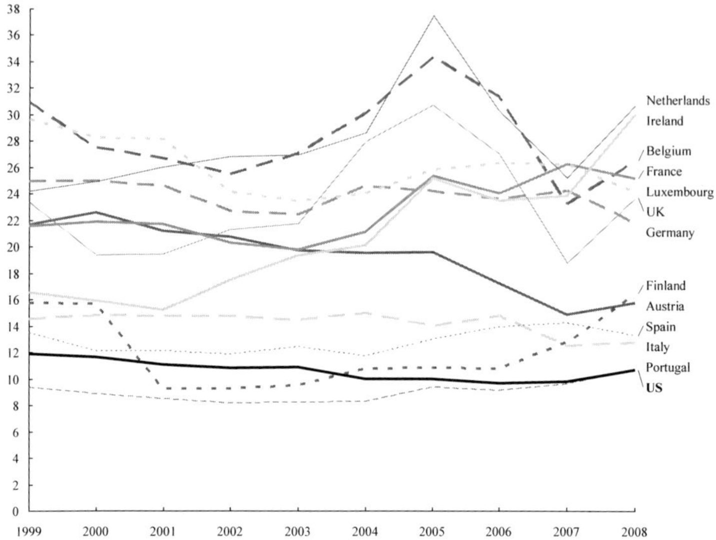

FIGURE 3: *Leverage ratios of Euro Zone, U.K., and U.S. banking systems*

Source: Author's calculation based on OECD Bank Profitability Dataset (2011); graph shows the inverse of non-risk-adjusted capital and reserve ratios for the consolidated banking system data by country

The driver behind this growth was to some extent regulatory arbitrage, which through an increase in assets (helped by securitization) outpaced the increase in risk-weighted assets (based on Basel I), thereby decreasing the regulatory capital required to be held as a buffer. With the resulting concentration of risks in banks' balance sheets or through guarantors of their SIVs' bonds, banking became collectively vulnerable to a systemic shock, i.e. a shock to a common exposure, which would reduce their capital buffers significantly. What compounded the risk was that banks had also tried to uplift profits through leverage and through financing their investments very short-term. As a McKinsey-Global Institute Study on de-leveraging after the crisis finds, there was and is a real preference for debt-financing in banking across the world (McKinsey Global Insitute, 2010). Apart from the tax benefits that debt receives, the main incentives for holding more debt identified are management incentives (as ROE is improved), implicit and explicit guarantees on deposits, which reduces cost of debt, lower transaction costs of debt, and the limited supply of equity capital. The theoretical underpinning is provided by Geanakoplos (2010c), who argues that leverage is a result of a class of buyers, who are willing to pay more for an asset (for, say, risk-preference) and will inefficiently drive up the value beyond fundamentals, thereby creating more collateral against which to borrow. This self-amplifying leverage cycle then similarly quickly can be wound down in the other direction ("manic-depressive" markets), as it is these very outlier buyers, who determine prices, who exit the asset market first, creating leverage risk for banks and investors. In addition to leverage, banks had accumulated substantial liquidity risk through "excessive maturity transformation"

(Hellwig, 2008). The above mentioned off-balance-sheet-conduits re-financed themselves through short-term money provided by money-market funds or other banks, which in turn required the AAA-ratings to provide this finance. Brunnermeier (2009) emphasizes this dynamic of downward liquidity spirals that require banks to engage in fire sales of assets as a reaction to a drop in asset prices. Such fire sales as a result of deleveraging in turn require further sales and lead to a decline in lending and borrowing. As lending channel dries up due to banks' worries about market liquidity and credit access on the money markets, banks' capital can erode and risks of bank runs increase. As, such liquidity risk is 'endogenous' to bank behavior and is transmitted between banks causing a loss spiral and the drying up of 'market liquidity'. To sum up, the new form of contagion in the financial system operated through the 'loss-spiral asset-price'-mechanism rather than through the classical domino theory, which assumes that direct exposures amongst banks, one of which might default, cause transmission of such effects. In one word: it was information contagion about fundamental similar exposures and fire sales rather than just real interconnections that caused the contagion between banks.

Such a form of contagion requires the collective exposure of systemically relevant financial institutions and banks to similar assets – or more simply put, regulation that enables banks to engage in 'mass equities trading' (Bhide, 2009) rather than simple loan creation and responsible maturity transformation. Bhide further argues that banks neglected their traditional business model of bank lending that was based on superior information and closely managed relationships due to regulatory changes. Financial economists and regulators shared the beliefs that mathematical models, arm's length relationships in corporate control, and the trading of risks through securitized assets would lead to a more efficient and more liquid handling of risks. A focus on 'hard' information that was quantifiable was favored over the more cumbersome collection of 'soft' information through direct communication with borrowers at the point of origination of a loan. As such, regulators were 'captured' on many levels: With banks under pressure in the 1970s due to economic shocks in inflation and more competition through money market funds, de-regulation set in the United States, repealing gradually the philosophy of the 1933 Banking Act, which had separated commercial from investment banking. Commercial banks were allowed to engage in the underwriting of securities and deal in mutual funds – more powers were later added in the 1980s such that in 1990 the Banking Law Journal stated that in reality the Glass-Steagall restrictions of the 1933 Banking Act had been repealed through "regulatory and judicial reinterpretation" (quoted in Bhide 2009, p-233). With increased competition from innovative business models such as mutual funds and declining profitability of traditional banking, securitization and trading with derivative investments multiplied manifold in the banking sector. In 1994 derivatives in megabanks accounted for more than 11 times the value of asserts, in 1997 credit default swaps were invented, and in 1999 the Gramm-Leach-Bliley-Act formally repealed the Glass-Steagall prohibition on combining banking and securities business in one entity. The latter Act was passed by the U.S. Congress at the initiative of Head of Treasury Larry Summers, who argued for the legislation out of competitive considerations: *"Today Congress voted to update the rules that have governed financial services since the Great Depression and replace them with a system for the*

21st century. This historic legislation will better enable American companies to compete in the new economy" (Labaton, 1999).[3]

As a result, commercial banks and particularly the megabanks took advantage of the new deregulation and grew their activities in trading of securities, such that the top five banks accounted for more than 80 percent of trading revenues in 2001 (Bhide, 2008). Profits of course rose strongly, largely due to the ability to take on more risk through new securities, higher leverage, and more short-term financing. However, the motivation for banks to "bet the house on housing" (Acharya & Richardson, 2009) in such a risky way, based on strong assumptions such as continuing rises in house prices and perfect ability to refinance has another reason in policy: Large complex financial institutions (LCFIs) were but all too aware that the only thing that could derail this bet would be a systemic event, which would affect many players and would require the central banks and regulators to act to save those players "too big to fail". As such, the assumption shared by economists that large institutions would act in their own long-term interest to maintain reputational capital was disproved by the Bear Stearnses, Merrill Lynches, and Lehman Brothers of this financial crisis (Acemoglu, 2009). Taken together, these U.S. institutions along with their European counterparts drove up the demand for securitized assets by so much, that risk premia on for instance subprime mortgages fell from 300 basis points in 2001 to 100 basis point in 2004 (Hellwig, 2008).

Globalization of de-regulation and spread to European banking

The globalization of these de-regulatory practices at least in the banking sector had taken effect through the political constellation behind the Basel Committee on Banking Supervision's principles of 'Basel I' and 'Basel II', where the U.S. saw the introduction of a model-based approach as a benefit to its own institutions in global competition (Hellwig, 2008). New regulation thus enabled all of these riskier investments into assets, which now would mathematically be assessed by the banks' own centralized risk management of banks, which supervisors then could only approve of or second-guess. Already at the time of the making in the 1990s, economists noted the risks of regulatory capture by the banks, namely that *"banks may find it desirable to develop models which serve not just for risk assessment and risk management but which serve also to minimize required capital, or, since you don't usually pursue two objectives optimally with one instrument, to develop models which serve to pursue some weighted average of these two objectives"* (Hellwig & Staub 1996, p.756). Hellwig continues that *"we are left with the paradoxical conclusion that on the one*

---

[3] The sponsors of the legislation argued in a similar vein, as the New York Times reported on November 5, 1999: "The world changes, and we have to change with it," said Senator Phil Gramm of Texas, who wrote the law that will bear his name along with the two other main Republican sponsors, Representative Jim Leach of Iowa and Representative Thomas J. Bliley Jr. of Virginia. "We have a new century coming, and we have an opportunity to dominate that century the same way we dominated this century. Glass-Steagall, in the midst of the Great Depression, came at a time when the thinking was that the government was the answer. In this era of economic prosperity, we have decided that freedom is the answer."
"If we don't pass this bill, we could find London or Frankfurt or years down the road Shanghai becoming the financial capital of the world," said Senator Charles E. Schumer, Democrat of New York. "There are many reasons for this bill, but first and foremost is to ensure that U.S. financial firms remain competitive."

hand the regulatory community sees a need to regulate risk in banking but on the other hand it is entirely dependent on the risk measurements provided by the banks themselves" (1996, p. 758).

The break-out of the financial crisis, particularly after the collapse of Lehman Brothers in September 2008, evidenced that deregulation and securitization had transformed the European banking landscape similarly strongly. The European banks due to their worse access to the originating mortgage banks, had become main investors along with the investment banks for the mezzanine tranches of securitized assets, which were riskier but also provided them with high yield. As a U.S. Congress assessment of the impact of the financial crisis on the European Union (EU) notes (Jackson, 2009, p.3):

"The financial crisis that began in the United States as a result of a downturn in residential property values quickly spread to European banks through effects felt in the market for asset-backed commercial paper (ABCP). European banks were either directly holding the securities or they were holding the indirectly through conduits and structured investment vehicles with similar holdings."

An analysis of the causes of the global financial crisis with a focus on Europe, Carmassi, Gros, and Micossi (2009) find that there is a paradox of why European universal banks were able to become more and more leveraged and over-exposed to toxic assets, despite generally being subjected to more stringent regulation. As such, lax regulatory oversight is cited also by these authors as a key root cause, which interacted negatively with loose monetary policy to set off the crisis in Europe. The 'De Lariosiére-Report' to the EU Commission, charged by the EU with advancing financial supervision in the EU based on the lessons from the crisis, identifies the competition motif as the main driver for the degree of yield-seeking observed in European banks (De Larosière et al., 2008, p.8):

"Exceptionally low interest rates combined with fierce competition pushed most market participants – both banks and investors – to search for higher returns, whether through an increase in leverage or investment in more risky financial products. Greater risks were taken, but not properly priced as shown by the historically very low spreads. Financial institutions engaged in very high leverage (on and off balance sheet) - with many financial institutions having a leverage ratio of beyond 30 - sometimes as high as 60 - making them exceedingly vulnerable to even a modest fall in asset values."

Importantly, the Report also states that this risk-taking was at least tolerated by regulation and overlooked by supervisors, who regulated those particular transactions far too lightly (De Larosière et al., 2008, p.10):

"These pressures were not contained by regulatory or supervisory policy or practice. Some long-standing policies such as the definition of capital requirements for banks place too much reliance on both the risk management capabilities of the banks themselves and on the adequacy of ratings. In fact, it has been the regulated financial institutions that have turned out to be the largest source of problems. For instance, capital requirements were particularly light on proprietary trading transactions while (as events showed later) the risks involved in these transactions proved to be much higher than the internal models had expected. (...) EU supervisors had a more difficult

task in assessing the extent to which exposure to subprime risk had seeped into EU-based financial institutions. Nevertheless, they failed to spot the degree to which a number of EU financial institutions had accumulated – often in off balance-sheet constructions- exceptionally high exposure to highly complex, later to become illiquid financial assets."

Finally and most importantly, the Report identifies the key failures of regulation, which are the *lack of 'macro-prudential' regulation and supervision* as well as a reluctance of nationally based supervisors and regulators to engage in actions, which could *endanger their competitiveness as a financial centre* (De Larosière et al., 2008, p.11):

"Regulators and supervisors focused on the micro-prudential supervision of individual financial institutions and not sufficiently on the macro-systemic risks of a contagion of correlated horizontal shocks. Strong international competition among financial centres also contributed to national regulators and supervisors being reluctant to take unilateral action."

Conclusion: The financial crisis 2007-9 as a crisis of regulated capitalism

When analyzing the economic dynamics behind the global financial crisis, there is structurally nothing new about this particular crisis – previous financial crises in Japan or the Nordic countries in the 1990s had also been based on abundant cheap capital, credit growth, leverage, asset price rises, and real estate bubbles (European Commission, 2009a). It is however the sheer magnitude and globality of its destabilizing effect, which as I argued it attained through global banking, that makes it the single most disruptive economic event since the Great Depression of the late 1920/early 1930s (Barry Eichengreen & Rourke, 2009) and gives this crisis a new quality. Moreover, when looking the close link between the destabilizing business choices, mainly in the form of excessive risk-taking, and the policies that encouraged (even if unintended) these choices, one needs to conclude that the financial crisis was indeed a global crisis of regulated capitalism, in which it was regulation and not capitalism that was the primary root cause (Friedman 2009). If one views banking regulation in this way, it is not surprising that one of the key responses of countries to the financial crisis has been the change in the public-private balance, as officials are now more and more taking back control over what used to be private regulatory initiatives, relying less on 'market discipline' and more on the taming of market forces (Helleiner & Pagliari, 2010).

There is a need to understand *regulation as a systemic root cause of the crisis*, requiring a systemic approach to understanding the "dialectics" of regulatory failure, as Friedman puts in it in his call for future research (p.168). Similarly, the 'Economist' in a special report on the world economy in the crisis assessed *"market fatigue"*, arguing that "it is the Anglo-Saxon model of deregulated and liberalized finance that has lost its mystique" (Economist, 2009). When combined, these two arguments make an important point, which this research aims to provide an analytical and empirical grounding for: Namely, that this 'dialectic' of regulation, in the following analytically denominated as 'regulatory preferences', derives from a particular role that the financial system is to take on within the economy, i.e. the financial system is regulated in such a way as to fulfill its function for the economic system. As such, I will compare the different financial stability dialectics and policies across the Euro Zone within the particular structure of a monetary union to shed light on the drivers and effects of these policies.

1

Introduction

"At this juncture, the impact on the broader economy and financial markets of the problems in the subprime market seems likely to be contained."

Ben Bernanke, Chairman of the Fed, Congressional testimony, March, 2007

"Life is a school of probability."

Walter Bagehot

1.1 Introduction of the research topic

1.1.1 Financial stability: Why does it matter?

The introductory quotes in combination with the below figure illustrate the relevance of financial stability policy in economic policy making in the 21st century very pointedly: Financial instability in the form of crisis is a very rare 'black swan'-type of event, but when it occurs it has a devastating effect on financial systems and economies at large. Because of this very rare and usually delayed occurrence of crises, financial stability policy also is subject to a very own political economy dynamic. As was shown in the prelude for the financial crisis of 2007-2009, financial instability often derives from murky policy choices over an extended time of exuberance that are and blurred in hindsight. This is why, paraphrasing from University of Chicago economist Raghuram Rajan, financial instability drivers such as excess credit growth have the exact payoff structure that politicians love: All the benefits of lax financial stability policy accrue now whilst the costs materialize much further in the future. Financial stability as an explicit policy goal really only has emerged in the last two decades as a response to the increasing volatility of financial markets and the high costs associated with the resulting, more frequent financial crises. As Andrew Crockett, the former head of the Bank of International Settlements (BIS), writes, a few years ago few people would not have been able to distinguish financial stability from monetary stability (Crockett, 2001). Indeed, it used to be the short-term stabilization of the economy during the 1960s and 1970s as well as ensuring price stability in the 1990s that took center-stage in the goals of central banks and economic policy-making. A look at the empirical reality illustrates why: The crisis frequency since 1973 has been twice that of the Bretton Woods and classical gold standard periods, only comparable to 'crisis-ridden 1920s and 1930s' (Bordo, Eichengreen et al., 2001). Crises are not longer or more severe in terms of output loss (this was prior to the most recent financial crisis) but certainly more frequent.[4]

---

[4] Interestingly they link this with the policy choices of capital mobility, the regulatory choice for the financial safety net as well as the implicit insurance against exchange risk that derives from an ex ante credible policy of pegging the exchange rate, leading financial and non-financial firms to accumulate excessive foreign currency exposures.

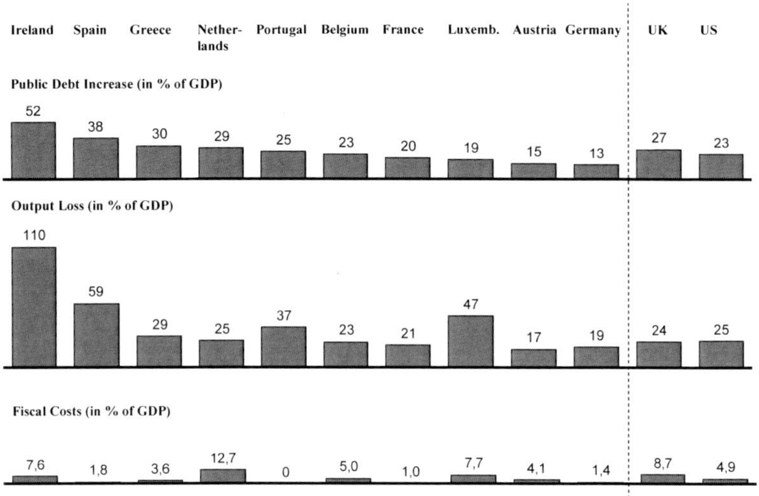

FIGURE 4: *Costs of the financial crisis in Euro Zone, U.K., and U.S.*

Source: Author's calculation based on data from Laeven and Valencia (2010); data for Finland and Italy not available

With respect to banking crises there has been only one in the period of 1945 up to 1970 but there have been 19 in the period from 1970 until 2000. The most recent financial crisis and the lack of foresight has triggered further research into the history of financial crises, reminding us that the notion of "this time is different" was false and contributed to the risk-taking prior to the most recent crisis (Reinhart & Rogoff, 2009). While Reinhart and Rogoff emphasize the recurrence of financial crises and the fact that there have already been other severe episodes of international financial crisis, their data also give clues with respect to the driver of this ebbing and flooding of volatility, namely, the increase in banking crises, which again seems to have been driven by the concomitant increase in capital mobility.

Different concepts of volatility and instability can be distinguished for analytical and measurement purposes: Volatility can be seen as the overall concept that for the purposes of economic phenomena can be defined as *"a measure of the possible variation or movement in a particular economic variable or some function of that variable, such as a growth rate"* (Aizenman & Pinto, 2005; p.2). Thus, volatility encompasses different phenomena of variance in economic/ financial returns including "structural or trend Volatility" as well as "crisis or boom" volatility, the latter of which differs in magnitude as it resembles a step change in deviation from "structural or trend volatility" (Hnatkovska, 2005). Thus, depending on the severity of the negative or positive deviation from the trend, volatility can trigger boom-and-bust dynamics as well as crisis. Financial crises again can be distinguished by their root cause as being either a) banking crises, b) exchange rate crises, c) sovereign defaults, or in few, dramatic cases as the most recent on as a mix of the above (Reinhart & Rogoff, 2009). The relevance of such banking crises for European economies has been shown not only in the most recent events of 2007-2009, but in fact there have been prior, severe experiences with financial and banking crises (see addendum II in the Appendix). Interestingly, the countries with such prior experience – notably Finland and Spain as Euro Zone countries – have fared relatively well in the current crisis, which shall be discussed at a later point.

1.1.2 The regulation of financial stability

To the extent that 'life is a school of probability', as the founder of modern central banking research Walter Bagehot puts it, financial stability policy is the management of these very probabilities with a focus on reducing the chances of a systemic crisis breaking out. The focus of my work in particular lies on the regulatory management of that kind of volatility and instability that can lead to financial crisis d*eriving from the financial system* and within that specifically from *banking*. In that respect Figure 4 illustrates the varying degree of success in the conduct of financial stability policy. When we add to that the dimension of variation in bank capitalization and leverage (see Figure 3 in the previous chapter), it becomes clear that financial stability is not just fate and a black swan type of event but rather is closely linked to *regulatory policy*. Yet, our understanding of this exact linkage and the political economy workings of regulatory policy is still relatively underdeveloped relative to the magnitude of its impact. A look at the definition of financial stability as a concept shows that. The table below summarizes a comprehensive review of various financial stability reports from central banks completed by Čihák (2006). He finds that central banks have not defined financial stability with the same operational precision and focus as other concepts such as price stability, which admittedly is a much less complex policy goal.

TABLE 1: *Comparison of price stability and financial stability concepts*

	Price stability	*Financial stability*
General definition	Clear	Range of definitions
Operational definition	Clear (variable and target), especially in inflation targeting	Typically not specified
Legal base for central bank's role	Based on law	Based on interpretation of law
Scope of central bank's responsibility	Full responsibility	Partial/ shared responsibility, exact boundaries in some countries unclear, in others delineated by a memorandum of understanding
Research	Well developed	Developing

Source: Čihák (2006)

This variation of conceptual and bureaucratic clarity between the two policy areas correlates with a variation in outcomes. Inflation today is widely regarded as under control and firmly in the hands of central banks, which have a clear mandate and an equally clear instrument. Financial instability on the other hand has been 'out of control' for the last years whilst the pursuit of it as a policy goal lacks all of the characteristics of monetary policy. This contrasts with the significant relevance that the absence of stability entails. Chant offers the following definition of financial instability:

"Financial instability refers to conditions in financial markets that harm, or threaten to harm, an economy's performance through their impact on the working of the financial system. It can arise from shocks that originate within the financial system being transmitted through that system, or from the transmission of shocks that originate elsewhere by way of the financial system. Such instability harms the working of the economy in various ways. It can impair the financial condition of non-financial units such as households, enterprises, and governments to the degree that the flow of finance to them becomes restricted. It can also disrupt the operations of particular financial institutions and markets so that they are less able to continue financing the rest of the economy" (Chant, Lai, Illing, & Daniel, 2003; p. 3).

This definition thus identifies financial instability as a shock that derives from or is significantly mediated by the financial system and impacts the real economy as a result through the described financial channels. As shown in the introductory chapter, this is where bank leverage – the economic parameter that banking regulation best controls - plays its crucial role. Whether the root cause of such a downswing in financial markets derives from the financial sector itself or not, the propagating mechanisms tend to be changes in leverage that can create contagion through asset prices or information channels, undermining the confidence in counterparties and financial contracts, impacting the financial condition of households, businesses, and financial institutions.

1.2 Research questions

Financial stability regulation therefore has a systemic role and is intimately linked to the 'breed of capitalism', institutional configuration of the economy in which the financial system is embedded. Hence, it follows that a regulator needs to internalize the effect of banking regulation not only in technical terms, i.e. its impact on the financial sector and its main protagonists such as large systemically relevant banks, but also needs to account for the role of banks in the financial system and the relation of the *financial system in the economy*. When looked at in such a way, it is clear that a more and more de-regulated financial sector, as in the United States prior to the financial crisis, is less and less likely to internalize its systemic role on the financial system and economy as a whole, as remarked by Hellwig (2008):

"[The] focus on yield at the expense of risk may be reinforced by governance mechanisms that rely on 'market discipline' in the name of 'shareholder value', and that the ease of measuring returns and of communicating about returns as opposed to measuring risks and communicating about risks introduces a bias in favour of

strategies that involve greater risk taking. (...) ...a system of 'market discipline' in the name of 'shareholder value' is unlikely to take into account the risk implications of the bank's strategy choice for its creditors and for the financial system as a whole."

It is this holistic perspective on regulation as a political economy phenomenon embedded in a particular variant of capitalism, which informs my research agenda. Hence I put regulatory action at the forefront of my work and inquire into the drivers and motivations of regulatory actions to learn more about a largely unexplored and under-researched type of policy actor in political economy and financial relations. Given this apparent gap in theory, which will be explored further in the next section, it is imperative to identify the kind of research questions that a political economy theory of banking regulation should answer. For this, one can turn to Persson and Tabellini's three classical tenets of economic policy-making (2002), which they specify as the three perspectives that a political economy theory of economic policy should contain:

- The *static, cross-sectional perspective:* Here one needs to understand the national banking regulator in its political and economic context. As such, this perspective by looking at the domestic sources of policy-making helps us explain the cross-national variation in regulatory policy-making.
- The *international perspective*: Understanding the interaction of national regulators in an international context and the nature of cooperation amongst them is the second important set of research, which is all the more relevant for a policy field as international as banking and finance.
- The *dynamic perspective:* Lastly a coherent political economy theory of banking regulation needs to show how banking regulation functions over time, given the exogenous political and economic influences that impact the regulatory and supervisory choice of stringency.

I employ these three analytical categories of political economy theorizing to structure my perspective of the regulator and inform my research questions. This perspective of the regulator in a varying and increasingly global context builds on the findings of Lütz (2002), who emphasizes the increasingly interactive role of the regulator in the globalized context. She finds that the regulatory role is defined by its relations and interactions with i) private actors, ii) the international level (Basel and the European institutions-) as well as iii) other states. In fact, I argue that in order to understand differences in regulatory action cross-sectionally, we need to understand the different ways in which private actors such as banks but also special interests in the non-financial sector economy interact with regulators to form regulatory preferences. Moreover I argue that the international perspective requires understanding of the way that regulators from different states interact with each other in particular in relation to the implementation of international standards. Thus, from comprehensive standpoint I derive three research questions, joining analytically three distinguishable tenets with the different relations of the regulator:

1) The *static, cross-sectional perspective:* What are the domestic sources of financial stability preferences and, building on that, why then do banking regulatory regimes and legal institutions of individual countries vary the way they do?

2) The *international perspective*: How can one explain the change in stringency in the application and implementation of international standards (i.e., Basel regulation) and the institutional change that it implies across the respective countries?

3) The *dynamic perspective:* How can one explain the variation in supervisory stringency over time that the crisis has evidenced?

1.3 Status of the literature and the 'gap' to be filled

The focus of these research questions is on questions that relate to the comparative or international political economy of finance and regulation. When engaged in a field of study as wide and with as many strands as political economy, it is in order to first lay out the specific body of political economy literature, which one intends to build on and contribute to in greater length, before turning to the status of the literature and the 'gap' in that literature that I want to make a contribution to.

1.3.1 The political economy approach to economic policy research

Political economy over the centuries of its existence has come to depict three different fields of research[5]: For Adam Smith and the other early moral philosophers that laid the ground for the economics discipline, political economy was equivalent to what today is termed pure economics, i.e. "the science of managing a nation's resources so as to generate wealth" (in Weingast & Wittman, 2006, p.3). Secondly, with the separation of economics and political science as separate disciplines in the late 19th century, in the twentieth century political economy usually came to refer to the study of the interrelationships of economics and politics – of states and markets (Gilpin, 2001; Strange, 1988). Thirdly and more recently, political economy has been used to describe the study of political behavior and institutions using the methodology of economics. This methodology regards the individual as the unit of analysis, assumes rational utility maximization as the best way to achieve goals, applies mathematical models and game theory to study problems, and uses statistical tools to explain patterns. This research employs a blend of the second and third category of political economy research. It reflects the second strand, as this research substantively looks at financial stability policy and regulation, which one could consider a 'natural' field of international political economy research at the intersection of the financial sphere (banking) with the political realm (regulation).[6] It reflects the third strand of political economy as it employs the model of the rational utility-maximizing actor and game theory to depict the various interactions of the regulator in its political environment.

The study of international political economy as a true interdiscipline (Lake, 2006; Walter & Sen, 2009) has a 'comparative advantage' in relation to economics in explaining actual policy choices and outcomes (positive understanding) rather than the understanding of what is best policy (normative understanding). In analyzing the

[5] For a good overview of the different research fields subsumed as political economy see Weingast and Wittman (2006).

[6] To the extent that banking regulation itself is a political phenomenon only, this research also has elements of the third category of political economy, i.e. as a methodology applied, as it employs an analytical model to the identification of the regulatory and supervisory utility function.

political determinants of regulatory preferences and policy choices cross-sectionally and over time it can build on a certain type of methodology as well (Alt & Shepsle, 1990) and fills a gap in the economics literature, as Pagano and Volpin find (2001; p.22):

"[Political economy of finance] helps us to understand why some countries end up with "poorly designed" financial institutions or "poorly enforced" financial regulation. Second, political economy can give us a clue as to when and why one can expect financial regulation or its enforcement to change over time. In other words, it guides us in the understanding of "financial reform" and of its feasibility. It does so by explaining which constituencies are sustaining a certain regulatory outcome, why they are currently dictating the rules, and how and why the balance of power can shift against them. Thirdly, besides explaining how pressure groups affect regulation, political economy takes into account how in turn regulation shapes and entrenches political constituencies via its economic effects."

The following sections briefly review the existing literature and provide an overview of the status quo of the relevant research. I argue that the financial crisis uncovered a void in both – political science and economics – in understanding financial stability policy and banking regulation's role in it. However, despite the shortcomings of the economics literature in this respect, the following overview also shows that the best theorizing on the sources of variation in economic policy practices, preferences, and institutions has come from combining insights from economics *and* political science, especially IPE/ OPE and comparative political economy, to accurately understand the most efficient 'best practice' but also to explain the variation in applying this 'best practice' due to political, distributional, and systemic interaction effects. The more recent approaches to IPE/OEP have benefited from the "rapprochement of IPE, comparative politics, and economics" (Walter & Sen, 2009) – that is from a critical and constructive engagement with other disciplines' contributions, in particular economics. This partial reversion to using economic theory for its rigor in deriving interests and predictions, has added an amount of analytical leverage that is considered useful for the research agenda of this paper.

1.3.2 State of the art of the political science literature

The financial crisis has painfully obviated a few literature gaps in the discipline of political science, which should receive greater scrutiny as a result of the crisis. One of those important agendas for future research, as David Singer and Layna Mosley (2009) conclude in a commentary on "The Global Financial Crisis: Lessons and Opportunities for International Political Economy", relates to the sources of domestic financial regulation (p.420-422):

"There is considerable cross-national and temporal variation in the manner in which national governments regulate their financial sectors. (...) Regulators themselves also differ across countries, in their ties to other government bureaucrats and elected leaders. Some regulators are relatively independent from political pressures and from the entities they regulate, while others are highly susceptible to partisan pressures or regulatory capture. In some nations central banks are responsible for bank supervision, while other countries have separate – and sometimes multiple – agencies

for bank supervision. Perhaps most importantly there are substantial cross-national differences in the content of regulation, including capital requirements, financial transparency, holding company supervision, and portfolio limitations. These regulatory differences are of interest for scholars of comparative politics as well as international relations, because disparate national policy requirements are potential drivers of international systemic risk. Given the diversity of national regulatory structures, multinational firms' incentives for forum shopping and regulatory arbitrage are significant. And given contemporary global financial interdependence, the system as a whole is vulnerable to financial instability within any individual country. (...) The global financial crisis laid bare the international consequences of domestic regulatory policies. Several areas are ripe for exploration, including the determinants of domestic financial regulation, the measurement of political independence of regulatory agencies, and more generally, the relative impact of domestic and international influences on national regulatory outcomes."

The following review confirms the existence of this large research gap on domestic and comparative financial and banking regulation in the literature. However I also find that certain elements required for such a theory exist in different branches of political science and can be built on. In particular three strands of research will be further examined in the following sections:

- Firstly, increasing mobility, velocity, and volatility of capital in the 1990s and 2000s gave rise to research on the *political economy of central banking and monetary policy*. A large strand of IPE has looked at the way that monetary policy can be used for macro-economic adjustment to monetary shocks and financial liberalization. Many of the relevant insights into the sources of monetary policy-making and stability preferences can be built on in the study of banking regulation.
- Secondly, from a *comparative political economy and Varieties of Capitalism-perspective* (VoC) there are relevant approaches to explaining variation in macro-economic stabilization polices. The VoC-contribution has illuminated how economies organize in certain economic policy areas and how they adjust to exogenous change (Hancke, Rhodes, & Thatcher, 2007), emphasizing the national variations amongst economies and the web of interactions of economic institutions, i.e. the institutional *complementarities* in the macro-economy.[7] This is particularly relevant, when we want to understand the impact that regulatory policy has on the wider economic system, through for instance differences in the role that bank finance plays for real economy, as I will argue at a later stage.
- Thirdly, more recent studies have made first advances into banking regulation to explain the *political economy sources of regulatory standards* (Singer, 2007) and the diffusion of certain regulatory policy paradigms (Simmons, 2001; Simmons, Dobbin, & Garrett, 2007). While this research has thus far has not produced a coherent theory of regulatory preferences that would account for the empirically

---

[7] Complementary relationships exist when the returns to one of the institutions to the economy increase with the existence of the other one.

observable variation in regulatory regimes, its analytical underpinning can be built on.

The Political Economy of financial stability and monetary policy

The macro-economic instability of the 1970s and 1980s required strong macro-economic adjustment to exogenous economic shocks. Valuable insights on the political determinants of financial liberalization choices, domestic interest formation, and central bank preferences have been gained from this. As financial interests led to a removal of capital controls and capital became increasingly short-term and mobile (Helleiner, 1994), the Bretton Woods-system of defending pegged exchange rates became more and more costly to defend – particularly in light of an expansionary fiscal and inflationary monetary policy of the United States. As investors were obviating the underlying imbalances of the system with different ‘attacks’ on currencies, central banks were left with few options other than periodic devaluations, which confirmed the assumed instability of the regime (Barry Eichengreen, 2008). Western countries opted for abandonment of the peg in exchange for exchange rate flexibility, making global competition for capital more intense, as financial centers around the world competed for international business.[8] The macro-economic effect of this liberalization of capital accounts was that economies were now connected through financial flows and would create policy externalities through their own macro-economic decisions, creating a world of more and more ‘complex interdependence’ (Robert O Keohane & Nye, 1977). The paradox of abandoning the Bretton Woods-system was therefore that policy autonomy in the long run was actually reduced rather than enhanced, as originally thought.

This transformative change in international finance posed new macro-economic policy dilemmas for central banks and domestic macro-economic policy making and in turn gave rise to a very relevant body of IPE/ OEP research on the dilemmas in decision-making, preferences of central banks, and the distributional implications of different policy choices. Departing from the insights of the national economy equilibrium Mundell-Fleming model (Fleming, 1962; Mundell, 1962), the new system of freely floating exchange rates implied that the national governments would loose fiscal policy as a lever over aggregate income in the long run. On the other hand central banks gained discretion over monetary policy back, which the exchange rate peg before had determined endogenously. Hence, IPE/ OEP research into the effect of the new international economic order occupied itself also with central banks as important actors, whose preferences and policy choices mattered substantially. Particularly relevant for our understanding of the preferences of central banks has been the finding, that central bankers face a basic dilemma of either fighting inflation credibly (tighter monetary policy) or contributing to employment objectives(looser monetary policy). With monetary policy being the far more effective economic policy instrument to stimulate the economy and employment, policymakers had an overwhelming incentive

---

[8] With the development of international financial markets and the integration of the funds from surplus countries (such as OPEC countries), the scale and velocity of financial transactions grew tremendously to a level in the 1970s, where financial flows were 25 times larger than trade flows (Gilpin, 2001).

to capture central bankers to conduct a rather loose monetary policy in favor of employment and at the expense of inflation. Thus, in a standard prisonner's dilemma policy game the wage-setters (trade unions) and the government are caught in a stable Nash Equilibrium, of expansionary monetary policy and expansionary inflation expectations. This reflects the *time inconsistency* problem of government policy in a democracy, where policymakers to win the electoral battle will often exploit short-term economic gains at the expense of long-term stabilization gains. In terms of central bank preferences the consensus became that central banks would be pressured by democratically controlled policymakers to adopt the clear preference for ensuring high employment rather than ensuring price stability. By implication, monetary policy needed to be delegated to an independent central bank that would serve as a commitment device, curtailing the influence of politics over it in terms of personnel, financing, and policy-making (Eijffinger & de Haan, 1996).[9]

This political economy prescription of independent central banks however fails to account for the variation of arrangements observed across countries in the post-Bretton Woods era as well as today.[10] With the post-Bretton Woods era an unprecedented variety of exchange rate regimes (fixed, floating, or currency union) and central bank designs (independence vs. dependence) originated (Bernhard, Broz, & Clark, 2002, p.701),[11] which produced new comparative political economy accounts to explain the variation in institutions and economic configurations.

Comparative Political Economy and Varieties of Financial Systems

Finding systematic explanations for the observed variation in economic institutions across countries is at the core of the contribution by the comparative political economists of the Varieties of Capitalism-school. In particular, the VoC-school has pointed out how macro-economic institutions interact with each other as well as with political institutional configurations on the national level.[12] A focus on complementarity in analyzing economic institutions underlies most of the VoC work.

---

[9] Central banks have in fact in many cases across the world become independent and are adopting an inflation-targeting approach based on certain rules, which specify what the central bank's preferences should look like (usually in some contrast to society's and the government's utility function).

[10] Because, indeed, as a review of the varying approaches to central bank independence in different countries by Eijffinger and Haan (1996) shows, countries deal very differently with the policy objectives, policy targets, and responsibility elements of central banks. While the Bundesbank had the support of government policy as a subordinate objective to price stability, the Reserve Bank of New Zealand had price stability as its sole objective. Also, they find that in the different measures of central bank independence (CBI) there is a large variation in the legal and non-legal independence afforded the central banks. Interestingly, the variation across countries is stable over time and there is relatively little change in the national arrangements of the central bank and no real trend towards independence between 1950 and 1989 – despite the clear social welfare implications of economic theory (Bernhard et al., 2002). With respect to the performance of independent central banks, the empirical evidence reviewed overwhelmingly finds that central-bank independence is negatively correlated with inflation, implying that indeed the theoretical proposition from economics holds in reality as well. Thus, the perplexing finding to be resolved remains the variation of CBI, monetary rules, and exchange rate choices across countries in the post-Bretton Woods era, despite a clear 'best practice' according to economic theory.

[11] While the largest industrial economies (the United States, Germany, Japan, and Britain) and the medium-sized developed countries (for example, Canada, Switzerland, Australia, New Zealand) opted for floating their exchange rates, European nations opted for a pegged exchange rate under the "Snake" and later for currency union in European Monetary Union (EMU). Austria and Sweden outside of that system also maintained tight pegs to the deutsche mark.

[12] For a an early and influential example of this approach to monetary affairs see Torben Iversen's (1998) analysis of the interaction of the monetary regime with national wage bargaining institutions.

Due to the centrality of complementarity in the VoC-school it is worth elaborating and defining here (Streeck, 2003; p.102):

"Complementarity is a relationship between at least two elements. Element E' is complementary to element E if its presence enhances the performance of E... More generally, complementarity of E' for E requires that E' assumes certain properties that match the properties of E, in the sense that the simultaneous presence of such properties in E and E' increases the performance of E... Complementarity may be mutual, i.e. E may be complementary to E' where E' is at the same time complementary to E... Complementarity may involve more than two elements interacting in a 'virtuous cycle' of mutual enhancement."

Thus, VoC conceptually emphasizes the interrelated configurations of subsystems of the economy, which however has largely been demonstrated for other realms of economic policy-making than finance such as welfare systems and social policy. The relevant VoC-contributions to systematic comparative financial system analysis rests largely on the 'patience of capital' and provides a useful classification into 'market-based' and 'bank-based' financial systems (Deeg, 2005). Deeg puts the financial system at the centre of a VoC-analysis, which he understands to comprise *"the banking system, securities markets, and elements of the corporate governance system"* (p. 169). He finds that different systems conform to a different type of logic, with market-based systems being *"characterized by arms length, deal-based interactions among firms, [...] based on explicit, contractually determined exchange and obligations"*, where banks operate according to a 'logic of exit'; This contrasts with the bank-based systems, which are based on *"longer-term, reciprocity-based interactions"* and *"implicit obligations and trust"* through *"board seats and equity investments"* that allow banks to operate by a 'logic of voice'.

Despite the centrality of this classification, which in essence rests on the variation in the 'patience of capital' institution, the actual literature elaborating on the implications of different financial systems for regulatory policy is more scarce. The literature has not developed a coherent concept of how banking regulation relates to the varieties of financial systems, what complementarities the conduct of banking regulation has to be mindful of or how and why banking regulatory institutions evolve and change over time. Rather the literature in the last ten years has debated the degree of transformation of bank-based systems towards market-based systems (Deeg, 1999, 2005; Hardie & Howarth, 2009; Krahnen & Schmidt, 2004; Vitols, 2004). Also empirically few comparative studies and to the best of my knowledge no comprehensive cross-country comparison of financial regulatory institutions applying such a VoC-perspective empirically exist. However, a deficiency of the relatively scarce VoC-literature on financial systems is that most of its studies focus on individual countries, a lot of times even zooming in on the German example as a 'pars pro toto'. An exception to this is Lütz (2003)'s contribution, which asks whether financial systems have produced convergence or divergence in banking regulation. Whilst her work not explicitly under the VoC-umbrella and rather under an explicitly historical institutionalist approach to explaining change, it reflects the VoC emphasis of of path dependency in the financial system evolution with the theory of veto points and complementarities. Her finding for the first half of the 2000s is that change in some convergence in banking regulation has taken place but within continued divergence of systems due to a path-dependent evolution of institutions from relatively divergent starting points. Also, Cioffi and Höpner (2006) provide some case studies of regulatory reform of finance capitalism and corporate governance regulation and show that political actors and particular their partisan sources matter in explaining institutional change. Domestic interests formed push factors that particularly drove center-left governments to engage in pro-market reforms in a pro-shareholder manner. Domestic factors such as a rise in private shareholdings and the emergence of a 'new middle' reflected a shift in domestic preferences that center-left governments picked up and that informed their policy-making towards gradual change. Such change has provoked cristicism of the VoC-approach's usefulness altogether. More moderate voices, however, have called not for an abandonment but rather an adaptation of the view of institutions and the nature of change within varieties of capitalism (Hancke et al., 2007; Streeck & Thelen, 2009).

Post-financial crisis this debate about the continuity or 'convergence in divergence'-analysis has picked up momentum again, with some authors challenging the existence of any 'varieties of financial capitalism'. Hardie and Howarth (2009) argue that financialization, i.e. the extent of internationalization and trading of risk, has driven the German and the French banking systems more and more towards an Anglo-Saxon type of market-based financial system. Their argument rests on the similar extent of exposure to systemic risk in the supposedly more protectionist German banking sector compared with the less exposed but supposedly more liberalized French banking system, which the crisis obviated. Securitisation and the 'originate to distribute'-model have transformed the nature of lending from bank-based to market-based – also in Germany and France. As bank operations have been financialized on both sides of the balance sheet, they have become more subject to risk-taking in trading activities, derivatives, and international retail-banking (asset side) and market-reliance for financing (liabilities). Consequently, due to the centrality of the financial system to the variety of capitalist system, they derive that *"financialization of German commercial banks and the LB has undermined the central position of the banks in the German model of capitalism"* (p. 1036).[13] As such, the argument goes, the 'bifurcation' of the German financial system into an internationalized and a domestic one, which Deeg attested, no longer applies and that first trends indicate also the 'Mittelstand' financing could be turning towards capital-market and foreign-based finance. These arguments open up an important research agenda about how financial regulation in an *integrating* financial market with a stronger role for capital markets affects the national regulatory regimes and policy paradigms. Again, however, these arguments rest on relatively sporadic empirical evidence and fail to account for the wider *financial system* (i.e., legal institutions, corporate governance mechanisms) and its very complementarities, which the VoC-approach assumes.

With respect to the prospects of a European model of financial regulation, opinions in the VoC-literature differ, particularly regarding the degree of regulatory convergence they observe across the various financial systems: Some research has found that post-financial-crisis the EU is getting its act together in creating a new appealing model of

---

[13] This argument largely rests on the the observation that the public sector-owned German Landesbanken (LBs) seeked higher yielding investments, such as securitized loans, to make up for their loss to cheap wholesale funding (having financed themselves with government guaranteed bond issues until 2005). This undermines the assumed functioning and legitimacy of an entire pillar of the German banking system.

financial regulation that is somewhat more 'managed' than the neoliberal pre-crisis consensus (Posner, 2010). Quaglia (2009) assesses the policy response by the European countries to the financial crisis as relatively homogeneous and 'Europeanized', as it was based on the British 'best practice' of bank re-capitalization and loan guarantees for troubled institutions. However, she also concedes that the differing configurations of the national financial systems and the links to the real economy were factors, which conditioned convergence in policy response and introduced an element of "persistence of different national institutional settings and policy legacies" (Quaglia, 2009; p. 1077). Hodson and Mabbett (2009) come to a different conclusion stressing continuity of national paradigms for the UK, as they find that New Labour's response to the financial crisis "remains rooted in the policy paradigm that it put in place after 1997". Other analyses of the reaction of the paradigmatic CME Germany and the paradigmatic LME Britain to the financial crisis also show that a clear and divergent national approach to financial regulation existed leading up to the crisis (Zimmermann, 2010). Germany, already in 2007 when hosting the G8-summit, had been a fervent supporter of a state-governed regulatory code for banks as well as other institutional investors such as hedge funds and private equity firms – both on a global level as well as on the EU-level.[14]

I find that this variation in findings owes in part to the lack of a more comprehensive cross-country comparison of the varying approaches to banking regulation based on more coherent empirical evidence. This type of a comparative cross-sectional and dynamic analysis of national banking regulation approaches, theoretically informed by the logic of complementarities and empirically tested using coherent data, is the core contribution of my work to the VoC-literature.

The Political Economy of financial stability and financial regulation

The recent IPE literature has picked up the topic of the political economy of financial stability with a stronger focus on banking regulation. Contributions have become more numerous and have centered on the many levels of regulatory decision-making: On the international level on the phenomenon of the rise of financial markets, sometimes called the 'financialization'[15] of the world economy (Epstein, 2005) as well as the international efforts towards regulatory harmonization through negotiated agreements (Ethan B. Kapstein, 1994; Simmons, 2001; Simmons et al., 2007; Singer, 2007); On the domestic level on the sources of regulation in bureaucratic and political incentives (Mosley, 2003; Singer, 2004a). The literature varies in theoretical emphasis i) in terms

---

[14] The motivation for such a stricter approach to regulation has been given by leading policy-makers through two arguments, as Zimmermann shows: Firstly, the German government has tried to use regulation "in defense of German capitalism" at large, trying to reform its economy and industrial core with the help of financial markets and private equity to break out of the network-based and less competitive patterns of the "Deutschland AG" (Höpner & Krempel, 2004). Secondly, the German finance ministry in particular has been stressing the importance of a competitive financial sector and 'Finanzplatz Deutschland' for its own sake (Lütz, 2003). Very importantly, Soskice uses these results to examine the preferences of central banks for three features in their *utility and preference function*: Firstly, the target of low inflation as an official mandate, secondly, the high weight attached to inflation deviations vis-à-vis unemployment, and, thirdly, an asymmetric response function, in which the central bank does not respond to inflation falling below its target. Applying that analogy to banking regulation should form part of the first analysis of how banking regulators' utility functions serve to fulfill their mandate.

[15] Epstein (2005) defines financialization as the *"increasing role of financial motives, financial markets, financial actors and financial institutions in the operation of the domestic and international economies"* (2005; p. 3).

of actors and ii) in terms of the diffusion of different policy paradigms. Explanatory accounts of international financial regulation have been mostly along one of three theoretical lenses: Inter-state or international power lines, domestic politics, or transnational forces (see the review by Helleiner & Pagliari, 2010). In terms of policy paradigm diffusion mechanisms IPE theorists have applied all different epistemologies ranging from constructivist theory of epistemic communities, learning theory, competition theory to coercion theory (Simmons, Dobbin and Garrett, 2007). As a result most IPE contributions tend to be a combination of a particular analytical focus (international level, domestic, transnational) with an emphasis on one or two of the mentioned diffusion mechanisms to explain international financial regulation.[16]

A continuity in this diverse body of political economy literature is the emphasis on a fundamental trade-off or 'regulator's dilemma'. Kapstein (1989) argued in the context of Basel I negotiations that globalization of finance regulators in an interdependent world have to cope with new challenges to domestic banks' competitiveness while ensuring national objectives such as financial stability. Also Kentaro (2003) examines the interaction of the domestic and international level by showing how regulators are playing a two-level game, in which they try to create leverage to resolve the basic regulator's dilemma: Trading-off the domestic interests in financial stability with the concern of the international competitiveness of its banks. Looking at the MoF of Japan he shows that regulators strategically employ the international regime to please both of their domestic audiences, banks and the general public/ consumers, by introducing international regimes that bind all countries and help them increase their win-set and leverage domestically whilst also strengthening the regulatory framework domestically to enhance their standing as a financial centre internationally.

Lütz (2002, 2003) in a regime theory-based analysis of the multi-level regulatory governance system then expanded on the nation-states' ways out of the regulator's dilemma. She contends that international regulatory standards are merely minimum standards, which the states have to build on in alignment with their national form of coordination. These forms of banking regulation in most states evolved largely in response to financial crises, varying from the U.S. pattern of a relatively state-based and fragmented policy to a Germany corporatist mode, or a Britain 'light-touch' form of regulation with a focus on the best-performing institutions. The enhanced role of capital markets and the way Basel II addresses it, however, does demand some convergence in regulation towards a more liberal form of self-regulation, as states apply the risk-based capital requirements jointly with the global players' internal models in a more flexible and interactive regulatory style. As a result of this mixed finding that leaves a role for national re-regulation, Lütz also disputes the 'race-to-the-bottom'-dynamic of capital markets, arguing that particularly the efforts of the Basel Committee since the 1980s have shown that banking regulation follows the logic of production standards and therefore are an important source of comparative advantage. While Lütz's contribution to the many levels of regulatory decision-making and the variation in organization of regulation on the national level is explicitly built on in my

[16] For a largely hegemonic and power-based approach see Kapstein (1992); For a rational choice account of regulatory policy as resulting from changes to the incentive structure , and changes in the information set see Simmons and Elkins (2004); For an blending of coercion and competition theory see Simmons (2001);

work, I contend that it requires elaboration based on the way that Basel has developed since then As I will show later, banking regulation despite the harmonization efforts on the global and European level still is a policy area with discretion in the domestic political as well as private realm – that is on the side of states and banks. Thus, my work expands this perspective and looks at the change in regulatory implementation and the evolution of banking supervision over time on the national level. In this way it furthers some of the work by Lütz (2003) on the diverse national reaction to the risks created by capital mobility and the change in the nature of risk from credit to market risk. Here Lütz also finds that divergence despite pressures for convergence prevailed due to national veto players and a persistent variation in national banking markets - variation in timing and implementation of the Basel accord are the empirically observable result.

Very influentially, Singer (2004; 2007) employs a principal-agent framework that puts the regulator and his domestic environment at the centre of analysis, using arguments from competition and coercion theory. He argues very much like Kantaro (2003) that international harmonization results as a resolution of the basic regulator's dilemma, which he sees as defined by the conflict between using regulation to either promote the competitiveness of the national financial industry (lax regulation) or to promote the confidence in the stability of the financial system (tighter regulation). The regulator maneuvers in a space of her "win-set" determined by the stringency of legislation that does not undermine competitiveness but also is strong enough to create financial stability. Exogenous shocks to international competitiveness or voter confidence in financial stability can decrease the size of the win-set and make legislative intervention more likely – a cost to the regulator that he will want to avoid. He shows that it is then that regulators seek international harmonization to increase the win-set again. Whilst his model and argument espouses the virtue of parsimony, which I want to build on, I find that one key element missing in his model: The dilemma assumes no role for the macro-economic role of banks in the economy, that is their important role as credit providers in the monetary transmission mechanism. This in my opinion is a significant shortcoming, which shows in particular when we apply his model to the European case, where financial systems are much more bank-dependent and therefore – aside from competitiveness considerations – regulators have to trade-off financial stability considerations with the wider implications for the economy and economic growth at large. Therefore, I argue that this model has to be amended to reflect the varying role of banks in the financial system and the economy, particularly in a more Europe-centered account of banking regulation in a monetary union.

Beyond this analytical and conceptual criticism, I find that Singer's account requires elaboration in terms of scope to make it applicable to wider questions of regulation that go beyond the mere genesis and revision of regulatory regimes such as Basel. While Singer convincingly argues that such regime derive from a simultaneous shock to the public interest in stability and the private interest in competitiveness, this still leaves a few central questions in the political economy of regulation unanswered. As the below table shows, for many regulatory situations and outcomes, the literature does not have a sufficient account of regulatory preferences and action, yet. To be precise, there are three gaps not only in his account of regulation but also in the literature at large that I find worthy of elaboration. Firstly, it still remains to be shown whether regulators within their 'win-set' actually do maneuver *in response to exogenous shocks* by accommodating and leaning against the wind (bottom-left and top-right corner of the matrix). Secondly, from a *comparative perspective* the key question is how regulators differ in their stringency of supervision when no exogenous shock to their utility function tempts them one way or the other (top-left corner). A review of the capitalization levels across banks in the Euro Zone suggests that there is large and systemic variation across countries, which theory thus far cannot systematically account for. Thirdly, the Singer argument, whilst developed over time with a focus on the evolution of the Basel regime, does not yet provide sufficient clues with respect to the supervision of banks *in a dynamic context*, which again in the absence of exogenous shocks might be subject to different dynamics just as monetary policy or fiscal policy have been shown to be.

TABLE 2: *Focal point of this research to date vis-à-vis existing related literature*

		Shock to financial stability	
		Weak	*Strong*
Shock to private interest	*Weak*	*Indeterminate* Regulation according to preferences/ institutions	*High* Leaning against the wind
	Strong	*Low* Accommodating	*Revision of regulatory regimes (focus of the Singer argument)*

Source: Author

Some recent important groundwork has focused on regulators as bureaucratic actors helping analysts comprehend the increasing abundance of networks and structures on the European or international level.[17] Other more theoretically informed accounts have focused on questions of accountability, stressing that the complex accountability story that assigns blame to institutions ranging from private credit rating agencies to irresponsible top-management in too-big-too-fail banks is likely to produce a piecemeal reaction to the financial crisis that originated from the regulators themselves (Singer, 2010). Both types of work however stress that the continued predominance of national and regional forms of regulatory action require more understanding of the national drivers of regulatory discretion and sources of domestic preference formation. Rosenbluth and Schaap's (2003) work that stands out and provides another take of domestic politics as a driver of banking regulation emphasizing the role of electoral politic in motivating politicians and consequently regulators to trade off the various domestic interests through regulation. Rather than calculating the optimal amount and type of regulation based on efficiency concerns, governments and their regulators act

[17] For an overview of the abundance of global and international networks and structures see Davies and Green (2008); for an overview of the European multi-level governance see (Quaglia, 2007, 2010);

on rules motivated by distributive political concerns. This model is based on the observation that regulation results as the interaction between *demand for regulation*, formed by the collective action capabilities of banks, bank clients, and labor, and *supply of regulation*, provided by politicians' reading of partisan preferences that result from how the democratic process aggregates preferences. In a centrifugal system of proportional representation and coalition government the politicians need only cater to a more specific group and will be prone to deciding policy in favor of special interests and less in favor of the median voter. In centripetal systems the reverse applies as politicians have to build wider majorities and will tend to serve them through for instance more competition in banking to provide lower cost services or higher-yield to consumers. This argument explains a fundamental difference across countries not in terms of economic differences and path dependencies but rather referring to political system differences that are stable over time. It therefore provides at least a first attempt towards establishing the 'micro-foundations' of the IPE-literature.

In a nutshell though one can summarize my review of the recent literature by stating that to date, despite the growing literature on this topic, too little work has been done on the actual micro-foundations of banking regulation and preferences that would allow us to explain the sources of variation in policy preferences systematically.[18] My work wants to contribute to the international and comparative political economy literature by filling this gap to explain the observed variance in leverage across countries using a coherent theory of regulatory preferences and utility functions.

1.3.3 State of the art of the economics literature

Economic theory provides a rationale for regulation in banking and has made inroads into understanding the role of regulation in the macro-economy. It still leaves the question of how national banking regulators fill the room for discretion unanswered. While there is a body of literature comparing financial systems that explains differences that emanate from different financial structures, this literature is not yet very connected to the literature on banking regulation. As such, the current research provides very few clues into how to adapt regulation to the specific financial sector and economy of a country and by itself is of limited use in explaining regulatory divergence across countries. However, rather than discarding it altogether, the economic literature reviewed in the below section certainly contains essential insights also for a political economy analysis to understand i) what economic dynamics make the case for regulation in the first place, ii) what role differences in financial system design play in that respect, and iii) how certain distributional outcomes in terms of how risk and return are shared across domestic economic actors in different financial systems.

To understand the role of banking regulation from an economic point of view, I will briefly review why the role that financial intermediaries play in the financial system is special and requires regulation. This section will then address the literature on the debate between the 'private' and 'public interest' view. Thirdly, the models looking at

18 This criticism is also already advanced by Kentaro (2003).

the regulator and his/ her preferences in the international context will be touched upon. I then conclude with the overarching finding that the literature has a gap regarding the real sources of domestic variation and divergence in regulatory approaches.

The Economics of financial intermediation and regulation

The main *purpose of banks and financial intermediaries* in general is to contribute to the efficient allocation of capital to its most productive use (for an overview of the microeconomics of banking see Freixas & Rochet, 2008). In doing so, financial intermediaries or banks create liquidity for assets and liabilities by diversifying to provide liquidity, transforming maturity, reducing risk, and reducing monitoring and search costs for borrowers and lenders (Howells & Bain, 2008). Banks as very specific intermediaries carry out a very important and impactful economic function, namely the creation of more money, i.e. assets and liabilities, which could – depending on consumer preferences – increase the spending and consumption pattern in countries. Efficient financial systems will at any given level of interest produce a higher willingness to borrow and lend and will, thus, lead to higher investment due to lower cost of finance. The transformation function also provides the most common definition of a bank, namely, as an *"institution whose current operations consist in granting loans and receiving deposits from the public"* (Freixas & Rochet, 2008; p.1). Others find that the defining emphasis is on banks' clear advantage over consumers in solving asymmetric information problems since they can engage in long-term relationships with borrowers and can economize on the costs of monitoring. For this school of thought the very existence of banks has been reasoned to lie in their ability to reduce moral hazard implicit in lending relationships through their characteristic role as 'delegated monitors' (Diamond, 1984).

However, finance theory shows that in order to fulfill their purpose optimally *regulation* is required. Apart from ensuring fair competition as in any industry, there are two specific elements to the nature of banks' provision of useful and efficient services that justify and even demand regulation by the government: Firstly, the presence of *information asymmetries and transaction costs* prevents single depositors from efficiently monitoring and controlling the actions of the bank. Specifically, it is the existence of adverse selection in the pre-lending process and moral hazard in the post-lending process, which is to be reduced through the existence of a well-governed system of financial intermediation (Mishkin, 2001). Since consumers deposit most of their savings with the bank, the solvency of the bank and the prudential management of the bank to that end need to be monitored by a representative – the regulator. This theory of the *'representation-hypothesis'* is developed in depth by Dewatripont and Tirole (1999) and then begs the question of how regulation as 'delegated monitoring' can best align incentives and produce a contract that addresses the needs of depositors. Were it not for these delegated monitors of regulators, consumers would in the event of an adverse shock to the banking system be very likely to cause a bank run, withdrawing all their deposits due to the uncertainty about the institution's health and stability. It is this logic that has led to the widespread adoption of the governments safety net for depositors, which effectively insure depositors against the loss of their assets and transfer the risk from the individual depositor to the government and the taxpayer. In imposing such a deposit insurance, governments create the next problem: Moral hazard. As depositors no longer exert effort to check the activities carried out by banks, there is a lack of market discipline on banks to prevent them from engaging in risky activities. A similar problem is created by the implicit 'too-big-too-fail'-policy of most governments, which means that most governments will stand ready to save and re-structure a failing bank, whose failure due to the size of its balance sheets would otherwise spell a larger disaster than the cost of saving it would. This again, ceteris paribus, increases the incentives for the management of large banks to engage in riskier activities. The focus of regulation in addressing this failure of incomplete markets lies in ensuring the *micro-prudential* soundness of banks and supervising their risk management to prevent failure of any deposit-taking institution.

Secondly, there is a systemic service or *public good* element to the provision of the payments and liquidity services for the economy, which is not internalized by the banks themselves necessarily (Freixas & Rochet, 2008). Whilst, in the past this element has usually been reduced to the creation of money and provision of a payments system, more recent insights from the financial crisis of 2007/8 suggests that this element of systemic risk provides a similarly if not more powerful rationale for the existence of banking regulation, which would have a *macro-prudential* focus on ensuring systemic stability (Acharya, Pedersen, Philippon, & Richardson, 2010; Bank of England, 2009; Brunnermeier, Crockett, & Goodhart, 2009; Hanson et al., 2010). This role is also justified by the fact that the central bank in the event of a systemic crisis is assumed to intervene as a lender of last resort (LOLR). This role demands intervention by the central bank to ensure that credit availability is not constrained too much to endanger the financial system and drain the entire economy.[19] Thus, where micro-prudential regulation addresses the problems of consumers due to the presence of asymmetric information, macro-prudential regulation addresses the risk of contagion and the problems for the entire financial and economic system that could result from a loss of confidence or contagious interbank dealings that would lead to multiple institutional failures.

The limitations of the micro-prudential approach to bank regulation have been outlined many times in the aftermath of the financial crisis, however, the main argument is worth rehearsing to understand the requirements towards regulation. The idiosyncratic perspective of micro-prudential regulation entails that banks are required to take corrective action to restore capital adequacy in response to an adverse shock. As such, the bank has two alternatives at its disposal in going about this, which however differ markedly with respect to the implication for the systemic stability of a financial sector: It can either *increase its capital base*, something that turns out to be rather difficult in situations of economic distress, or it can *decrease its asset holdings*, which in turn will lead to *credit crunches* and further *fire sales* of assets (Hanson et al., 2010). Such fire sales of assets create the externality of self-perpetuating liquidity spirals as asset prices drop, which again lead to reductions in lending and borrowing (Brunnermeier et al.,

---

[19] Already over a century ago Walter Bagehot introduced the benchmark on how central banks should do this to minimize the problems of moral hazard and protect public financial means as best possible in such situations (Bagehot, 1897). His recommendations as summarized in Prati and Schinasi (1999; p.20) included that central banks "1) lend only to illiquid institutions that are solvent, 2) let insolvent institutions fail, 3) lend speedily, 4) lend only for the short-term, 5) charge penalty interest rates, 6) require good collateral, and 7) announce these conditions well in advance of a crisis".

2009). As the lending channel dries up, the entire banking system is faced with problems of market liquidity and credit access on the money markets. A second reason is given by the Bank of England (2009) and relates to the systemic tendency of the banking sector to take on too much risk and leverage in good times, which leads to a correspondingly strong downward swing. This is corroborated by the theory of the leverage cycle (Geanakoplos, 2010c). In a nutshell, in both cases banks do not internalize the systemic effects that their own actions have on other institutions, which provides a rationale for a macro-prudential approach to regulation.

The important implication is that regulation, that is the stringency of capital adequacy rules, has systemic effects, which through a change in bank leverage and lending spill over into the real economy. Since these effects vary, countries have generally catered financial regulation to country needs through discretion of the national regulator. This resulting national variation and the impact on regulatory incentives remains under-researched.

The public and private interest view of regulation

To provide a more theoretical rationale for variation in the practice of regulatory policy the economics literature of regulation has offered two contrasting views: The *public interest view* assumes that governmental regulators simply apply the economic concepts to achieve maximum efficiency in markets. Applied to banking regulation this means that the "banking system allocates resources in a socially efficient manner and performs well the other functions of finance" (Barth, Caprio, & Levine, 2006; p.18-19). The *private interest view,* very prominently formulated by George Stigler (1962) in the context of energy regulation, empirically and theoretically establishes that regulators are subject to capture by organized industry interests and over time will be prone to being too lenient and easy in applying regulation. For banking regulation this view will similarly expect that bank regulators will succumb to the interests of banks in having capital adequacy requirements and risk management enforced more loosely.

This new political economy theory in banking regulation contends that policymakers will take into account and pursue private interests next to their public interest mandate. Empirical evidence gathered on the actual practice of banking regulation and supervision in various countries overwhelmingly supports the private interest view of discretionary application of banking principles (Barth et al., 2006). The authors find no relationship between regulatory restrictiveness and the level of financial development in countries. However, they do find that government ownership is correlated with reduced competition and that countries with more open, private sector-oriented supervision tend to have greater bank development, consistent with the notion that public oversight informed by private interests negatively affects banking industry efficiency. Moreover regulatory restrictions on banking activities are associated with instability just as deposit insurance is associated with an increase in systemic risks. With regard to bank efficiency neither supervisory power nor capital regulation are significant in terms of impact on net interest margin, whilst private monitoring is associated with greater bank efficiency. On the contrary, tighter restrictions on bank activities boost interest rate margins by protecting vested industry interests.[20] Interestingly, while the authors observe that the political system of a country and the practices in supervision and regulation are correlated, very little can be found on the sources of these institutions and the mechanisms through which private interests manifest in political systems.

What would be needed is a coherent political economy theory on the way that private interests institutionalize their demands in financial systems and financial regulation. Rajan and Zingales (2003) offer a political economy view of financial development, which goes some way in that direction. Their theory maintains that the private interests of financial incumbents but also industrial incumbents manifest themselves through an opposition to trade openness and consequently financial development. The main countervailing mechanism, the interaction with which determines outcomes, is the lack of opposition that incumbent banking can organize when there is financial entrants and producers that require cheaper, arm's length finance through markets. The development of financial systems up until 1913 and its 'great reversal' until the 1990s can be explained this way, something that structural theories referring to time-invariant factors such as the law and finance view cannot really explain: Governments after the Great Depression gained more control over financial markets and the banking system, became suspicious of markets and nationalized and limited competition, producing new incumbents, who would block liberalization for a long time. This 'great reversal' was then followed by the famous rise of industrial capitalism through largely oligopolistic, where few large firms increase in scale and scope (Chandler, 1994). With the gradual liberalization as of the 1970s markets returned to the fore and led to innovative forms of finance such as private equity or hedge funds and instruments such as securitized assets, making finance more available. The resulting increase in competition also led to a concomitant shift in corporate governance towards a market for corporate control, as capital was disciplining management for the optimal use of and return on the assets invested in.

Other views tend to concur with this, in the sense that they see regulatory policy as not always welfare-enhancing, yet, very little exist in terms of why and through what processes such regulatory preferences are formed. One approach suggests that the interplay of politics and economics and the ability to organize collectively needs to be taken into account (Kroszner & Strahan, 2001). According to such an approach, once the private sector interests and partisanship have influenced the implementation of legislation-process, there will be little role for consumer interests. Thus, private interests, well-organized in compact organizations are able to extract rents from the regulation at expense of more dispersed groups. The key factors driving such interest organization are the ability to organize the beneficiaries, the dispersion of the cost, i.e. the disadvantaged, and the ratio of benefits to costs, which if high enough makes costly organization worth while. Kroszner and Strahan test the role of various interests in the regulatory policy-making process and find that, additionally, ideology of the

[20] Also in bank lending corruption in lending does not decrease with an increase power of supervisors - official power is instead positively correlated with corruption in lending. Again, firms in countries with private monitoring exhibit lower levels of corruption in lending. As a result, a balancing of regulation with private market monitoring is recommended as the authors constitute that there is no trade-off between reliance of official supervision and private sector monitoring imposing market discipline.

dominant political party also plays a role. As such, industry interests and the de-regulatory ideology of the governing party find common ground at the expense of unorganized consumer interests to determine regulation in a suboptimal equilibrium from an efficiency and welfare-enhancing point of view. With respect to the reaction to the recent crisis, similar private interests also seem to have affected the regulatory legislative, as voting patterns and support for the Foreclosure Prevention Act and the Emergency Economic Stabilization Act have been related to the degree of constituent default exposure as well as to campaign contributions from the financial industry (Mian, Sufi, & Trebbi, 2011).

International regulatory competition and varying regulatory stringency

The very specific finance literature occupied with the variation in regulatory standards, capital levels, and risk-taking can be grouped into three fields. A first branch on the systemic level has theorized the impact of regulatory variation in the presence of relatively open international financial markets discussing the 'race to the bottom'-argument; A second branch has asked what impact varying regulatory policies have on risk-taking; A third and very scarce branch has made first empirical endeavors into explicating the sources of regulatory variation. It is my intent to make a political economy contribution to complement this growing literature with a theoretical and empirical account that more systematically incorporates the role of varying regulatory institutions and financial systems. The current literature does not sufficiently account for institutions theoretically, but first empirical work has shown that they matter and yield significant correlations.

In terms of the *consequences of regulatory interaction*, a prominent view pertains that competition amongst states will trigger the infamous 'race to the bottom'. Sinn (2004) argues in a game-theoretical model that regulation favors the small and organized groups over the large and unorganized interests and therefore tends to be socially inefficient, particularly, when competition for a mobile factor of production, like capital, is introduced. Since the regulatory target function maximized remains a national one, regulators will produce externalities such as systemic risk and will regulate insufficiently. There will be an undersupply of regulation due to the international externality that risk-seeking banks will impose on foreign lenders of domestic banks, which governments will not internalize. Such competitive laxity has also been found to be an important root cause of the most recent financial crisis, as regulatory agencies relaxed standards, certified opaque financial products prematurely, and supervised banks only mechanically in a concern for their financial centre's competitiveness internationally (H.-W. Sinn, 2010). A related but different externality argument has been developed against the background of the EU regulatory and supervisory infrastructure by Stolz (2002). She argues in her model that the two main purposes of regulation, the protection of depositors and the avoidance of excess systemic risk, are not reflected the same way in the national regulator's incentive structure or utility function. Supervisors that are only accountable to their own jurisdictions, as is the case, will regulate the former at the expense of the latter, since they are not penalized as much for the production of systemic risk. The resulting stringency of regulation will be at an inefficient level, given the ease at which systemic risks can be transmitted through the interbank money market, cross-border establishments, and cross-border lending. Similar conclusions are also reached in other papers, diagnosing very much the same incentive problems on the European (Schoenmaker & Oosterloo, 2008; Schüler, 2003a, 2003b). They also find more empirical evidence for a marked increase in cross-border externalities that regulators do not internalize. Due to the fundamental dis-incentives to regulate systemic risks they argue that ad-hoc improvised cooperation between national authorities will lead to under-provision of public good of bailouts. On a more normative level these papers propose alternative institutional solutions, which lead to incorporation of more systemic information into the regulatory rationale. These solutions vary in the degree of centralization of regulation as the authors assign different value to the role of local information and proximity to the banks. While some suggest a model of national supervisors with much more institutionalized cooperation and information-sharing Stolz suggests a common European supervisor that internalizes all relevant information in its utility function. Policy proposals post-financial crisis have also echoed this view particularly where macro-prudential oversight is concerned (De la Dehesa, 2009).

A small but growing strand of literature has examined *the link between regulatory policy and risk-taking in financial systems*. Basel II's provision for bank discretion in choosing between the internal ratings based approach (IRB) and standardized approaches has been shown to add to risk-taking incentives (Hakenes & Schnabel, 2006). The fact that using an IRB approach is costly and therefore only practical for large banks, which can then reduce their capital holdings against their lending, introduces fierce competition for smaller banks, which in turn will have higher incentives to take on risk. This theoretical moral hazard argument thus assumes that regulation under Basel II not only produces lower capital holdings for larger banks but also relatively higher risk-taking in financial systems at large. Whilst this moral hazard argument points out some of the limitations of Basel, which will be elaborated here as well, it does not provide sufficient theoretical basis for the observed cross-country variation in regulatory stringency and capital ratios. Empirical work on the variations in risk-taking across countries as evidenced by the financial crisis has pointed out that this cross-country variation in risk-taking and capital cushions is real and significant (Beltratti, 2009). These findings corroborate the view that banks were pushed by their boards to maximize profitability through higher risk-taking, as banks with higher pre-crisis returns had significantly higher losses in the crisis. The role of regulation shows up to be significant as countries with oversight have a better performance in the crisis.

With respect to the *sources of the observed variation in regulatory stringency*, the literature is still scarcer. Fonseca and Gonzalez (2006) provide a cross-sectional empirical analysis of varying capital buffers across countries and find that banks that have more market power and are less constrained by market discipline hold lower capital buffers. Regulation in their analysis enters positively if it encourages disclosure practices and limits the engagement in overly risky activities. Brewer, Kaufman, and Wall (2008) also look at variations in bank capital structure as a function of regulatory variables. They distinguish bank-specific and more macro-economic/ regulatory factors and find that both drive differences in capital ratios. Their more encompassing dataset allows them to distinguish the varying effects of different public policy and regulatory factors on bank leverage. Next to espousing the fact that bank equity differs significantly across countries, their key contribution lies in the finding that banks maintain higher capital ratios in countries with smaller banking sectors. However, both of these studies lack a real theoretical underpinning and satisfactory political economy accounts of why these established correlations hold and how institutions shape regulatory preferences and action.

1.3.4 Conclusion: The need for an integrated political economy theory of banking regulation

Having reviewed the general and banking-regulation-specific approaches from the economics and finance, political science, and comparative political economy literature, I would like to briefly summarize the gathered insights to, firstly, establish *what the gaps in the literature are*, secondly, recap *how the existing theory still can inform the resulting approach* to ensure that this research ties in with existing work, and, thirdly, *show how this research intends to innovatively fill the gap left by the existing literature*.

In terms of the research gap, it has been shown that the existing literature has not yet provided a comprehensive theory of regulatory action. Despite first efforts at explaining regulatory action, there is no coherent account of regulatory preferences that would more systematically explain the sources of regulatory deviation across countries (*cross-sectionally*) as well as explain the sources of change in a dynamic context (*over time*). However, regulatory differences are an important phenomenon in finance since they provide opportunities for arbitrage and with integrated financial markets can lead to a competition for laxity producing systemic risks as their main externality. The financial crisis has evidenced this clearly. To cite Mosley and Singer (2009; p.421) on new research opportunities in IPE once more: *"The field of IPE has generally not appreciated the fact that cross-national differences in domestic financial regulation have international repercussions. While the open-economy implications of domestic policy areas such as central banking, taxation, and even welfare spending have garnered substantial attention, the political economy of domestic financial regulation has remained curiously outside the traditional confines of the IPE field."* I would add that there is a lack of accounts establishing systematically how the different *role that banks take on in the various financial systems* and *economies* should influence the regulator's preferences and actions. Providing such political economy micro-foundations of regulatory action to understand their role in regulatory capitalism better and to comprehend the sources of varieties of financial systems better is the main contribution that this research aims to make.

To fill the identified gap in the literature, a coherent model of regulatory action needs to be formulated, incorporating the important insights from the reviewed literature. I therefore summarize the findings from the above reviewed literature, which I intend to critically engage with, build on, and expand as follows:

- Firstly, new political economy studies in banking regulation have established that regulators consider public and private interests in formulating policy. The element of concern derives from the regulator's public mandate as well as an certain relevant private interests such as bank competitiveness. For regulation in its globalized context this has been encapsulated in the regulatory dilemma, that is the trade-off between maintaining competitiveness on the one hand and preserving the confidence of consumers and the stability of the financial system on the other hand (Dell'Ariccia & Marquez, 2006; E.B. Kapstein, 1989; Ethan B. Kapstein, 1992; Lütz, 2002; Singer, 2007).

- Secondly, regulatory harmonization efforts such as the Basel Accords are therefore mostly seen as attempts of regulators to provide a 'level playing field' that allows them to exert discretion within a certain 'winset' (Singer, 2007). Very little though is said about either the other factors such as the interests of firms and individuals in continued credit access, which shape these outcomes. Nor is there much theorizing on the shape that implementation of these standards is likely to take on the national level.
- Thirdly, with respect to the variation in regulatory laxity there is neither an consensus in the economics literature nor a satisfactory political economy account of the drivers behind this variation. Economics does not suggest very specific best practices but rather acknowledges the variation in approaches based on the nature of the market failures and the type of financial system. Political economy research has shown that this discretion can then, depending on the preferences and incentive structure of the regulator, be used for public and private ends; Proponents of the public interest view suggests that this discretion is likely to be motivated by concerns for maintaining micro- and macro-prudential behavior in the financial sector; proponents of the private interest view suggest that this discretion is more likely to fall prey to organized lobbying interests of the financial sector (Barth et al., 2006); First political economy attempts to explain the drivers of such observed patterns of laxity and stringency point to domestic interests and processes of preference formation that – mediated by political institutions - ultimately determine which view will be right for which country. These studies are however based on very limited countries and data points (Rosenbluth & Schaap, 2003) and require further theoretical basis.
- Fourthly, in terms of the cross-sectional variation in either the economy or the financial system the varieties-of-capitalism and the comparative finance literature have provided very powerful and theoretically rich accounts that, whilst not yet addressing the sphere of banking regulation sufficiently, can be built on. These accounts show that regulatory preference formation is likely to be shaped the structure of the financial system (bank- vs. market-based), the consequent specializations and asset-specific investments of firms, and the way that banks are embedded in the wider structure of economic institutions. The role of complementarities producing path dependence and divergence need to be assessed against the economic drivers of change producing convergence to understand the degree of policy convergence.

1.4 Research design

This research wants to fill the gap in the literature by providing a coherent theory of regulatory action within its institutional context across countries and over time to explain the observed variation. It is argued that banking regulators need to be understood as actors that operate and interact in the context of domestic financial systems and legal institutions as well as international policy networks, which together shape their preferences and constrain their regulatory and supervisory actions.

1.4.1 Theoretical framework

Availing itself of both, economics and political science theory of institutions and purposeful action and interaction, this dissertation aims to provide a general political economy approach to studying banking regulatory and supervisory action. aim to develop such a coherent political economy and institutionalist account of banking regulation sequentially, covering the questions set out earlier, which were derived from Persson and Tabellini's (2002) three classical tenets of economic policy-making, which the below table summarizes and complements with the theoretical lens and the specific application of this research. Borrowing the individualistic focus and rational-choice assumptions from economics, this research derives the preferences of economic actors (financial stakeholders across financial systems) and identifies their interests towards policy or regulation, treats institutions as mechanisms of interest aggregation, and where necessary analyzes patterns of bargaining and outcome distribution among the (national or international) actors involved (Lake, 2006). Founding the regulatory action in a micro-theory of political economy preferences for 'public interest objectives' and 'private interest objectives', this research analyzes if and how the such we can explain what one could call varieties of financial stability preferences and regulatory and supervisory policies in banking. Thus, next to an analysis of the economics of banking and regulation, political institutions and strategic interactions within institutional contexts are relevant to determine the available policy strategies from a regulator's point of view, the relative costs, and the discretion in choosing from these options.

TABLE 3: *A three-step political economy approach to financial stability and banking regulation*

Analytical step in theory development	*Theoretical lens/ focus*	*Application in this research*
1. Deriving economic preferences and interests (cross-sectional)	Individualistic rational choice analysis	Derivation of financial stability preferences and interests of key financial stakeholders (depositors, shareholders, and creditors)
2. Aggregate preferences and interests (cross-sectional)	Institutional analysis, including political science assessment of power relations, and interactions	Analysis of preference and interest aggregation looking at the financial system and its legal institutions such as creditor, shareholder, and depositor rights
3. Derive outcomes based on interactions and bargaining (cross-sectional and dynamic)	Game theoretical analysis of interactions	Devise game-theoretical models to depict the key interactions of the financial stability agent (i.e., banking regulator)

Source: Author

This theoretical framework's focus on deriving policy preferences and outcomes from individual actors' interactions within a certain institutional context is consistent with the main tenets of Fritz Scharpf's (1997) actor-centered institutionalist approach to policy research. [21] Actor-centered institutionalism research departs from the assumption that actors, policy makers, regulators, and firms alike act as rational individuals, whose strategic options are shaped but not determined by the institutional environment This entails of course the analysis of the political economy of institutions, which in the tradition of institutionalist accounts puts institutions center stage in explaining economic performance. Douglas North (1990, p.3) defines institutions as *"the rules of the game in a society or, more formally, are the humanly devised constraints that shape human interaction."* Such a political economy account explicitly acknowledges and stresses the central role of institutions and the way they shape human action and interaction, changes in them, and their impact on economic performance across countries and over time. Because institutions vary across countries, as for instance the varieties of financial systems do, we would expect differences in regulatory action and interaction to follow. Moreover, in a dynamic context these institutions are assumed to constitute an element of continuity and path dependence, in other words *"we have no reason to assume a convergence towards one 'best' solution. Institutional development is path-dependent in the sense that where you end up is strongly influenced by where you started from"* (Scharpf, 1997, p.41). Hence, if there are significant differences in the financial and economic systems of countries, we would expect them to correlate with varying regulatory approaches that change and evolve but retain some of their cross-national variation despite that change.

1.4.2 Research variables

Dependent variables

Regulatory action and stringency across financial systems is the main outcome that this research wants to explain. I argue that it can be understood as a causal chain that contains the following analytically separate elements, each of which will be a dependent variable in one of the following chapters:

DV1: *Regulatory preferences and regulatory stringency* (cross-sectionally), which then shape the different opportunity sets and utility functions, and define the costs and benefits of a course of regulatory action for the regulator;

DV2: *Change in regulatory stringency with respect to the implementation of internationally agreed regulatory standards*, which is closely related to institutional change in regulation, since most domestic institutions today are constrained and shaped by international standards;

DV3: *Change in the enforcement of regulation and the practice of banking supervision* as it pertains to changes in capital adequacy levels over time (and across countries);

---

21. The actor-centered institutionalist account provides a framework that *"conceptualizes policy processes driven by the interaction of individual and corporate actors endowed with certain capabilities and specific cognitive and normative orientations, within a given institutional setting and within a given external situation"* (Scharpf, 1997, p.37). Whilst actors are thus one key focus of this approach, actor constellations, interactions, and the institutions that shape all of the above are key as well to determining policy choices and economic outcomes.

As is the aim of this research, these three variables together form a micro-founded theory of preferences and action that can be analyzed in a cross-sectional and time-series context for its 'goodness of fit' and impact on economic outcomes such as leverage and systemic risk. In a first static cross-sectional context, the main *dependent variables* are the *national preferences* of the Euro Zone countries' regulatory and supervisory institutions in banking when entering the Euro Zone with the introduction of the euro in around 2001/2002. While variation in 'regulatory paradigms' is often cited to be a significant and relevant phenomenon in European financial governance (Quaglia, 2010), no coherent theory of preference formation and regulatory action seems to exist to the best of my knowledge. In a dynamic context I then look at the impact of regulatory action on *regulatory and supervisory outcomes* – given exogenous changes, which are of particular interest in a largely 'asymmetric' monetary union.[22] Such exogenous changes can of course impact regulatory action through a change to one of the variables of its utility function. For the Euro Zone these exogenous change factors analyzed are driven by financial integration, which increases cross-border effects as well as competition between financial systems.

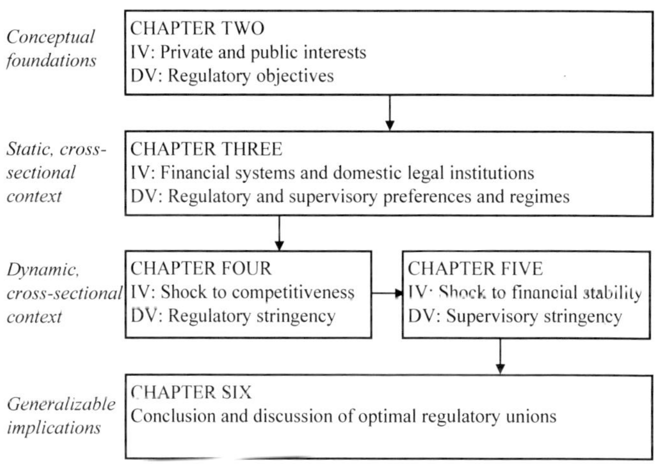

FIGURE 5: *Research design and chapter contents*

Source: Author

Independent variables

To provide such a coherent theory of regulatory action, this research employs independent variables that are derived from a view of regulatory action as purposive behaviour. Policy actors pursue policies, I argue, as political economy strategies that

[22] For a discussion of the various institutional asymmetries in the fiscal and wage setting context across countries see Enderlein (2004); for the manifestation in a 'one size fits none'-policy of the ECB see Enderlein (2005).

reflect their preferences as well as their strategic interactions with private actors and other national regulators on the international level. Thus, both, institutions and interactions, are essential to my argument. Due to these assumed interdependencies of regulatory action I employ game theoretical rigor, where it seems necessary to demonstrate how interactions of varying preferences and interests translated into outcomes. In defining the games, the actors, and their interests, economic analysis and theory is used to determine how actors will benefit or loose from an economic policy or regulation and what efforts to 'lobby' politics they are likely to exert. Actors are therefore usually grouped based on the identity of their preferences or interests with one another. Economic theory thus has a key role in determining the distributional implications of policy, which in the case of banking regulation would be the bearing of risk or expected gain or losses that can be forwarded either to shareholders, to depositors or to creditors. Building on a solid foundation of economic theory, preferences and interests can thus be derived in a very robust and analytically stringent way, which also lends new political economy theory its "distinctive nature and, indeed, explanatory power" (Lake, 2006, p.764). The specific variables employed are:

IV1: *The interaction of the regulators with private and public interests, the strength of each being conditioned by the institutional setting of the national financial system.*

As such, the first interaction that this research will analyze is the interaction between *private and public interests in the domestic institutional setting of the financial system* to establish how it shapes regulatory preferences. Here the key actors are the depositors, who constitute the public interest in financial stability, and the private agents, that is banks' shareholders and recipients of credit, who will be shown to have somewhat conflicting interests. The relative strength of their interests varies by country and is defined by the complementary configuration of national financial systems. Legal institutions provide credible commitments that ensure a certain stability of these preferences and, thus, allow private and public interests to converge around a certain stable approach towards regulation.

IV2: *The interaction of the national regulator with other national regulators within the international institutional policy environment*;

At the international level regulators from different financial systems with varying preferences interact to deal with the externalities of their national regulation on the stability and competitiveness of other countries' banking systems. In the field of financial stability policy international regimes or institutions are relevant due to the presence of international externalities arising from the actions of one state for another. The relevance of systemic risk creation in one state's financial system for the stability of another state's financial system is a clear example of this and provides the rationale for the existence of international bargaining forums such as the 'Financial Stability Forum', the 'G20' or the 'Basel Committee'. Depending on whether or not cooperative outcomes can be attained, regulation, as is shown, can take the shape of a 'race to the bottom' or a 'race to the top'. Here the credility of international institutions drives the dynamic on the international level either towards one or the other.

IV3: *The interaction of supervisors with monetary policy and private interests over time given the preferences and instruments of the regulator/ supervisor*;

Regulators have to implement the agreed regulation through the actual practice of supervision, which results from their *dynamic interaction between supervisors and banks*. Supervisors can set banks' expectations about what levels of leverage and risk will be acceptable and banks can decide whether or not they deem such signals credible and will set their own leverage – using the afforded discretion of internal capital adequacy models – accordingly. All of these, partially sequential, interactions within the respective institutional contexts matter in explaining the variation of regulatory and supervisory stringency across countries and over time. The various chapters pick each of these links up individually, describe the actor configurations, the games played, and the theoretical predictions and empirical evidence along these causal claims.

1.5 The main argument

Most centrally my research finds that national-level differences in financial systems and related institutions explain and drive variation in regulatory financial stability policy across countries and over time. I show that regulators are facing a complex trilemma of policy objectives that can be irreconcilable in the short to medium term, forcing them to make important trade offs with financial stability. The 'impossibility trinity' of policy objectives in the case of banking regulation consists of the simultaneous pursuit of i) financial stability, ii) national bank competitiveness, and iii) credit availability to the domestic credit-reliant economy.

At the heart of the trilemma lies the tension created by the regulation of capital adequacy for stability purposes, the centerpiece of bank regulation, and the economic adjustment mechanism that banks have to follow to comply with such (more or less stringent) leverage regulation. As capital adequacy is regulated more tightly, banks have to adjust and de-leverage either by increasing their capital holdings or by cutting down on their risk-adjusted lending activities. These two very different adjustment mechanisms are both costly to private interests, which therefore creates a two-fold tension with the public interest of financial stability. The former adjustment mechanism is costly for banks, as it harms their relative profitability and competitiveness vis-à-vis less strictly regulated banks; The latter adjustment mechanism is costly as it reduces credit availability to the economy, which therefore reduces output below potential. It is this latter effect of bank regulation on credit availability and the economy, which has been largely ignored by the political economy literature, as it has been primarily occupied with the tension between stability and competitiveness. However, as we turn our focus towards quite a number of European bank-based financial systems, the key function of credit provision to the economy becomes central to our understanding of regulatory preferences in a comparative context. I show that regulators across varying financial systems hold different preferences for each of the three objectives, which they derive from complementary configurations of the macro-economy and in particular the financial system. The relative degree of bank-reliance as well as the relative influence of legal financial stakeholder rights shape regulatory preferences for these objectives and allow a clustering of countries according to these preferences.

The effects of such a trilemma are amplified in the context of a monetary union, which becomes evident particularly in a dynamic context. Due to its institutional governance the Euro Zone is a monetary union but not at the same time a regulatory union. Banks still remain largely domestic, thus leaving national regulators exposed to various political and private pressures in their conduct of discretionary regulatory and supervisory policy. As private interests tend to be well-organized relative to the diffuse public interest in stability, regulatory and supervisory stringency *over time* can be subject to two types of dynamic phenomena, which can induce a relative relaxation of stringency. Firstly, increasing financial integration as under monetary union amplifies the effect of *variation in implementation of international and European-level regulatory standards* and can lead to competition of laxity. I show that indeed there is a differentiated but nonetheless downward trend in stringency in central regulatory standards over time, which can be linked to the degree of openness and exposure of financial systems to each other's regulatory standards. Secondly, *variation in the underlying financial systems and credit reliance causes differential exposures to monetary policy shocks in a monetary union.* As regulators in countries like Spain or Ireland, which experienced very strong shocks to stability through excessively low interest rate credits, are exposed to such shocks, the political economy pressures to avoid clamping down on such credit booms build up. Hence, the implication for regulation is that supervisory stringency over time can relax, as the political economy support for 'leaning against the wind' dwindles. This can be a crucial driver of persistent bank leverage and, thus, explains a key element of the 'boom' and 'bust'-cycles, which we have witnessed in certain countries of the monetary union. As such, the trade-offs behind the trilemma can become amplified by the asymmetric effects of financial integration and a common monetary policy with however differential effects.

My argument is developed in the respective chapters as follows:
Chapter 2 discusses how national banking regulators in a monetary union with integrating financial markets are faced with a trilemma between attaining financial stability, keeping domestic banks internationally competitive, and fueling growth and with ample credit. This trilemma is the result of

- *the multi-dimensional nature of financial stability policy*, which unlike price stability policy is a less clearly measurable policy field that makes banking regulation a very complex task and a classical field of 'quiet' politics;
- *the resulting capture of the regulator by private interests for bank competitiveness and credit access for domestic growth,* which are traded off with financial stability, making banking regulation deeply political;
- the limited *instruments and capabilities available* to address these multiple objectives in a purely stability-oriented way, leading to inevitable trade-offs and a potential 'overstretching' of regulatory financial stability policy - particularly if its regulatory policy is not supported by strong, rules-based macro-prudential instruments, which address the macro-economic effects of banking regulation and allow some coordination with monetary policy;

Chapter 3 shows how national regulators preferences and their use of regulatory instruments in response to the trilemma has historically been conditioned by complementary configurations of the financial system that reduce the salience of one of the three objectives and hence leave the regulator with a trade-off between two remaining objectives. The resulting three stylized regulatory approaches that can be found are:

- The *'relationship' finance approach*, which assigns a strong role to banks in providing finance to the economy and providing intertemporal risk-sharing through large universal banks; creditors and depositors rights are more strongly developed, while lower shareholder rights and the institution of 'patient capital' (including in some cases state owned banks or cooperatives) reduce the salience of competitiveness;
- The *'competitive self-regulatory' finance approach*, which is most compatible with a hybrid financial system, that produces very highly competitive banks as well as good access to credit through both banks and markets; creditors and shareholders have strong institutionalized rights, while limited depositor rights/ deposit insurance limits moral hazard, which along with strong market-side surveillance is key in providing financial stability;
- The *'arm's length' finance approach*, which is associated with the market-based financial system, which relies less on banks for credit access but instead employs markets as institutional vehicles for corporate finance and risk-sharing; shareholders and depositors are stronger here reflecting the focus on bank competitiveness and financial stability, while the salience of 'credit access' as a regulatory objective is clearly reduced due to the mentioned presence of deep and liquid capital markets;

Chapter 4 analyzes how increasing financial integration, as follows the introduction of a monetary union, went far enough to induce institutional change in the various national financial systems but has not produced truly 'European' banking, thus, leaving the financial systems 'caught in transition'[23] and causing asymmetric political economy shocks due to national competitiveness considerations.

- The *financial integration* pattern after EMU has proceeded at different speeds, creating more cross-border traffic in the case of banking but failing to create truly pan-European banks and instead leaving banking more domestic than European.
- The *national variation in implementation of international and European-level regulatory standards* at the same time has laid the foundations for an 'unlevel playing field', causing national regulators to react to each other's regulatory stringency.
- The *resulting shocks to national competitiveness* have led to institutional change and in the crucial area of capital adequacy definition has led countries on average reducing their stringency of capital definitions over time, consistent with the 'race to the bottom'-hypothesis.

Chapter 5 looks at the way that regulation can be enforced in an asymmetric monetary union. Differences in the countries economies can cause asymmetric shocks to stability through excessive credit growth in certain countries, limiting the political economy

---

[23] A similar argument is also made by Enderlein (forthcoming) in "Lost in transaction: German banking and the financial market crisis" focusing in particular on the incomplete transition of the German financial system.

support in these countries for national discretionary banking regulation in 'leaning against the wind'.

- The Euro Zone is an *asymmetric monetary union*, which means that while there is one real interest rate there are varying levels of inflation across countries and, thus, real interest rates, causing varying shocks to credit supply across the union.
- The *variation in bank-reliance and credit-reliance of the national financial and economic systems* again causes these shocks to lead to varying demands for credit expansions and bank leverage across the Euro Zone.
- The *resulting positive shocks to credit and economic output* put high political economy pressures on regulators, who in the absence of rules-based regulators instruments will find it hard to commit to a hawkish policy stance.

In *Chapter 6* I conclude with a reflection on the degree to which the Euro Zone constitutes an 'optimal regulatory union' as well as with a discussion of the implications for political economy research and policy.

2

Trading off financial stability: A political economy perspective on European banking regulation

"There is no such thing as a free lunch."

Fundamental economic principle; as a quote often attributed to Milton Friedman

The previous chapter outlined the main theoretical underpinnings that will inform this approach to the political economy of banking regulation. This chapter wants to complement this with a first look at the formation of regulatory preferences for financial stability policy. The infamous insight of economics that "there is no such thing as a free lunch" also applies to financial stability policy, as I argue. Instead financial stability policy is a multi-dimensional policy space with many stakeholders and principals bargaining over the optimal use of a very limited set of instruments. Due to the lack of political salience that financial stability policy enjoys in tranquil economic times it lends itself particularly well to capture – the more so the more important the role of banks is in the financial system. In particular in the institutional setup of the Euro Zone with one monetary policy but varying financial systems and preferences this can lead to excessive bank leverage and financial instability as seen in the financial crisis of 2007/8. I develop this argument subsequently as follows:

- Firstly, this chapter opens up the analytical space defining the *overall public interest or mandate,* which regulators are assigned, namely, defining the *goal of financial stability*. As will be shown, the breadth of the policy objective and its interrelations with other policy mechanisms, that do not necessarily relate harmoniously with it, make the pursuit of financial stability through banking regulation a very complex task, which increases the political burden of decision-making in the national regulatory realm.
- Secondly, a political economy perspective of *financial stability policy objectives* shows that in the absence of a one-dimensional and measurable policy objective (e.g. as inflation for price stability policy) the regulator is also subject to *capture*[24] *by private interests, which are traded off with financial stability*, making banking regulation deeply political. A brief review of regulatory mandates and financial stability reports across the Euro Zone confirms that beyond financial stability all regulatory bodies explicitly or implicitly consider other objectives in their policy conduct.

24 This terminology of 'capture' is used to reflect the concept of the role of private interests in regulation, which is theoretically very well-developed by the regulatory economics literature and dates back to the work by George Stigler (1962; for an overview of his impact see Peltzman, 1993). However, it is not to imply that regulators across the Euro Zone are engaged in fraudulent or corrupt activity – instead it is my view that is the channels of intellectual and political capture are much the drivers of 'captured' behaviour. It is in this way that I employ the term to avoid "devaluing the efforts of many overworked and underpaid public servants around the world" (Davies, 2010a).

- Thirdly, I discuss the role of *national banking regulation in the context of monetary union and the European multi-level financial stability governance.* I show how the Euro Zone differs distinctly in how it separates the use of monetary policy and banking regulation on the European and the national level, respectively, limiting the role of the ECB (in particular pre-crisis) to price stability and assigning the financial stability mandate largely to national regulators, which in some but not all cases of course are the central banks.
- Fourthly, I show that in this particular setup national regulators have limited *instruments and capabilities available,* since they can only maneuver their instrument of regulatory and supervisory stringency along the various objectives assigned to (or expected of) them. I argue that this can cause potential conflicts or 'overstretching' of regulatory financial stability policy, particularly if it regulatory policy is not supported by strong, rules-based macro-prudential instruments, which address the macro-economic effects of banking regulation and allow some coordination with monetary policy.
- Finally, I conclude with a presentation of the *regulatory trilemma,* which I argue can result from an gap between the regulatory mandate and objectives and the institutional setting of the national banking regulation in an integrating monetary union, which leaves too many trade-offs to be resolved at the national level with only one regulatory instrument available. I argue that the way countries deal with this trilemma gives us insights about their regulator preferences and is a useful analytical tool to trace financial stability policy in a comparative perspective. The existence of the trilemma and its dynamic over time will force national regulators to either i) find national complementary institutions, which reduce the salience of certain objectives for the regulator (e.g., 'patient capital to reduce the salience of bank competitiveness) or – in particular in the face of exogenous shocks – ii) to unintentionally neglect financial stability due to the overly strong pre-occupation with other conflicting regulatory objectives.

2.1 Financial stability

Banking regulators are assumed to pursue the public interest of financial stability (as well as potential private interests, as we will see later), which therefore firstly requires (i) a definition of financial stability, (ii) an understanding of the different elements of financial stability that the regulator needs to ensure.

2.1.1 Financial stability defined

Financial stability as a policy goal emerged more in response to the consequences of its absence and the challenges posed by systemic risks. The financial stability profession has for a long time been doing without a proper definition of financial stability, instead emphasizing it as a negative concept (i.e., the absence of financial instability). However, it is appropriate to ask: What defines financial stability in a positive sense? Schinasi (2004) suggests five principles that are defining of financial stability and therefore inform his definition of financial stability: 1) Financial stability is a broad concept relating to the entire financial system; 2) Financial stability also should encompass the functioning of finance in the economy including monetary aspects such as the payments system; 3) It includes that a financial system should handle imbalances naturally; 4) It should be embedded in the well-functioning of the real economy; 5) Financial stability takes place along a continuum, i.e. it is dynamic and composed of many elements of the financial system, not all of which have to be in a stable state at all times for financial stability to be present. These principles inform the financial systems approach taken in this paper and are very congruent with Schinasi's following comprehensive financial stability definition:

"A financial system is in a range of stability whenever it is capable of facilitating (rather than impeding) the performance of an economy, and of dissipating financial imbalances that arise endogenously or as a result of significant adverse and unanticipated events" (Schinasi, 2004; p.8)

This definition also sheds some light on the trade-offs that the practice of regulating for financial stability entails: Firstly, the role of the financial system as opposed to the financial sector only is emphasized, which implies that the regulator needs to take a systemic perspective. This, as we will see in the next section, is complicated since the regulatory toolkit is mainly on the level of the institution. Secondly, this systemic perspective of a "facilitating financial system" requires the regulator to trade off various interests – particularly those of the financial firms versus those of the other participants in the economy, i.e. households and non-financial firms. Thirdly, "dissipating financial imbalances" in most cases will involve intervention the regulator against short-term market forces, which will involve a trade-off of efficiency vs. stability, as Schinasi finds as well (2004).

A particularly relevant case from a regulatory point of view of course is the situation, when such financial instability derives from the inherent instability of the banking sector itself. Most analysts agree that these types of risks are the ones that brought the financial system 'on the brink' during the recent financial crisis. Two sources of financial instability that are endogenous to the financial system can analytically be distinguished: Individual failure of a single financial intermediary (Schinasi, 2004) and systemic failure of many parts of the financial system (Crockett, 2001), both of which we will turn to next.

Micro prudential level. Instability of a financial institution

There are two elements to the justification for regulating and supervising individual banks: One is the fact that they hold consumers money in deposits, which is covered by deposit insurance. As such government and the general public hold a de facto contingent claim (having sold a put option on the bank's assets), which creates significant problems of moral hazard. The second element is that banks by themselves tend to be inherently instable and prone to risk taking. Since the previous chapter has already established the first element, namely that banking regulation at the level of the individual institution is justified to limit the moral hazard created by the deposit insurance, this element will not be rehearsed here. Instead I would like to dig deeper into the inherent instability of banks and explore why what problems micro-prudential regulation needs to address as a consequence to prevent instability on the institutional level.

The starting point is the economic vulnerability that is inherent in the business model of banks, which derives from the fact that banks transform the maturity of assets and end up holding illiquid assets to provide liquid liabilities to their customers (Freixas & Rochet, 2008). This creates a structural mismatch of the term structure of assets and liabilities also called *liquidity risk*. Moreover, banks tend to be highly leveraged, i.e. hold a high amount of liabilities in relation to capital to finance their assets when compared to non-financial companies – this represents another source of *liquidity risk*. Next to these financial structure risks, there are risks that derive from the nature of the business banks engage in, lending, borrowing, and investing, which is subject to a host of information asymmetries that create further risks. As such, banks are exposed to *credit risk* regarding counterparties, *yield risk* regarding the development of interest rates on their assets and liabilities, and *market risk* regarding returns in trading. Moreover, as any business, banks are subject to *operational risks* that derive from potential failures of their internal processes and staff, including management (Ware, 1996). The Basel Committee defines risks in banking in very similar terms, adding only risks such as concentration risks and country transfer risk as additional categories of risk in their 'Core Principles' of banking supervision (Bank for International Settlements, 2006), which in nature however are very related to general credit or counterparty risk.

Coupling these inherent risks with the observation that the government has extended a safety net along with deposit insurance in nearly all countries, the rationale for regulation is clear. Bank regulation tries to regulate and supervise these inherent risks and instabilities through its micro-prudential level of regulation. While the tools will be analyzed in a later section, it is already possible to the basic trade-off that banking regulators face when addressing these instabilities of financial intermediaries: Ceteris paribus, the stricter that bank regulators with the intention of increasing consumer confidence in the banks that serve them, the more they will reduce the short-term profitability of a bank. This is because short-term profitability in competitive markets to a large extent derives from engaging in riskier activities such as short-term financing, leveraging, and high-yielding investments in risky assets. Hellmann, Murdock, and Stiglitz (1997) show for developing countries how a policy of *financial restraint* that actually restricts banking competition to create rents leads to more prudential behavior and better development. Small interventions for instance in the deposit-rate setting can increase franchise value and "will increase their own equity stakes and make these institutions behave in a more proprietary way" (p.165). Thus, given that profitability leads to the accumulation of capital and franchise value (the main insurance against risky behavior), the regulator has an interest in bank profitability, will take this trade-off very seriously, and is unlikely to always err on the side of caution. As such, the regulator has a discretionary space to make complex trade-offs between two legitimate goals of banking regulation, profitability/ competitiveness and stability, to ensure the micro-prudential functioning of banks.

Macro-prudential level: Instability of a financial system

The more recent systemic-risk-literature has examined the system-level inherent financial instability and has tried to break down the components of financial instability in terms of the *systemic risks* that can emanate from the banking sector itself. The similarity of these two concepts, systemic risk and financial instability, can be grasped when comparing the Federal Reserve Governor Daniel Tarullo's definition of systemic risk to the above definition of financial instability:

"Financial institutions are systemically important if the failure of the firm to meet its obligations to creditors and customers would have significant adverse consequences for the financial system and the broader economy." (quoted in Brownlees & Engle, 2010; p.2)

Essentially then, financial institutions themselves can be a source of financial instability if they are important enough to the system through their production of systemic risk. But what constitutes systemic risk? Classical finance theory as in the Capital-Asset-Pricing-Model (CAPM) distinguishes two types of risks in any firm: Idiosyncratic risk, which is specific to a firm and which diversification strategies can eliminate, and market or systematic risk, which is related to the covariance of the stock returns with market returns, something that can not be diversified away and therefore needs to be compensated through higher returns (for an overview see Ross, Westerfield, & Jaffe, 2002). Systemic risk is related to the latter type of systematic risk in that covariance of individual returns with market returns form an important element of systemic risk measures. However, most recent systemic risk measures go beyond that to account for other systemic sources of risk apart from covariance. The prominent "CoVaR" systemic risk measure suggested by Adrian and Brunnermeier (2008) is centered on the observation that co-movement tends to increase during financial crisis and spreads looses around financial system. Hence, their measure of systemic assesses co-variation along with other factors such as leverage rather than individual value at risk (VaR) only, as the current micro-prudential measure of VaR does. Systemic risk creation in a world of Basel II, where only VaR is measures, is the perfect arbitrage strategy as it allows institutions to turn their risk into an externality whilst receiving higher returns. Basel II is undermined due to the low correlation between VaR and CoVaR. Their suggestion therefore is to measure systemic risk through the measurement of the value at risk of any institution, conditional on the other institutions being in distress, i.e. conditional on other institutions' return being at their VaR-level. This measures the degree to which a particular institution is exposed to risk spillovers from other institutions during a crisis. Macro-prudential regulation should help financial institutions to internalize these externalities that their actions create for the financial system, for instance measuring and penalizing each portfolio's increase in CoVaR. The focus of this approach thus is more on tail risk rather than mean returns, which are measured in systematic risk.

Central to the new work on systemic risk measurement is the concept of excessive leverage or under-capitalization, which most authors agree to be a key driver of systemic risk. Work by economists of the NYU Stern School of Business on providing a definition of systemic risk (Acharya, 2009; Acharya et al., 2010; Brownlees & Engle, 2010) departs from the observation that systemic crises are constituted by an undercapitalization of the financial system, which in turn implies that the systemic-risk component for each bank, the systemic expected shortfall (SES), is equal to *"the expected amount a bank is undercapitalized in a future systemic event in which the overall financial system is undercapitalized. Said differently, SES increases in the bank's expected losses during a crisis"* (Acharya, Pedersen, Philippon, & M Richardson, 2010; p.3). So the main focus in this definition is the expected loss of capital that a firm occurs in an extreme tail end situation of overall market returns, i.e. a crisis. Systemic expected shortfall is expected to increase in the variables *leverage, volatility of asset returns, correlation of asset returns, and tail-dependence*. Thus, the role of the regulator from a systemic risk point of view would be to make firms *internalize these externalities* through for instance a tax or a related tool, which would be based on the marginal contribution of each firm to the total SES. This indeed is the concept that underlies the measurement of systemic risk on a firm level, suggested by Acharya et al., which breaks down the total SES in percentage terms for each institutions and shows empirically how these values explain the pattern of the financial crisis of 2007-9 rather well. Thus, co-variance of returns, leverage, excessive volatility in returns, and tail-dependence resemble common measures of systemic risk, which can create instability from the banking sector itself.

2.1.2 Financial stability as a policy field

Financial stability as a policy field, I argue, is defined by i) its public good characteristics; ii) a very high diffusion of these benefits as well as well-organized special interests; iii) its relatively low political salience in times of stability, which enable private interests to penetrate into the regulatory objective function.
The public good nature of financial stability provides the rationale for government intervention in financial stability through the regulator. Economics sees a role for government in the production of certain goods, in this case the production of micro- and macro-prudential behavior for the sake of stability, when these goods can be classified as *public goods*. The theory of *public goods* defines two criteria that these type of goods have to satisfy, which are non-rivalry and non-excludability (Stiglitz, 2000). Applied to the case of financial stability these two criteria suggest that indeed financial stability is a public good: Financial stability is

- *non-rivalrous* in that consumption of financial stability by one actor (e.g., banks, depositors, firms, and households) does not subtract from the amount of financial stability available for consumption by other actors in the same system, and
- *non-excludable* in that financial stability is a common pool resource, from which no consumer can effectively be excluded.

Particularly the latter point makes financial stability as a public good problematic, as free-riding on the provision of public good becomes a profitable possibility for each and every market participant in the national context as well as each and every country in the international context. The likely result of non-excludability of a public good will therefore be an *inefficient under-provision* of this good due to such free-rider problems, which in turn justify a role for government in regulating the production of financial stability.

A political economy analysis along the lines of Olson's theory of 'collective action' (Olson, 1965) suggests that capture is a very likely and relevant phenomenon in banking regulation indeed. The theory of collective action posits that the pursuit of the public interest through the provision of a non-excludable public good such as financial stability is particularly at risk, when the costs of its absence are diffused and the benefits of not providing it are concentrated. In the case of banking regulation and financial stability, this is indeed the case: The group affected most by the absence of financial stability consists of a large number of depositors and taxpayers, who will find it difficult to organize for their interests, since they are facing large costs to organizing. On the other hand, the interests of bank shareholders are material to each of the relatively small groups, which implies that as self-interested rational actors they will organize and lobby for their collective interests. In the case of debtors and even leveraged households again one can find small groups with clear interests (such as firms or the real estate sector), who will find it in their interests to further those private interests. As such, it is likely that these interests – under particular institutional settings - can find their way into the objective function of policy-makers.[25]

How and when can these interests be inserted into policy? From a political science perspective it is the *low political salience*, in particular in times of relative economic prosperity and financial stability, when banking regulation and related policies receive relatively little attention, which makes this policy area particularly open for the insertion of non-public good interests. Political salience matters in the political economy of democratic polities, as Pepper Culpepper (2011) shows. Culpepper shows for a variety of political economies that 'noisy' politics differs significantly from 'quiet' politics. As such, many regulatory areas of high political economy relevance are subjects of 'quiet' politics and are thus actually subject to strong business influence due to the low salience that they enjoy with respect to public and media attention, hence, decreasing the political involvement in the resolution of these regulatory issues. Culpepper's methodology rests on the analysis of news media mention of different topics to determine salience. I am interested to show that financial stability policy varies over time, since it has the property that it can turn from an issue of low salience into high salience, when the effects of unsuccessful financial stability policy materialize in financial crisis.

As an indication of this, Figure 6 below shows the distribution of 'financial stability' searches in Google over time, indicating the intuitive point that indeed a relatively 'quiet' area of political economy only generates public attention, when its policy fails to live up to its financial stability mandate. Throughout the 'great moderation', financial stability policy and banking regulation enjoyed low salience. This makes them subject to the rule of 'quiet politics', in which private interests play a much stronger role. As Culpepper outlines, lobbying capacity, the role of expertise and private interest committees, as well as influence over the tone of media coverage all

[25] Empirical reality bears this argument as the European case evidences: In the aftermath of the financial crises the new stricter regulatory initiatives in the European Parliament found so much resistance in the form of lobbying and information provision on the likely costs to competitiveness, that parliamentarians organized a counter-balancing lobby themselves. As the Financial Times reports (Hönighaus, 2010), parliamentarians of all parties complained that the horror scenarios on the likely consequences of regulation were not matched with data and information on the benefits. The fact that this perception is no singular incidence is evidenced by the fact that the new expert group on banking matters at the European Union consisting of 40 members contains 37 representatives from the financial industry (Tagesspiegel, 2010). To overcome such collective action and resulting information problems, parliamentarians have therefore themselves initiated a lobby group themselves by the name of "Finance Watch", which is supposed to provide them with balancing information (Frankfurter Allgemeine Zeitung, 2011), indicating the relevance of private interests in the objective function of legislators and, thus, likely also the regulators.

shape 'quiet' politics in a different way from 'noisy' politics. Thus, in such an area of 'quiet' politics with a multi-dimensional and complex policy objective such as financial stability it is likely that private and political interests towards the regulatory are likely to penetrate. The pre-dominance of such private interests in the context of banking are a well-known phenomenon, which led the famous banker Mayer Amschel Bauer Rothschild to conclude decades ago very candidly that *"the few who understand the system will either be so interested from its profits or so dependent on its favours that there will be no opposition from that class"*.

To briefly corroborate the relevance of such private interest efforts towards regulators, it is worthwhile turning to the arguments directed towards regulators from organized private interests such as bank lobbies in the context of changes to leverage regulation. A study commissioned by the German banking lobby, the Bundesverband Deutscher Banken, and directed at policymakers is very informative in this context as it analyzes the impact of an increase in the leverage ratio in these exact terms (Frenkel & Rudolf, 2010):[26]

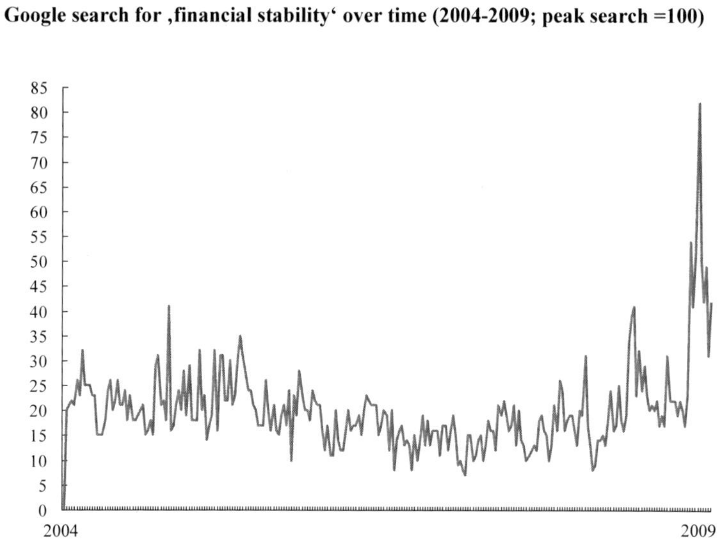

FIGURE 6: *Financial stability as a 'quiet'/ low political salience policy field*

Source: Author based on Google Analytics data (2011) using global data for the time between January 2004 and the end of 2009

26 For a rebuttal of these views see Admati, DeMarzo, M. Hellwig, and Pfleiderer (2010).

- Firstly, it is argued, the macroeconomic impact of a more stringent leverage ratio will lead to a *reduction in credit*, since capital will be hard to come by. This impact will be particularly hard for the German small and medium sized businesses, which are particularly loan-dependent.
- Secondly, the likely reaction of banks across countries will be to turn to other sources of income such as capital market-related activities that could involve higher risk-taking, which would put German banks at a *competitive disadvantage*.

The suggested path of action for regulators is to therefore at least negotiate a longer transition period for German banks to implement such a leverage ratio, which – by correlation or causation – is exactly the outcome that the agreed Basel III leverage ratio has yielded. Similar debates have been taking place also across the Atlantic, where influential banker Jamie Dimon voiced his concerns about the likely impact of stricter capital rules on the largest banks, including JP Morgan, which he manages, in a more than candid way, alluding to the very impact on the economy and competitiveness of American banks (Braithwaite & Jenkins, 2011):

"I think any American president, secretary of Treasury, regulator or other leader would want strong, healthy global financial firms and not think that somehow we should give up that position in the world and that would be good for your country. (...) I'm very close to thinking the United States shouldn't be in Basel any more. I would not have agreed to rules that are blatantly anti-American. Our regulators should go there and say: 'If it's not in the interests of the United States, we're not doing it'."

Thus, a political economy perspective needs to look at financial stability policy and banking regulation as a policy area with a high degree of stakeholder influence, subject to a multiplicity of objectives, which are likely to go beyond the pure public good objective of financial stability itself. This argument should of course not be overstated. Regulators by and large still have financial stability on their minds, but they are also subjected to other influences. It is the threat of political intervention, should financial stability policy rise to become an issue of political salience, that keeps the regulators 'on their toes' and makes them acknowledge the legislature's interests. This, as Singer also points out, is most likely to most influential way that political accountability conditions the degree of influence of the political realm on the preference function of the regulator:

"To minimize the possibility of legislative intervention, the regulator must take into account the legislature's preferences. Regulations that are too lax (e.g., low minimum capital levels for financial institutions) will ultimately contribute to faltering firms and a crisis of confidence among voters, triggering a swift intervention by elected officials" (2007; p. 23).

2.1.3 Conclusion

I propose two important takeaways from this conceptual and political economy discussion of banking regulation:

- Firstly, the analytical breakdown of financial instability, its increasing occurrence and very real consequences, and the inherent nature of the financial system to produce systemic risk have driven home the important point that this is an area *that requires regulation to reduce the production of this harmful externality.* Financial stability on the other hand has all the features of a public good, in that its consumption is non-rival and non-excludable, which implies that it justifies government intervention to ensure the adequate level of production of it.

- Secondly, the vast concept of financial stability proposed shows that regulators, in providing this public good, will also look beyond the immediate scope of the stability of a single financial intermediary or even the system as a whole. In formulating banking regulatory policy as a 'non-salient' policy topic (most of the time), the regulator will be subject to strong private interests, which lobby for the competitiveness of the financial system and the credit access for the real economy, creating a multi-dimensional policy function for the regulator. Since there might be conflicts between these goals, it will be important to understand what *specific objectives banking regulators have to pursue as well as what tools they have at their disposal* in pursuing their objective function. This will be analyzed in the next sections.

2.2 Regulatory policy objectives

Financial stability remains, as was shown, a vast and somewhat opaque concept that goes beyond price stability and encompasses the stability of individual financial institutions as well as of the financial system and the wider economy. Given that regulators themselves as well as the objectives that they pursue are deeply embedded in the financial system at large and the wider economy, it is worth examining the *comprehensive set of regulatory objectives* that banking regulators are faced with in practice. Complementing the already discussed 'public interest' rationale for regulation, a 'private interest' view of regulation is presented. A political economy model of regulatory objectives needs to capture both dimensions of regulatory preferencs: The *public interest* preferences that provide the economic rationale for what works and what doesn't work in regulating a system for financial stability; also, the *private interest* preferences that reflect banks and beneficiaries of bank policy such as debtors, that have special interest towards the formulation of banking regulation; Therefore the following section provides an integrated political model of banking regulation, firstly, reviewing the economics perspective towards regulation (equivalent to the public interest view) and then, secondly, complementing it by the political science perspective of likely special interests towards regulation (equivalent to the private interest view) to arrive at an overarching point of view. This proposed model then is suggested to yield higher explanatory power, as it better reflects the real mandate of banking regulators and allows variation in the importance of each objective across countries (contingent on the strength of preferences for the respective objectives) and over time (contingent on exogenous shocks and the degree of insulation of the regulator from these shocks, which relates to institutional design). What emerges from this comprehensive review of financial stability objectives and policy is that banking regulation is indeed "more of an art than a science", requiring complex trade-off decisions among three types of regulatory objectives using instruments that always have repercussions on more than one of the regulatory objectives. As such, it can be concluded that financial stability policy is deeply political as by necessity it needs to trade off potentially conflicting economic objectives and respective stakeholder interests with each other to formulate policy.

2.2.1 The public interest view: The regulator as delegated monitor for financial stability

A *public interest view needs* to depart from the economic analysis of market failures that need to be corrected to provide net welfare gain. Banking regulators are conceptualized as economic institutions that serve to correct specific market failures that would arise in 'unfettered markets'. From an economic point of view there are three specific market failures that require regulatory responses:

- **Anti-competitive behaviour**: Due to the high relevance of scope and scale economies in banking, banking has a high tendency towards conglomeration and anti-competitive behaviour, which begs regulatory action to create an efficient and competitive banking system (Beck, 2008; Matutes & Vives, 2000).
- **Information asymmetries**: Financial intermediaries rely on funds from their depositors (and to a lesser extent on shareholders) – since depositors are fragmented and have little individual incentive and ability to monitor banks in the presence of deposit insurance, regulators act as delegated monitors for depositors to overcome information asymmetries through regulation and supervision.
- **Systemic financial instability**: Financial intermediaries are inherently instable due to the natural liquidity, credit, market, and operational risks, which they expose themselves to. As financial intermediaries' business consists of key economic functions such as ensuring the payments system, asset transformation, risk management, and the solution of information asymmetries in lending, the instability of a single systemic institution or the entire system at large creates repercussions for the wider economy. Therefore the bankruptcy and wind-down of certain large institutions is not economically feasible and should best be avoided through regulation and supervision.

The latter market failure is obviously the one that is of most interest given the focus of this research. Yet, the other objectives interact with this objective in an important way (e.g., 'too big too fail' results from a lack of competition) and should, thus, not be forgotten. In the particular case of the European Union, competition regulation however is separate from financial stability regulation and thus does not fall under the mandate of financial regulators but instead is the task of specialized competition authorities at the national and European level. The role of monitoring banks with respect to information asymmetries (often called 'conduct of business'-regulation) and the pursuit of financial stability are in the realm of national financial regulators. In the pursuit financial stability, banking regulators would be serving as agents of their principals, which consists of the following largely overlapping stakeholder groups:

- **Depositors**: Bank depositors have a natural *interest in the stability of the individual bank* with which they hold their deposits and can therefore be expected to lobby for strong deposit insurance rights with high coverage and low (or no) co-insurance on their part.

- **Taxpayers**: To the extent that deposit insurance and the implicit insurance of 'too-big-to-fail'-banks by governments forwards the costs of a failing institution on to public debt, taxpayers of course hold *similar interests as depositors* as they jointly would have to cover (as they have done in many countries in the financial crisis of 2007/8) the costs to instability through the fiscal guarantees and liquidity injections that national central banks and finance ministries provide.

In theory, these market failures would be addressed by stringent regulation and, given that regulators would want to err on the side of caution as representatives of their principals, one would expect a rather *overly stringent level of regulation*. However, banking regulation in reality does not take place in a vacuum and therefore is subject to other stakeholder interests beyond those of the general public as well, which result in a trade-off with the stability goal.

2.2.2 The private interest view: The regulator as captured agent for credit and competitiveness

The *private interest view* departs from the key stakeholders or interest groups and their respective interests in the provision of goods by the banking system. Two groups of private stakeholders can be distinguished analytically, even though in reality of course individual members of society might find themselves belonging to more than one group – a reality though that any interest group analysis in politics needs to contend with.

- **Banks' shareholders**: Banks and their shareholders, as has been established by banking theory, hold very different interest to bank depositors, as they have an *interest in a profitable banking enterprise* also through risk taking at the expense of financial stability. Thus, competitiveness of the banking sector is the key interest, which - in the presence of international competition from foreign banks – also comprises an interest in a competitive financial centre and as few regulatory dis-advantages towards competitors as possible.
- **Banks' debtors and creditors** (firms and households): Bank debtors hold a strong *interest in stable, affordable access to funding*. As such, they are more affected by the systemic impact of the banking system through their access to funds and their own exposure to the financial markets through banks – their interest in financial stability thus relates more to the systemic stability of banks and the financial system. It is this objective, which is most malleable and subject to government intervention, since the banking system can effectively be leveraged to promote certain social objectives as a "source of off-budget finance to fund initiatives for which they chose not raise taxes or to borrow" (Allen & Herring, 2001, p.12). Particularly housing finance but also credit to the credit-dependent or exporting part of the economy are examples of such initiatives by government.

When combining the two views, three regulatory objectives can be derived: The objectives of a stable banking system, a competitive (profitable) banking system and financial centre, and a growing economy with sufficient credit access together form what I propose to be the most salient regulatory political economy objectives, the strength of which will of course vary across countries.

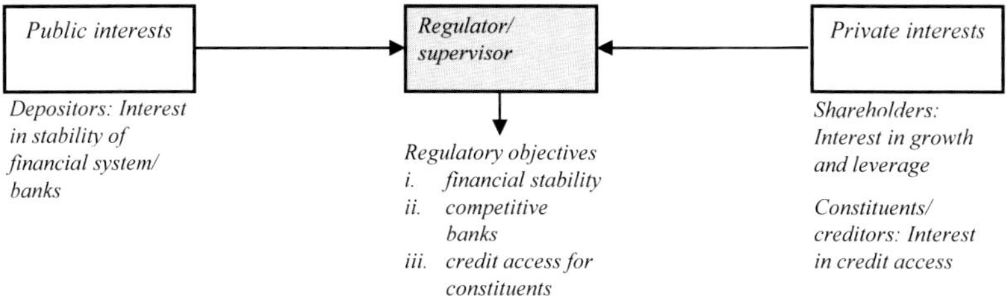

FIGURE 7: *Private and public interests and resulting regulatory objectives*

Source: Author

2.2.3 National regulatory mandates

To verify whether the three assumed objectives of banking regulators do reflect the actual policy priorities, I look at the banking regulators in the Euro Area and - due to their relevance in the financial sphere - the United Kingdom and the United States. One indication for the relevance of these three objectives is their mention in the official regulatory mandate of the regulatory and supervisory institutions of the Euro Zone countries. This stress on official mandates reflects the fact that regulators as non-elected officials will of course require a mandate for their courses of actions. At the same time, this rather legalistic stance should also not be exaggerated, given that regulators have to operate in a political environment, where interests are voiced through many different channels, which are likely to be considered regardless of whether the official mandate assigns an official role to the interests or not.[27]

A look at the mandates of banking regulators in the Euro Area shows that there is a certain variation across different official mandates, which emphasize different aspects of the above mentioned three regulatory objectives over others. Table 4 emphasizes this by pointing out the relative official importance that the mandate of the national regulators puts on these respective objectives. Evidently, the financial stability objective is named as the overriding shared objective across all regulators. However, regulatory mandates are formulated very broadly (D Masciandaro, Quintyn, & Taylor, 2008) and as such are often complemented by other objectives reflecting the role of a profitable banking system and an efficient access of the economy to finance. Thus, the analysis of these mandates (see table below and addendum III in Appendix) shows that indeed all three objectives find mention across the Euro Zone. Moreover, even in those cases, where the other objectives next to financial stability are not reflected in the wording of the regulator's mandate, they receive special mention and attention in the official financial stability publication (see Table 4),

[27] This view was emphasized in interviews with a former senior regulator as well as a former chief economist from leading regulatory and financial stability bodies in major G8 counties, who both emphasized that mandates are always relative and only partially insulate an institution from relevant and organized interests beyond that mandate. One interview partner describe them rather as "fig leafs" to hide behind on specific occasions but as insufficiently strong for doing so n a continuous basis.

thereby reflecting the relevance as an (implicit) objective of the regulatory institution.[28] Thus, all Euro Zone regulators are faced with a similar set of objectives even though the official importance attached to them varies.

Upon closer inspection it becomes clear though that the official mandates are unlikely to be an exhaustive or entirely accurate reflection of the actual policy priorities that the regulators in these countries hold. As an example of a major - if however non-Euro Zone – financial system, the UK's Financial Service Authority's mandate makes no mention of ensuring the competitiveness of the City of London, the world's leading financial centre and banking stronghold and contributor of 16 % of income tax and 11% of UK corporate tax (McKinsey & Company, 2008).

TABLE 4: *Regulatory mandates and objectives*

(● *= official mandate;* • *= reflected in financial stability report)*

Country	*Regulatory institution*	*Financial stability*	*Profitable & competitive banking*	*Efficient access to credit*
Austria	Oesterreichische Nationalbank (OeNB)	●	•	•
Belgium	National Bank of Belgium	●	•	●
Finland	Bank of Finland	●	•	●
France	Commission Bancaire	●	●	•
Germany	Deutsche Bundesbank/ BaFin	●	●	•
Greece	Bank of Greece	●	•	•
Ireland	Central Bank of Ireland	●	•	●
Italy	Bank of Italy	●	●	•
Luxembourg	Commission de Surveillance du Secteur Financier	●	•	•
Netherlands	De Nederlandsche Bank	●	•	•
Portugal	Banco de Portugal	●	•	●
Spain	Banco de Espana	●	•	●
United Kingdom	Bank of England	●	•	●
United States	Federal Reserve (& other regulators)	●	•	•

Source: Author (based on table/ addendum III in Appendix)

[28] The legitimacy of interpreting the mention of such considerations as an indication of them being an implicit objective of the regulator is supported by the fact that regulators themselves look to mandates and documentation of other central banks as indications of their priorities. A speech by the Fed's Vice Chairman at the time Roger Ferguson (Ferguson, 2002) on the role of financial stability as an objective makes reference to the same kind of approach by comparing other countries' implicit objectives to the ones of the Fed.

However, competitiveness considerations, as a former leading FSA regulator shared, do enter the regulatory equation in different semi- and unofficial ways: Firstly, the FSA has a committee of industry representatives, which can insert their interests and concerns on competitiveness and profitability through these channels. Secondly, and probably more importantly regulators can be subjected to socialization and idea diffusion processes causing intellectual capture, which implies that they will incorporate certain considerations and points of view without necessity of inclusion in an official mandate. In the case of the FSA, its former Chairman Sir Howard Davies (Davies, 2010a) commented on the issue of intellectual capture as follows:

"While I would strongly argue that the FSA in my day did not favor firms unduly, it is perhaps true that we – and in this we were exactly like US regulators – were inclined to believe that markets were generally efficient. If willing buyers and willing sellers were trading claims happily, then, as long as they were "professional" investors, there was no legitimate reason to interfere in their markets."

This of course makes the job of the political economy analyst somewhat harder since one needs to look further than the actual mandate in deriving actual policy preferences in a comparative way. In the following chapter I therefore relate the financial system, its stakeholders, and the respective legal institutions to each other to derive a more realistic picture of the regulatory preferences. For now we can constitute that indeed the three objectives discussed seem to be very relevant for regulators across the Euro Zone and comparable relevant financial systems. Moreover, it seems that regulators seem to see some degree of trade-off between them since no single regulator makes explicit mention of all three objectives in the official mandate, even though all of them make at least implicit reference to these considerations at least in their financial stability review. The next sections analyze how the three types of regulatory objectives are reflected in the European multi-level governance for financial stability, what actual instruments are available to regulators, and how the application of these instruments relates to the regulatory objectives.

2.3 Financial stability governance in the Euro Zone

This section wants to illuminate the main political economy implications of the complex governance of banking and financial services in the Euro Zone to establish how the division responsibilities and powers puts the *national banking regulators center stage in banking regulation and supervision*, how these actors *organize banking regulators and hold them accountable* in very different way, and how this *opens regulators up for the insertion of private and political interests*. I do not aim to be comprehensive but rather would like to analytically establish the context, which informs the model of regulatory preferences and action and lays the groundwork for an analysis of regulatory policy-making in the following section.

When it comes to financial stability governance two dividing lines have been driving intense political economy debate and have triggered successive rounds of reform and restructuring within the European financial polity: Firstly, with increasing financial integration and concomitant increases in cross-border externalities to financial regulation, the question of which parts of financial stability policy should be at the *European vs. the national level* has taken center-stage. Secondly, as financial instability has shown its more and more devastating impact on the Euro Zone, having severely impacted on monetary policy and the mandate of central banks, the debate about whether such functions are best located with *central banks vs. regulatory authorities* has gained renewed currency along with the question of *how regulators should be held accountable and how independent* they should be made.[29] I will firstly analyze the governance structure that shapes the *interaction of monetary policy with banking regulation* and will then turn to the questions relating to the *institutional design of the regulator*.

2.3.1 The European Central Bank's limited role in financial stability

As Table 5 below shows, the governance structure of financial stability does vary significantly across countries. In the case of the Euro Zone's monetary union the use of these the two relevant financial stablity instruments is decided on at different levels, with banking regulation and supervision (largely) residing at the national and monetary policy at the supranational level. The United States also has a rather complex and fragmented governance structure, which however comes closer to the integrated approach to monetary policy and the regulation and supervision of banks. As the Fed was founded in response to the Great Depression and the failure of banks, it has been given more tasks that relate to financial stability than the ECB, comprising the regulation and supervision of banks, which it shares in conjunction with the Office of the Comptroller of the Currency (OCC), the Federal Deposit Insurance Corporation (FDIC), the Office of Thrift Supervision (OTS), and the state-level reserve banks (Federal Reserve, 2011). Who becomes the actual supervisor of a financial institution is then determined by the nature of the financial institution's business. Yet another regulatory governance configuration is the UK's model of separating monetary policy and banking regulation and supervision into the Bank of England's (BoE) and the Financial Service Authority's (FSA) responsibility. This model of separation of financial stability policy responsibilities and increasing specialization of the regulator and supervisor in its tasks was a response to the blurring of boundaries in financial markets driven by the integration of banking, securities, and insurance businesses. As such, the creation of the FSA as a separate institution from the BoE has become known as the 'integrated' model even though of course in relation to financial stability policy this model is more of a separate model that relies on the effective coordination of monetary policy with banking regulation. It is this apparent failure of coordination and communication between the BoE and the FSA on macro-prudential issues, which has now come under closer scrutiny post-financial crisis and has created doubts with respect to the efficacy of this model (House of Lords Economic Affairs Committee, 2009). Of course each of the described models has received close scrutiny in relation to the obviated negligence towards systemic risks in the lead-up to the 2007-2009 financial crisis.

---

[29] This debate is embedded in a more general and ongoing discussion of how to best organize banking regulation, covering issues such as the degree of independence from ministries of finance (MoF), legitimacy, and the design of the regulatory institutional structure. I will discuss these issues, when I analyze the role of national institutional structure in regulatory credibility in Chapter 4.

TABLE 5: *Euro Zone financial stability governance in comparative perspective*

Financial stability policy element	*Euro Zone*	*United States*	*United Kingdom*
Monetary policy	European Central Bank (ECB) No LOLR responsibility	↑	Bank of England (BoE)
Banking regulation	-2008: National central banks (NCBs) and regulators Since 2010: NCBs/ regulators with European Banking Authority (EBA)	Federal Reserve, OCC, OTS, FDIC, and regional Federal Reserve Banks ↓	Financial Services Authority (FSA)
Interaction between monetary policy and regulation	Weak coordination through multi-level governance (especially pre-financial crisis) including C	Responsibility lies with the Board of Governors; consistency of supervision is ensured through the Federal Financial Institutions Examination Council (FFIEC)	Stronger coordination (with variance throughout the period of 1999-2008)

Source: Author

Yet, the collective failure of all three alternative models has also cast some doubt on the relevance of pure formal governance structures as explanatory variables for systemic risk creation alone. As such, this section is interested more in the impact of the Euro Zone's specific governance de-centralized and coordination-heavy structure on national banking regulators' incentives and capabilities in the conduct of regulation and supervision. This is particularly relevant, since - as the below above indicates - there is a theoretical and practical alternative governance arrangement for a monetary union, which would entail creating a centralized regulatory union of some shape.

The role of the European Central Bank is central for the Euro Zone's financial stability governance due to its complete control over monetary policy. However, its mandate, whilst considered to be the legally most independent central bank in the world (Quaglia, 2008), mainly relates to price stability. In the realm of regulatory financial stability policy its official role has been bordering on the irrelevant, since it has had remarkably little official role in supervision and regulation as a separate actor. The only role for the ECB and the Eurosystem in the supervision of individual banks and the stability of the financial system foreseen by the EC Treaty is defined in Article 105(5), which reads that the Eurosystem shall *contribute to "the smooth conduct of policies pursued by the competent authorities relating to the prudential supervision of credit institutions and the stability of the financial system"* (European Central Bank, 2006). The ECB is of course indirectly involved through the European System of Central Banks (ESCB), composed of the central banks of the EU member states, to conduct monetary policy through this Eurosystem. Thus, to the degree that there exists a congruence of central bankers and regulators at the national level, there is some degree of indirect involvement or connection through these central bankers that are also regulators. However, the Eurosystem's tasks according to Article 105(2) of the EC Treaty and Article 3.1 of the Statute of the ESCB do not comprise any regulatory competences. These statutes confer the competences of a) defining and implementing monetary policy, b) conducting foreign exchange operations, c) holding and managing official foreign reserves of the Euro Area member states, and d) promoting the smooth operation of payment systems. Hence, with the possible exception of the latter, no explicit financial stability competence is conferred on the ESCB either. Its direct role is related to three functions, which form its 'contribution' to prudential supervision and the stability of the financial system:

- Promoting cooperation between central banks and supervisory authorities on supervision and financial stability
- Performing an advisory function under Articles 4 and ESCB Statute 25.1
- Cooperating with other fora in Europe

In pursuing its goals, the above mentioned Banking Supervision Committee as an ESCB committee has formed the core forum for a common perspective on financial stability and supervision issues. While the Community has clearly made bank supervision a national mandate based on the principles of 'home country control', 'minimum harmonization', and 'mutual recognition', one clause does enable a potentially more involved role for the ESCB and the ECB provided that member states do see this need: Article 105(6) of the EC Treaty and Article 25.2 of the ESCB Statute specify that *"specific tasks concerning policies relating to the prudential supervision of credit institutions and other financial institutions with the exception of insurance undertakings"* may be conferred upon the ECB, provided that the EU Council with assent of the EP decides to do so (European Central Bank, 2006).

The ESCB is thus de facto subordinate to the national governments when it comes to financial supervision and stability European banking. There are two political economy arguments for this unique type of decentralized financial stability governance: Firstly, the ECB's limited role in financial stability is related to its limited fiscal mandate, which prevents it from becoming a lender of last resort (LOLR). This is a stark difference to the Fed and the Bank of England, both of which have the capacity to act as lender of last resort (Vives, 2001). As such, the Fed can step in to save failing banks and correspondingly also has the ultimate say in supervision towards the other regulatory bodies. In the Eurosystem it has been the understanding that national central banks (NCBs) would be the relevant actors to do so in the case of a bank failure.[30]

[30] In fact Wim Duisenberg commented on this in 1999 in relatively clear words: "The ECB's contribution to financial stability, and in particular the question of the provision of emergency liquidity to financial institutions in distress, is another issue upon which the interest of the European Parliament is focused. Allow me to explain some of the main considerations in this regard. The main guiding principle within the Eurosystem with reference to the provision of emergency liquidity to individual financial institutions is that the competent national central bank would be responsible for providing such assistance to those institutions operating within its jurisdiction. The ECB does, however, have to be informed of this in a timely manner. In addition, in operations of relevance to the single monetary policy, the decision-making bodies of the Eurosystem will be involved in assessing the compatibility of the envisaged operations with the

Secondly, the answer can largely be found in the long-standing and still debated pre-financial crisis consensus of economists that central banks have no business in financial stability beyond their contribution through fighting (retail price) inflation and (in the case of the US Fed) stabilizing output growth (Chadha & Holly, 2011).[31] This line of argumentation also forms a powerful argument against the central bank's role in supervision: The strong reputation that central banks have developed for credible inflation fighting can indeed come under stress, if other mandates are assigned to the central bank.[32] Empirical political economy research has shown that indeed the additional role of a central bank as a banking supervisor does negatively impact on the conduct of monetary policy and vice versa. Copelovitch and Singer (2008) show that the countercyclical conduct of monetary policy and the pro-cyclical conduct of regulation indeed do not go well together. They show for a sample of 23 countries that inflation is less likely to be the focus of central banks when they also have to focus attention on banking regulation, which incentivizes them to look out for financial stability and profitability. Conditional on the choice of the exchange rate regime and size of the banking sector, inflation is systematically higher in countries where central banks have dual goals. Vice versa, Ioannidou (2005) shows for the case of the United States, that the one institution in supervision also responsible for monetary policy, the Fed, is affected by the conduct of monetary policy, in that it relaxes banking supervision whenever it steps on the breaks, i.e. tightens, monetary policy. Such compensatory 'banking policy' behavior cannot be shown for the other two supervisory institutions, suggesting that no business cycle effect or the like is behind this observation. Other work by Schoenmaker and Goodhart (1992) corroborates these findings and confirm that two policy objectives in parallel can create situations, where they interact with each other in a trade-off fashion.

With the financial crisis this governance structure has seen some tendencies to change in particular in the realm of macro-prudential supervision in the future. The exact changes and how likely they are to be effective will be subject of the outlook on the financial crisis and the resulting institutional changes to European banking supervision in a later chapter.[33]

2.3.2 National regulators' strong role in financial stability policy

National regulators and supervisors

As in many policy areas of the European Union, the governance of the financial sector is a system of multi-level governance, in which the national regulators are only one – if however the most important – actor, but no longer have the exclusive privilege to

---

pursuit of monetary stability. In the case of a general liquidity crisis resulting from a gridlock in the payment system, for instance, the direct involvement of the Eurosystem could be expected." See Vives (2001,p.63).

[31] For a practitioner's perspective on the limited role of central banking in financial stability see the speech by Fed Vice Chairman Ferguson (2002), who reflects in a very similar fashion as Bernanke and Gertler about this issue.

[32] As the 2010 sovereign debt crisis in Europe and the involvement of the ECB through its purchase of Greek and Irish government bonds on the secondary market has shown, this concern about its perception as an independent, credible inflation fighter has indeed split central bankers from politicians, who demanded a higher involvement of the ECB.

[33] For instance the creation of a European Systemic Risk Board (ESRB) is a direct consequence of the analysis of the weaknesses of the European supervisory system by the de Larosiére Group, which found that macro-prudential oversight of the financial system within the Community in order to prevent or mitigate systemic risks was required (European Commission, 2009b).

shaping policy anymore (Quaglia, 2007, 2010). Within this multi-level governance different actors are assigned different mandates as well as different powers: In general terms the European level has been assigned the mandate to organize cooperation amongst regulatory and supervisory bodies, particularly where cross-border issues and financial stability are concerned, and to converge the different practices towards a more European model. In practice regulators however have regarded these European fora more as platforms for rather technical implementation discussions with very little binding effect.[34] The national level has maintained its mandate to regulate the domestic banking sector and to conduct the supervision. In terms of powers, Quaglia (2010) finds that the EU Commission has been most influential in agenda-setting, national political authorities, who mostly cater to their national industries, are most influential in decision-making stage, and financial supervisors are most influential in implementation stage.

The general approach to banking regulation and financial supervision in the EU has been based on three key principles that were already enacted in the Second Banking Directive of 1989:

- *Single banking license*: Banks that are licensed in one member state are able to establish a branch operation in another member state without requiring approval from the host country's supervisor
- *Home-country control:* The responsibility of supervision lies with the home supervisor in the country of origin of the bank, which cooperates and coordinates with host supervisors
- *Mutual recognition:* Getting approval from the home supervisor implies that the bank has supervisory approval in all other member states

Despite the right to offer banking services in other EU countries through branches with a single banking license, many banks maintain subsidiaries and multiple banking licenses. In 2006, 44% of banks' daughter entities (branches and subsidiaries) in EU countries were subsidiaries (McKinsey-internal study). Wholesale banking activities, international by essence, are sometimes performed through branches but retail banks are often full subsidiaries with a separate banking license, are sometimes inherited from an acquisition, and are generally perceived as a positive signal of having an 'anchor in the country'. Still, the general principle of home-country control has implied that the national supervisor's regulatory and supervisory actions can have a bearing on the bank's business abroad, thereby creating an externality on another country's banking system.

Thus, the inherent problem in banking supervision in an integrated financial market is an incentive problem: Supervisors that are only accountable to their own jurisdiction (and, say, ministry of finance) will not internalize the systemic risk or contagion effect that their own actions and those of domestic banks could have elsewhere (Schüler, 2003a, 2003b; Stolz, 2002). As a result, there have been many suggestions and also approaches to creating a European-level governance that institutionalizes a level of coordination among these nationally focused regulators and supervisors, effectively

[34] Author's interview with a former senior regulator from one of the major national regulatory bodies.

creating a division of labor where the European level is pre-occupied with macro-prudential concerns of contagion and systemic risk and the national level is concerned with the micro-prudential supervision of banks.

Whilst this division of labor has been a persistent feature of European financial governance, this shouldn't mask the significant amount of change, progress, and Europeanization in this realm as well. Progress and integration in the financial sector has been rather slow due to the sensitive economic role that the financial system plays in the economy. The diversity of financial systems, to be explored in the next section, has created a situation where significant financial integration and regulatory convergence is likely to produce winners and losers due to the differential competitive implications of such policies, making integration based on Pareto-improving policies such as in trade liberalization less likely (Guiso, Jappelli, Padula, & Pagano, 2004). Thus, integration at the European level has been less pronounced than in other areas and has taken the form of more complex committee structures, as Quaglia (2010; p.31) confirms: *"Partly because of the substantive differences of national economic structures and partly because of the diversity of domestic preferences, regulatory and supervisory frameworks have retained distinctive features across the EU, even though some convergence has taken place. (...) it is clear that the progress towards market integration, regulation, and supervision varied over time until the late 1990s: it has been more advanced in banking and less so in insurance and securities markets."*

Following the issuance of the 5-year Financial Services Action Plan (FSAP) and the realization that greater cooperation was needed also in the governance of financial services, the *Lamfalussy Report* in 2001 initiated the move to today's committee-based system of governance and was implemented throughout 2003 and 2004.[35]

2.3.3 Comitology between the ECB and national regulators

The pre-financial crisis Lamfalussy architecture governing banking regulation for macro-prudential topics relating to rules and cooperation between supervisory authorities comprises four levels of committees for decision-making. Level 1 works according to the Community method and decides on high level or general rules legislation put forward by the Commission after consulting with the level 3 committee. Decisions are made in co-decision mode with the ECOFIN Council, consisting of the ministers of finance of the various member states and the European Parliament (EP). These high-level rules are then detailed in the technical level 2 committee, where qualified majority voting (QMV) is applied and the working mode is generally less political, unless undecided issues are passed down from level 1 (Quaglia, 2007). Level 3 consists of the advisory committees and is mainly charged consulting the Commission, ensuring information sharing, and the consistent implementation of legislation on the national level. The level 4 committee then mainly focuses on the compliance of member countries with the passed legislation.

---

[35] The fact that progress was made then, in political economy terms can be attributed to the influence of large, competitive, international banks, which allied with domestic decision-makers and the supranational Commission to drive financial integration forward despite resistance from small, non-competitive, domestic banks, which had most to loose from integration. The Commission, as the engine of integration against a background of competition from U.S. banks and with the support of European large banks, put financial market integration on the agenda.

Within this comitology process different committees at the EU-level have governed financial services in banking, securities, and insurance. For banking this governance consists of the European Banking Committee (BSC), the Committee of European Banking Supervisors (CEBS), the Banking Supervision Committee (BSC), and the European Financial Conglomerates Committee (FCC). The European Banking Committee works by QMV, even though de facto consensus is the decision rule (based on interviews by Quaglia, 2010), and provides its advice to the Commission in implementing legislation – mainly the Basel II Accord in the last years but also the issues of cross-border mergers and supervisory arrangements. The Committee of European Banking Supervisors (CEBS) is composed of the national regulator's representative as well as a central bank representative, when the latter is not identical with the former, and is tasked with a) advising the Commission either at the Commissions request or on the Committees own initiative in particular for the preparation of draft implementing measures, b) contributing to a consistent implementation of EU directives and to the convergence of member States supervisory practices, c) promoting supervisory co-operation particularly with respect to the exchange of information (CEBS, 2002). The committee also aims to work on a consensus basis and otherwise also decides by QMV. 'Opt-outs' in such cases require countries that do not oblige in implementing decisions to explain their position under a complain or explain procedure. The Banking Supervision Committee comprises banking supervisors from all EU countries and assists the European Central Bank (ECB) in the drafting of legislation and the Eurosystem in the conduct of prudential supervision of banks and financial stability. The role of the BSC mainly lies in the financial stability realm and thereby has a more systemic or macro-prudential focus. The FCC is composed of member state representatives from the finance ministries, also decides by QMV but seeks consensus, and works on the role of large, cross-border conglomerates to cope with the challenges emanating from an increasing conglomeration trend. [36] Additional working groups with the various sectoral committees for the insurance and securities sector exists.

Due to the weakness of European institutions (pre-financial crisis) in the realm of financial stability regulation and supervision the BSC and the CEBS have been most influential in shaping policy convergence (Quaglia, 2008). In the absence of real supranational institutions and regulations it is rather the 'softer' forms of influence such as ideational policy paradigm diffusion that have shaped the 'European' model of financial stability policy. As the following discussion of financial stability instruments will show, the impact from a technical policy point of view has been limited in that very little additional capabilities relevant to the three policy objectives were created.

[36] Thus, whilst due to the tendency towards consensus decision-making the preferences of each country are relevant, it is likely that countries will ally in group sizes of similar preferences to ensure that their cumulative voting power will influence the final outcome in case of the required QMV decision-making mode.

2.4 Financial stability instruments

There are two types of instruments whose impact has been most directly linked to financial stability outcomes: Monetary policy and banking regulation.[37] While the exact impact of each instrument is still debated in the literature,[38] there has been an emerging strong consensus that both instruments are relevant for financial stability. Because of its complex relationship with price stability the policy instruments available and the institutional responsibility for financial stability policy tend to overlap with those of the monetary authorities (Oosterloo & de Haan, 2005). In many cases the mandate for banking regulation and financial stability has been resting with central banks, since the banking system is a key part of the monetary transmission mechanism. In the case of the Euro Zone the question of the control over financial stability instruments is peculiar: The European Central Bank controls European monetary policy as a supranational entity but has had a very limited financial stability mandate and thus also almost no regulatory and supervisory function. The national regulator as a result faces the opposite dilemma with no control over monetary policy as a stabilizing instrument to cope with particular exogenous shocks to bank competitiveness or the credit supply. To better understand the implications of this setup for the regulatory actors' capabilities, comparative political economy research needs to also inquire into the policy instruments available in different countries to attain those objectives.

This section analyzes the implications of monetary union on the use of the regulatory instrument, elaborating the differently theorized mechanics and impact of each instruments in relation to the political economy objectives of financial stability policy. I find that in the *absence of objective-specific regulatory instruments* in the sense of the Tinbergen principle, regulators find themselves in a position where they have to trade off policy goals to make *specific policy choices at the expense of one of the regulatory objectives*. As a result, the two key instruments in financial stability policy – monetary policy and banking regulation – are detached from one another and instead only coordinated through a relatively complex multi-level governance structure. This implies that regulators will be faced with increasing trade-offs amongst the regulatory objectives identified, which jointly create a regulatory trilemma.

2.4.1 Monetary policy

While central banks in the last years have indeed 'perfected the conduct of monetary policy' (Goodhart, 2010) when measuring their success in terms of price stability, their use of this instrument for other purposes has been more restrained and often also excluded from their mandate.[39] The conventional, more 'Tinbergenesque' view of "one policy goal – one instrument" on monetary policy (Borio & Lowe, 2002) has

[37] There is of course also a valid argument for fiscal policy as a long-run driver of financial stability as unsustainable government debt can drive instability. Fiscal policy however is controlled by very different actors and its use evaluated under very different considerations. It is thus not the focus of this analysis of regulatory and central banking action.

[38] The specific impact that each type of policy instrument has is of course subject to intense debate, as many contributions on the monetary and banking regulatory nexus already prior to the financial crisis (Garcia Herrero & del Rio, 2005; Oosterloo & de Haan, 2005; Padoa-Schippoa, 2002) but in particular after the crisis as part of a whole new debate about the future of central banking discuss (Davies, 2010b; B Eichengreen, El-Erian, Fraga, & Ito, 2011; Levine, 2010).

[39] Of course these mandates with the sole focus on maintaining price stability have also only evolved over time, as an excellent historical analysis of central banking by Charles Goodhart (2010) shows.

suggested that financial stability should rather be left to banking regulation, which has been seen to control the more 'pure' financial stability instruments. Monetary policy in this view can be considered 'second-best' in pursuing financial stability, as indicated in the table below. The limitations the instruments available to central banks in financial stability have been voiced very pointedly by Mervin King of the Bank of England (House of Commons Treasury Committee, 2009, p.95):

"We were given a statutory responsibility for financial stability in the Banking Act, and the question I put to you in February at this committee, to which I have not really received any adequate answer from anywhere, was: what exactly is it that people expect the Bank of England to do? All we can do at present, before a bank is deemed by the FSA to have failed, is to write our Financial Stability Report and give speeches. They are important. We have our next Financial Stability Report coming out on Friday. These are important things, but, in the end, I do not believe that people change their behaviour simply because we publish reports."

Others have argued that this narrow view disregards the importance of the interaction between the two instruments, which is crucial in shaping stability outcomes (Borio & Lowe, 2002; Padoa-Schippoa, 2002).

TABLE 6: *Conventional view on monetary and regulatory policy instruments*

(● *= primary use;* ● *= additional use or impact)*

Instrument	*Price Stability*	*Financial Stability*
Monetary policy strategy	●	●
Short-term interest rates	●	●
Money market operations	●	●
Standing facilities	●	●
Public and private comments	●	●
Banking regulation	●	●
Banking supervision	●	●
Payment systems	●	●
Emergency liquidity support	●	●
Crisis co-ordination	●	●

Source: Author adapted based on Padoa-Schippoa (2002)

Next to the well-documented effect on price stability, monetary policy instruments have been discussed for their effect on two of the three objectives that banking regulators have to take into consideration:

- Firstly, through the manipulation of the money supply monetary policy *can have a stabilizing or stimulating impact on credit access and economic output*. There have been two challenges towards this assumed affect: The first challenge by the monetarists around Milton Friedman has cast doubt on such effects due to the 1) lagged impact of monetary policy, 2) the inability of policymakers to determine the right state of the economy, and 3) the policymakers' focus on smoothing interests rates considering real rates making it likely pro-cyclical and thus destabilizing (M. Friedman & Schwartz, 1963). The second challenge has come from the rational expectations camp, which has questioned the stimulating impact of expansionary monetary policy due to the ability of private agents to anticipate this and build this into their expectations (Lucas, Robert E., Jr. Sargent, 1980). However, this criticism has been addressed by the Keynesian analysts of monetary policy, who see an increase in the money supply ceteris paribus will lead to an expansion of real economic activity (in the short run) even with rational expectations (see Fischer, 1977; Phelps & Taylor, 1977).[40] It is beyond the scope of this analysis to go into depth into this debate. Yet, despite some contention, it is still generally assumed that in the open-economy context monetary policy can influence real economic outcomes in the short run and can be used as a policy tool to stimulate economic activity in a output-stabilizing way using the channel of credit supply – the exact effect however is likely to be a contingent one, depending on many features of the economic and financial system such as institutions and expectations. Thus, the debate in recent years has focused on the monetary transmission mechanism and the variation in financial systems (Borio & Zhu, 2009). An entire stream of 'bank centric' monetary policy research on the work of Bernanke and Blinder (1992) and Kashyap and Stein (1994) amongst othershas emphasized more the role of the financial sector and the 'bank lending channel' in shaping the impact of monetary policy on output and inflation building. They show that because of the special nature of bank credit as relationship lending, which allows banks to overcome information asymmetries in relation to otherwise non-creditworthy customers, there is a special credit lending channel, which affected the conduct of monetary policy. Hence, to the extent that there is variation across time and financial systems in the role of this channel, the impact of monetary policy is going to vary substantially as well. This of course is a highly relevant insight with respect to the European Monetary Union, which has been shown to be composed of very different financial systems with rather different banking channels as well.[41] As Kashyap and Stein put it (2002; p.4):

"The special response of banks to changes in monetary policy is their lending response (not just their role as deposit creators). Thus, the ambiguity over what constitutes money is much less important. For this mechanism to operate, it is essential that some spending that is financed with bank loans will not occur if the banks cut the loans (that is, there is no perfect substitute available for a bank loan). One basic prediction is that the firms and individuals whose creditworthiness is most difficult to gauge (that is, those borrowers about whom information is imperfect) will be most dependent on banks for financing. Because these borrowers

---

[40] For a summary discussion of the empirically proven impact of monetary policy on real economic variables such as output and inflation see Walsh (2003).

[41] For a survey of the variation in European financial structure at the time and a discussion of its monetary policy implications see Kashyap and Stein (2002) and Hartmann, Maddaloni, and Manganelli (2003)

face the extra cost of raising funds from third parties, they are not indifferent about the composition of their liabilities. Banks have a particular advantage in lending to such borrowers because they can specialize in information gathering to determine creditworthiness."

It is the varying nature of the financial system that drives how the impact of credit access and monetary operations relate to the central role of banks in lending decisions and their special information that they gather from overcoming information asymmetries through relationship lending. This factor will be all the greater, the more bank-based a financial system is.

- Secondly, monetary policy tools have been discussed for their *effect on financial stability* above and beyond price stability in that it affects key variables such as leverage and asset prices, which are key factors in producing bubbles and hence instability (see Borio and Lowe for an overview, 2002).[42] This view has also been debated with most monetary economists pre-financial crisis maintaining that flexible inflation targeting rather than intervening in financial markets through a direct responsibility for them is the best framework for achieving macroeconomic stability and financial stability (B. S. Bernanke & Gertler, 2000). This argument against such use has been that the strong effect of asset bubbles on the real economy takes place through changed access to credit and investment, which is given based on collateral on those very assets. As central banks try to react to asset price bubbles, they create expectations of increasing interest rates leading to declining asset values and output gaps. Firstly, this would require a superior degree of information, which also practitioners of monetary policy have long been denying, as for instance Otmar Issing, the ECB's chief economist at the time, disputed the „comparative advantage over market participants to dare such a judgment" (Otmar Issing, 2003). Secondly, from a macro-economic point of view it is argued that this approach is dominated by a stronger focus on inflation, leading to superior results than if the central bank were to focus on instability. In the prominent Bernanke and Gertler view, allowing excessive leverage to build up is also a failure of regulatory and tax policy, which should discourage this, since the effects of the bubble on real activity depend on the leverage ratio. This view very much reflects the conventional wisdom of monetary policy as a second-best instrument for financial stability, which sees price stability only as a necessary condition for stability – not a sufficient one. The other school of thought has argued that inflation as such is under control and very likely the major battle of the next years lies in controlling asset price volatility. According to this school of thought it is the combination of low inflation, rising asset prices, and economic growth that causes 'exuberant' expectations and through this interaction lays the foundation for a bubble (Borio & Lowe, 2002). Proponents of this school have argued that in particular due to the insufficient existence of prudential tools, monetary policy can be an additional instrument in attaining financial stability or at least in preventing the evolution of financial instability. They argue that

---

[42] The literature on asset prices and credit has already developed prior to the financial crisis with major contributions by authors more skeptical (Ben Bernanke from the U.S. Fed) and more enthusiastic (e.g., Claudio Borio from the BIS) about the benefit of a more financial stability-oriented monetary policy (B. S. Bernanke & Gertler, 2000; Borio & Lowe, 2002; Kindleberger & Aliber, 2005).

financial imbalances in aggregate are not as hard to identify as skeptics have assumed, since there are certain regularities that include "periods of strong credit growth, booming asset prices and high levels of investment", which "almost invariably lead to stresses" (Borio & Lowe, 2002, p.26). Thus, instabilities materialize over time very much in line with existing models of bubbles like the ones developed by economic historians such as Kindleberger and Aliber (2005) and can be spotted and averted through decisive 'leaning against the wind'.[43] Again recent literature has examined the role of the varying financial structure in shaping the role the monetary policy plays in impacting asset prices with some controversy about the degree of impact. As such, Maclennan, Muellbauer, and Stephens (1998) find a relatively strong role of differences in housing and financial market institutions in the EMU, which would naturally affect asset price-oriented monetary policy as well. Assenmacher-Wesche and Gerlach (2008) for the period of 1987-2006 find a more moderate effect of financial structure variation in monetary policy transmission to residential property and equity prices. All in all however again a stronger effect of monetary policy on the financial stabiltiy of bank-based systems has been assumed, which again relates to the very credit channel identified earlier.

To summarize: There are two potential economic objectives for regulators above and beyond price stability towards which monetary policy could theoretically contribute: i) Credit access and output as well as ii) financial stability and asset prices. However, economic convention and practice has been very skeptical about this use of monetary policy and, hence, the Euro Zone model of central banking has not included them in the official mandate of the ECB. Also, current research lays emphasis on how *domestic financial institutions and the structure of the financial system* condition the impact of monetary policy.

TABLE 7: *Impact of monetary policy on policy objectives in different financial systems*

<table>
<tr><td></td><td></td><td colspan="3">Policy objective</td></tr>
<tr><td></td><td></td><td>Financial Stability</td><td>Bank profitability and competitive-ness</td><td>Credit access</td></tr>
<tr><td rowspan="2">Nature of financial system</td><td>Bank-based</td><td>Potential impact preventing excess bank credit growth</td><td>No contribution</td><td>(Indirect) impact through 'bank lending' channel</td></tr>
<tr><td>Market -based</td><td>Potential impact preventing excess asset price rises</td><td>No contribution</td><td>(Indirect) impact through 'equity price' channel</td></tr>
</table>

Source: Author

[43] With the costs to instability having been evidenced so dramatically in the financial crisis of 2007-2009, the latter view has gained more support and research has focused on the how monetary policy could potentially be transformed to work towards financial stability. Today the conventional vie is thus under pressure, as central banks have had to realize 1) the costs of 'writing a put' on financial activities by (implicitly or through 'constructive ambiguity') guaranteeing to inject liquidity and buying up distressed assets; 2) seeing their the ability to conduct monetary policy for price stability objective impaired due to the higher variability in inflation outcomes and the threat of persistent deflation (E. W. Nier, 2009). Pre-financial crisis however such frameworks were not in place in either the Euro Zone, the UK or the US.

In particular the nature of the banking system as a transmission channel for monetary policy and source of financial instability has a role in how monetary policy impacts on output and financial stability in individual countries. With the integration of monetary policy in the Euro Zone as a supranational instrument and a "one size fits all"-monetary policy, this instrument is lacking as a national instrument to cope with exogenous shocks. As a result of this limited use and scope of the monetary policy instrument, there is added stress on the prudential regulatory and supervisory controls such as capital requirements in the pursuit of the mentioned objectives. Therefore I will now turn to the regulatory instruments' impact before discussing the coordination between the two instruments.

2.4.2 Banking regulation and supervision

In contrast to monetary policy practice, which rests on a well-developed if however sometimes conflicting body of theory, the terms of reference for banking regulation are more uncertain (Padoa-Schippoa, 2002). While recommendations tend to oscillate between discretionary and non-discretionary elements (Dewatripont & Tirole, 1999), some common ground on the effects of common instruments of banking regulation has been established in the last two decades and shall now be reviewed with respect to their effect towards the mentioned objectives.[44]

Most of the focus has traditionally been on the *micro-prudential aspect of regulation* as systemic effects were largely seen to derive only from the failure of single institutions, understating the effect that systemic events themselves could have. To illustrate the nature of regulatory instruments' effects we will look at the most central instrument of prudential regulation, which are capital adequacy requirements imposed on banks.

- Capital adequacy requirements are designed to contribute to *financial stability* in a very straightforward way: More bank capital increases the bank's share of losses absorbed through equity, thereby a) decreasing the chances of default due to a capital buffer, and b) giving banks more "skin in the game" and thus changing their incentives.
- The *effect* of capital adequacy on the *competitiveness of banks and credit availability* has been generally discussed as very strong, since differences in leverage regulation impact on the cost of banking in that country – a higher degree of leverage ceteris paribus will allow banks to earn a higher return, as discussed earlier in the simplified model of regulatory impact on banks.[45] As Hellwig puts it candidly: *"Economizing on equity", the catch phrase of the*

---

[44] There is a second important differentiation with respect to the degree of intervention that the available regulatory tools represent (Crockett, 2001). Empirical research has shown a higher reliance on prudential norms and supervision rather than crude intervention in recent years (Barth et al., 2006). As such, we would expect to see variation in these tools over time reflecting the respective thinking and preferences in banking regulation. For now the focus is more so on the actual regulatory instruments (high degree of intervention) and less on the norms of supervision, mainly because the latter are more complex to observe. Differences with respect to the way that these tools are exactly applied in the supervisory practice, how they are shaped by overarching paradigms (such as for example the 'light touch regulatory style' practiced in the UK), and how they are employed across countries also give a good clue as to the variation in regulatory paradigms, indicating varying preferences as well. I will come back to this at a later point.

[45] The political economy of this impact was already discussed as the regulatory dilemma by Kapstein (1992).

industry, is really a euphemism for a strategy that tries to capture the excess returns to equity that are associated with high leverage. If the balance sheet is forty or fifty times equity, even small margins between asset returns and refinancing costs can be turned into substantial returns on equity." As an illustration of the significance of regulatory tightening and the recent introduction of Basel III have been estimated by McKinsey & Company (2011) to cost a total of 12-13 percentage points of profitability whilst also de-leveraging the financial system substantially, which of course was the intention of this exercise but goes to show what level of political determination needs to be in place to create such regulation.

- The effect of bank regulation on *credit access to the economy and, ultimately, output* is contingent on the banks' decision and financial structure. As banks have to de-leverage in the face of stricter capital adequacy standards, they face the choice between 1) increasing capital or 2) unwinding some of their credit positions. In the latter case such a reaction will reduce the growth of credit to the economy and might thereby slow economic growth in the same way that a surprise decrease in liquidity due to a monetary policy shock would. Lobbyists tend to emphasize on this 'credit crunch' argument as an academic study by academics for the German Bundesverband Deutscher Banken on the impact of a stricter leverage ratio evidences. Economists have rightly pointed out that the de-leveraging effect of a higher stringency in regulation is not automatic but instead contingent on the very decisions by banks that I just described and that regulators could engage in more determined action forcing re-capitalization rather than de-leveraging.[46] However, given the conventional wisdom pre-2007 that banking regulation was supposed to be 'principles-based' and had no role in intervening in banks' decisions to issue equity, it is hard to imagine how a regulator would prevent this effect from taking place from a political economy perspective. Such broader political economy considerations will be the stronger the larger the expected de-leveraging effect is, which again is a function of the bank reliance of the economy, i.e. the discussed 'bank lending channel'.

Thus, from a political economy perspective there is no free lunch in the use of regulatory instruments more stringently. The choices by the regulator involve certain trade-offs with respect to its three regulatory objectives making regulation inherently political due to its distributional implications on the financial stakeholders. The political economy considerations again seem to be related to the underlying interests and the structure of the financial system. When comparing the impact of CARs to the impact of monetary policy (assuming a role for the credit channel) they seem like close substitutes.

---

[46] Hellwig (2010) stresses this point: "Higher equity capital requirements do not mechanically limit banks' activities, including lending, deposits taking and the issuance of liquid money-like, informationally-insensitive securities. Banks can maintain all their existing assets and liabilities and reduce leverage through equity issuance and the expansion of their balance sheets. To the extent that equity issuance improves the position of existing creditors and/or it may be interpreted as a negative signal on the bank's health, banks might privately prefer to pass up lending opportunities if they must fund them with equity. The "debt overhang" problem can be alleviated if regulators require undercapitalized banks to recapitalize quickly by restricting equity payouts and mandating new equity issuance."

TABLE 8: *Impact of banking regulation on policy objectives in different financial systems*

		Policy objective		
		Financial Stability	*Bank profitability and competitiveness*	*Credit access*
Nature of financial system	*Bank-based*	Impact through 'leaning against the wind'	Impact contingent on other countries' stringency	(Indirect) impact through 'bank lending' channel
	Market-based	(Smaller) impact through 'leaning against the wind'	Impact contingent on other countries' stringency	(Limited) impact through 'equity price' channel

Source: Author

The real difference of course is that banking regulation has a more direct bank competitiveness impact, which the regulator needs to take into account and has no further impact on price stability or money supply beyond the bank lending channel.

Of course the list of regulatory instruments is long and goes beyond CARs. Each of the instrument could require its own impact study, since their impact is likely to vary somewhat with factors like the level of development of banking systems (Barth et al., 2006). However, a rough categorization of the instruments allows at least a tentative look at the degree of impact of various prudential instruments on the three mentioned regulatory objectives. Mishkin (2001) identifies nine elements of prudential regulation and supervision: 1) *Restrictions on asset holdings and activities*, which relate to the moral hazard incentives due to the lack of depositor monitoring; 2) *Separation of banking and other financial service industries*, which in addition the risk for banks also resembles the risk of overextending the safety net to non-bank-institutions in real estate or investment banking (as the financial crisis proved); 3) *Restrictions on competition*, which are important to ensure the continued profitability as a source of capital as well as an incentive to manage the institutions with a long-term focus on the franchise value (K. C. Murdock, Stiglitz, & Hellmann, 2000). 4) *Capital requirements*, the central elements of regulation, which aim to create accountability in the bank for the risk taken on by increasing the amount of capital that the bank has at stake and therefore to loose. 5) *Risk-based deposit insurance premiums*, a much less practiced form of making banks internalize the risks they pose to taxpayers, by charging them fees depending on the risks taken on; 6) *Disclosure requirements*, which aid the process of imposing market discipline by making the dealings of banks more transparent; 7) *Bank chartering*, a process of selectively granting bank licenses to limit the adverse selection effect of having very risk-seeking entrepreneurs open and run too many banks; 8) *Bank examinations*, which form the basis of prudential regulation to ensure that banks also comply with the regulations set out; 9) The *supervisory approach*, which is less focused on ensuring only the compliance with certain regulations but tries to assess the bank's risk management practices more holistically to deal with the more dynamic risks that result from the more intensified dealings of banks in trading and underwriting. Based on a similar categorization as the above one, some commonly applied instruments are analyzed in a table in the Appendix (see addendum V) with respect to their impact on the three regulatory objectives.[47] Whilst this analysis does not claim to be exhaustive and definite, its tentative conclusions illustrate one seemingly trivial but nonetheless important point: The trade-offs hypothesized earlier are very real also for other instruments - no instrument serves all three objectives at the same time. Thus, even within the pure regulatory instruments available, conflicts can arise with respect to the objective function that they are supposed to serve.

2.4.3 Macro-prudential regulation and supervision

With the advent of the financial crisis the 'land in between', referring to central banks and regulators and the shared macro-prudential policy instruments between them, has become the focus of analysis. As BIS economist Claudio Borio (2010;p.1) put it fittingly, paraphrasing Milton Friedman: *"We are all macro-prudentialists now."* In fact, most evidence for the use of macro-prudential instruments still remains tentative as the Bank for International Settlement finds (2010).[48] As shown earlier, the Euro Zone governance of this area pre-financial crisis has been very comitology-oriented with little tangible policy impact. The number of existing macro-prudential instruments has been very small with some countries like Spain leading the way through their early adoption of dynamic provisioning, as a strategy to increase capital requirements and 'lean against the wind'. To illustrate this void of policy instruments pre-financial crisis this section will review the 'land in between' to derive the political economy implications of the depicted financial stability governance of the Euro Zone.

The financial crisis has triggered a lot of research into what a macro-prudential approach should contain (Bank of England, 2009; Brunnermeier, 2009; Brunnermeier et al., 2009; Hanson et al., 2010). Macro-prudential instruments re-define the regulatory perspective means by "calibrating regulation from a system-wide or systemic perspective, rather than from that of the safety and soundness of individual institutions on a stand-alone basis" (Borio, 2010, p.2). Thus, macro-prudential policy by its nature has a wide impact on the interactions between financial institutions, markets, market infrastructure as well as the wider economy (Bank for International Settlements, 2010). Macro-prudential regulatory instruments serve to complement and fine-tune regulation and monetary policy towards the goals of financial stability on the systemic level, thereby also impacting on the objectives of a well-functioning payment system and monetary transmission system, competitive banks, and stable access of the economy to sources of finance.

As Table 9 shows, macro-prudential tools can complement monetary and micro-prudential instruments to attaint financial stability and fine-tune the pursuit of it with other objectives. The way I conceptualize macro-prudential instruments here is as 1) a

[47] See Allen and Herring (2001) for an in-depth discussion of these instruments.

[48] In a BIS survey with 33 central banks a large number of practitioners still find macro-prudential policy to be murky and proved to have very different definitions of what macro-prudential policy contained. However, the importance of macro-prudential policy was underlined in its most wide application of measures to limit credit supply to sectors prone to excessive credit growth. For an overview of current application see Borio (2010) and Bank for International Settlements (2010). (Borio, 2010)

coordination mechanism between monetary policy and banking regulation, which serves to create mutual benefits for the conduct of each (Bank of England, 2009; Borio, 2010; Caruana, 2010); 2) a main mechanism to support prudential regulation in leaning against the cycle and making existing regulation such as capital adequacy more cycle-sensitive and sophisticated to address risks that materialized in the last crisis. Specifically in terms of instruments the macro-prudential approach aims to address the different sources of vulnerability of the financial system that arise across time across different sections of the economy (Borio, 2010).

TABLE 9: *Macro-prudential policy and its impact on the coordinated conduct of monetary policy and banking regulation*

Macro-prudential instruments[49] for coordination	■ *Information: Information exchange between central bankers and regulators; Identification and measurement of systemic risks* ■ *Pro-cyclicality/ capital charges: Countercyclical capital buffers linked to credit growth; Countercyclical provisioning* ■ *Interconnectedness: Capital surcharges for systemically important banks* ■ *Liquidity: Liquidity requirements / funding; Contingent capital; Loan-to-deposit requirements; Loan-to-value (LTV) ratios* ■ *Other: Direct controls on lending to specific sectors; Limits on currency mismatches*	
Impact on financial stability policy	Macro-prudential instruments can limit the political economy costs of financial stability policy by limiting discretion of the regulator to regulate too laxly/ set monetary policy too loosely.	
Specific impact on monetary policy and banking regulation	*Impact on conduct of monetary policy* Reduces the political economy costs of 'leaning against the wind' ■ Reduces the impact of financial frictions on credit supply and ability to conduct monetary policy ■ Official interest rates probably need not move as much as would be required	*Impact on conduct of banking regulation* ■ Limits the degree to which regulators have to 'lean against the wind' due to easy credit or 'risk-taking'-channel of monetary policy ■ Reduces macro-economic destabilization as a cause of financial instability

Source: Author based on publications by the Bank of International Settlements and Bank of England

Across time the instruments aim to cope with the inherent pro-cyclicality of the financial system and through for instance time-varying capital charges. In terms of the different sections of the financial system and their relative contribution to financial instability the macro-prudential approach calibrates existing instruments to reflect the differential contribution to systemic risks.

[49] The above mentioned list of instruments is not necessarily exhaustive, yet, it reflects the most important instruments that have been debated post-financial crisis. A very prominent and coherent approach to macro-prudential regulation has been suggested by Hanson, Kashyap, and Stein (2010) and contains six elements. At the heart of these proposals are in most cases automatic mechanisms that make capital charges more anti-cyclical, create new sources of capital such as contingent capital, and that consider the other systemic risks such as the shadow banking system and the real economy.

Two cautionary remarks in the context of this analysis are required: Firstly, macro-prudential policy should not be mistaken as a 'pars pro toto' for financial stability policy. This would undermine the role of other policy instruments such as monetary policy and micro-prudential regulation and at the same time overstate the role that macro-prudential instruments can play as supplementary instruments. Secondly, whilst clearly contributing towards financial stability, macro-prudential policy also has some secondary effects on the other objectives, which implies that from a regulatory point of view there is no 'free lunch' in applying them. However these instruments do reduce the costs of 'leaning against the wind', which is an important advantage, as will be discussed later.

2.4.4 Political economy implications

I now summarize the political economy implications of the reviewed financial stability governance and instruments analysis:

- Two generic types of instruments are available in theory to banking regulators: Monetary policy (second best) and (micro-)prudential regulation, which today are increasingly being bridged by instruments of macro-prudential regulation to coordinate the conduct of the two. Mapping the instruments along the trilemma, we can conceptualize monetary policy as directly impacting on objectives banking profitability and credit access with an indirect impact on financial stability; Micro- and macro-prudential banking regulation directly impact on all three objectives. *The structure of financial systems* matters, as it impacts the degree to which the 'bank lending' channel and, thus, credit access as well as financial stability are impacted. Thus, regulators across different financial systems are likely to have different preferences in how they apply discretionary regulatory and supervisory policy.
- In the absence of objective-specific instruments (Tinbergen, 1952)[50] there can be a trade-off along the three objectives, which derives from the likely trade-off between financial stability, a competitive banking system, and domestic growth and economic output considerations. Moreover restrictions on banking business and bank lending can reduce credit availability for local borrowers to the detriment of the objective of efficient access to credit for the economy. This implies that the pursuit of financial stability needs to be traded off with bank competitiveness and credit availability objectives. The analysis shows that *regulatory instruments available do not operate in an objective-specific way* but instead create trade-off decisions for the regulator.
- *Under monetary union and the special European governance of financial stability*, national regulators are faced with an amplified trilemma through the integration of the national financial systems and the delegation of the monetary policy instrument to the European level. Whilst macro-prudential instruments and the coordination of European monetary policy and national regulation promise to alleviate some of the risks to financial stability and reduce the political economy costs of such a stability-oriented policy, such an explicit financial stability-

[50] The Tinbergen principle simply states that every policy objective has to be matched with a policy tool.

mandate was not given to the European Central Bank nor were many macro-prudential instruments in place. In the absence of macro-prudential regulation prior to 2008, national central banks and regulators effectively had one policy instrument, namely (micro-)prudential regulation, to address the three potential policy objectives. This suggests that national banking regulation in an integrating monetary union such as the Euro Zone is a policy task that involves a high amount of political economy trade-offs for the regulator.

2.5 The regulatory ‚trilemma'

The previous analysis culminates in a central analytical contribution of this research: Banking regulators in the short- to medium-term are faced with a trilemma. This trilemma results from the fact that regulators only have one real instrument to trade off their *public interest* objective/ official mandate, i.e. financial stability, and their *private interest* objectives, i.e. banking competitiveness and credit availability. Even outside of a monetary union, as in the case of the U.S. or the U.K., regulators still face a trilemma, as the second instrument of monetary policy still can be insufficient to address all three objectives at the same time, and, since to date monetary policy and banking regulation often have not been used in a coordinated fashion. The below figure shows the regulatory 'trilemma' or impossibility triangle graphically: All three objectives are potentially relevant and desirable but yet the regulator cannot attain them all at the same time.

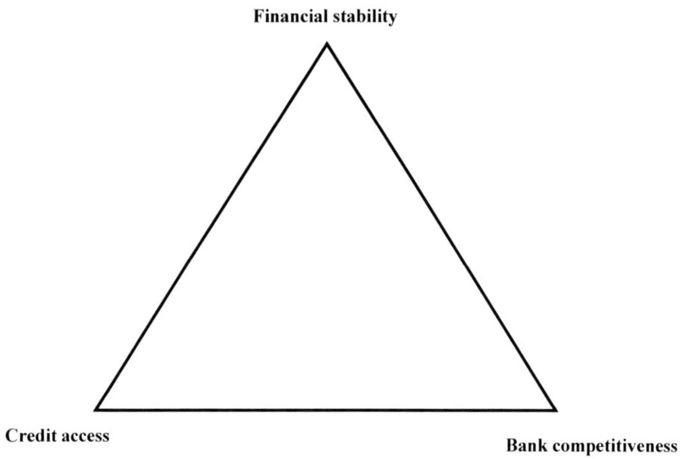

FIGURE 8: *The regulatory 'trilemma'*

Source: Author

Underlying the trilemma argument is the tension created by the regulation of capital adequacy for stability purposes and the economic adjustment mechanism that banks have to follow to comply with such regulation. The trade-offs behind the trilemma are very real not only in an economic sense but also in the way that regulators have to formulate policy. Well-known as the 'regulator's dilemma' the trade-off between financial stability and bank competitiveness, this trade-off has long occupied the political economy literature (E.B. Kapstein, 1989). The contribution of the trilemma is the third dimension of credit availabilty, which builds on the basic insight, that banks have two ways of adjusting leverage: Increasing capital, which reduces the return on equity, profitability, and/ or lending, which limits credit availability in the macro-economy. The latter dimension however plays a central role in the day-to-day conduct of regulation and supervision, as it is a main argument advanced by studies commissioned by the banking lobby to prevent regulators from tightening leverage regulation.[51] They argue that strict leverage regulation constrains credit availability as banks have to curtail lending activities. This of course needs to be qualified, as banks theoretically still have the option of increasing capital, as Admati, DeMarzo, Hellwig, and Pfleiderer (2010) point out. They counter the argument advanced by the lobby with an argument for why bank equity is not *socially* expensive, since it would remove implicit subsidies and distortions currently in place. However, from a political economy perspective it is clear that bank equity is *privately* expensive to private interests of banks, which are better organized than the public interest.

First empirical evidence has shown that domestic credit availability indeed remains a concern for national regulators in particular in moments of crisis. Using data from the recent financial crisis, Aiyar (2011) demonstrates that in response to a contraction in foreign funding resident subsidiaries and branches of foreign-owned banks reduced lending by a larger amount than domestically-owned banks. The proposal by Andrew Haldane, executive director of financial stability at the Bank of England, in August 2011 echoes this relevance of credit creation in regulation, as he proposed a temporary cut to bank capital adequacy requirements in order to stimulate credit to the economy (Alexander, 2011). The assumption of course behind this stimulation is that the capital ratios could then be increased again once economic growth had picked up – an assumption that will be challenged in Chapter 5 of this research.

This trade-off between stability and credit availability/ liquidity takes on a special significance in the context of monetary union with national banking regulation. Outside of a monetary union as the Euro Zone, monetary policy can be used to limit the detrimental effect that more stringent regulation has on the availability of credit and the competitiveness of banks. This still leaves the central banks and regulators though with two instruments and three objectives, which still makes the trilemma a relevant concern. However, inside a monetary union and an integrating European financial market, stringent regulation might even face trade-offs with both private interests as banks and bank capital can relocate due to decreased competitiveness or as banks can deleverage in the face of stringent regulation, which reduces credit availability. Thus, under monetary union the logic of the trilemma not only forces them to surrender one objective in the short term (as would be the case with monetary policy as a national policy instrument) but also to accept certain trade-offs in the pursuit of the other two objectives, since they still could often relate in a negative way to each other with only one instrument at hand.

[51] For an example of this line of argument see a study commissioned by the German bank lobby Frenkel and Rudolf (2010).

This section formulates a simple, formal model, which explicates the relationship between the regulatory utility function and the bank leverage adjustment mechanism, which is at the heart of the trilemma argument. As regulators have to decide the stringency of regulation, they change the degree of bank leverage permissible. Since this directly impacts on private interests in competitiveness and credit availability, the decision to regulate more or less stringently should also reflect the relative role of private and public interests in the regulatory utility function, which would allow us to model this utility function for comparative purposes. The following section develops this in a more mathematical fashion for analytical purposes.

A simple model of regulatory action

This section employs a more formal model of the regulatory utility function for the sake of analytical rigor and then derives the relevant proposition regarding the role of regulatory preferences. This analytical model accounts for the describe private interests in a single private interest variable, which then allows us to model the regulatory trilemma as a trade-off between two objectives, for which only one instrument – regulatory stringency – is available.

Regulatory utility It is assumed that the regulator of country *a* maximizes a utility function that consists of both, a public interest objective as well as a private interest objective. For the simplicity of the argument, the two private interest objectives of bank competitiveness and domestic credit access are therefore lumped together. This is based on the assumption that laxer regulation by the banking regulator creates rents in the form of either excess profits for banks or excess credit for constituencies, the form of which depend on the specific relaxation of regulation. Conceptually the two are very similar though, which analytically justifies this simplification for the sake of this analysis[52]. The regulatory disutility function below specifies what the regulator tries to avoid through her regulation: Firstly, the *stability objective,* referring to the expected costs arising from instability (e.g., in the form of deposit insurance for the taxpayer), which are assumed to be a direct function of the excess leverage of the bank and are denoted by S_i. Secondly, the *private interest objective* P_i, representing bank profitability or alternatively the deviation from the credit/profitability demanded by political constituents/ banks, as denoted by P_e:

$$DisU_{regulatori} = \alpha_i S_i^2 + \beta(P_e - P_i)^2 \qquad \text{with } P_i \leq P_e \quad (2.1)$$

[52] There are three specific reasons that merit such a depiction of the trilemma as a dilemma: Firstly, the trade-off, as is shown, exists between the stability objective and each of the private interest objectives, respectively, - not between the specific type of private interest objectives themselves. Thus, the real implications of this trade-off can still be derived when reducing the objective function to the two components.
Secondly, the trilemma implies that countries will have to make a choice for two of these goals at the expense of another policy goal, making the two-dimensional objective function adequate for the analysis.
Thirdly, the economics behind the policy objectives link the two private interest objectives in a very clear and direct way, thus making a combination of them in one variable sensible: Bank competitiveness derives from bank profitability, which relies either on higher margins or higher volumes of bank activities. Since regulators in an open market can only influence leverage by allowing higher volumes of lending, there is a direct link between bank profitability and credit access to the economy. These objectives therefore can be subsumed under a single variable for the sake of the formal argument.

Importantly, both elements of the equation, the public and the private interest term, have a relationship to leverage and can be broken down further to show that relationship.

$$S_i = L_i \qquad \text{with } L_i = \frac{E_i}{k_i} \quad (2.2)$$

$$P_i = \theta P_e + cL_i \qquad \text{with} \quad \theta \leq 1 \quad (2.3)$$

Thus, in (2.1) L_i denotes leverage in country *i*, which is by nature defined as the amount of assets held relative to capital, usually as a factor of equity, and which can be defined with respect to capital stringency k_i as shown in equation (2.2). In this case stability is assumed to be purely dependent on the amount of leverage of banks – of course a somewhat parsimonious assumption that does, however, reflect much of the current literature on systemic risk that sees leverage as the clearest link to financial instability (Acharya & Richardson, 2009; Geanakoplos, 2010b). The fact that the term is squared shows that increases in leverage above have a disproportionately negative effect on the cost function of the regulator. The same applies to the second term, which reflects the deviation from the private interest in credit availability or profitability of banks.

In (2.3) the term P_e denotes the expected level of private interest in bank profitability/ credit for constituents, which is really the same in a model where banks only generate profits from the amount of credits they give for a given amount of capital. This expected leverage term for now is an exogenously given term that largely relates to the nature of private interest representation and the financial system (as Chapter 3 will discuss). Thus, regulators are assumed to want to keep their banks competitive and credit flowing to constituents. As equation (2.3) shows, this can be achieved through the degree of leverage that banks in a system hold, which can be converted into bank profitability/ credit for constituents with factor c. Since we restrict the values of P_i to be strictly less than P_e , we are assuming that there generally is demand for more leverage and bank profitability, which seems to reflect the reality of the last years quite well, when leverage and financialization increased across many countries manifold with no visible saturation effects. Importantly, the respective weight on these objectives is captured by β, which represents supervisory preferences, i.e. the degree to which the regulator is 'captured' or pre-occupied with concerns that are not financial stability, with α denoting the weight put on preserving financial stability.[53]

Banks finance themselves with deposits and equity, denoted by D_i and E_i , respectively. Banks invest their equity and deposits into credit C_i.[54] This means, banks maximize the difference between returns R_i from making their loans C_i and incurring

[53] This also reflects the specification of other existing models, all of which have a varying combination of these two objectives with some measure of preferences (see for instance Schüler, 2003b).

[54] This excursion on the role of banks is inserted to illustrate the mechanism through which capital adequacy regulation and regulatory stringency operate. It reflects the conclusions of similar models such as the one by Dell'Ariccia & R. Marquez (2006), who also show that banks will only hold the absolute minimum amount of capital required.

costs for deposits and capital paid in. To the extent that returns do not fluctuate over time, profitability is driven by the amount of credit that banks can lend. Banks then maximize a profit function that looks as follows:

$$\Pi_i = (R_i(C_i,) - (1 - k_i)\partial C_i - k_i \rho C_i \quad (2.4)$$

With respect to capital adequacy regulation as denoted by k_i, banks will always want to hold the minimum amount of capital (which is equal to the regulatory capital), given that the respective costs of equity and deposits (captured by ρ_i and δ_i) differ in that $\rho_i \leq \delta_i$, reflecting the fact that deposits are generally easier to raise than equity.[55]

In their pursuit of profits, banks will determine the optimal amount of capital by maximizing function (2.4) with respect to k_i, which by itself will be too low, since banks in the presence of deposit insurance will not internalize the losses, which go beyond the equity put into the bank. As a result of this, banks will therefore economize on the amount of capital they hold, which makes the equilibrium amount of capital held by banks equal to the regulatory capital:

$$E_i = k_i C_i. \quad (2.5)$$

For simplicity we can set capital in the system $E_i = 1_i$, which then allows us to re-arrange

$$L_i = C_i = \frac{1}{k_i} \quad (2.6)$$

The important implication for the stability goal of the regulator is that the stricter (higher) capital adequacy regulation is, the more 'skin in the game' banks will have, but the less profitably they will be and the less they will lend. Since capital is costly, the higher stringency will also have costs for each firm, showing that there is indeed a trade-off, which then needs to be optimized by the regulator according to preferences.

The optimal regulation and level of capital The mechanism through which the crucial trade-off for the respective objectives works is the stringency of regulation. Regulators make choices on the level of capital adequacy regulation and, thus, leverage for the banks in their own jurisdiction, the home country *i*, which are denoted by L_i.[56] Since leverage is the inverse of the share of capital to assets (i.e. the identity shown in 2.2. holds), this could also be formulated as regulators choosing the level of

---

[55] This assumption goes back to the fact that in the financial sphere the Miller-Modigliani-theorem does not hold. The theorem states that the actual source of funding (equity or loans) should not matter, since lenders will adjust the interest rate for the additional risk they take on in the case of higher leverage, which will yield the same costs of funding. However, due to the limited liability that banks in effect have in the presence of deposit insurance and government bail-outs that save lenders, equity is the scarcer factor, as equity does run the risk of being wiped out in the case of failure. See Goodhart (2010;p.13ff) for this as a reason for declining capital in the 1980s; see Bebchuk and Spamann (2009) for how this increased risk-taking as bankers were taking out larger amounts of bonuses in the phase of 2000-2008.

[56] Of course the Basel regime has made some effort towards harmonizing this decision across countries. However, since there is discretion under Basel I and II in setting both the level of capital adequacy requirements as well as the definition of what constitutes capital, this in essence can be regarded as a sovereign decision by each regulator.

capital adequacy k_i with the same results. Banks are obviously the subjects of this regulation and due to the higher costs of equity capital have no incentive to hold more capital than required. To derive the optimal level of capital adequacy from the regulator's point of view, we take equations (2.5), rearrange for C_i and plug this into (2.1), and then maximize with respect to L_i, which is the factor that regulation can influence through instrument k_i. The result is:

$$L_i = \frac{(1-\theta)c}{(\alpha + \beta c^2)} P_e \qquad (2.7)$$

Equation (2.7) allows us to derive some very interesting results that can guide the further analysis. Since $(1-\theta)$ is always positive as are all the other terms in (2.7), the degree of leverage in the system is positively related to the *level of private interest* P_e (in bank profitability/ credit access) that the regulator can observe. Thus, the theoretical model illustrates analytically the *direct trade-off* between *private interest*, that is rents accruing to certain interest groups, and the *public interest* in the stability of the financial system as posited in the trilemma, which works through the *stringency of regulation*.

Result T*here is a negative relationship (i.e. trade-off) between the public interest objectives of financial stability and private interests in banking competitiveness and access to credit, respectively.*

Implications for regulatory trade-offs

The previous more formal engagement with the regulatory utility function and private actor profit maximization analytically corroborates the trilemma. Regulators have to trade off the public interest in financial stability, which therefore – somewhat contrary to intuition – makes them less risk-averse or less restrictive in leverage regulation than in the absence of such private interest objectives.

The relationship between leverage and bank profitability is positive and of course inherent in the business model of leveraged banking. When we turn to some stylized facts regarding the nature of leverage in determining bank profitability we see some interesting patterns indicating the relevance of leverage regulation in shaping profitability outcomes: Banks across different countries of course play a different role in the financial system and, hence, take on different amounts of leverage depending on the riskiness of their activities, regulation, and many other factors. Figure 9 below indicates this for a single year (2007) to illustrate the differential role that leverage plays in banking across different countries.

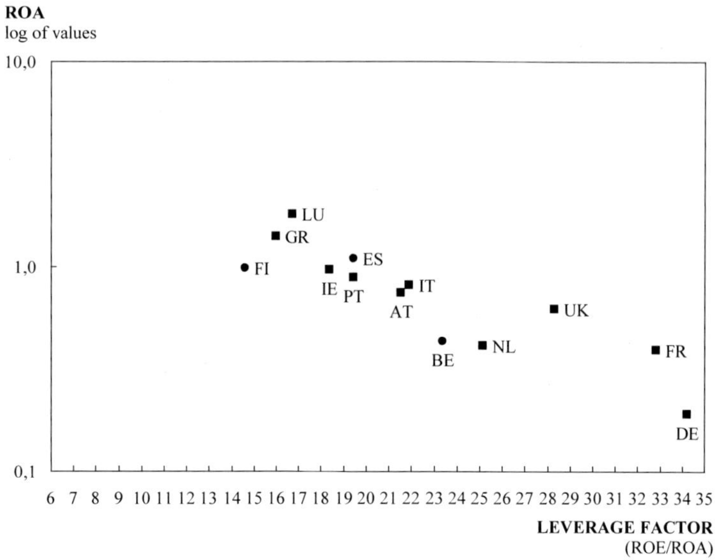

FIGURE 9: Leverage and return on assets across financial systems in 2007

Source: Author based on ECB data; Note that the above shown relationship becomes even stronger, when including more non-Euro Zone European countries in the sample

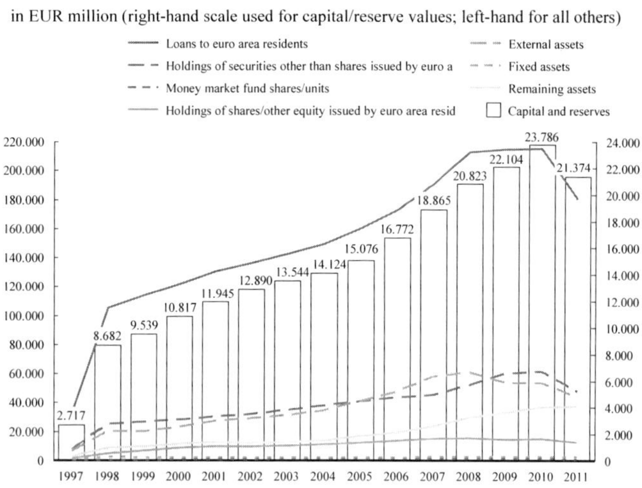

FIGURE 10: *Development of aggregate Euro Zone balance sheet's asset side*

Source: Author based on ECB data

With respect to the relationship between credit availability and leverage a short elaboration is useful to point out the particular relevance to the Euro Zone. While a detailed analysis of the shape and nature of de-leveraging and the differential role of leverage in driving bank profitability is beyond the scope of this section, some stylized facts serve to make the point. Figure 10 shows Euro Zone banks' aggregate balance sheet in absolute terms over the last 14 years, for which this data is available. What the data shows is that despite the stronger increase in securitization and non-Euro Zone lending activities, the role of lending by banks still constitutes the overwhelming activity of banks with an average of 55% in 2011, a point at which de-leveraging has already proceeded strongly. Also, the data indicates the very close relationship of capital and lending, highly significant of course by virtue of the regulatory relationship, which shows the extent to which bank lending is constrained and enabled by capital stringency regulation. Leverage and the degree of credit access for most bank-reliant European system are thus closely related dimensions, between which regulatory stringency effectively functions as a type of tap.

How does this help us explain regulatory action? In the absence of shocks, the existence of only one instrument implies that this trade-off will be decided based on national preferences along the trilemma.[57] It is assumed that countries will surrender the one policy objective, which is least dear to them. The next chapter will therefore inquire into how these trade-offs differ across financial systems and what the drivers of regulatory preferences are.

[57] This logic of prioritizing amongst three conflicting policy trade-offs is also applied in other policy areas. For social and employment policy see for instance Torben Iversen's work (2005).

3

What drives the banking regulator? Varieties of financial systems and regulatory preferences

"Shareholders are stupid and impertinent. Stupid, because they entrust their money to people they do not adequately control. Impertinent, because they ask for dividends and thus even want to be rewarded for their stupidity."

Carl Fuerstenberg, German banker, (1850-1933)

"We do not view the company itself as the ultimate owner of our business assets but instead view the company as a conduit through which our shareholders own assets."

Warren Buffett, Chairman of Berkshire Hathaway.

The previous chapter has shown that regulatory preferences are central to determining which two of the three regulatory objectives a country's regulator is – ceteris paribus – going to favor at the expense of the third. This chapter develops a theoretical and empirical derivation of such sources of regulatory preferences in a cross-sectional fashion. I argue that institutional features of the financial systems shape the particular set of objectives and preferences along the trilemma that the regulator is likely to hold. As the introductory quotes show very candidly, financial systems vary and assign very different degrees of power and influence to the various financial stakeholders. Most centrally, shareholders in more coordinated market economies and historically bank-based systems have generally been viewed as 'patient capital' whilst it was bankers often in the form of 'Hausbanken' who had a very central role in shaping the economy. On the other hand, liberal market economies with market-based systems and a strong emphasis on shareholder value have given banks much less leeway, constraining them to 'arm's length' relationships with each other and their customers. This chapter systematically examines these systemic configurations, clusters countries accordingly, and shows that such a 'varieties of financial systems'-approach yields insights into regulatory preferences, regulatory complementarities, and, (to the extent that complementarities are 'sticky' institutions) real regulatory outcomes:

- In the first section I dismiss a popular alternative proposition that links regulatory preferences with the way that *banking regulation and supervision is set up organizationally*. Much of the academic debate of the last ten years has focused on the organizational design questions of regulation, which however seem to have very little explanatory value by themselves in explaining financial stability outcomes in particular in relation to the financial crisis. However, a systematic analysis of the institutional variations still yields some measure of the degree to which Euro Zone regulators and supervisors are lacking in real independence from private and political interests, which therefore allows some conclusions with respect to the ability of these regulators to commit to a hawkish regulatory stance over time – a topic that I analyze in depth in Chapter 5.

- Secondly, I propose that *preferences for risks and stability* can instead be derived in a comparative perspective looking at the institutions underlying the varying *financial systems*. These include the degree of *bank-reliance of the economy* and the corresponding *legal institutions* that provide stable expectations for regulatory action over time are *shareholder rights, depositor rights, and creditor rights*. These can be taken as institutionalized contracts that reflect regulatory preferences across countries, which reflect the respective strength that is afforded to these financial stakeholders in different financial systems. I maintain that these institutions matter not only because they confer certain stable expectations upon stakeholders, but especially since they alleviate some of the political economy burden by reducing the salience of some of the trade-offs that the trilemma poses to the regulators.
- Thirdly, this chapter *demonstrates empirically the significance of this assumed relationship* clustering countries based on their specific financial systems and institutionalized financial stakeholder rights. I show that, with a few exceptions, there is indeed a complementarity between financial system configurations and financial stakeholder rights. The resulting clustering of countries yields very insightful regulatory regimes, which I argue reflect different financial system preferences and institutional configurations to creating financial stability whilst maintaining competitiveness and credit availability.
- Fourthly, the *link to banking regulation outcomes* is established by discussing each regulatory regime in turn and defining i) the way that the prioritized regulatory objectives are pursued, and ii) how a particular institutional configuration allows the regulator to de-prioritize the other objective due to its lower salience and it being addressed by certain institutions (as is the case in presence of 'patient capital' with profitability considerations). I corroborate this link empirically for various regulatory outcomes with particular emphasis on the variation in capital adequacy and *leverage ratios across financial systems*, which I show to vary largely in line with the predicted financial system and regulatory regime clusters.

3.1 Regulatory preferences across financial systems

Since regulatory preferences are likely to vary along financial systems, the use of regulatory discretion will vary across countries as well. Of course there are situations, when regulatory behavior across countries will tend to converge. In particular, when faced with strong exogenous shocks to private interests, even very stability-oriented regulators are likely to temporarily surrender the pursuit of financial stability by lowering regulatory stringency. Vice versa, the same applies for the case of strong shocks to stability. In these cases we are likely to see an 'accommodating' or a 'leaning against the wind'-policy across countries. However, in the absence of exogenous shocks, that is in times when financial stability policy is a non-salient area of quiet politics, we require insight into regulatory preferences to explain policy choices and outcomes.[58] In order to fully explain regulatory action across countries, we need to systematically analyze the identified factors from equation (2.7) in a comparative way. The previous chapter derived the regulatory utility function based on the concept of the trilemma, which forces regulators to trade-off objectives using the instrument of regulatory stringency.

$$DisU_{regulatori} = \alpha_i S_i^2 + \beta(P_e - P_i)^2 \qquad \text{with } P_i \leq P_e \quad (3.1)$$

Again we define the public and the private interests as before (see section 2.4 for details).

$$S_i = L_i \qquad \text{with } L_i = \frac{E_i}{k_i} \quad (3.2)$$

$$P_i = \theta P_e + cL_i \qquad \text{with } \theta \leq 1 \quad (3.3)$$

Accounting for profit-maximizing banks and maximizing regulatory utility with respect to the minimum amount of leverage held by banks we get the following result:

$$L_i = \frac{(1-\theta)c}{(\alpha + \beta c^2)} P_e \quad (3.4)$$

The previous chapter has already outlined the proposition that this resembles a trade-off between private and public interest. I am now interested in deriving the role of the crucial drivers of regulatory stringency, which we can then further examine in a comparative way.

Firstly, *regulatory preferences*, that is the level of α or β, drive the stringency of regulation, as a higher weight on the public interest of financial stability (α) will decrease leverage, whilst a higher level of private interest (β) will increase leverage through the interaction with c^2.

Proposition 1 *The stringency of policy instruments, which affect the degree of leverage that banks can hold, is directly related to the regulatory preferences of a country.* To the extent that these preferences are embedded in regulatory institutions, which differ across countries, the stringency of regulation will *vary systematically with regulatory institutions.*

Secondly, the role of the parameter c shows that there are features of the financial system that affect the ability of the regulator to affect macro-economic outcomes such as bank profitability or the degree of credit access to the economy. The higher c, i.e. the degree to which a *regulatory-influenced variable* such as bank leverage can be converted to benefit private interests, the more this will affect regulatory outcomes such as leverage. We can think of this as the 'credit channel' or the way in which banks are embedded in the type of capitalism that a country's institutional configurations make up.

Proposition 2 *The structure of the financial system, that is the degree of bank-reliance of an economy, is a major driver of regulatory stringency and the degree to*

58

which private interests that will demand credit access and bank competitiveness as relevant dimensions of regulatory policy-making.

These two propositions together suggest that regulatory stringency varies along with the strength of institutions as well as the nature of the financial system of a country.

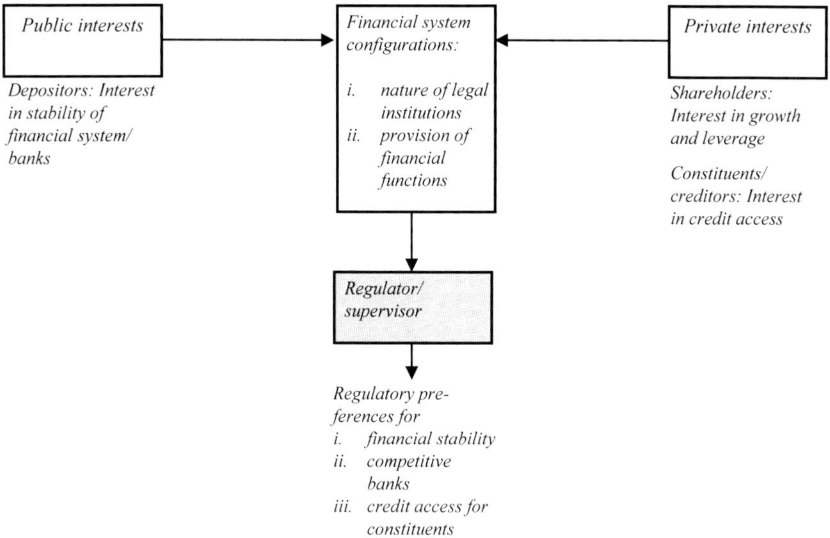

FIGURE 11: *Aggregation of regulatory preferences through institutional configurations*

Source: Author

So, how can we analyze these institutional and financial system features to derive regulatory preferences? Given the obvious importance of preferences in shaping regulatory action, it is curious to see that very little research exists on systematically deriving regulatory preferences across countries. There are two forms of institutional variation across countries that lend themselves to an institutional analysis of regulatory preferences: Firstly, one can analyze institutions in the more *organizational context* and focus on the way that the differences in organizational setup of the regulatory bodies and central banks across countries shape regulatory preferences and stability outcomes. While I maintain that this is likely only to be a mediating factor, I pursue this avenue and review some of the literature and key empirical outcomes in the next section. The second form of institutional variation is more systemic in focus and looks at the way that *the broader context of the financial system* is key to understanding the transmission of risk and, hence, the interrelations of financial stability with the real economy. Here I build on the comparative financial systems- and variaties of capitalism-literature, which shares an inherent neo-institutionalist focus on the interrelations of institutions and the systemic effect of those through consistency, coherence, and complementarity channels. I argue that this helps us understand how the varieties of financial systems impact on regulatory preferences, because it is within this institutional context that bureaucratic decision-makers are likely to look to the fit of an economic idea or policy with the key economic, political, and ideational factors that prevail in the country in deciding which regulatory and supervisory policy style to adapt and which policy objectives to prioritize at the expense of one other policy objective (Hall, 1993).

3.2 The varying organization and accountability of national regulators

As shown, in the Euro Zone it is the national level where regulatory and supervisory bodies carry out the supervision of banks and decide on the stringency of implementation of regulatory standards. In the banking regulatory sphere it is the finance ministries, central banks, and (where they exist) the specialized banking regulators, that are the main national actors. To the extent that these national institutions can shape the way that national regulatory actors form their preferences (through interactions with private actors but also in interaction with the other involved policy actors) it is natural to turn to these institutions first in trying to derive cross-sectional regulatory preferences. In addition these actors of course also sit in the respective European level committees to represent their countries, thus, 'multiple-hatting' as national actors and as banking-diplomats in negotiating with other European supervisors and regulators (Quaglia, 2010). To the extent that the organization and accountability of national regulatory actors shape their interactions and in particular their independence from private and political interests, it is insightful to analyze them in a cross-country fashion for further insight into the degree to which these interests are likely to penetrate regulatory preferences. National regulators and supervisors in the Euro Zone are very differently organized across the various European countries, varying from completely independent supervisors to totally integrated supervisors, located either in- or outside of central banks, and given varying degrees of political independence.

3.2.1 Organizational design of the regulator

With respect to the appropriate way to organize regulation and supervision every country has to answer two related questions (Llewellyn, 2005): i) What is the desired role of the central bank? And: ii) What is the appropriate degree of integration of supervision across the three sectors of the financial system, i.e. banking, securities, and insurance? Each of those will briefly be discussed in turn and then applied to the cases of the Euro Zone countries.

With respect to the first question, the reasons for having the *central bank involved in financial supervision* relate to the natural focus that the central bank lays on and the experience it has with financial stability in its pursuit of monetary policy as well as its role as lender of last resort, which give it a direct stake in the effect of macro-prudential policy. Generally the reasons for central bank involvement therefore are (Charles Goodhart & Schoenmaker, 1995; Donato Masciandaro, 2005):

- Synergies and economies of scale in supervising stability of the financial system and individual firms jointly
- Information advantages due to responsibility for monetary operations
- Solvency information coupled with responsibility as lender-of-last-resort
- Authority and credibility of the central bank
- Ability to resolve conflicts of interests with monetary policy internally
- Ability to recruit skilled supervisors due to reputation of central banks

The most controversial one of these benefits is clearly the relation to its mandate in monetary policy and the trade-offs and reputational risks associated with sharing this mandate with a mandate for financial supervision – a point very related to the above discussion on the role of central banks in focusing on asset price bubbles. This controversy has occupied the discussion of banking regulation and supervision for the last years and has been suggested as one of the core issues in banking regulation (Mishkin, 2001). Whilst a discussion of the exact relationship between the two policy areas is still to follow, suffice it to say that the two policy instruments are very related and have a significant amount of overlap in terms of effect. Most countries exhibit some overlap of personnel or are even institutionally joint with respect to the respective agencies responsible for monetary policy and regulation and thus would have some potential conflicts of interest (see addendum VII in the Appendix).[59]

With regard to the second dimension of institutional design, the *integration of financial supervision across the various sectors,* the main debate has related to the changing nature of finance and banking. As such, the emergence of conglomerates and financial innovations that transgress the former sectoral demarcations of finance, make the organization of supervision along banking, securities, and insurance lines less effective in today's financial systems. Hence, integrated supervision has emerged as an alternative to sectoral supervision.

TABLE 10: *Typology of institutional regulatory structure/ design*

		Role of the central bank	
		Central bank (exclusively) responsible for systemic risks in banking regulation	*Central bank not (exclusively) responsible for systemic risks in banking regulation*
Financial authority conlgo-meration	*Single regulatory authority*	Integrated mega-central bank	Single financial authority/ regulator
	Multiple regulatory authorities	Twin-peaks model	Institutional or functional approach (less common today)

Source: Author

[59] For a more extensive economic discussion of the subject see the classical piece by Bernanke and Gertler (2000). For a political economy discussion of the relationship between the regulatory agency and the central bank see for instance (Ioannidou, 2005)(Schoenmaker & Goodhart, 1992)

When we combine the two choices along the two dimensions of institutional design, we can derive a typology of four institutional structures. Each separate approach in the following will briefly be discussed for their implications on financial stability policy-making building on the insights generated by a review through the Group 30 (De la Dehesa, 2009):

- **Institutional or functional approach:** This approach has historically been the dominant one in many Euro Zone countries, given that the market landscape for banking, securities, and insurance used to be largely separate, deeming a separate regulatory structure (based either on institutions or the nature of the underlying transaction/ functions) feasible. With increasing interaction between banking and trading due to the conglomerization of finance and the blurring of product lines the requirements for coordination have increased so much that this approach is generally not deemed practical anymore.
- **Integrated mega-central bank:** This institutional configuration is also not a very common one, since it requires the central bank to also be responsible for supervision of securities trading and insurance business – areas in which it historically has not developed the same amount of expertise as it has in banking. Also, as mentioned before, the political economy of institutional power suggests that a concentration of powers and responsibilities in the already very independent and powerful central banks will likely not be pursued by governments and finance ministries. Ireland thus remains an exception to the rule, which is most likely explained by the smaller size of the economy and the well-documented intimate relationships between the different policy actors, which allow coordination and checks and balances preventing excessive power concentration. In fact, as the first Chief Executive of the Central Bank and Financial Services Authority of Ireland Liam O'Reilly states in a review of the regulatory reform process in Ireland of 2003 (O'Reilly, 2004): *"The supervisory structure adopted by Ireland addresses not only the macro but also the micro regulatory issues facing a small open economy. The interlinkages among monetary policy, financial stability, prudential supervision, and consumer protection are being coordinated in a unique, efficient, and innovative way. The structure enables us to provide the regulatory service the government requires in a manner that meets customer needs, is responsive to industry, and uniquely suits the institutional structures and relative size of the Irish financial sector."*
- **Single financial authority/ regulator:** The integrated regulator model is one of the more stable configurations that has emerged in response to the financialization of banking and the general blurring of boundaries between the three sectors of finance. This approach employs one universal supervisor to overlook all types of financial institutions, which proves to be particularly effective in the context of small financial markets and high degrees of conglomerization since it reduces the likelihood of regulatory arbitrage or a failure to coordinate. Challenges arise when the complexity increases due to the size and complexity of financial markets, as the depth of financial products is more difficult to manage within one supervisory institution. The introduction of the Financial Services Agency (FSA) in the UK, initiated by the then incoming Labour Government under the auspice of Gordon Brown in 1997, is the model case of such a regulator separate from the Central

Bank. The motivation according to the FSA's former vice president Howard Davies was based on the changing nature of the financial landscape and the will to relieve the Bank of England of potential conflicts of interest with its mandate for price stability (Davies, 2004).

- **Twin-Peaks Model:** The second stable and more current configuration is the twin-peaks model, which derives its name from the separation of tasks along the two types of objectives that regulators are often assigned: i) The supervision of the conduct of business (with a micro-prudential and consumer focus) and ii) the supervision of systemic risks (with a macro-prudential and economy focus). This model tries to get the best of two worlds in that the central bank retains the responsibility for the systemic risks while the regulatory agency is assigned the micro-prudential focus on conduct of business and prudential regulation. The case of Australia illustrates the choice for the twin-peaks model as a choice triggered by a changing environment, in which technological change, changing customer needs, and de-regulation would trigger new challenges to stability and competition of banks. The twin-peaks model was seen as most suited to provide more accountability of the agencies, more effective and consistent regulation across sectors, and a more efficient and competitive financial system. The very structured approach taken to the review of regulation thus resulted in a clean new model of regulation, favouring different agencies for different objectives and thereby splitting regulatory and supervisory responsibility for banks into the two peaks.

As the above discussion shows, different models seem to be applicable to different financial environments. From a political economy perspective, what emerges is the concern of policymakers not to make regulators too strong and independent, as is the case with the integrated mega-central banks model. Thus, the combination of a central bank role for financial stability and regulation as well as the tendency to increase in integration in regulatory powers together make for a policy dilemma regarding the institutional structure of supervision: Prioritizing financial stability by assigning financial supervision to the central bank is generally not perceived to be compatible with integrating financial supervision across all sectors. The reason generally accepted in this debate is that otherwise the central bank, generally relatively independent, would accumulate excessive power and control over the financial system by regulating, making monetary policy, and being the chief actor in crisis management, which in political economy terms is generally not favored by the ministries of finance in most countries. Moreover, making the central bank this predominant player is perceived to extend the lender-of-last-resort responsibility to all financial intermediaries rather than banks only, which would create more moral hazard in the financial system. To establish the prevalent models in the Euro Zone, the figure below replicates the empirical findings by Masciandaro (2004, 2005) for these countries, mapping the concentration of supervisory powers, as measures by a Financial Authorities Concentration Index (FAC Index) with the degree of central bank involvement in financial supervision, as measured by the Central Bank as Financial Authority Index (CBFA). I also add the costs of the financial crisis 2007/8 to derive the potential impact of the organizational structure on financial stability outcomes.

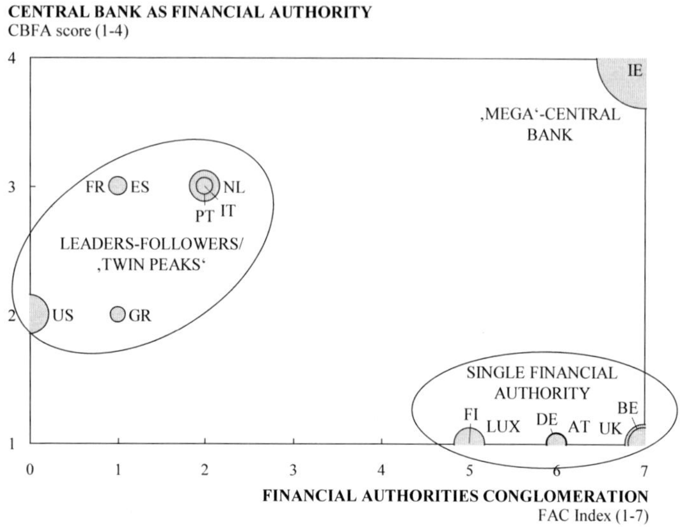

FIGURE 12: *Organization of banking regulation and costs of financial crisis across countries*

Source: Author based on CBFA and FACE data by Masciandaro (2004, 2005) and cost of financial crisis data by Laeven and Valencia (2010)

Like Masciandaro, I find that the various countries are more and more clustering into two groups, which either concentrate powers but then do not charge the central bank with supervision or which spread powers across multiple institutions and then do assign supervisory tasks to the central bank. With the exception of Ireland, which has concentrated supervision with the central bank, the European countries are similarly polarized and have either opted for a *single financial authority* regime or a *leader-followers* framework with a role for the central bank. However, neither of the above mentioned models seems to have played a determining role in preventing financial instability from arising. For each of the three prevalent, above shown models of regulatory organization we can identify countries with severe systemic crises and high costs of the financial crisis. As such, the United States and the Netherlands have espoused a model that gave the central bank a role in banking supervision, yet, experienced not only institutional failure but also a systemic crisis with costs of 25% and 16% of GDP, respectively. On the other hand, the United Kingdom and Belgium had concentrated banking regulation and supervision with a specialized integrated financial authority and similarly experienced deep systemic crises and institutional failure at 25% and 18% of GDP, respectively. Lastly, Ireland with the most powerful and integrated central bank and regulator experienced the strongest systemic crisis in terms of the costs to GDP, which have been estimated to add up to 156% of GDP.

From the literature and a review of recent financial stability outcomes across countries no superior model of regulatory organization emerges (D Masciandaro, 2007). This implies that we cannot assume to derive direct financial stability preferences form regulatory design. However, a pattern of not assigning too much independence to the regulator seems to emerge, which indicates that policymakers have been hesitant in giving regulatory policymakers too much leeway in determining financial stability policy. To verify this tentative finding, a closer look at the design of regulatory accountability and independence is warranted.

3.2.2 Political accountability/ independence of the regulator

Beyond organizational structure the other important source of regulatory institutional variance across countries is accountability and the complementary dimension of independence of the regulator.[60] The question is: To what extent do countries keep a check on their banking supervisors and organize accountability to depositors and their elected representatives, on whose behalf they carry out their regulation and supervision? Singer describes the role of the check on and intervention in the delegated regulator's action by the politicians as "the bane of the regulator's existence" (2007; p.22):

"The agency (or the 'agent') is generally capable of making frequent modifications to the regulatory environment for firms – such as altering prudential supervisory protocols, tightening capital adequacy rules, and changing reporting requirements – but rarely are these changes prompted by observable pressure from elected officials. However, if the outcome of a regulator's policy choices run counter to the interests of elected leaders, the legislature – as the principal – can intervene and enact new policies (...) The prospect of intervention by legislators therefore creates ex ante constraints on a regulator's range of policy choices, which ensures that the principal can maintain some control over the agent."

The democratic accountability of regulators is important as it provides legitimacy and at the same time ensures the (degree of) alignment of goals between the regulator and elected representatives of the general public. At the same time, regulatory independence is often espoused as a virtue to allow the regulator to make politically difficult decisions that are however considered to be in the long-run public interest. As such, Masciandaro, Quintyn, and Taylor (2008, p.834) discuss de-politicized accountability and independence of the regulator as an important institutional feature to ensure that financial stability can actually be carried out against the multiplicity of regulatory objectives:

"Accountability arrangements for independent financial regulatory agencies must necessarily be more complex than for independent central banks owing to their multiple, and harder to measure, objectives and the existence of a multiple principals environment. It has been further argued that from the social welfare standpoint independence and accountability should not be regarded as mutually exclusive but are complementary to the extent that well-designed accountability arrangements can help to buttress agency independence."

---

60 The argument that accountability and independence are really complementary features and condition regulatory policy in the same way is advanced extensively in Masciandaro, Quintyn, and Taylor (2008) and is discussed later on.

Hence, the regulator is caught between a strive for independence to maximize the amount of discretion with respect to regulating and supervising especially in times of stability and low salience of financial stability policy, however, has to anticipate the legislative response and intervention should the regulatory agent fail to accommodate its principals. Given this incentive structure of the regulator, it becomes clear that how countries organize the structure and accountability of national banking regulators could have an impact on how preferences of regulators and banking supervisors are formed. The easier political intervention is, the more a regulator should anticipate this in its regulatory policy-making and therefore the more she will pay more attention to influential and potentially salient private interests as well, since these might also trigger intervention, when they fail to be addressed.

The below figure summarizes the relative independence and accountability constellations for the regulators and supervisors of the Euro Zone and the United Kingdom (U.S. data is not available). Again a holistic analysis of the implications of regulatory accountability and independence is beyond the scope of this section. However, I am interested in the relative degree of insulation of national regulators from channels of private interests such as the influence from the industry as well as the political realm.

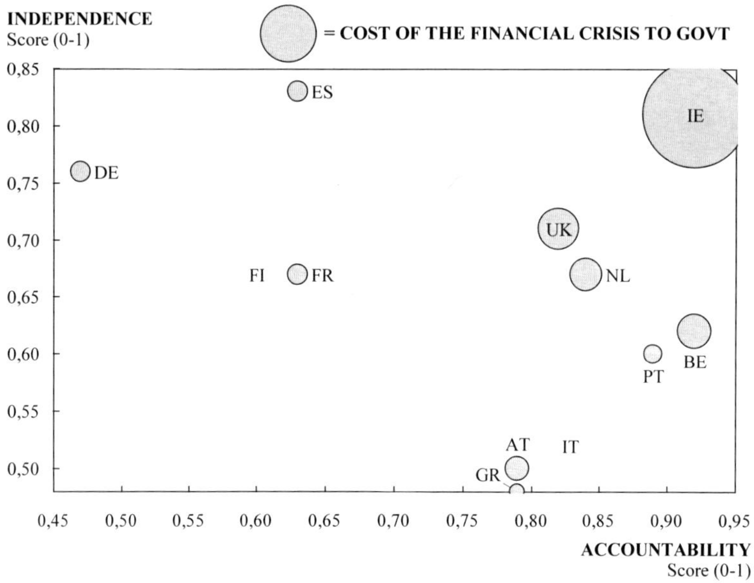

FIGURE 13: *Independence and accountability of banking regulation and costs of financial crisis across countries (on the horizontal accountability axis, higher scores indicate limited accountability)*

Source: Author based on data by D Masciandaro et al. (2008) and cost of financial crisis data by Laeven and Valencia (2010)

To the extent that mandates do not already focus regulators on objectives beyond financial stability, it is through political and lobbying pressures that regulators would have to be influenced to mind these objectives. Analysis of the pattern shows that countries largely again fall into two categories with respect to the independence and accountability of their regulators: Some countries including Germany, Spain, France, and Finland make their regulatory bodies very independent but hold them accountable in more stringent manner. Other countries have the opposite constellations including Greece, Austria, Italy, Portugal, and Belgium. The United Kingdom and the Netherlands fall in-between with relatively high accountability and independence. Thus, when one excludes the special case of Ireland, there actually is a negative correlation between the two dimensions: Countries either advance independence at but then hold regulators more accountable or they limit independence but then make them less accountable. Again Ireland stands out as the regulator with the highest total degree of independence and lowest accountability.

When we add the dominions of the financial stability outcomes, measured by the costs of the crisis, we also cannot establish a clear pattern: The formally most independent and also least accountable regulators of Ireland, the United Kingdom, and the Netherlands all had rather important failures of individual banks under their watch, which in the case of Ireland were also clearly linked to regulatory oversight and politically induced lax regulation (Regling & Watson, 2010). Hence, the *de iure* independence particularly in small states as Ireland with high proximity of government, regulators, and business does not necessarily translate into *de facto* independence. Thus, independence and accountability can be particularly relevant when it comes to the conduct of financial stability policy in a financial system not affected by shocks to the regulatory objective function. Hence, we need to look further when trying to derive the sources of regulatory preferences, realizing however that in general full independence of the regulator remains illusionary for the reasons stated above.

3.2.3 Conclusion

Much of the academic debate has stressed the design and accountability of regulatory bodies as key drivers of financial stability outcomes. Even post-financial crisis political economy scholars have argued that the maintenance of a regulatory and supervisory function in the central bank with its strong record of independence has led to lower levels of systemic risk as evidenced in the pattern of crisis in 2007/8 (De la Dehesa, 2009). My findings about the role of regulatory organization and financial stability policy and outcomes are not consistent with this view. Instead they rather reflect the findings of work by Masciandaro, Quintyn, and Taylor (2008):

I base my view on two distinct findings:

- Firstly, looking at the empirical record it is hard to derive a pure relationship between the way that *responsibilities are assigned to the monetary and regulatory institution and the performance in terms of financial stability*. Whilst Ireland and Greece suffered deep systemic banking crises, Italy came out of the crisis largely unscathed – yet, both have the central bank in charge of banking regulation. I shall therefore take into account another dimension of regulatory institutional design to arrive at a more holistic view of structure.

- Secondly, *formal institutional accountability is not sufficiently instructive to explain the emergence of financial instability* through regulatory capture. Most countries *do not make their banking regulators and supervisors fully independent* from a political and legal point of view and thus leave certain channels of influence for the political and private sphere to shape regulatory policy towards desirable political objectives – the tolerance for higher consumer leverage to further home ownership in the United States is one example that can be found in the recent post-crisis literature (R. Rajan, 2010). Apart from that even in countries with already high existing levels of independence, this has not yielded superior financial stability outcomes but on the contrary has also left them open to intellectual capture and overly lax regulation.

Based on these findings I conclude that whilst independence and accountabilty are important for regulators to be able to 'lean against the wind', it is the complexity of the objective function in relation to the means available, which shapes regulatory stringency and financial stabilty outcomes. Due to the nature of regulatory mandates and the multi-dimensional policy conduct of banking regulation, regulators will have to consider other objectives in the pursuit of financial stability regardless of the degree of independence or accountabilty afforded to them. This is where banking regulaiton differs distinctly from the conduct of monetary policy. As I showed earlier, in some cases this works officially through mandates and in other cases inofficially or through intellectual capture as evidenced by the focus of financial stability reviews. As such, it is when the multiple objectives together form a multiplicity of trade-offs that banking regulation becomes an insolvable problem and is likely to fall short of its financial stability purpose. However, preferences that shape this choice are likely to derive from more systemic institutional configurations rather than simple organizational choices. This is what the next sections will look at.

3.3 Financial systems and the varying role of banks across countries

In the following I argue that institutional configurations at the systemic and not the organizational level drive regulatory actions through important path-dependent complementarities of financial systems. Such an approach is based on the neo-institutionalist approach to financial systems, which tries to capture the different factors that together constitute the political economy system, within which the regulator operates, and depicts the economy as a holistic system composed of *complementary subsystems*. This perspective is to be differentiated from a purely functional perspective, which regards the provision of these essential functions as key to financial systems with very little room for complementarities between these functions.[61] The fundamental neo-institutionalist concepts also transport themselves to the realm of regulation and financial systems, even if the latter research areas are much less developed than the research into other questions of fiscal, wage bargaining, and monetary macro-economic adjustment. In fact, already in the seminal work on the varieties of capitalism by Hall and Soskice (2001; p.52) it reads:

---

[61] Such a functional account is best described by one of the main functionalist proponents Robert Merton (Merton & Bodie, 2005; p.26): *"When studying the dynamics of financial systems, it is best to adopt an analytical framework that treats functions rather than institutions as the conceptual anchors."*

"The approach to comparative capitalism developed (...) provides another way of specifying how states will define their national interests in international economic negotiations. It suggests that their stance toward new regulatory initiatives will be influenced by judgments about whether those initiatives are likely to sustain or undermine the comparative institutional advantages of their nation's economy. Governments should be inclined to support such initiatives only when they do not threaten the institutions most crucial to the competitive advantages their firms enjoy."

This shows the value of a neo-institutionalist approach in complementing other political economy approaches: Varieties of capitalism specifies very clearly how domestic preferences are formed along competitiveness considerations of the domestic industry and how (co-)specific investments create pressures for path dependence. Given the divergence in comparative advantages of nations, the resulting differences in investments made and competitive advantages conferred onto firms, it is logical that most VoC-approaches also assume and predict a divergence of regulatory initiatives and implementation practices. As Zimmermann (2010; p.124) argues in his recent account of varying approaches to financial regulation: *"The CPE argument is very attractive because it systematically introduces country-specific variables based on structural characteristics of national economies into the analysis, opening the black box of the state."* Thus, in this approach it is the *financial system* that drives the country-specific approach to financial regulation.

3.3.1 Financial systems: Varying financial stability configurations across countries

What constitutes a financial system? Schmidt and Tyrell distinguish the *financial sector* from the *financial system* (2003, p. 3):

"The narrow concept is that of the financial sector. We define the financial sector as that part – or sector – of an economy, which offers and provides financial services to the other sectors of the economy. It consists of the central bank, other banks, non-bank financial institutions, organised financial markets and the relevant regulatory and supervisory institutions.
The broader concept is that of the financial system. It can be defined in general terms as the interaction between the supply of and the demand for the provision of capital and other finance-related services."

This more systemic view, in contrast to a narrower functional view, emphasizes the role of *complementarities* and *consistencies* of subsets of this system.[62] The financial systems literature treats the definition of financial systems as surrounding three topics in financial relations: The way 1) wealth is accumulated and income is transferred over time; 2) the way businesses finance themselves and they way that corporate governance is exercised; 3) the way that risk is managed (R. H. Schmidt & Tyrell,

[62] From a VoC-perspective one might add to these three subsystems the fourth subsystem of corporate strategy, which in the firm-centered VoC-perspective is shaped by the institutional complementarities. In fact in an earlier print of their concept, this broader view of the subsets is defined, comprising the financial sector, different financing patterns (saving and investment), different corporate governance arrangements, and systemic variations in corporate strategy (R. H. Schmidt, 1999). Thus, these four different subsystems and their respective polar choices within the subsystems open up different combinations along which systems can differ.

2003)(R. H. Schmidt, 1999). There is a congruence between these financial sub-systems of the neo-institutionalist view and the functionalist view. The comprehensive theoretical comparison of financial systems by Allen and Gale (2001a) also discusses that three systems reflect the different provision of the three basic functions of any financial system. Allen and Gale discuss how financial intermediaries and markets differ in their provision of the key functions of 1) asset transformation, 2) producing information for optimal resource allocation, 3) risk sharing.

The comparative financial systems literature has made more inroads into the specifics of comparing financial systems. in terms of a coherent neo-institutionalist or systemic account of how varieties of financial systems provide their essential functions.[63] Most prominently economists Allen and Gale (2001) set out to develop new theories based on comparing financial system development across the world. Their main argument is that different responses to incomplete markets and instability have shaped the financial systems differently. Their account assumes that *„markets and intermediaries are alternatives that perform more or less the same functions in different ways and perhaps with different degrees of success"* (Gale & Allen, 2001a; p.17). Where the neo-institutionalist account differs from the functionalist account is in that it presumes the existence of *complementary* choices along these subsystems: Clearly the savings and investment patterns (banks vs. financial markets) will determine to a large extent the role of banks and financial markets in the financial sector, creating a natural correspondence between these two subsystems (Schmidt, 1999). Given that corporate governance patterns (insider-control vs. market-control) tend to co-vary with the type of financing, it also seems intuitive to assume a correspondence of corporate control and the financial pattern, for instance the systematic coincidence of a bank-based system and a system of insider-control. The complementarity between the *financial system* and the *economy* works through the channel of *corporate strategies* (radical vs. gradual change). These have been shown by the VoC-literature to co-vary systematically as well (Peter A Hall & Soskice, 2001), depending on the 'patience' of capital, which tends to be higher (lower) in bank-based (market-based) financial systems and then tends to favor incremental (big-leap) change in strategy and innovation. Thus, the classification the systemic finance literature is consistent with the *liberal* vs. *coordinated* capitalism-literature as it tends to group countries similarly along the *market-based* vs. *bank-based* financial system divide, if, however, based on a more systemic and comprehensive analysis of its various linkages between the subsystems. It therefore fits our approach of locating banking regulation within the wider economic and political context of the financial system and the economy.

The two complementary configurations that the neo-institutionalist approach to financial systems identifies, ***the market-*** and ***the bank-based financial system***, identify some key design choices (and implicit trade-offs) along the different functional elements of a financial system:

---

[63] The most comprehensive approach to defining a framework for comparative analysis has come from a small branch of the economics discipline itself. With a focus on the German financial system as well as the convergence of systems in Europe Reinhard Schmidt has authored a series of papers and books, which provided a systemic perspective on what constitutes a financial system and how they can be analyzed in comparative perspective (Krahnen & Schmidt, 2004; R. H. Schmidt, 1999; R. H. Schmidt & Tyrell, 2001, 2003).

- *Asset and maturity transformation* can take place either through *financial markets* or through *financial intermediaries* – mostly *banks*. In reality of course the co-existence of the two institutional forms is mostly the case. Inspite of that, clear differences in the degree of intermediation can be found across countries (see actual data below). Market-based economies tend to transform their assets through markets (sometimes of course aided by financial institutions) whilst bank-based systems have higher intermediation ratios, that is a higher share of claims vis-à-vis the banking sector vs. other economic sectors. The general flow of funds in the classical bank-based system sees flows from households to firms through financial intermediaries, whilst in the market-based system this flow tends to go through financial markets in the form of securitized financial instruments (R. H. Schmidt & Tyrell, 2003).
- *Corporate governance,* that is *information provision and allocative efficiency* about firms in their role as borrowers and equity investments, differs along a spectrum of *insider-based* governance and *outsider-based* governance (Clarke & Chanlat, 2009). The *insider-based,* often also called stakeholder-oriented, form can mostly be found in bank-based economies, where banks serve to overcome the informational asymmetries that result from a large share of small and medium-sized firms, which are not publicly listed and traded and therefore make equity investments by private investors more difficult. Close long-term relationships between banks and firms, often bolstered by equity investments and supervisory board presence by bank managers, therefore serve to monitor management decisions and produce information, which enables banks to make profitable long-term lending and investment decisions on behalf of investors. In the *market-based*, also called shareholder-oriented, system on the other end of the spectrum, an outsider-based system of governance is made possible by high disclosures requirements as well as a high share of firms traded in capital markets.
- *Risk sharing* in these two systems differs along a spectrum of *intertemporal risk-smoothing* to *cross-sectional risk-sharing. Intertemporal risk-smoothing* represents the concept that financial intermediaries, for example historically in Germany and France, can smoothen out earnings shocks resulting from non-diversifiable market risk over time – facilitated usually by an accounting system, which does not mark their assets to market (Gale & Allen, 2001b). Hence, households, who hold a large share of their savings intermediated by banks, will be able to smoothen out risks through the 'shock absorber' of large financial institutions. In the *cross-sectional risk-sharing* model, on the other hand, households have a larger share of risks on their own balance sheets and can optimize the risk allocation through cross-sectional risk-sharing, that is through the forwarding of risky assets through 'securitized' claims, which are traded on capital markets.[64] This development of different financial systems in Europe has mainly been shaped by the imperfections of capital markets, which exhibited the

64 The oil shock of the 1970s is given by Allen and Gale as such an example of a correlated change in stock prices, which was felt much less in household spending in the bank-based systems of Germany, France, and Japan than in the market-based systems of the U.K. and the U.S.. As competition in banking is more intense in countries like the U.K. and the U.S., therefore banks have to compete with financial markets for returns and will be less able to smoothen. Given the trends towards the market-based system, a subject of analysis in a later chapter, such competitive pressures tend to increase as well in the EU and the Euro Zone.

inherent instability of financial markets in Europe in the 18th and 19th century, leading to the development of bank-based systems in continental Europe.

3.1.2 Legal institutions: The varying strength of depositors, creditors, and investors across countries

New political economy has espoused the role of domestic interests that shape preferences in economic policy-making on the national level, showing that regulation is often a reflection of the varying strength of domestic economic and political constituencies (R. Rajan, Zingales, & Economic, 2000; Singer, 2004b; Verdier, 2001). This new political economy thinking sees policymakers, very much like this work does, as self-interested agents, who respond to political incentives rather than acting as benevolent social planners alone (Pagano, 2001). Such new political economy thinking aims to allow inference regarding the development of markets and explaining regulation and its economic effects on constituencies. Since regulators will therefore respond to differences in constituencies, the respective strength they are afforded by the financial systems' legal institutions should therefore allow us to derive the strength of the underlying interests as an indication of a country's regulatory preferences. The law and finance literature (La Porta, Lopez-de-Silanes, Shleifer, & Vishny, 1998) has had a very significant impact in deriving more systematically such cross-country differences in legal institutions with respect to how companies are financed and governed, thus illuminating better the real economy-finance nexus of investors, creditors, and depositors in different legal traditions. The literature maintains – much in keeping with the comparative financial systems-literature – that different systems across countries favoring different types of financial stakeholders work quite well. As such, there is an implicit assumption about the complementarity of such legal institutions to other systemic configurations. Moreover the literature distinguishes the differential role of banks and markets across legal traditions, which implicitly links this literature with the financial systems literature. This link, however, to the best of my knowledge has not been done explicitly. Hence, the following will summarize the insights on the role of these legal institutions in finance based on the law and finance-literature and will relate it to the complementary financial system that is best supported by such institutions, which then should give us a good indication of the more systematic regulatory preferences of a country.

A *bank-based financial system* is built around strong financial intermediaries, which based on private information can make continuous credit available to the firms they lend to – usually small and medium sized enterprises (SMEs). Thus, in bank-based financial systems relationship finance is likely the most important function of financial intermediaries, as SMEs rely largely on external debt for financing their investments (Elsas & Krahnen, 2004).[65] In order to provide such finance more extensively, banks need to have a stronger say in the case of default of one of their clients, which implies higher chances of recovering their loans through reorganization in case of bankruptcy. Otherwise debtors will anticipate ex ante that lenders will not be in a good position to

65 This is consistent with those approaches that have derived financial system choices as the 'Anglo-Saxon' and the 'German-style' financial system as equilibria choices, based on the presence of moral hazard and variation in the respective bargaining power of lenders and borrowers and corresponding demand for monitored or un-monitored loans (Baliga & Polak, 2004).

renegotiate credit ex post and moral hazard and, consequently, adverse selection on the side of the borrowers will result (Gale & Allen, 2001b). To overcome this time inconsistency problem strong creditor rights are needed to in commit the lender to an aggressive stance. This is the case in the German insolvency code for instance. In the German financial system the insolvency code has allowed banks, particularly the relationship lenders called *Hausbanken*, to be involved in the case of a workout, which implies that out of the bankruptcy cases analyzed by Krahnen and Elsas (2002) only 6,5 % of all cases really end up going into bankruptcy proceedings immediately, while 37% of cases undergo restructuring workouts and another 56,5% experience no such serious treatments. Thus, if relationship finance and access to credit is a priority for a financial system, as assumed in the bank-based system, it is likely to find that regulation will strengthen creditor rights and have weaker shareholder rights: Strong creditor rights facilitate the bank's ability to create long-term relationships through increased powers over their debtors while on the other hand more limited investor rights facilitate the provision of more 'patient' capital from shareholders, which allows such a long-term perspective.

What prediction can we make about the extent of depositor rights, which reflect the focus on stability? Financial stability in bank-based systems is organized along institutional lines, where banks represent the anchor of risk management. Financial intermediaries smoothen risk out over time (Gale & Allen, 2001b) but are also subject to institutional euphoria (R. G. Rajan & Zingales, 2002). Because financial intermediaries take such a pre-eminent position in the financial system, depositor rights are likely to be more limited. Two arguments support this prediction: Firstly, larger financial institutions create larger potential liabilities for governments, which would explain why governments would tend to limit their own exposures (at least formally) through more limited deposit insurance and depositor rights. Secondly, banks' interests will be better organized in a financial system with large FIs, which would likely limit depositor rights. These lower depositor rights are, however, not necessarily a reflection of a lower valuation of stability. Instead, in this configuration strong banks with a lot of rights vis-à-vis creditors and depositors are assumed to provide financial stability through lower default and better risk-smoothing over time. Thus, the following proposition can be formulated:

Proposition 3 *Bank-based financial systems will have relatively stronger creditor rights, weaker shareholder rights, and weaker depositor rights.*

A *market-based financial system*, on the other hand, will have much stronger shareholders rights, which are a reflection of the stronger role of investors in these financial systems and will be accompanied by weaker creditor rights – a reflection of the more restricted powers afforded to financial institutions. Since financial markets provide credit through bonds only with a short-term interest at arm's length, re-negotiation of credit lines is not a priority for the design of regulation. As an example, the U.S. financial system has historically had quite a lot of banks in a relatively fragmented banking system, where each of the banks on average plays a smaller role than the European counterparts. Since financing in the market-based system can take place through capital markets, banks are not the only source of corporate finance and hence will not need to be equipped with overly strong creditor rights – a reflection moreover of their more limited influence in the United States' financial system.

Depositor rights can be assumed to be stronger given the relative weakness of banks and given that the logic of the bank-based system does not apply. Hence, the proposition regarding the *market-based financial system* is:

Proposition 4 *Market-based financial systems will have relatively weaker creditor rights, stronger shareholder rights, and stronger depositor rights.*

In a very highly developed financial system with strong financial institutions *and* deep capital markets, we will expect strong creditor and shareholder rights at the same time. Because of the strength of both banks and investors, we are unlikely to see either a relationship-finance-configuration, since shareholders will demand higher and more short-term returns, which contradicts the nature of the risk-smoothing system. Rather, strong creditor rights as well as strong shareholder rights can be seen as reflections of an interest in profitable, competitive, and powerful banks that are competing with capital markets. Hence, in such a competitive system the regulator is likely to want limit the moral hazard that the introduction of extensive deposit insurance rights would likely create for banks. Hence, the presence of strong shareholder and creditor rights will likely come at the expense of depositors' interests and instead reflects a reliance on market forces and the self-regulating market in creating financial stability.

Proposition 5 *Very developed and competitive hybrid financial systems with both – strong financial markets and financial institutions - will have relatively stronger creditor rights, stronger shareholder rights, and weaker depositor rights.*

TABLE 11: *Complementary configurations of financial systems and legal institutions*

		Relative strength of interest in bank competitiveness (relative strength of shareholders relative to creditors and depositors)	
		Low	*High*
Relative strength of interest in credit access (relative reliance on banks for provision of financial functions)	*Low*	*Other financial systems:* Non-captured/ developing finance	*Market-based systems:* 'arms-length'-finance
	High	*Bank-based systems:* 'relationship' finance	*Hybrid systems:* 'competitive self-regulating' finance

Source: Author

3.1.3 Conclusion

When joined with the insights from the law and finance-literature, the *neo-institutionalist approach* can help illuminate the link between financial systems and legal institutions. I suggest that the legal institutions relate to the financial system and its subsystems in a *complementary and consistent fashion*. Different financial systems perform functions differently and have different legal institutions to support this configuration, which again reflect differences in the strength of domestic financial stakeholder interests. Such a complementary account of financial systems and regulatory institutions is given in the table above and to be subjected to empirical tests in the following section. These configurations should then provide evidence with respect to how a regulator's preferences are likely to be influenced by the financial system and its main actors.

3.4. Empirical clustering analysis

3.4.1 Financial system clusters

Clustering Variables

How can the Euro Zone financial systems be categorized? An empirical look along the three subsystems should give clues with respect to how bank- vs. market-based the respective financial systems were in 2000. [66] The key variables employed to make such a classification are:

Asset and maturity transformation is measured through the variable *SIZE* based on the data and variable specification strategy of World Bank economists (Levine, 2000) as the log of *stock market activity* and *stock market size* relative to *bank credit* to provide an indication of how relevant markets versus banks are to intermediation in the economy. A more intermediated and hence bank-based financial system will therefore see lower values, whereas a market-based system will have higher values. *ACTIVITY* is introduced as a second measure of the prevalence of markets vs. banks, this time however measuring the log of the relation of stock traded versus credit provided (Levine, 2000).

The risk sharing sub-system[67] as a variable also differs along the bank-based versus market-based continuum and hence is captured by the same two variables. Again, as before, higher values for *SIZE* and *ACTIVITY* indicate a larger reliance on capital markets for financial transactions (and thus also for risk-sharing), whereas higher reliance on intermediaries indicates also a higher reliance on inter-temporal smoothing. Admittedly, this measure is second-best to a real measure of for instance securitization vs. loans or risky asset vs. non-risky asset holdings by households – however, data limitations do not allow for such measures to be gathered consistently across all sampled countries.[68]

Corporate governance as a sub-system is captured by two variables, that measure the dominant corporate governance approaches: Stakeholder vs. shareholder orientation is measured through the variable *EMPLOYEE RIGHTS*, which denotes the OECD measures for employee protection. Stronger stakeholder orientation, as for example in the corporate governance of German companies, which give employee representatives the right to co-determination through seats on the supervisory board, will be reflected in stronger employee rights and therefore higher values of this variable. Insider-based vs. outsider-based control is measured

---

[66] This year is chosen to have a departure point far enough in the past to derive developments since but near enough to allow inference about the implications of recent financial integration.

[67] As such, this operationalization does not assume something like a cultural aspect that would justify higher risk-taking in some countries over others, which for instance Charles Kindleberger seems to suggest, who found (Kindleberger & Aliber, 2005; p.54): *"The speculative temperament may differ among countries."*

[68] In fact, the European Central Bank, at the time of writing, was still in the process of filling this gap to provide household-level data across its Member Countries through a Household Finance and Consumption Network (HFCN). Data results could then be used to validate the risk-measures used here.

by the concentration of *OWNERSHIP*, where lower values reflect smaller average equity holdings, that is a higher dispersion of equity shareholdings. Because the insider-based system gives less information to shareholders, more dispersed and smaller shareholdings are more indicative of a higher degree of outside control market-based corporate governance. This reflects work done by Perotti and von Thadden (2003), who stress the inter-linkage of the financial sphere and the system of corporate governance and its roots in the median voters' preference for corporate risk-taking. In their model of the political economy of bank- or market-based dominance, preferences of the median voters depend on their own interest in defending their holding of human capital vs. actual capital. Depending on this, their choice will vary in favour of either protecting labour income from risk (i.e., in favour of a bank-based system of less corporate risk) or alternatively voting in favour of an equity-dominated system (that favours higher returns to accumulated or invested wealth, i.e., pension savings etc.).

A look at the raw data in Table 12, based on which the above variables are measured and constructed, is instructive to see how systematic the countries do differ within each sub-system (for a graphical mapping of these variables see addenda IX and X in the Appendix).

TABLE 12: *Financial system features across countries*

Country	*Asset transformation and risk-sharing*			*Corporate governance*	
	Stock market capitalization relative to GDP	*Stock traded relative to GDP*	*Bank credit relative to GDP*	*Employee rights (1-4)*	*Ownership concen-tration (0-1)*
Austria	16%	5%	99%	2.21	0.58
Belgium	80%	16%	78%	2.18	0.54
Finland	266%	170%	51%	2.09	0.37
France	111%	82%	81%	2.98	0.34
Germany	72%	56%	115%	2.34	0.48
Greece	110%	66%	42%	3.5	0.67
Ireland	79%	15%	97%	0.93	0.39
Italy	58%	71%	71%	2.51	0.58
Luxembourg	174%	6%	96%	N/A	N/A
Netherlands	175%	176%	126%	2.12	0.39
Portugal	57%	48%	118%	3.67	0.52
Spain	81%	170%	90%	2.93	0.51
United Kingdom	192%	127%	121%	0.68	0.19
United States	164%	326%	49%	0.21	0.2

Source: Author based on data from Levine (2000) and OECD

With respect to their reliance on financial institutions and capital markets for *asset and maturity transformation* and *risk-sharing*, countries in 2000 still differed significantly. Whereas Finland and the United States clearly rely much more on capital markets in their financial dealings, as reflected in their stock capitalization ratios, continental European countries have a much stronger reliance on financial intermediaries, as evidenced by their much higher credit-to-GDP-ratios. Some countries like the Netherlands, the United Kingdom and Luxembourg have relatively large banking systems *and* capital markets and therefore can be seen as evidence that a co-evolution of capital markets and banking systems is possible – there need not necessarily be a mutually exclusive reliance on one or the other. In the *corporate governance* sphere, we see an even clearer divergence: The Anglo-Saxon countries, on the one hand, rely on market-based outside corporate control with low ownership concentration and low employee (insider) rights; the continental economies, on the other hand, rely on a stakeholder-oriented insider-based form of corporate control with high ownership concentration and strong employee rights. Whilst the corporate governance literature of the last years has pointed out the slow erosion of this dichotomy (Enriques & Volpin, 2009; Goyer, 2009; C. Lane, 2009), the facts for the year 2000 still bear out a clear pattern reflecting this polarization. Thus, the financial sub-systems indeed do seem to reflect systematic key differences in the underlying financial claim flows as well as differences in institutional setups, which seems to make a clustering of financial systems along these sub-systems feasible.

Clustering approach and statistical validation of approach

For the systematic aggregate clustering of financial systems, based on the three sub-systems, a statistical clustering methodology is employed. For the purpose of the clustering I measure the two respective variables for each dimension using standardized z-scores. To ensure comparability of the different variables I standardize the values through a z-transformation based on the following formula:

$$z_{gi} = \frac{x_{gi} - \bar{x}_i}{s_i}$$

with z_{gi} being the standardized value for object g and s_i being the empirical standard deviation observed for the variables. The resulting variables express the number of standard deviations that the variable of each object is away from the sample mean of the variable (Bacher, Pöge, & Wenzig, 2010).

Clustering analysis systematizes the forming of groups of classification objects based on homogeneity criteria, which satisfy the conditions that a) there is sufficient homogeneity *within the cluster* (along the mentioned dimensions) and b) there is sufficient heterogeneity *between the clusters.*[69] One limitation of this approach clearly is the limited number of objects (13 countries in this case) in relation to the amount of dimensions. Hence, we have a relatively low ratio of objects to variables of only 3.25 (13 countries and 4 variables). However, the strength of the relationships along the variables and the theoretical depth supporting it seem to balance this out.[70]

---

[69] See Bacher, Pöge, & Wenzig for an extensive discussion of this methodology (2010).

[70] The Pearson correlation figures confirm that (see Table 7.8 in Appendix) and would even justify dropping two of the variables employed. I choose to include them here to reflect certain existing differences between the variables.

The classification method employed is a *deterministic partitioning clustering procedure*, which relies on an existing set of classification categories (as opposed to a procedure that is more explorative and looks to determine the number of clusters). This seems legitimate, since neo-institutionalist and law-and-finance theory provides a very convincing account for the nature of these classification categories and the resulting number of clusters (i.e., market- vs. bank-based financial systems) and since the descriptive raw data seems to bear out the relationships assumed.

A few tests are required to validate the appropriate choice of the clustering strategy: Firstly, a look at the screeplot reveals insights with respect to the optimal (and ideally low) number of clusters that can explain a high share of the variance: The screeplot, relating the Eigenvalue and the number of clusters, shows that a clustering of the countries into two or ideally three clusters yields very high explanatory power, which is not improved anymore by increasing it to four or five clusters. Thus, this is largely in line with the assumed clustering approach according to which countries will fall into the bank- or market-based cluster, but could of course also have intermediate hybrid financial systems, which have characteristics of both systems along the three sub-systems. Hence, it makes sense to at least derive also a three-cluster solution given that there is a meaningful interpretation to this three-cluster-grouping of financial systems. Secondly, when conducting a principal components analysis and conducting a significance analysis of the three-component solution we get a Kaiser-Meyer-Olkin-score is at 0.53, which is above the 'rule of thumb' threshold of 0.4 and the significance level is highly significant at the 0.02 level. This assures us that indeed the clustering along these variables can yield significant results even though we of course have to take some caution due to the described small N-issue.

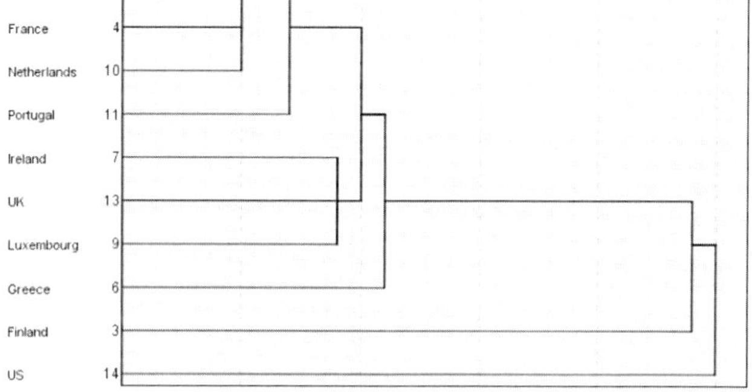

FIGURE 14: *Dendogram of the financial system hierarchical clustering analysis*

Source: Author based on calculations using SPSS v.19

Thirdly, a *hierarchical clustering analysis* is employed to validate the chosen classification strategy. The hierarchical classification strategy yields results, which allow further judgment on the appropriate number of clusters based on the values of the variables. The results of this approach can be seen in the dendogram above: The two cluster-solution seems to group the bank-based European financial systems versus the market-based financial system of the United States and Finland. With a three-cluster-solution we can derive from the dendogram that there are financial systems such as the UK, Luxembourg and Ireland, which share a lot of characteristics as hybrid financial systems and which lie in-between the market- and the bank-based systems.[71]

Deterministic clustering results

The results of the deterministic partitioning cluster analysis corroborate our first findings: The three-cluster-solution separates market-based financial systems of the United States as well as Finland from the bank-based continental European systems and Ireland. Apart from Finland, no other European bank system in 2000 can be identified as sufficiently market-oriented, despite the growth of capital markets across European financial systems in the 1990s. The United Kingdom and Luxembourg as strong financial centers for capital market activities are classified as hybrid systems. In line with our theoretical discussion of the complementarity of different sub-systems, for each variable we see different directions of the coefficient for the bank- and market-based cluster. This indicates that indeed complementary choices can be verified in empirical reality, which provides us with some confidence that the financial systems approach is suitable for deriving regulatory preferences due to relatively stable and path-dependent configurations that prevail over time and therefore drive the choice of regulatory institutions and regulatory stringency across countries.

3.4.2 Legal institution clusters

Clustering Variables

Turning to the shareholder vs. creditor-orientation of a country's legal institutions we can turn to a set of comparative existing indicators: The data used to measure shareholder and creditor rights across countries have been compiled by La Porta, Lopez-de-Silanes, Shleifer, and Vishny (1998), who already composed an index based on this data, the logic of which is replicated in a table in the Appendix (see addendum XV). Depositor rights are based on the data gathered by Demirgüç-Kunt, Karacaovali, and Laeven (2001), who compiled comparative data on the most important dimensions of deposit insurance globally. Here an index for comparative purposes still had to be composed, which was done based on the methodology explained in the table in the Appendix (Table 7.10). Importantly, these indexes, particularly the deposit insurance index, are not meant to be normative in that a higher value necessarily denotes a better practice than a lower value. They are purely descriptive to differentiate different institutional practices with respect to financial regulation.

---

71 In fact Greece also seems like a hybrid system based on the clustering analysis. However, Greece is still by far the least developed financial system analyzed here and hence has a much lower developed banking system as well, which requires different interpretation of the data.

A look at the raw data in Table 3.5 below already provides some first clues regarding the assumed relationship between the variables to each other (see addendum XI in the Appendix for a graphical representation): No country has very high or very low values across all three dimensions, as the logic of the trilemma with the implicit trade-offs suggests. Moreover, the assumed differences along financial systems lines seem to hold, as a look at the paradigmatic cases of the United States (market-based system), Germany (bank-based system, and the United Kingdom (hybrid system) confirms: The United States is the country with strongest shareholder rights (along with the United Kingdom) as well as strong depositor rights but relatively weak creditor rights. This can be seen to be consistent with the idea of consumer and depositor protection as well as shareholder value but an inherent skepticism of strong banks. Germany as a bank-based system, on the other hand, has the opposite type of rights structure, as hypothesized in the above discussion. The UK with its highly developed banking system as well as capital markets stands out as a hybrid system, that has strong shareholder and creditor rights but weaker depositor rights. This is indicative of the moral hazard concern that has been going around the UK's financial regulation, which would indeed arise when investors and banks are already strong and have to be competitive in the presence of competition from the capital markets.

TABLE 13: *Financial stakeholder rights across countries*

Country	*Shareholder rights (index 0-6)*	*Creditor rights (index 0-4)*	*Depositor rights (index 0-6)*
Austria	Low (2)	High (3)	Low (3)
Belgium	Low (0)	Med (2)	High (4)
Finland	Med (3)	Low (1)	High (4)
France	Med (3)	Low (0)	High (3)
Germany	Low (1)	High (3)	Med (3)
Greece	Low (2)	Low (1)	High (4)
Ireland	High (4)	Low (1)	Med (3)
Italy	Low (1)	Med (2)	Med (3)
Luxembourg	N/A	Med (2)	Low (2)
Netherlands	Low (2)	Med (2)	Med (3)
Portugal	Med (3)	Low (1)	High (4)
Spain	High (4)	High (2)	High (4)
United Kingdom	High (5)	High (4)	Low (2)
United States	High (5)	Low (1)	High (6)

Source: La Porta, Lopez-de-Silanes, Shleifer, and Vishny (1998)

An analysis of the hierarchical clustering plot suggests that the continental European countries indeed fall into somewhat different groups: The bank-based financial systems at the center of Europe around Germany, the Benelux, Austria, and Italy are in one group, which judging by Table 13 are all more creditor-oriented and have relatively strong depositor rights. Then there are the more Southern and peripheral bank-based financial systems around France, Spain, Portugal, and Greece as well as Ireland, which share some attributes with the United States in that they are more shareholder-oriented. Lastly, the United Kingdom stands out as the most different financial system. Again, the paradigmatic cases seem to confirm that indeed there are trade-offs along the trilemma, which financial systems seem to respond to differently through institutionalization of stakeholder rights.

Clustering approach and statistical validation of approach

A more methodical and comprehensive look through another formal cluster analysis illustrates this result for the entire sample. As before, the cluster analysis minimizes the differences within the clusters and maximizes differences between them. The variables used to create our classification for the clusters are the values along the three categories of rights (shareholders, creditors, and depositors). As before, a *partitioning clustering procedure*, which relies on an existing set of classification categories, is applied to determine these clusters in a deterministic way (see Bacher et al., 2010, for a discussion of this procedure and its applicability). This time the first test for significance, the KMO-score, shows a value of 0.52, and the Bartlett-significance level is only at 0.24 (see Table 7.12 in Appendix). This indicates that the clustering of the countries here does not capture all of the variance in the way that countries design their financial stakeholder institutions/ rights. Yet, because of the strong theoretical underpinning for such a grouping, an indicative clustering analysis still seems to be the best approach for grouping countries in a meaningful way, even if one has to be somewhat more cautious in interpreting a country's membership to such a cluster. A look at the screeplot (see addendum XIII in Appendix) suggests that three clusters seem to do the best job of explaining the variance, since there is still a substantial gain in explanatory power when moving from the two- to the three-cluster solution. Also, the dendogram from the hierarchical clustering analysis indicates that such a grouping will likely separate the special case of the United Kingdom from some more shareholder-oriented countries around the United States and some more creditor-oriented countries around Germany, which corresponds to the assumed relationship. Hence, continuing with the clustering approach despite its more limited statistical significance seems sensible.

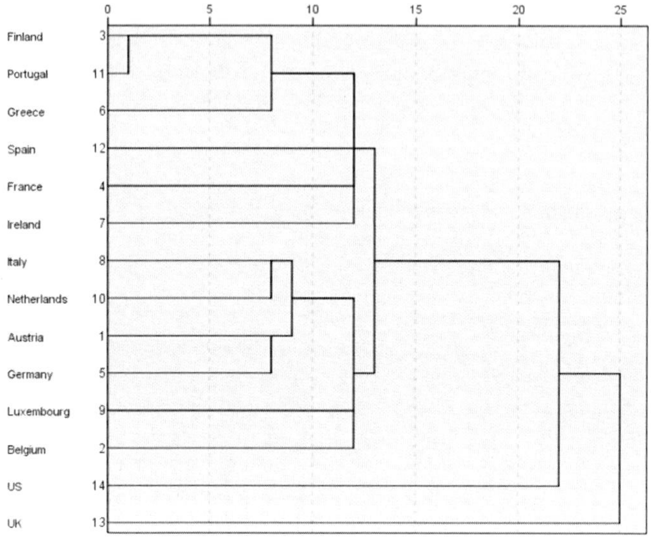

FIGURE 15: *Dendogram of the legal institutions hierarchical clustering analysis*

Source: Author based on calculations using SPSS v.19

Deterministic clustering results

The result of the clustering analysis is largely consistent with the hypotheses developed above: For the three-cluster solution the classification of the different countries is largely along financial system lines, however, with some deviations from the original classification from the prior section, which require explanation.

- The first cluster comprises the countries that have weaker shareholder and depositor rights but stronger creditor rights. As expected, the *creditor-oriented financial systems* around the paradigmatic case of Germany including Austria, Belgium, Italy, Luxembourg and the Netherlands (as a hybrid financial system with strong banking intermediation) can be grouped according to this logic.
- A second cluster of *shareholder-oriented financial systems* then forms around the paradigmatic case of the United States, joint by the similarity of having relatively strong shareholder and depositor rights but weak creditor rights. These countries are financial systems with strong capital markets such as Finland (market-based system), and also countries with a developing capital market but still a stronger reliance on banks such as the Mediterranean economies around France Spain, and Portugal. The latter countries have historically relied on bank intermediation and are still classified as bank-based systems but have made concerted efforts through transformations of their financial systems in the 1980s and 1990s towards developing capital markets. The special case of Greece also falls into this category with a similar structure of rights as well as a financial system that is still underdeveloped – in the banking and the capital market sphere.

- Finally, the third category comprises the special case of the United Kingdom, which as a highly developed *hybrid financial system* has strong creditor *and* shareholder rights but rather weak stability-orientation as denoted by the depositor rights. This reflects the argument that strong depositor protection in the presence of strong shareholders and banks would create moral hazard with excessive risk-taking. Hence the market is better left to self-regulate. Interestingly, when moving from the two- to the three-cluster solution, the United Kingdom emerges as a special classification cluster by itself, in addition to the above categories. Since this special case has a very meaningful interpretation in the context of the trilemma, being a very competitive financial centre with high focus on competitiveness, as it has been serving as a model for many countries aspiring to have strong capital markets along with strong banking markets, it makes sense to keep this additional cluster.

The predictions thus far have been very accurate in particular for the paradigmatic cases Germany, the United States, and the United Kingdom. A high correspondence of financial system configurations and financial stakeholder institutions can be identified. The trilemma seems to hold here, since all countries in the three groups assign higher priority to two of the three stakeholder groups over a third one. The most significant departure from the prediction relates to those Euro Zone financial systems, which have stronger shareholder and weaker creditor rights than assumed: These are in particular the Mediterranean economies of France, Spain, Greece, and Portugal, which seem to emulate the shareholder-oriented approach of the United States in terms of legal institutions but otherwise are still bank-based financial systems much like the German one. How these countries can be classified will be discussed in the context of the joint analysis of financial systems and legal institutions in the next section.

TABLE 14: *Financial system and legal institution variables and clustering results for the Euro Zone countries, the United Kingdom, and the United States*

Country	*SIZE (bank-reliance relative to markets)*	*ACTIVITY (bank-reliance relative to markets)*	*Asset-transformation and risk-sharing system*	*Employee rights*	*Ownership concentration*	*Corporate governance system*	*Financial system cluster*	*Shareholder rights*	*Creditor rights*	*Depositor rights*	*Legal rights orientation (private interests/ depositors)*
Austria	High	High	*Banks*	High	High	*Insider*	*Bank-based*	Low	High	Low	*Creditors*
Belgium	High	High	*Banks*	High	High	*Insider*	*Bank-based*	Low	Med	High	*Creditors*
Finland	Low	Low	*Markets*	Med	Low	*Outsider*	*Market-based*	Med	Low	High	*Shareholders*
France	High	High	*Banks*	High	High	*Insider*	*Bank-based*	Med	Low	High	*Shareholders*
Germany	High	High	*Banks*	High	High	*Insider*	*Bank-based*	Low	High	Med	*Creditors*
Greece	Low	Med	*Hybrid*	High	High	*Insider*	*Bank-based*	Low	Low	High	*Shareholders*
Ireland	High	High	*Banks*	Low	Low	*Outsider*	*Bank-based*	High	Low	Med	*Shareholders*
Italy	High	High	*Banks*	High	High	*Insider*	*Bank-based*	Low	Med	Med	*Creditors*
Luxembourg	Med	High	*Hybrid*	Low	Low	*Outsider*	*Hybrid*	N/A	Med	Low	*Creditors*
Netherlands	Med	Med	*Hybrid*	High	Low	*Hybrid*	*Bank-based*	Low	Med	Med	*Creditors*
Portugal	High	High	*Banks*	High	High	*Insider*	*Bank-based*	Med	Low	High	*Shareholders*
Spain	High	Low	*Hybrid*	High	High	*Insider*	*Bank-based*	High	High	High	*Creditors*
United Kingdom	Med	Med	*Hybrid*	Low	Low	*Outsider*	*Hybrid*	High	High	Low	*CRED..-&-SH.-oriented*
United States	Low	Low	*Markets*	Low	Low	*Outsider*	*Market-based*	High	Low	High	*Shareholders*

Source: Author's clustering estimation; data based on Levine (2000), OECD, and La Porta, Lopez-de-Silanes, Shleifer, and Vishny (1998)

3.4.3 Joint cluster of financial systems and legal institutions

Lastly, a final clustering analysis is conducted to generate clusters that consider both, financial system and legal institution, configurations. Since I have identified some degree of overlap and complementarity between the above classifications, there should be some related principal components in the data, which a clustering analysis can rely on in minimizing within-cluster variances in these components. Since these clusters aggregate the way that financial systems rely on banks for the provision of key functions *and* the relative strength of financial stakeholders, these clusters should be particularly insightful from a political economy perspective on financial relations.

Again, I apply the same step-wise approach to clustering the data to allow for some judgment in determining the optimal number of clusters. A look at the screeplot (see addendum XX in Appendix) shows that the 'optimal' number of clusters would be three clusters. To verify whether this also serves the analytical purpose of explaining differences among Euro Zone countries (vs. differences with the UK and the US) I conduct the hierarchical clustering analysis, which yields the dendogram shown in the figure below.

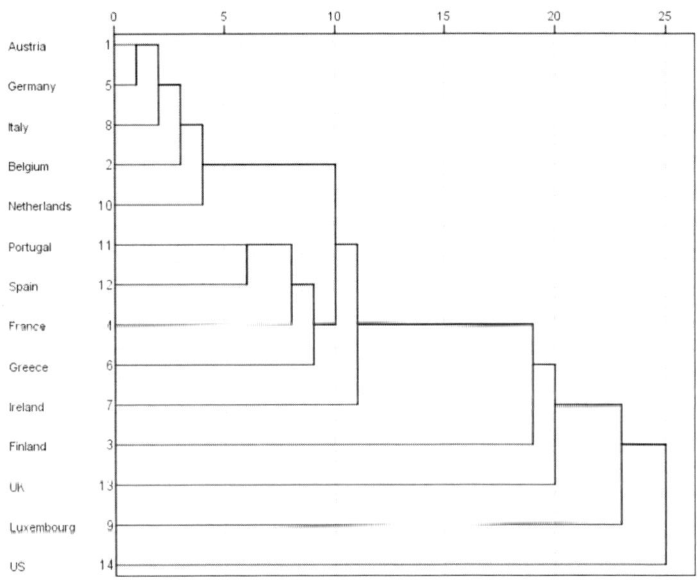

FIGURE 16: *Dendogram of the joint financial system and legal institutions clustering analysis*

Source: Author based on calculations using SPSS v.19

The dendogram suggests that a three-cluster-solution is likely to be insufficient to account for the identified differences amongst the core European financial systems and the peripheral European financial systems. The clusters indicated by the above diagram separate the market-based and hybrid financial systems of the US and Finland and the UK and Luxembourg from the bank-based systems of the continent. However, a fourth cluster would also allow us to differentiate the somewhat different peripheral financial systems with a much higher shareholder-orientation from the other bank-based continental systems with a creditor-orientation. Hence, I conduct also a four-cluster analysis to see whether these differences are then accounted for. Since the variables employed are the same seven variables as prior, the correlation matrix (see Appendix) only yields additional insight with respect to the interactions between the financial system and the legal institutions variables. Only one correlation at .77 stands out as being higher, which is the correlation between *ACTIVITY* and *depositor rights*. The more market-based a financial system is, the more it seems to provide for depositor rights, which again is consistent with the idea that a) regulators are likely to be subject to higher capture in bank-based systems and b) moral hazard concerns are more prevalent amongst legislators and regulators the bigger the role of banks in the economy is. Again, a look at the KMO-value of .48 and particularly the Pearson-coefficient of significance of .001 suggests that a clustering of the countries based on these variables is permissible and should yield meaningful and relatively homogenous groupings (see Table 7.14 in Appendix) . The deterministic clustering analysis yields a four-cluster solution with groupings of countries as shown in Table 3.5 below.

TABLE 15: *Aggregate financial system clustering and regulatory orientation*

Approach to financial stability[a]	*Country*	*Financial system*	*Legal institutions*
'Credit-availability'-oriented relationship finance	*Austria*	Bank-based	Creditor-oriented
	Belgium	Bank-based	Creditor-oriented
	Germany	Bank-based	Creditor-oriented
	Ireland	Bank-based	Shareholder-oriented
	Italy	Bank-based	Creditor-oriented
	Netherlands	Bank-based	Creditor-oriented
'Stability-oriented' relationship finance[c]	*France*	Bank-based	Shareholder-oriented
	Greece[b]	Bank-based	Shareholder-oriented
	Portugal	Bank-based	Shareholder-oriented
	Spain	Bank-based	Shareholder-oriented
'Arm's-length' finance	*United States*	Market-based	Shareholder-oriented
	Finland	Market-based	Shareholder-oriented
'Competitive self-regulatory'-regime	*United Kingdom*	Hybrid	Creditor-and-SH.
	Luxembourg	Hybrid	Creditor-oriented

Source: Author's clustering estimation

a Regulatory orientation is assumed to follow from the role of banks in the economy (financial system configuration) and the respective strength of financial stakeholders.

b Greece is a special case, since its banking system is relatively underdeveloped. Hence, its interpretation is much more limited and this classification should therefore be taken with caution.

c Classification as 'stability-oriented' is based on fact that depositor rights in these countries are very strong relative to private legal rights, as table 14 evidences.

The classification not surprisingly yields the four clusters that already manifested in the hierarchical clustering:

- One cluster of continental European countries conforms to the ***'relationship'-finance*** regime, which complements a bank-reliant financial system with a set of legal institutions that provide creditors with strong rights towards debtors and at the same time insulates banks somewhat from short-term market pressures as it limits shareholder rights. The slight outlier in this context is the Irish financial system, which technically due to its shareholder orientation in corporate governance could also be placed with the other peripheral countries, yet, the deterministic clustering analysis classifies it as a 'relationship'-finance regime. This implies that the similarities in the risk-sharing and asset transformation realm outweigh the dissimilarities in the corporate governance sphere.
- The diametrically opposed cluster is the ***'arm's length'-finance***-regime of market-based countries such as the United States and Finland, which are not as reliant on banks for virtue of deeper capital markets and have more shareholder-oriented institutions as well as stronger deposit insurance.
- Yet a third category is the ***'self-regulatory'***-regime, that juxtaposes strong shareholder rights with strong creditor rights. It seems to be applied mostly in very competitive hybrid systems such as the United Kingdom, where banks have to compete with liquid and well-developed capital markets. Luxembourg is grouped with the United Kingdom due to its very similar financial system, which interestingly shows that strong financial centers, well-known also for the agglomeration of other financial services, seem to rely on a different configuration of financial intermediation and legal institutions altogether, which reflects the belief in 'self-correcting' markets. This is also complemented with a view of deposit insurance as a potential source of moral hazard, which explains the lower rights extended to depositors (thus, also limiting the role for regulators).
- Lastly, the peripheral financial systems and France can be distinguished as bank-based relationship finance systems with a slightly stronger ***'stability-orientation'*** in a fourth cluster. This cluster deviates somewhat from the classical 'relationship' finance cluster in that the configurations of the financial system and the legal institutions at first sight do not conform to the stylized variants of relationship capitalism that have been discussed thus far. However, due to the relative homogeneity of the countries within this cluster and the meaningful heterogeneity to countries from the 'relationship'-finance cluster I keep this variant and will elaborate it further in the following. This is consistent with the finding by Hall and Soskice who in their original VoC-work also found that the Mediterranean countries to be in a more *"ambiguous position"* as they *"show some signs of institutional clustering as well [...] with specific kinds of capacities for non-market coordination in the sphere of corporate finance but more liberal arrangements in the sphere of labor relations"* (P.A. Hall & Soskice, 2001, p.21). These bank-based financial systems with stronger shareholder orientation are most alike as they all have high depositor rights relative to the private interests and, thus, a relatively stronger role for the regulator in ensuring financial stability compared to the other countries entrenched in their legal institutions. Amongst these countries *Greece* stands out as the least developed financial system with a

relatively smaller role for banking than the other Euro Zone countries and a lower development of both, shareholder and creditor, rights. Its relatively strong deposit insurance scheme makes Greece also a more stability-oriented regime on paper, however, due to the described differences in financial depth and development I choose to treat Greece separately as a special case.

3.4.4 Conclusion and evaluation of findings against hypotheses

The empirical analysis is largely consistent with the concepts derived in the earlier part of this chapter and as laid out in *propositions 1 to 5*: The cross-sectional analysis of the financial systems and legal institutions has yielded meaningful groupings, which provide some confidence that financial system configurations indeed shape the role of banks across countries in very different way and are, thus, likely to influence the regulatory choice to a significant degree *(propositions 1 and 2)*. Moreover, the joint analysis of these two dimensions has shown that strong complementarities exist between the way that financial functions are supported by banks and the degree to which financial stakeholders' rights are institutionalized across countries *(propositions 3 to 5)*. Countries can meaningfully be grouped along the financial and legal systems yielding certain regulatory approaches or logics of action. The analysis has also yielded some interesting conclusions with respect to the nature of certain the financial systems of France, Spain, Portugal, and Greece. They exhibit a slight variation from three approaches, as they combine elements of the continental bank-based system with a legal shareholder-orientation but, yet, also show a high stability-orientation through relatively stronger deposit insurance. Thus, their regulatory role is subsumed under the 'stability-oriented' approach but will have to analyzed in a more 'explorative' way in the following, as this configuration has not yet been covered adequately in theory.

3.5 Regulating along a trilemma: Three stylized regimes

Banking regulation in the wider political economy context of the financial system and the economy needs to be seen as classical economic policy-making rather than a pure technocratic exercise in applying internationally agreed regulatory standards. In the following I will discuss two elements of each regime:

Firstly, this section wants to establish not only the way the main regulatory instrument (capital stringency) is applied but also what *complementary economic policy instrument or market constellation* is required for this approach to function. The previous chapter has outlined that banking regulation and supervision in a dynamic context can really only contribute *one instrument*, namely the stringency of regulation (as well in a more limited way though monetary policy), to the pursuit of the identified three most salient regulatory policy objectives. The described stylized regulatory approaches have their origin in particular economic configurations, which hence have left an institutional and regulatory legacy. Secondly, I will discuss how policymakers across countries use different *regulatory approaches* complemented by additional institutions to address the various objectives behind the trilemma.

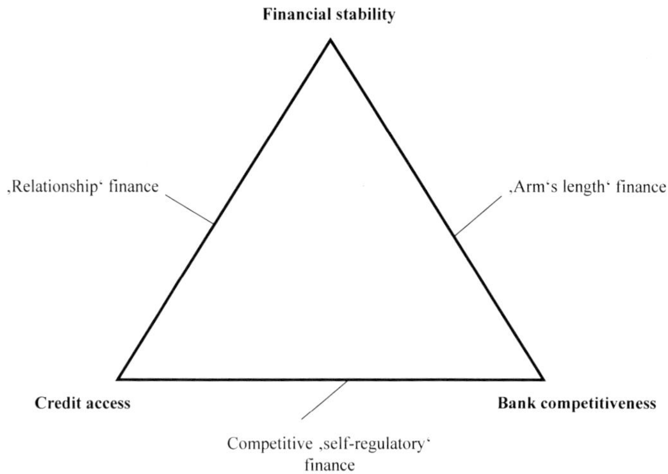

FIGURE 17: *Three regulatory regimes along the trilemma*

Source: Author

The above figure illustrates the distinct regimes along the regulatory trilemma – a stylized and of course somewhat simplified classification.[72] What I argue is that the respective financial system configurations actually represent different 'solutions' or consistent responses to the trilemma, since each financial system configuration produces certain institutions, which reduce the salience of one of the three objectives, which therefore do not have to be addressed by policy as explicitly. In the 'relationship' finance regime the institution of 'patient capital' (including some level of state ownership or cooperatives in banking) has historically reduced the salience of profitability and competitiveness considerations somewhat for policy makers. In the 'competitive self-correcting' regime the equivalent is the strong market discipline that is enabled by the higher reliance on ratings and market-side surveillance as well as an effort to reduce moral hazard-inducing policies such as extensive deposit insurance. As a consequence the regulator can focus on ensuring the efficient and competitive functioning of markets rather than 'micro-managing' banks' risk-management. Thirdly, the 'arm's length'-finance approach relies on stronger capital markets for the availability of credit to the economy and therefore regulation is less bank-dependent in this respect and more focused on the remaining objectives of financial stability and bank competitiveness.

[72] This typology wants to emphasize parsimony over completeness and capture a great deal of the variation in regulatory styles, which to the best of the author's knowledge, to this day has not been reflected in a real categorization, reflecting both intent and likely stringency in the use of instruments by the regulator.

TABLE 16: *Regulatory regimes and their 'resolution' of the trilemma*

Regulatory dimension	*'Relationship'-finance*	*'Competitive self-correcting' finance*	*'Arm's length'-finance*
Financial stability	↑	*Market discipline/ lower moral hazard reduces salience of this objective*	Objectives managed with the instrument of regulatory stringency/ monetary policy
Credit availability	Objectives managed with the instrument of regulatory stringency/ monetary policy ↓	↑	*Capital market presence reduces salience of this objective*
Competitiveness	*'Patient capital' reduces salience of this objective*	Objectives managed with the instrument of regulatory stringency/ monetary policy ↓	Objectives managed with the instrument of regulatory stringency

Source: Author

The trade-offs implicit in the trilemma will require regulatory actors particularly in the face of political and private interest pressures to trade off objectives accommodating certain special interests at the expense of less salient objectives. To create a certain degree of predictability and coherence in this policy, regulators will likely follow certain regulatory approaches or regimes, which are catered to the key institutions of the financial and legal system, as analyzed above, and which exhibit certain non-time-variant features.

3.5.1 The 'arm's length'-finance regime

Defining the complementarities of the regime

Regulatory bodies that prioritize 'competitiveness of banking' and 'financial stability' over ensuring ‚credit access' are likely to do so in the context of an 'arm's length'-finance regime. The focus on competitiveness is thus most consistent with a market-based financial system with a large share of financial services in total value added, making the relative contribution of the financial system large enough to justify a focus on competitiveness due to the relative contribution of the financial sector to total value added. This approach most likely to prevail in the market-based financial system, where *shareholders* are backed by a strong legal institutionalization of their rights and where *creditors* are not favored by any type of regulatory arrangements, since the market and its price signals are assumed to allocate credit efficiently. Next to an emphasis on efficiency, this system also limits the powers of banks through the presence of strong *depositor rights*, which in particular in the United States are indicative of a strong tradition of consumer protection. Consistent with this description, Rajan (2001, p.473) depicts the characteristic features of the 'arm's length' financial system as:

"In an arm's-length system, by contrast, the firm will be able to tap a wider circle of potential lenders because there will be more widespread financial information about it. The loan will be contracted for a specific period, and the interest rate will be a

competitive one that will compensate the lender for time and the risk of that particular loan."

The complementary configurations of this regime that allow the regulators to focus more on other objectives relate to the presence of deep capital markets and/ or the complementary use of monetary policy to facilitate credit access through other means than the leveraging of banks. Again, the United States is the paradigmatic example, where monetary policy is of course still a sovereign instrument of economic policy-making and, importantly, is explicitly also charged with domestic economic output and employment considerations.

Regulatory implications

This regulatory approach works to ensure profitable banks for the relatively strong shareholders and ensures financial stability at the same time through a *relatively high capital buffer*. Stability is realized since banks have to have sufficient 'cushion' to draw on in the event of a credit event or other negative risks materializing. As such, capital levels should be kept relatively high to ensure that the 'arm's length'-finance holds shareholders and managers accountable for their risk-taking policy. The lower concern with credit availability and the presence of capital markets thus can lead the regulator to disregard the detrimental impact that lower leverage levels have in this respect. With respect to *activities regulation*, market-based financial systems and 'arm's length'-finance approaches have historically tended to restrict banks more strictly from engaging in overly risky activities such as securities activities to promote financial stability and in order to level the playing field and prevent universal banks, equipped with access to cheap and government-secured deposit financing, from competing with real estate, securities, and insurance companies (Mishkin, 2001). This has for instance been evidenced in the United States' Glass-Steagall Act of 1933, which separated commercial and investment banking, and which was only repealed through the Gramm-Leach-Bliley Financial Services Modernization Act in 1999 to increase competition in these other sectors.

3.5.2 The 'competitive self-correcting'-finance regime

Defining the complementarities of the regime

In the self-regulatory type of regime the regulator focuses on both, a competitive banking system as well as a growing credit-fueled economy, thereby implicitly giving least explicit attention to financial stability objective. Certain institutional and actor configurations allow the regulator to play more of a market-facilitating role, which essentially plays to the self-correcting features of markets. Of the countries analyzed here, the UK and its regulatory body the FSA best reflects this type of a 'self-regulatory' regime: In terms of regulatory style, informal and frequent contact to market participants, market-friendly and principles-based regulation, as well as a focus on triggering the efficiency of its banks are some of the cornerstones of the FSA's approach (Frach, 2007). This regulatory philosophy of course since the failure of Northern Rock in 2007 has clearly come under strong scrutiny, receiving criticism from the current head of the FSA, Adar Turner, who called the pre-Northern Rock style of regulation "a competent execution of a style of regulation, and a philosophy of regulation which was, in retrospect, mistaken". The most important expression of the less explicit focus of this regulatory style on financial stability is of course the intellectual capture behind the 'self-regulatory' philosophy which former FSA Chairman Howard Davies puts into words as follows (Davies, 2010a, p.2):

"While I would strongly argue that the FSA in my day did not favor firms unduly, it is perhaps true that we – and in this we were exactly like US regulators – were inclined to believe that markets were generally efficient. If willing buyers and willing sellers were trading claims happily, then, as long as they were "professional" investors, there was no legitimate reason to interfere in their markets. These people were "consenting adults in private," and the state should avert its gaze. We now know that some of these market emperors had no clothes, and that their activities, far from benign, could result in severe financial instability and generate serious losses for taxpayers, not to mention precipitating a global recession. That has been a grave lesson for regulators and central banks."

However, despite the obviated shortcomings and apparent neglect of financial stability in this approach, it is important to analyze the logic of this regime's complementarities, as it has been very influential and prevalent across countries in the last ten or fifteen years. The Turner Review, which the Chancellor of the Exchequer asked the new FSA's Chairman (and successor to Callum McCarthy) to conduct lists the philosophy of this regulatory approach as follows (House of Commons Treasury Committee, 2009; p.13):

"The FSA explicitly stated, according to Lord Turner, that it was not the function of the regulator to cast questions over the overall business strategy of firms. Lord Turner himself, upon arrival at the FSA, found this approach "surprising". He attributed this approach to a global philosophy of regulation, which "was based upon too extreme a form of confidence in markets and confidence in the ideas that markets were self-correcting."

However, I argue that indeed such a regulatory regime and philosophy did not develop by chance but instead was conditioned by the complementary financial system and the way that financial interests were entrenched in the described legal institutions. As such, the belief in functioning of self-correcting markets was supported by a strong role for shareholders in making reasonable business decisions, which were not to be second-guessed by regulators, who again were supposed to act with more judgment and moderation. In fact, the term "light touch" regulation usually associated with this regime originated with *political* actors interested in making the City of London more competitive and was thus an interpretation of the regulatory 'self-regulatory' or 'principles-based' approach to regulation.[73] This view of the regulatory regime is supported by the assessment of the House of Commons Treasury Committee's assessment, which also contextualizes the "faulty regulatory philosophy of bank supervision" as "part of a wider political philosophy" and deems this interpretation as "to us plausible". An important element of this regulatory regime is the belief that strong explicit deposit insurance and concomitant regulatory intervention is likely to insert 'moral hazard' into the actions of private actors. As banks in the hybrid financial

---

[73] Interview with a former senior regulator of the FSA and a banker from the City.

systems such as the United Kingdom or Luxembourg act in the presence of strong financial markets and due to laxer activities regulation (see below) are allowed to trade in these markets, they engage in more risky activities. Stronger deposit insurance when extended to risk-taking financial institutions of course creates the well-known phenomenon of moral hazard, which then again can result in financial instability. Again, with hindsight this regulatory philosophy was of course proven to be misled in the presence of too-big-too-fail financial institutions, which regardless of the level of explicit deposit insurance could rely on implicit government guarantees and bailouts. However, the concern with moral hazard shows clearly in the below statement by Mervin Allister King, governor of the Bank of England (House of Commons Treasury Committee, 2009, p.95):

"Deposit insurance from central bank liquidity facilities are properly confined to deposit-taking institutions. In my view, it is unwarranted that those same institutions, funded in substantial part by taxpayer protected deposits, be engaged in substantial risk-prone propriety trading and speculative activities that may also raise questions of virtually unmanageable conflicts of interest."

Thus, the self-regulatory approach, relies on the ability to wind down financial institutions, which have taken on excessive risks and therefore have encountered liquidity or solvency problems. Hence, limitations to moral hazard, which can result from either the presence of banks that are 'too big too fail' or from a lack of activities regulation, are an essential feature that complement a more 'hands-off' approach to regulation.

Regulatory implications

The regulatory implications for the competitive 'self-regulatory' approach can be defined based on the prior discussion: With respect to bank capital regulation this regime shows its focus on ensuring credit availability and competitiveness through lower levels of capital held. Competitive efficient markets and incentive-compatible limitations on deposit insurance are supposed to ensure that financial stability is not dismissed entirely. Still, the self-regulatory regime constitutes a much more aggressive and competitive approach to capital adequacy regulation, which sees smaller 'capital buffers' and rather emphasizes the role of the supervisor and market forces in ensuring financial stability. With respect to activities and conglomerate regulation I argue this approach is complemented by much more stringent regulation than the 'relationship' regime. The latter relies on large universal banks and thus lower levels of activities restrictions for intertemporal risk-sharing and diversification benefits. The 'self-regulatory' regime on the other hand is reliant on low levels of 'moral hazard', which implies that it should prevent banks from engaging in what can be considered overly risky activities for deposit-holding and (partially) insured financial institutions. Thus, the 'self-regulatory' approach is very compatible with and sympathetic to a higher level of activities regulation as well as a limit on the 'too-big-too-fail'-problem, which stricter financial conglomerate regulation should help avoid.

3.5.3 The 'relationship'-finance regime

Defining the complementarities of the regime

The choice for the stability of the financial system and for the continued access of the economy to stable sources of credit implies a choice against banking competitiveness as a key driver of regulatory policy. Thus, the natural focus of the regulator becomes the soundness of the financial institution and its interfaces with the real economy. This largely prudential regime focuses on the stability of the financial institution, but it also utilizes the discussed regulatory tools to ensure that the banking system serves the needs of the wider economy . In doing so it therefore can serve the political interests of a particular constituency to whom credit is provided. To the extent that this regime relies on banks extending a continually high volume of loans due to long-term relationship considerations rather than short-term profitability considerations, it needs to take place in the context of lower levels of competitive intensity and/ or limited *shareholder rights* and strong *creditor rights*. Hence, it mostly reflects the environment, which has been characterized as 'relationship-finance' by the comparative financial systems literature (Allen & Gale, 2001). As Rajan (2001, p.473) puts it very aptly in his description of the nature of the business judgment relating to credit extension under this system:

"In a relationship-based system, a bank will have close ties with a potential borrowing firm, perhaps because of frequent past contacts or because of ownership links. In assessing the borrowing needs of the firm and its ability to pay interest and principal, the bank will consider not only the firm's current debt-servicing capability, but also its long-term ability to repay and the various non-contractual levers the bank can push to extract repayments. (...) Limitations on competition in a relationship-based system do not just give the financier power, but also strengthen his incentive to cooperate with the borrower."

The need for credit access and leverage for growth stabilization usually is assumed to come from a particularly bank-reliant real economy, which usually comprises a larger number of small- and medium-sized firms (SMEs). Whilst 'relationship-finance' can take place also in the market-based system (e.g., through venture capital), the financial system that is most complementary to this regime is the 'bank-based' system, where banks also service customers with a long-term perspective based on insider information and supported by strong creditor rights. And whilst the outcome, higher leverage than one would prudentially allow under a stability-oriented regime, might be similar to the 'arm's length'-finance regime, the motif for this policy as well as the distributional effects are very different.

The factors enabling and complementing the effectiveness of this regime relate to the *intensity of competition* and the *openness of the economy*. Since the regulator can not necessarily ensure that banks can indeed stay competitive and stable through higher margins, this regime is somewhat limited in the face of a severe competitive pressures. In order to facilitate this focus of banks on their otherwise less lucrative lending activities, this strategy could give more consideration to the profitability and competitiveness of banks in a number of ways such as restricting competition between different types of financial intermediaries or by boosting their international competitiveness through tougher regulation on foreign banks. Restricting competition can take place by for instance tolerating higher profit margins on specialized areas of business (deriving e.g. from oligopolistic positioning or factor specificity), which then can either be paid out as dividends or can create a profit buffer through retained earnings for bad times that can smoothen out the inherent volatility of banking business.[74] In the face of intense cross-border competition, such as a small economy might face it with EMU and financial integration, this regime is likely to become unfeasible or at least unsustainable in the medium term.

A second but today less often applied complementary institution is of course government-ownership of banks or even cooperative banking systems. These particular variants of banking still conform to the above described 'patient capital' logic of lending in high volumes at relatively low risk and return. Because of the inherent patience of shareholders of these banks (taxpayers and members of the cooperative), their management can engage in more long-term relationship-based lending activities that next to a more modest profitability objective have a strong lending and stability focus and are designed to allow certain constituents to have enhanced credit access. Thus, by their very nature these business models are complementary to a relationship-finance regime and also still find application in the paradigmatic case of the German financial system.

3.5.4 Two varieties of relationship finance and regulatory orientation in the Euro Zone

Before discussing what these complementarities of the 'relationship finance' approach mean for the regulatory approach, I would like to briefly elaborate two specific varieties of the relationship finance approach, which I suggest add more explanatory power to the specific context of the Euro Zone. The trilemma suggests that there can be three different institutional configurations that countries can choose from in trying to accommodate two of the three regulatory objectives. These are the three clusters that the empirical analysis has yielded, which were discussed above. However, in addition to that the empirical clustering analysis has also shown that breaking down the relationship finance cluster further into two variants creates two meaningful types of relationship finance, which have slightly differential emphasis on regulatory objectives and also differ slightly in their institutional configuration.

In the following I discuss the regulatory implications of two variants of the 'relationship' finance approach separately. Within the relationship-finance approach certain bank-based Southern European countries (France, Spain, and Portugal)[75] can meaningfully be distinguished from some Northern European countries, as the two groups exhibit certain differences, particularly in their legal institutions, which reflect different preferences. The more Southern European countries share a similar history as having had a more stability-oriented regulatory approach and, thus, exhibit less

[74] This latter strategy of using profits as a stability buffer in essence reflects elements of the regulatory approach described by Hellmann, Murdock, and Stiglitz (1997), who advocate a policy of financial restraint for low-depth financial systems at the expense of competition and efficiency in the financial sector to reduce moral hazard and create micro-prudential stability.

[75] Greece would count in as well but is excluded due to the relative under-development of its banking system.

captured regulatory configurations with relatively strong depositor and relatively weaker creditor rights, which provide for a stronger role of the regulator vis-à-vis the banking system. Therefore I will treat these countries as manifestations of the more 'stability-oriented' and interventionist regulatory regimes that however also have elements of the relationship-orientation of traditional bank-based systems. This is helpful to add a bit more granularity in terms of distinguishing different approaches within the Euro Zone, rather than grouping almost all bank-based financial systems in a single cluster.

The 'credit-availability-oriented' variant of relationship finance

Germany, Italy, the Netherlands, Belgium, Ireland, and Austria are bank-based systems with a strong traditional relationship orientation. In these countries the main private interest that finds its way into regulation is the strong credit-reliance of the real economy, which traditionally has been less capital-market-oriented, despite the falling and rising tide of capital market-based financing for small and medium-sized companies through the 'new markets'.[76] Regulation in such historically more *bank-based continent* has been less restrictive regarding the *activities of banks*, allowing banks to engage in securities, insurance, and real estate activities in addition to their core function of retail or commercial banking. This has brought about the dominant *universal banking model* coupled with a strong element of relationship banking towards banks' corporate clients. This regulatory regime also has a financial stability component, which rests on the idea that financial stability can be ensured through the diversification of income streams to allow for inter-temporal return smoothing and the sheer size of the resulting financial conglomerates. Since banks are mainly supposed to engage in lending for higher credit availability, *capital levels* will be lower to facilitate such additional credit. In order to ensure that this does not lead to a competitive race to the bottom, in which universal banks take on too much risk, one also has historically seen lower levels of competition or even (in the case of Germany for instance) high levels of government ownership as a logical complementary regulatory configuration.

The 'stability-oriented' variant of relationship finance

While the bank-based European financial systems of France, Spain, and Portugal share this basic relationship finance orientation, they have a somewhat different variation of this regime, which I argue mainly shows in a slightly more interventionist and stability-oriented form of regulation. Such a 'stability-oriented' approach rests on a somewhat different institutional configuration of relationship finance than in the other European, Northern European bank-based economies with stronger roles afforded to both shareholders as well as regulators. The strength of these two stakeholder groups counters the otherwise inherent dominance of banks in bank-based financial systems. The three financial systems empirically grouped under this regime here are characterized by strong deposit insurance schemes as well as medium to strong levels of shareholder rights, which is contrary to the complementarities that most scholars of political economy have theorized for bank-based systems. This configuration in all three financial systems is the outcome of conscious financial system transformation

---

[76] For a discussion of the rise of the new markets in these economies see Posner (2009).

programmes in the 1980s and 1990s, which intended to make these financial systems more competitive and shareholder-oriented, as has been well documented by the comparative political economy literature. Whilst these reforms have been generally labeled as 'pro-market'-reforms, the more liberalized financial sector still has a legacy of the previous more 'stability-oriented' approach towards finance through the presence of stronger deposit insurance rights, as the data shows. Historically the countries in this cluster have pursued policies that included strong interventions in the management of banks and credit to advance domestic growth considerations through active if however selective 'credit regulation policies'. Perez (1998) shows that in contrast to Italy or Germany, Spain and France pursued policies that allowed them to based their post-war growth to a certain extent on cheap credit (versus export-led growth) that then led to a preference for higher inflation monetary policy in contrast to the price-stability-oriented monetary policy of Germany. With the disinflationary focus of central banks that took hold in both countries with progressing capital mobility, problems emanated from this loose monetary and interventionist regulatory stance, as it created highly leveraged economies, which were unwilling to go along with austerity stance of governments. Thus, this explicit 'credit regulation policy' retreated and opened the path for financial sector liberalization, the results of which are visible in the data analyzed here. In the French case this was also accompanied by the creation of new sources of credit access for firms through the strengthening of capital markets and the concomitant shareholder rights. Spain saw a more gradual reform due to oligopolistic banks, which prevented a similar competition from capital markets.

In the case of Spain and Portugal the presence of state-owned banks and savings banks further document the continued role of the state in financial relations to affect domestic growth outcomes. While creditors are relatively important due to the continued bank-reliance of the financial systems (despite the rise of financial markets over the last years), their powers are limited by shareholders with strong say and regulators with a more 'hands-on'-view of regulation. As evidence that these countries indeed did regulate more stringently above and beyond what the Basel standards required of them, Pinho (2009) shows how in France, Spain, and Portugal the loan loss provisions for banks are set by regulators rather than by banks themselves (as in Germany for instance). Also, regulators in these countries have shown to have been more conservative than regulators in the United States or the United Kingdom with respect to the dynamic treatment of provisioning regulation, which led both Spain and Portugal to adopt 'dynamic provisioning schemes' to prevent the emergence of excessive lending. Thus, these instances indicate that despite their relative bank-reliance these countries limit bank power somewhat through shareholder rights and a more 'stability-oriented' stance towards regulation.

When it comes to the use of regulatory instruments, not surprisingly, I argue that the 'stability-oriented' regime is characterized by a more stringent use of *capital adequacy* regulation and supervision. This simply relates to the increased stability focus of the regulator and the lower powers of banks in this regime for. Thus, we can expect a somewhat higher restrictiveness towards the activities of banks, since regulators are likely to take a less sympathetic view towards the engagement of banks in excessively risky activities.

3.5.5 Conclusion

In summary, I argue that regulators across countries will hold different preferences as they pursue their main objectives using their regulatory and supervisory discretion. These preferences are likely to be institutionalized in relatively stable and non-time-variant regulatory regimes, of which I introduce three types along the trilemma as well as a special fourth kind that really is a variant of the 'relationship'-finance regime. Not only the existing institutions condition the regulatory choice and preferences but also i) other complementary configurations required to make the stylized regulatory regimes work in practice and ii) the regulatory stringency with respect to capital adequacy. The below table summarizes these relationships for all of the regimes: Each regulatory regime is a set of coherent policies and institutions that suit the path-dependent institutional legacies of the financial system, that is the degree of bank- vs. capital market-reliance as well as the legal rights of the key financial stakeholders.

TABLE 17: *Regulatory regimes and complementary institutional configurations*

	'Relationship'-finance		*'Competitive self-correcting' finance*	*'Arm's length'-finance*
Regulatory dimension	*'Credit-availability'-oriented*	*'Stability-oriented'*		
Financial stability	Low activity and conglomerate restrictions for diversification and inter-temporal risk-sharing	Some activity and conglomerate restrictions *High stringency on capital adequacy*	Low deposit insurance coverage and high conglomerate restrictions to reduce risks of moral hazard High market-side surveillance	High activity and conglomerate restrictions *High stringency on capital adequacy* High market-side surveillance
Credit availability	*Low stringency on capital adequacy*	Some capital markets/ liquidity separate from banks Monetary policy	Co-existent and intertwined banks and capital markets (lower activities restrictions)	Deep capital markets/ liquidity separate from banks Monetary policy
Competitiveness	'Patient capital' and state-owned/ cooperative banks	'Patient capital' and state-owned/ cooperative banks	↑ *Low stringency on capital adequacy* ↓	Limitations on foreign competition (above and beyond high activity and conglomerate restrictions)

Source: Author

As such, the stringency of capital adequacy regulation can differ in different regimes, since, firstly, countries place a different emphasis on the different objectives that regulation can attain, and, secondly, since different complementary regulatory institutions can be in place that condition the optimal choice of capital adequacy to attain these objectives. As such, capital adequacy levels in bank-based and 'relationship'-finance regimes are lower mainly for reasons of credit availability, while in competitive 'self-regulatory' regimes the same adequacy levels reflect the pre-occupation with competitiveness considerations. In 'stability-oriented' and 'arm's length' regimes capital adequacy is generally handled more strictly since credit availability can be ensured through (varying levels of) capital markets and/or the use of monetary policy.

Before turning to the forces of change, which have challenged these complementary configurations throughout the 2000s in particular, I will however review the empirical evidence to check for the relevance of these stylized models and predictions.

3.6 Regulatory stringency outcomes

This section applies the developed typologies of regulatory regimes to explain variations in regulatory stringency outcomes across financial systems and to examine the extent to which the assumed complementary configurations were prevalent across financial systems in the Euro Zone, the United Kingdom, and the United States. I corroborate empirically the argument made earlier that it is "financial systems, not organizational design", which matters in shaping regulatory preferences and outcomes:

- To that extent I, firstly, show that the *financial system's institutions*, i.e. the typology developed in this chapter, add significant explanatory value with respect to the observed high variation in capital stringency and regulatory stringency outcomes along the dimensions analyzed.
- Secondly, this section concludes with an outlook on the institutional fitness of the different regulatory regimes in a dynamic context when faced with exogenous shocks. I conclude that almost all Euro Zone countries have been missing important regulatory institutional configurations to cope with these shocks adequately.

3.6.1 Regulation and supervision across regimes

To measure regulation outcomes I discuss the variation in the central instrument of *capital adequacy/ supervision* (measured by actual equity in relation to assets) around the year 2000, which is more flexible and dynamic because of the higher degree of discretion which supervision can apply within the confines of a given body of regulation. I also look at the key *regulatory* institutions such as *capital definition as well as activities restrictions and conglomerate restrictiveness*, which are less flexible regulatory institutions and therefore less easy to change over time. They therefore differ somewhat from the more flexible instruments, which I have discussed earlier, but should therefore also reflect the complementary configurations that were hypothesized.[77]

The *degree of conglomerate and activities restrictiveness* are based on indices as developed by Barth, Caprio, and Levine (2006). The activities restrictiveness index measures the extent to which banks are allowed to engage in insurance, real estate, and securities activities while the conglomerate restrictiveness index reflects the extent to which insurance companies, banks and non-financial firms can engage in investments and controlling stakes with each other to create financial conglomerates.

Capital stringency measures the varying definitions of what banks could make count towards regulatory capital, which under Basel was allowed to differ across countries.

Lastly, *banking supervision* is measured by taking the average level of capital adequacy using Tier 1 equity relative to total assets in the year 2000 based on OECD bank profitability data. This measure therefore differs from regulatory definitions of capital adequacy, since these already include the risk weighting negotiated into Basel regulations, which were intended to undo some of the financial system differences in regulatory treatment, and thus give a relatively skewed impression of the actual capitalization of an entire banking system.

Table 18 shows the relevant regulatory data, which I will now discuss by regime (for more extensive data see addendum XXIII in the Appendix). I find that the paradigmatic cases of each regulatory regime seem to fit the institutional configurations that have been described previously while some significant deviations are instructive, as they allow to derive likely paths of institutional change and adaptation.

'Credit-availability-oriented' relationship-finance countries

Looking at the paradigmatic 'relationship'-finance country of Germany we can see the predicted very de-regulated pattern of activities regulation. This is in line with the universal banking model that relies on very few restrictions on bank activities. Also other continental bank-based and 'relationship'-finance financial systems such as Austria and the Netherlands have a similar reliance on the universal bank model and similarly exhibit only few restrictions on insurance activities. A very similar pattern is visible when we look at the dimension of financial conglomerate regulation, which is highly correlated with the degree to which activities are regulated, since both dimensions relate to the extent to which large banks and bankassurance companies can engage in finance across various product categories to form large financial conglomerates. However, there are some important deviations from the pattern in individual countries, which include Belgium, Ireland, and - in one dimension - Italy which in 2000 were more strictly regulated in activities and conglomerates regulation (in the case of Italy only with respect to the latter dimension). Following the logic of

[77] Particularly since I look at their status in the year 1999/2000, which precedes the implementation of important institution-converging European-level legislation such as the FSAP, the Conglomerates Directive, and the Capital Requirements Directive.

the trilemma this would impose higher competitiveness costs on the regulator to the extent that in particular these relatively smaller financial systems of Belgium and Ireland have been exposed to stronger financial integration in the early 2000s and, thus, had to compete with other countries that afford their banks more access to profitable other activities.

Turning to the dimension of capital regulation and banking supervision, we can see that four of the countries including the paradigmatic case of Germany have relatively laxer standards of how capital is defined and on a scale of 1-10 define capital with values between 5 and 6 also hold relatively lower levels of capital, which measured in simple equity-terms are far below the Basel level of 8%. This is expected, since a too stringent definition of capital and enforcement of capital requirements would likely receive strong scrutiny and lobbying from private interests, which would point to the de-leveraging effect of higher capital requirements. Whilst there are two deviations from this pattern with Austria and Belgium, we can see that these cases do not differ that much, when we look at their actual capitalization levels as measured by the supervision-variable. Both Austria and Belgium hold only 4.7% and 3.8% of equity capital against their assets, which shows that they similarly as bank-based financial systems rely on the enhanced intertemporal risk management and diversification benefits of large banks to ensure financial stability. However, again the significant deviation from the pattern of comparable financial systems suggests that a change in regulatory institutions for competitiveness considerations is a likely consequence for these two countries.

'Stability-oriented' relationship finance countries

Spain as the most paradigmatic country of the 'stability-oriented' cluster has medium to strong activities and financial conglomerates restrictions, which are somewhat higher than the other more de-regulated bank-based systems of the 'relationship'-finance cluster but still lower than the United States' regulations. In terms of capital adequacy and capital stringency Spain clearly differs from the other Euro Zone countries, since it has both, a more stringent definition of capital, that includes no other forms of assets to be added to capital other than cash and government securities, as well as a higher equity ratio that at 8.3 is around twice as high as those of the other Euro Zone economies. The same applies to the Portugal, which has somewhat tighter regulated but still in the medium end of the spectrum in terms of activities and conglomerate regulation but also has much lower levels of leverage and more stringent definitions of capital than the 'relationship'-finance systems.

France's regulatory configurations differ more strongly from Spain's and reflect more so the 'self-regulatory' regime with lower activities and medium conglomerates regulation as well as lower levels of capital held by banks at only 4.6% and a less stringent definition of capital that allows assets other than cash and government bonds to be counted as capital. This very deviant pattern is in line with the more recent varieties-of-capitalism literature on institutional change, which has observed that France has been slowly unwinding its coordinated capitalism and has been moving swiftly towards a more liberal market economy (Culpepper, 2011).[78] In fact from a financial regulation perspective it is interesting to note that on the regulatory dimensions analyzed here, France is nearly identical with the United Kingdom. Yet, due to the still existing and systematic differences in bank-reliance, financial sector reliance, and also regulatory philosophy we would expect certain more systematic differences to materialize over time, which would justify keeping them in distinct categories. Still, the transformation of the French financial system becomes visible when looking at banking regulatory configurations as well.

'Self-regulatory'-finance countries

The United Kingdom similarly along with Luxembourg as examples of 'self regulatory' regimes impose similarly few restrictions on the regulation of banks. Along with the lower regulated countries of the 'relationship'-finance regime in 2000 these countries had the least regulated regime with respect to the activities that banks were allowed to engage in, restricting only the engagement of banks in certain insurance activities. With respect to financial conglomerate restrictiveness there is a somewhat higher degree of restrictiveness that reflects the described stance towards financial conglomerates as potential sources of moral hazard that can undermine the 'self-correcting' nature of market participants.

In terms of capital stringency both countries are in the medium to lower end of the stringency spectrum. In the case of the United Kingdom this lower stringency derives from a more lenient initial capital definition that allow certain forms other than cash and government securities to be counted as capital as well as a more lenient application of Basel I with respect to revaluation gains, 100% of which were allowed as part of capital. In the case of Luxembourg similarly more diverse sources of capital were permitted whilst also risk weights were not designed to vary with market and credit risks at the time, thus, resulting in a lower score on stringency.

'Arm's length'-finance countries

On the other extreme lie the United States with very high activities restrictions, particularly in real estate, and a similarly stringent treatment of financial conglomerates. The United States again most clearly differs from the European regulatory setup and also from the other more market-oriented financial system of Finland. Its activities regulation in particular derived from the legacy of the Glass-Steagall Act of 1933, which separated commercial and investment banking, and which leads the U.S. to score much highest on the activities restrictions dimension. Of course it was exactly around the time analyzed here that institutional change was taking place as well in the United States, leading amongst other things to the already discussed Gramm-Leach-Bliley Financial Services Modernization Act, which would lift many of the restrictions still in place here. Still, the data for 1999 shows that the United States conforms to the assumed 'arm's length' configuration that due to the presence of deep capital markets can regulate bank activities.

---

[78] The transformation of the French economy from a 'financial network economy' to a 'financial market economy' was already discussed in the literature of the early 2000s and has since been debated. See Morin (2009) for an overview.

With respect to capital stringency the U.S. finds itself at a slightly above average level of stringency, which derives from not acknowledging assets other than cash and government securities as capital, distinguishing it from the more laxly regulated countries. However, the U.S. did allow banks to use borrowed funds as capital, which of course increases the potential linkages that can result (and did materialize) in a systemic crisis, when these borrowed funds have to be withdrawn. Capital adequacy levels in the United States were still at 9.1%, which far exceeds the average capitalization of the continental European banks, and conforms to our earlier assertion that the 'arm's length' regime is less inclined to let banks leverage up since it is less reliant on it as the sole credit channel. Finland shares at least these attributes and with a capitalization level of 10.8% also has a less leveraged banking system than the other more bank-based financial systems in the Euro Zone. In terms of activities and conglomerates regulation though, Finland resembles the universal banking model with lower activities restrictions and lower restrictiveness towards financial conglomeration. Thus, while Finland within the European varieties of financial systems comes closest to the United States as a market-based system and in bank leverage reflects the 'arm's length'-regime, it still shares certain features of the universal banking tradition with the European financial systems.

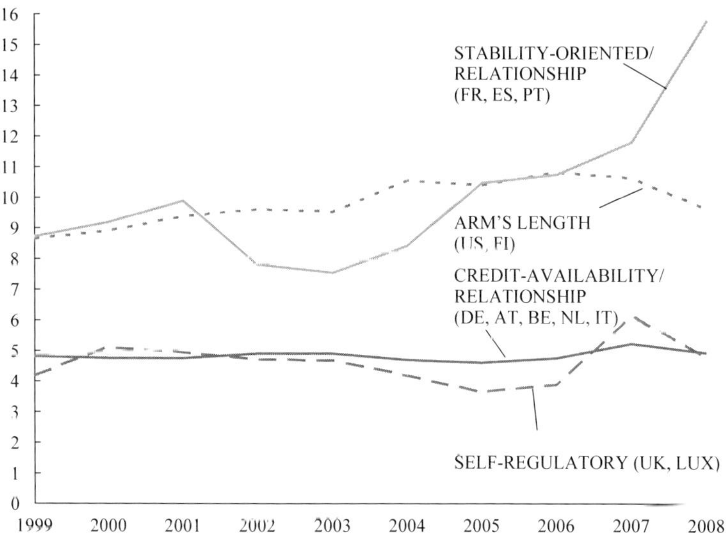

FIGURE 18: *Capital adequacy over time by regulatory regime cluster (weighted average of equity, taken as capital and reserves to total assets)*

Source: Author based on OECD bank profitability data

TABLE 18: *Regulatory institutions for the Euro Zone, the United Kingdom, and the United States in 2000*

Financial system	*Country*	*Activities restrictions*	*Financial conglom. restrictions*	*Capital stringency*	*Supervisory stringency/ CAR levels*[a]
	Austria	4	5	10	4.7%
	Belgium	7	8	9	3.8%
	Germany	3	4	6	4.1%
	Ireland	6	7	6	6.6%
'Relationship' -finance-regime	*Italy*	7	5	6	6.8%
	Netherlands	4	4	5	3.8%
	Weighted cluster average[b]	*4.7*	*4.7*	*6.3*	*5.0%*
'Competitive self-regulatory'-regime	*United Kingdom*	4	7	7	5.1%
	Luxembourg	4	6	7	3.6%
	Weighted cluster average[b]	*4.0*	*6.8*	*7.0*	*4.8%*
'Arm's-length' finance	*United States*	9	9	7	9.1%
	Finland	5	4	5	10.8%
	Weighted cluster average[b]	*8.9*	*8.9*	*7.5*	*9.1%*
	France	4	7	7	4.6%
'Interven-tionist' regime	*Greece*	7	6	4	N/A
	Portugal	6	8	5	11.8%
	Spain	6	5	9	8.3%
	Weighted cluster average[b]	*4.9*	*6.4*	*7.0*	*6.7%*
	Total weighted average[b]	*5.9*	*6.6*	*6.8*	*6.3%*

Source: Author based on data from regulation indexes by Barth, Caprio, and Levine (2006) and capital and reserves data from the OECD (2011) "Bank Profitability" survey

a Capital adequacy here measured as real equity (Tier 1 capital; no regulatory definition) as a share of total assets in 2000

b Countries weighted by the relative share of banking assets in relation to cluster or total of countries, respectively.

3.6.2 Conclusion

Different financial systems with varying degree of bank and market reliance as well as variations in financial stakeholder rights reflect different preferences for financial stability. These preferences find expression in the respective strength of certain financial stakeholder groups, as institutionalized in shareholder, creditor, and depositor rights, and shape the way the financial systems try to regulate along the trilemma.

As this chapter has shown, one can indeed meaningfully group the Euro Zone countries as well as the United Kingdom and the United States based on their financial systems along the three distinct approaches suggested by the trilemma as well as a fourth variant to distinguish certain bank-based financial systems with different legal institutional origin from each other. The financial systems and concomitant regulatory approaches of Germany (bank-based and ''relationship'-finance' approach), the United Kingdom (hybrid system and 'competitive self-correcting' approach), and the United States (market-based system with 'arm's length'-finance regime) and Spain (bank-based system with 'stability-oriented' regime) provide guidance as paradigmatic cases, around which one can group the other financial systems and regulatory approaches. In line with neo-institutionalist economics and political economy predictions, this regulatory approach produces certain institutional comparative advantages, since it inclines the regulator to cater her regulatory approach to the financial system and stakeholder groups: Regulators will try and identify complementary regulatory instruments and adapt their stringency of use of these instruments to attain their somewhat conflicting objectives in the most efficient (least costly) way.

This chapter has also established an empirical link between the nature of the regulatory approach, the financial system, and the restrictiveness towards and particularly the degree of leverage of banks. Different preferences materialize in varying regulatory outcomes regarding capital levels, capital regulation and (somewhat less clearly though) in financial conglomerate as well as bank activities restrictiveness. This is particularly reflected in the paradigmatic cases of Germany, the United Kingdom, Spain, and the United States but also in some of the other countries' groupings. In fact, a look at leverage over time (see Figure 17), measuring the average level of equity held against assets, shows that this cross-sectional differences for the cluster averages remains relatively stable over time. Whilst there is some change in capitalization within these clusters and across time, the average level of these distinct financial systems differs significantly and persistently all the way into the financial crisis and also beyond. This is in line with the predictions of the trilemma and the theoretical linkage between system structure and optimal policy-making from a political economy perspective developed earlier in this chapter.

Thus, whilst it could be shown that significant cross-country deviations in capitalization exist and persist due to structural differences there is of course further room for empirical analysis: More granular time series data on a bank-level could allow researchers to further elaborate this link. This picture also reflects the aggregate picture of the early 2000s, looking at the financial systems of the time at a time, when financial integration was on the rise but yet not as progressed as ten years later. It will be interesting to monitor the potential convergence of financial systems closely, in particular the way that particularly big institutions across all financial systems have become much more interbank-market reliant and somewhat more diversified in their asset management activities. This could converge banking and financial system structure further.

Against this background of financial integration, the relevant question to be answered in the next chapter will be to see if and how the interaction of financial regulators has affected these patterns of regulatory decision-making, regulatory institutions, and institutional comparative advantage that we could still identify here for the early 2000s.

4

International cooperation or race to the bottom? Banking regulation in an integrating financial market

"Operations can be moved globally and capital can be accessed globally. It's not arbitrage to thwart [regulation], it's about a need to compete with rivals."

Lloyd Blankfein, CEO of Goldman Sachs, Financial Times, September 29th 2010.

"The United Kingdom's experiment in a strategy of 'light touch' regulations to attract business to London from New York and Frankfurt ended tragically. (...) We want to avoid another race to the bottom around the world."

Timothy Geithner, U.S. Secretary of the Treasury, New York Times, June 6th 2011

The prior discussion has advanced the argument that banking regulators have to make economic policy trade-offs based on their regulatory preferences, which derive form the nature of the financial system. As was shown, national banking regulators do not operate in a vacuum, but instead are faced with the interaction of domestic private interest influences that in many cases conflict with the original financial stability mandate assigned to them. Similar things can be said for the role of the national regulator in its international context. Hence, this chapter builds on the established theoretical framework and expands the horizon to look at the interaction of national regulators with each other in an international context, where banks compete for capital and investment in increasingly open economies based on their relative competitiveness. The quote by Goldman Sachs banker Blankfein underlines how this strive for competitiveness will inevitably drive banks to engage in regulatory arbitrage to maximize the degree of permitted leverage to compete with rivals. As such, regulators can either commit to leveling the playing field through strict implementation of international standards such as Basel, or they can engage in a competitive race for laxity, as was the case for some areas of regulation in the time period leading up to the financial crisis of 2007/8, as the quote of the U.S. Secretary of the Treasury Geithner indicates.

The key driver shaping the outcome of international regulatory interaction again is the institutional setup and the resulting incentives for policymakers. As such, this chapter opens up the theoretical model for the interaction among regulators with different regulatory preferences and makes predictions about the likely trajectory of international regulation given these interactions. The conclusions are the following:

- Firstly, I derive theoretically that *differences in regulatory preferences and, thus, regulatory outcomes* between countries (as existent in the Euro Zone) negatively affect the likelihood of international cooperation the *more the two financial systems are integrated with each other.* Thus, from a theoretical perspective international cooperation in an integrated financial market with, however, strong variations in financial systems and regulatory preferences creates strong political economy demands for regulatory institutional change towards national regulatory policy.

- Secondly, I find that *financial integration* after EMU has proceeded at different speeds, creating more cross-border traffic in the case of banking but failing to create truly pan-European banks and instead leaving banking more domestic than European. This integration coupled with the *national variation in implementation of international and European-level regulatory standards* at the same time has laid the foundations for an 'unlevel playing field', causing national regulators to react to each other's regulatory stringency.
- Thirdly, I show that the *resulting shocks to national competitiveness* have led to institutional change. In the crucial area of capital adequacy definitions in affected countries I find on average a reduction in stringency of capital definitions over time, which is more consistent with the 'race to the bottom'- than the 'race to the top'-hypothesis. Also other regulatory institutional change seems to be consistent with this 'competitiveness'-argument.

4.1. Modeling international regulatory interaction

This section derives very specific propositions about how the interaction of varying regulatory preferences on the international level, facilitated by the *ongoing integration of financial and banking markets*, shape regulatory outcomes on the international level, which then are executed through supervision at the domestic level (the subject of the next chapter). Hence, whilst this chapter departs more from the perspective that the path-dependent structure of the domestic financial system shapes international regulatory outcomes, the interaction between the different financial systems on the international level of course also has repercussions for the optimal level of regulation at the domestic level. The approach taken here is informed by the 'interdependence' - literature in international political economy, which posits that the increasing level of economic interlinkages between countries make economic policy-making a strategic interaction rather than a purely domestic affair (R.O. Keohane & Nye, 1997). This justifies the use of a game-theoretical model for analytical rigor to derive testable propositions about the outcome of such interaction.

There is a rich body of literature on international interaction and coordination in economic policy-making, which this section builds on analytically in the formulation of the game-theoretical model. While there is an abundance of such models on policy coordination in particular in fiscal and monetary policy, in terms of substance it is surprising to see how few models have been developed to capture the dynamics of banking regulation in an integrating financial market.[79] Some few models however do exist, which in a more rigorous and parsimonious fashion have produced some very relevant insights on the dynamics of regulatory interaction. The existing models have

[79] This conclusion is shared for instance by Sinn (2002), who also ventures to apply the systems competition theory to the realm of banking regulation.

usually i) focused on the externalities of domestic regulation in the international context as well as ii) on the role of private interests in the regulatory utility function, whilst some models also iii) have debated the question of whether a race to the bottom exists.

As an example of the first category, Schüler (2003a) uses a principal-agent model of banking supervision in Europe, where the regulator acts as agent for the taxpayer in supervising banks but is also subject to potential capture by the banking industry that she is supervising. Banks that have an upside from risky returns but no downside due to deposit insurance have an incentive to lobby for less strict regulation. Taxpayers appoint regulators to take care of their stability interests but have little information about the actual work carried out by the regulator. Self-interested regulators now have a public interest (stability and banking profits) and a private interest (bureaucratic gambling, covering up etc.). [80] He concludes that

"firstly, supervisors may not take into account the externalities on the other country's financial system and economy as a whole. Secondly, the regulatory agents may not sufficiently monitor the cross-border activities of financial institutions. Thirdly, regulators may not deliver relevant information to the other supervisor" (p. 17, 2003).

With respect to the second category, the trade-off between private and public interests, Singer (2004; 2007) suggests a principal-agent framework that puts the regulator and his domestic environment at the centre of analysis, which then serves as the explanation for why international level regimes are created. He argues very much like Kantaro (2003) that international harmonization results as a resolution of the basic regulator's dilemma, which he sees as defined by the conflict between using regulation to either promote the competitiveness of the national financial industry (lax regulation) or to promote the confidence in the stability of the financial system (tighter regulation). The regulator maneuvers in a space of his "win-set" determined by the stringency of legislation that does not undermine competitiveness but also is strong enough to create financial stability. Exogenous shocks to international competitiveness or voter confidence in financial stability can decrease the size of the win-set and make legislative intervention more likely – a cost to the regulator that he will want to avoid. Because regulators cannot influence either how competitiveness or confidence are hit by shocks, they seek international harmonization to cope with these shocks and increase the win-set again. In this framework the regulator is a private interest actor that does not look to mitigate global systemic risk but instead is a clearly incentivized actor embedded in the domestic political economy. However, for the purpose of understanding international regulatory interaction, the model has a serious shortcoming or at least requires extension. Given Singer's focus on regime genesis, it provides very little guidance with respect to regime evolution and the question whether regulatory interaction over time (in the absence of simultaneous shocks) produces a race to the bottom or a race to the top.

[80] From this he derives also a few recommendations in Schüler (2003b) that conclude that current structures of cooperation also with the innovations of the then planned Lamfalussy framework among European financial supervisors would be insufficient incentive – instead it would take a European observatory of systemic risk, which in fact turned out to be valid.

A third category of models have analyzed the effect of international competition on regulatory and legal outcomes. These models have largely been developed in other policy spheres such as capital taxation or environmental regulation and have in some cases been more doubtful about the actual existence of a race to the bottom (e.g., (Basinger, Brook, & Hallerberg, 2004; Plümper, Troeger, & Winner, 2009). Instead some models find that domestic norms and veto players can restrain such a race dynamic and will sustain a certain level of taxation or regulation. Due to the nature of banking regulation as a 'quiet' area of politics, these considerations have a lower relevance for banking regulation. In the realm of banking regulation, that is regulatory stringency competition, the most relevant formal model is provided by Dell'Ariccia and Marquez (2006). In their model of regulatory interaction they look at two countries with different preferences towards regulation under different regulatory regimes, one time under a centralized regulator and one time under a decentralized regulator. In line with Schüler's model they find that countries with asymmetric preferences towards competitiveness and stability will produce an inefficiently high level of systemic risk externalities as the externality on foreign banks is not internalized. Moreover they endogenize the decision of regulators to coordinate, assuming different regulatory preferences in creating regulatory dynamics to show the situations under which a 'race to the bottom' can come about. The key conclusion from their paper is that under a decentralized regulatory system with increasing financial integration a reduction of regulatory standards can result – a result, which is even amplified if one incorporates higher mobility of bank headquarters, since regulators then have to compete even harder for factors of production to locate in their jurisdiction, which leads them to lower stringency.

How does my model relate to these existing models? With respect to the first two findings, the externalization of systemic risk creation as well as the trading off of public and private interests, the formal model developed in this research very much builds on existing work. The model departs from a view of the national regulator as that is driven by domestic rather than systemic considerations, which include private interests. However, I also assume that the international interaction of regulation will naturally have an effect on regulatory action, which is why these models require further elaboration. With respect to international interaction the formal model developed in the following makes room for the possibility of an international regulatory regime, which countries can join to coordinate at a higher level of stringency. The model itself will determine what factors shape the likelihood of such cooperation, while the ensuing empirical analysis will provide insight into the real values of these factors and, thus, the likelihood of such cooperation.

4.1.1 A simple open economy model of regulatory interaction

The objective of this section is to review and integrate these insights into a simple game-theoretical model of regulatory interaction, which is consistent with the developed theory of differing regulatory preferences and suitable to deriving predictions for the impact of financial integration and financialization. Regulatory utility is assumed to follow the disutility function introduced in Chapter 2:

$$DisU_{regulator\,i} = \alpha_i S_i^2 + \beta (P_e - P_i)^2 \qquad \text{with } P_i \leq P_e \qquad (4.1)$$

where the public and private interest terms, S_i and P_i respectively, are defined as

$$S_i = L_i \qquad \text{with } L_i = \frac{E_i}{k_i} \quad (4.2)$$

$$P_i = \theta P_e + cL_i \qquad \text{with} \quad \theta \le 1 \quad (4.3)$$

Again L_i denotes the public interest in avoiding excess leverage in country *i*, whilst the private interest in profitability or alternatively additional credit provided to constituents is denoted by P_i and P_e. We know that the optimal level of regulatory stringency, say capital stringency, and resulting leverage is:

$$L_i = \frac{(1-\theta_i)c_i}{(\alpha_i + \beta_i c_i^2)} P_e \quad (4.4)$$

Taking the inverse of L_i equals:

$$k_i = \frac{(\alpha_i + \beta_i c_i^2)}{(1-\theta_i)c_i P_e} \quad (4.5)$$

Thus, countries' regulatory stringency will differ in the closed economy context only based on the level of credit demand/ profitability expectations as denoted by P_e, financial stability preferences, which shape the regulatory approaches with varying values of α_i and β_i. Lastly, the degree of convertibility of leverage into private interest benefits c_i is an important parameter as well.

Now we can modify this model slightly to incorporate the role of financial integration and the resulting interaction between regulators. We can insert the role of financial integration to derive its impact in the context of regulatory preferences. Financial integration in the model enters through its effect on bank competitiveness and profitability, as it affects the amount of lending that banks can do abroad and therefore also the amount of competition they have at home. In an integrating financial market, both factors – the public interest and the private interest – are shaped by international lending and competition, which reacts to the stringency of foreign regulation. Regulators are still assumed to follow a disutility function as described in (4.1), except that now the respective degree of financial stability (i.e., leverage) and private interests (i.e., credit availability or bank competitiveness/ profits) are assumed to be influenced by domestic regulation as well as by the foreign regulation. Hence, from the point of view of country *i* we specify that the two factors are simple functions of domestic and foreign regulatory stringency ($L_i; L_j$)[81]:

Financial stability in an integrating market As the substitutability of domestic and foreign bank services increases and more lending abroad takes place, the financial instability externalities of domestic regulation increase. This is in line with the findings of Stolz (2002), who in her model of supervisory incentives shows that

[81] This reflects the result from Chapter 2, that regulatory stringency is the direct link between regulation and stability outcomes, that is credit and leverage in the economy.

national banking problems can easily spread through the interbank lending market, evidencing how nationally anchored regulation can produce classical instability externalities to other countries. With her model of the home-country control and accountability of regulators limited to their own jurisdictions she shows that in a system with home country control (such as the European system) an *inefficient level of regulation for cross-border effects and contagion* will result. Thus, we incorporate this effect through the inclusion of foreign leverage L_j in the stability objective equation (4.2) of the national regulator and we insert a weighting factor for the relative weight of domestic and foreign bank leverage in the financial system.

$$S_i = c_i L_i + d_i L_j \tag{4.6}$$

Bank competition and international lending in an integrating market In a similar way private interests are of course also impacted by the financial integration of markets, which mostly challenges bank competiveness as it makes the competition for lending more international. Hence, as banks abroad are allowed to leverage up more heavily than national banks, they become more profitable and competitive and can threaten domestic banks either through takeovers or undercutting domestic banks' offerings. From a national regulatory and political economy perspective such competition works contrary to domestic private interests. One effect of internationalizing bank competition that is somewhat at odds with this effect deserves some discussion: Of course to some extent foreign lending is positive as it increases the amount of credit available to domestic constituents, which serves private interests. However, regulators can be assumed to have a domestic lending bias, that is prefer to have credit granted by domestic banks, since foreign lending is less resistant to crisis and tends to evaporate relatively quickly in times of distress (Aiyar, 2011).[82] As such, foreign leverage enters the domestic private interest equation (4.3) with a negative prefix for now, which of course needs to be empirically substantiated later.

$$P_i = \theta P_e + cL_i + dL_f \tag{4.6}$$

The respective parameters represent the relative importance of domestic (c) versus foreign (d) regulatory stringency for country i and are assumed to be the same as in equation (4.5). The same functions of course are assumed to hold for country j in a symmetric fashion.

Determining the optimal reaction function for country *i* We can now specify the optimal reaction function, maximizing (5.1) for country i with respect to given country j's regulatory stringency level k_j and the above given relationships between credit, leverage, and regulatory stringency. [83] This reaction function is:

$$L_i = e_i + f_i L_j \tag{4.7}$$

with the two parameters of this function being defined as follows:

---

[82] This is a central finding of Aiyar's study based on the most recent financial crisis evidence.

[83] For a more extensive discussion of this and other related results regarding policy coordination in the international economy (and specifically the role of different models of the economy) see Frankel and Rockett (1988).

$$e_i = \frac{(1-\theta)b_i}{(\alpha_i + \beta_i)c_i} P_e \tag{4.8}$$

$$f_i = \frac{(\beta_i - \alpha_i)d_i}{(\alpha_i + \beta_i)c_i} L_j \tag{4.9}$$

What we see is that the optimal strategy of country *i* as reflected by functions (4.7) to (4.9) is not only related positively to the degree of private interest, but is now also clearly dependent on L_j, which derives from the level of stringency of regulation in the other country *j*. This is of course expected and reflects the nature of the strategic interdependence of banking regulation in an integrating financial market. However, at closer inspection it is interesting to identify the factors that determine the direction of the reaction, that is the slope of the coefficient f_i. As we can see from equation (4.9), the direction of the reaction to country *j*'s stringency of regulation relates solely to the relative weight that the regulator places on α_i and β_i, i.e. public and private interests respectively. Thus, because laxity in another country has mixed effects on a country's financial system, on the one hand increasing financial instability through spillovers and on the other hand decreasing national banks' competitiveness, the optimal reaction depends on the relative weight that regulators assign to stability vs. private interests.

Based on these results we can now derive relevant propositions.

Proposition 1: National regulatory stringency in an integrating financial market, given equations (4.1) to (4.9), is

- related to the *level of regulation of other countries*;
- *the more impacted by other countries' stringency the more the two financial systems are integrated with each other* (due to the parameters *d* and *e*, which measure relative role of the *domestic economy* in the denominator, and the openness parameters in the numerator;
- affected by *national regulatory preferences*, that is the strength of private and public interests in the regulatory objective function, which will determine the direction of the regulatory reaction.

To derive some equilibrium outcomes we can now map the reaction functions of two countries graphically. Assuming somewhat differing preferences and thus different slopes across the two countries this can be depicted as below in the figure below. We can see that the two reaction curves intersect at point *A* and yield a certain amount of disutility for both regulators. In the absence of institutions, which help sustain coordination or cooperation for a different outcome, this is the Nash Equilibrium, since it reflects the best strategies available given the other regulator's strategy. It is thus the point of tangency between the two countries' utility curves. The above example in the graph is of course only illustrative and not exhaustive, since any combination of preferences, level of private interests, and financial integration will yield different results. It does however serve to illustrate how the international interaction through the channel of financial integration can shape optimal regulatory reactions at home and, as a result, leverage and financial stability outcomes across countries.

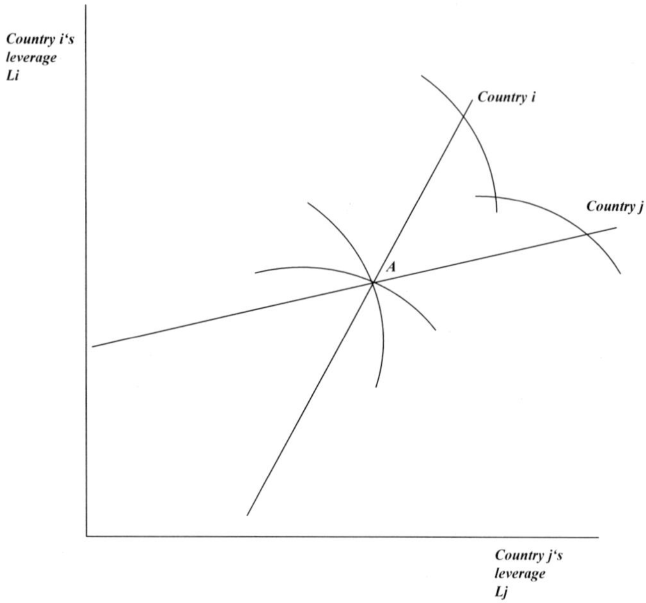

FIGURE 19: *Regulatory reaction curves and equilibrium leverage outcome: Two countries with given level of private interests and relatively higher financial integration*

Source: Author

In this example with relatively similar regulatory preferences (which favour private interests over stability) and with higher financial integration we see a steeper reaction curve to foreign regulatory stringency decisions, which yields an equilibrium level of leverage at A, which is the intersection of the best response curves and thus constitutes a Nash Equilibrium.

4.1.2 The role of international institutions in regulatory interaction

The Nash Equilibrium A could theoretically be improved upon in a Pareto-optimal fashion, if we were to move South-West direction of the diagram towards lower levels of leverage (i.e., higher levels of regulatory stringency) in both countries, which would help facilitate higher stability through reduced leverage externalities, leaving discretion for the attainment of private interests by each national regulator. The space between point A and the two reaction curves can in fact be bargained on in international negotiations. From bargaining theory we know that the points of tangency of the utility curves yield a coordination path of different possible negotiated outcomes such as point B as depicted in the below figure. For these outcomes to be truly attainable and stable equilibriums it takes institutions to sustain them, since if left to their own devices countries will naturally have to assume rational behaviour and optimal strategies on the other countries' part and thus will end up with the Nash Equilibrium A. Thus, in a repeated context this game has potentially more solutions or stable equilibriums than outcome A (such as B), the attainability of which depends upon the strength of international institutions.

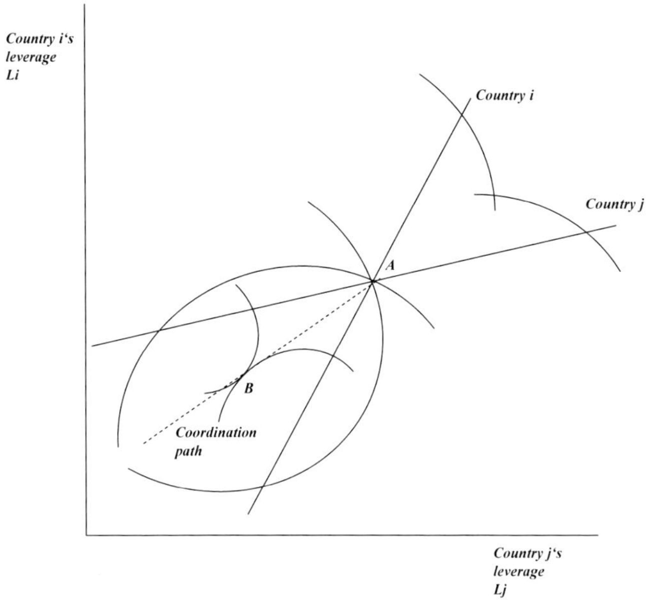

FIGURE 20: *Potential equilibrium outcome in the presence of international institutions*

Source: Author

Proposition 2: Regulatory cooperation with international institutions. The outcome of the regulatory interaction, that is the resulting level of regulatory stringency across financial systems, will depend on international institutions, which enhance the ability of regulators to coordinate on a higher level of stringency than would result from their interaction in the absence of institutions.[84]

The presence of weak institutions or even countries outside a regulatory union, thus, not subject to the described institutions, will further add to the 'race to the bottom'-dynamic, as they will be able to have laxer regulation than the members of the regulatory union and will therefore have no incentive to join since they can effectively compete for banking business now. This is a relevant issue due to the United States' decision - as the major financial system – not to implement Basel II immediately but to

[84] This is in essence the result of this model as many other models of international regulation, which can be depicted as a classical non-cooperative game of the prisoner's dilemma form. With each country pursuing an independent regulatory regime, country *j* with a lower stability preference will find it its dominant strategy to be lax, in response to which it becomes optimal for country *i* to follow suit and be lax as well. This leaves the countries in a competitive race for regulatory laxity, which would eventually culminate in countries reaching point A, which is the Nash Equilibrium in the absence of cooperation. With increasing integration and repeated interaction, the demand for a coordinated outcome and institutions to stabilize this outcome will increase.

lag implementation, making them the temporary outsider to the Euro Zone countries, who agreed to implement Basel II earlier.[85]

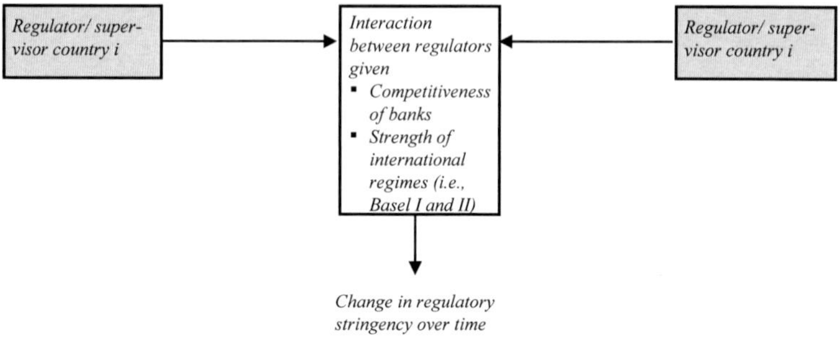

FIGURE 21: *Change in regulatory stringency as an outcome of international regulatory interaction*

Source: Author

4.2 Financial integration in the Euro-Zone

In European as in global financial relations the stylized fact is that financial integration since the late 1990s has increased immensely in almost all dimensions. Particular for the case of the Euro Zone there were conscious policy choices that drove such integration through the introduction of European-level legislation and policies such as the Financial Services Action Plan (FSAP), the Financial Conglomerates Directive, and of course the introduction of European Monetary Union (EMU). All of these reforms have in common that they removed national instruments to limit competition or impose activities and conglomerate restrictions to a significant degree and, thus, led to a more harmonized model, which, hence, should also challenge the regulatory configurations of the individual Euro Zone countries and in particular those countries, whose regulatory model relied on a certain amount of activities and conglomerate restrictions. Still, despite this conventional wisdom, financial integration is a vast concept that has a qualitative (type of integration) and a quantitative dimension (how much integration in each market). Hence, a brief discussion of financial integration in the Euro Zone, its progress and its limitations, is required to inform my following analysis of its effect on banking.

There have been two parallel trends in financial markets in the last two decades that have had a significant influence on the nature of banking and regulation in almost all markets, certainly though in the Anglo-Saxon and European markets: One is the integration of markets across borders and the other is the financialization of banking. Both of these trends have challenged the ability of national regulators to regulate according to their preferences, since they have created larger externalities to domestic regulation, have challenged existing business models and comparative advantages, and have changed power relations to favour banks and financial institutions vis-à-vis their national regulators due to the ability to engage in regulatory arbitrage. To understand how financial integration has challenged the specific comparative advantages of

[85] See R. J. Herring, 2007, for a discussion of the reasons for this decision.

certain financial systems and what that implies for the regulator in turn, we will take a brief look at the facts of European financial integration. While integration thus describes the increase in cross-border interaction between the financial systems, financialization describes the increasing role of capital markets in finance, which has transformed the nature of banks. Given the transformative impact of capital market development such as securitization and the increase in trading by financial institutions and banks rather than individuals, it is fair to say that *"investment has become institutionalized"*, as Financial Times editor John Authers finds in his analysis of "The fearful rise of markets" (2010). Because financialization to a large extent has enabled integration, it makes sense to start with the analysis of financialization and then move on to integration to see how this development got transported into the European financial systems.

4.2.1 Financialization

Financialization here is understood as the increasing importance and dominance of capital markets in financial systems, affecting also the centers of European banking. The origins of the financialization of banking can be traced back to the United States as the mother of the market-based financial system. The U.S. increased their market focus for financial activities on both sides of the financial institution's balance sheet: On the one hand the introduction of money market funds in the 1970s and their rise in the 1980s led to greater competition between deposit money banks and money market funds for cheap sources of funding, as depositors invested their money preferably into the higher-yielding money market funds rather than the insured but lower-yielding deposits of banks. The volume of funds flowing into these funds exceeded USD 1 trillion in 1997 and reached USD 3.8 trillion in 2008, creating the de facto shadow banking system around the world (Authers, 2010), which had access to plenty of cheap money and was seeking new targets. The total of the shadow banking system, then including also investment banks, hedge funds, and off-balance-sheet vehicles exceeded the size of the banking sector in the United States in 2009. Thus, competition in the U.S. increased markedly as financial markets deepened and new financial institutions discovered more unregulated ways of competing with banks. The targets of this cheap money were, on the asset side, supplied by the securitization of debt obligations.

These securitized assets essentially separated debt origination and debt holding under the infamous originate-to-distribute-model, pressuring banks even further through the competition by institutional investors. These structured financial products made their way from the United States to Europe directly and using the highly developed market of the United Kingdom as a hub. As ties to the Anglo Saxon more market-based financial systems have intensified, the large scale import of many securitized financial products soared and made private debt assets the largest of all asset groups in European banking (McKinsey Global Institute, 2008). While in the United States, non-bank institutions started competing with banks and drove financialization, banks in Europe had to adapt to maintain their pre-dominant position. It is therefore widely acknowledged that in the last ten years since 2000 there has been a real transformation of the European financial landscape, which has been accelerated by the introduction of the euro (for an extensive discussion of this transformation see Hartmann, Maddaloni, & Manganelli, 2003).

Private bond market capitalization (as % of GDP)

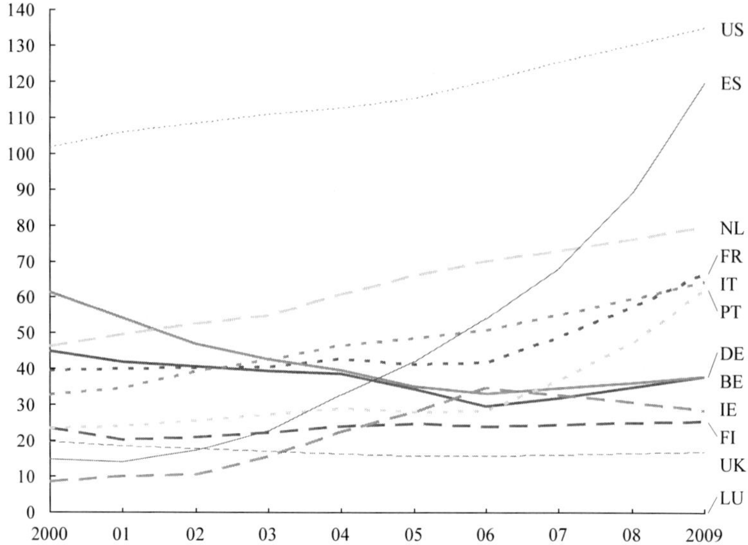

Stock traded 2000-2009 (% of GDP)

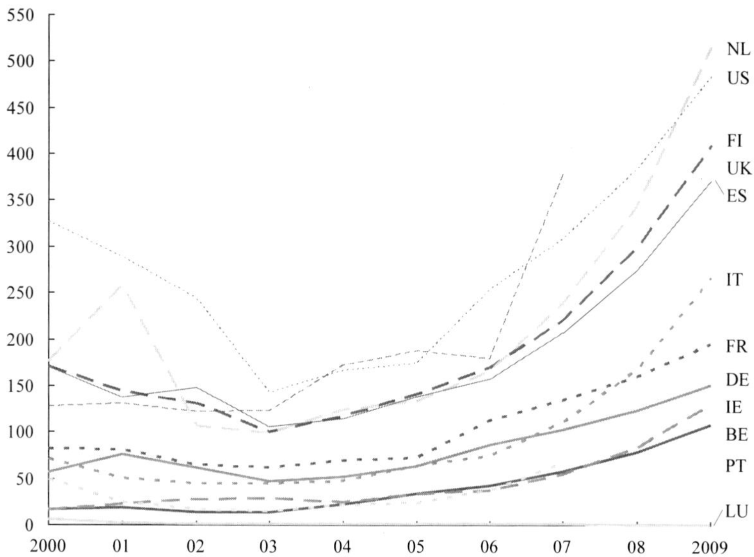

FIGURE 22: *Development of capital markets across Euro Zone, UK, and US*

Source: Author based on IMF data

The above figure shows a clear pattern of increasing bond market reliance across the Euro Zone, even if the level of the United States as a market-based systems remains out of reach. Clearly, markets have taken on a bigger role and have reduced the degree of intermediation in the Euro Area, positioning the Euro Area as a whole more and more as a hybrid system in between a bank-based and market-based system, as ECB economists find as well:

"*...the Euro Area financial structure is placed somewhat in between those of these two countries [United States and Japan], with financial institutions playing an important role, but with market based instruments developing further. (...) The importance traditional banking intermediation from deposits to loans has diminished. Capital markets have considerably developed. Many financial innovations have emerged and at the same time we have witnessed a substantial shift toward institutionalized management of savings*" (Hartmann et al., 2003; p.5-7).

The data indeed confirm this view of the Euro Area moving towards a hybrid financial system. Looking at the private bond market capitalization one can see an increase in the issuance of bonds in many countries across the Euro Zone over time, indicating that firms are indeed accessing other sources of funding rather than loans from their respective *Hausbanken* or *relationship lenders*. This indicates that with the euro introduction indeed non-bank institutions issued more bonds to diversify their funding sources – however, they did not substitute bank lending. Some exceptions to the rule are the German and the Belgian bank-based system, where in fact after the first wave of market orientation in the late 1990s levels even declined for some time. Moreover a stronger role of stock markets can be derived from the across the board increase in stock market capitalization and stock value traded in relation to GDP. Yet, the picture is not unanimously showing a market-orientation, as the volume of loans has been growing on the bank-side as well.

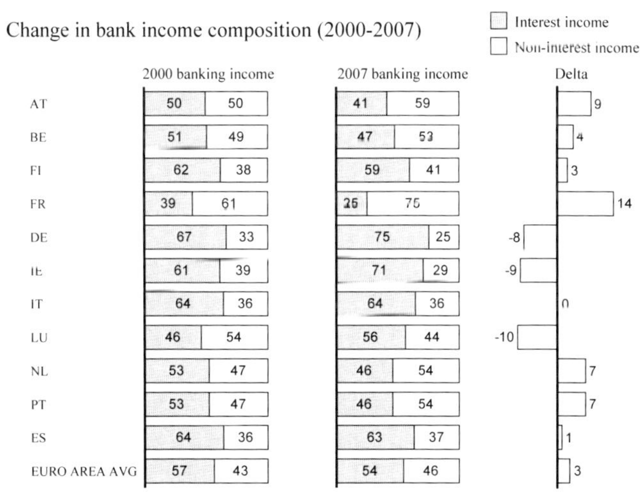

FIGURE 23: *Change in bank income composition in the Euro Zone in 2000 and 2007*

Source: Author based on OECD bank profitability data

Hence, when looking at the impact on banking business models and the relevance of different sources of income we still see an important, if slightly declining, share of interest-based income. The below figure shows interest and non-interest income as a share of total bank income for the years 2000 to 2008. Most banking systems have indeed seen their non-interest share of income from securities-related activities increase despite an increase in lending activities as well, which shows that indeed market-related activities have become more important for European banks as well.

4.2.2 Financial integration

The internationalization of finance and the financial integration it has brought about has been going along with a general swelling up of global financial assets. Whilst global financial assets skyrocketed from USD 48 trillion in 1990 to a high of USD 194 trillion in 2007, the share of cross-border capital flows went from USD 1 trillion in 1990 to USD 10.5 trillion in 2007 (McKinsey Global Institute, 2009) – of course taking somewhat of a nose-dive with the financial crisis of 2007/8 again. Similarly, the Euro Zone financial market has been growing to comprise financial assets of USD 43.8 trillion in 2007 and integrating in the same time period. Financial integration is defined by the law of one price. This implies that interest rates on different products and in different markets should - *ceteris paribus* - converge. To that end it makes sense to decompose the effect of this financial integration into its components of integration in financial markets, credit markets, financial institutions, and financial products to get a more differentiated picture. Financial markets in the Euro Zone have generally developed and integrated relatively well, owing also to the increased liquidity and choice that a common financial market with a single currency provides (European Commission Internal Market and Services, 2005). However, equity markets still show some sign of domestic bias, as country effects still weighed more heavily than sector effects. This is confirmed by Jappelli and Pagano (2008), who put this down to the presence of institutional barriers to integration such as the costs for cross-border trades arising from the fragmentation of the clearing and settlement system. Bond market integration on the other hand proceeded relatively quickly, as a look at the government bond market spreads reveals, showing remarkable convergence to a level that with hindsight can almost be termed overly ambitious, given the development of certain countries' creditworthiness. However, also indicators like the beta-convergence have confirmed this strong degree of integration of bond markets (European Commission, 2005). The size of the interbank market assets doubled in 8 years, indicating that indeed interbank lending has become a more important channel of funding and with that also of contagion. As the European Commission finds in its integration report (2005; p.5): *"The unsecured money market reached a stage of "near-perfect" integration almost immediately after the introduction of the euro. In addition, the repo market is highly integrated albeit to a lower extent."*

Credit and retail markets have however not integrated as quickly, which Pagano and Jappelli put down to the heterogeneity of borrowers and the local nature of the information that lenders need (2008). The authors also confirm the persistence of interest rates differentials in medium- and long-term loans in the corporate and consumer credit market.

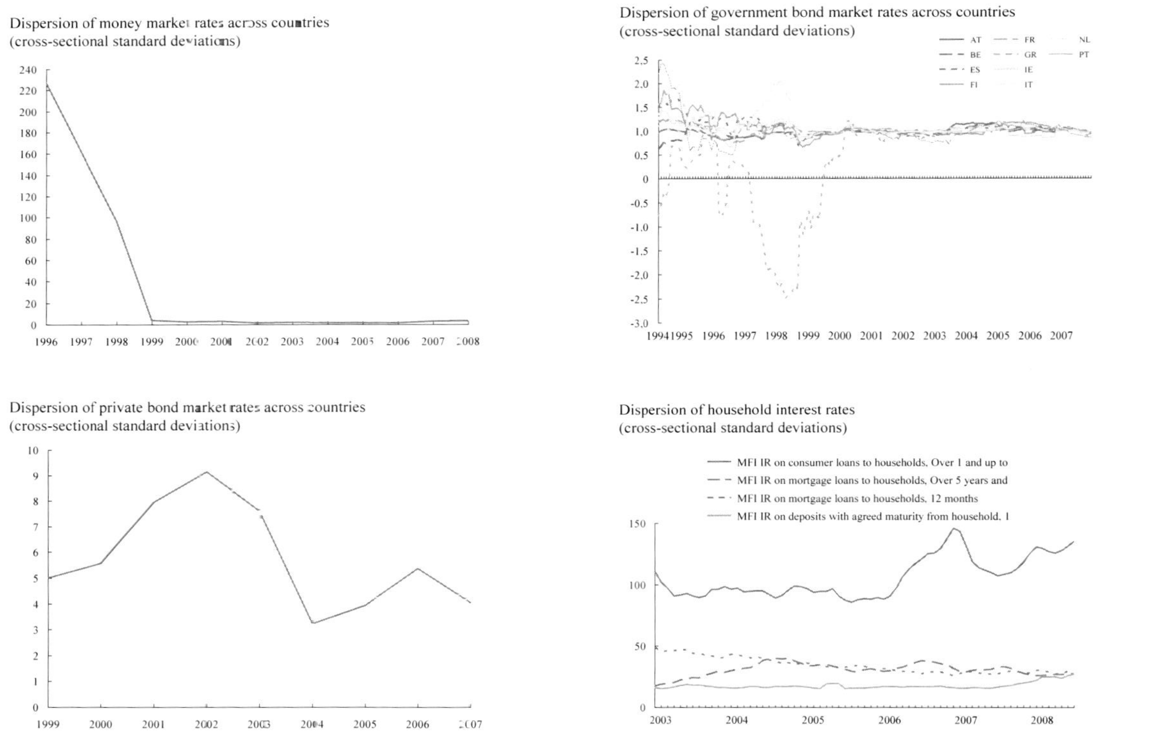

FIGURE 24: *Progress in financial integration in the Euro Zone by financial market segment*
Source: Author based on ECB data

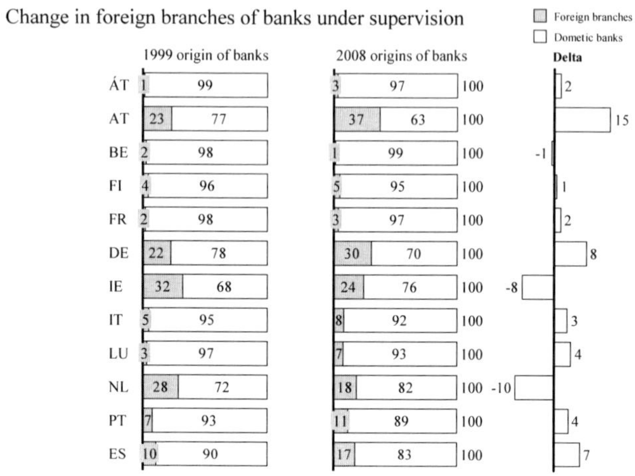

FIGURE 25: *Origin of banks under supervision across Euro Zone countries*

Source: Author based on ECB data

As evidence of that we can see the relatively wide dispersion of different household credit rates in the table above, which shows that the law of one price does not yet hold across European retail banking markets. In terms of institutional integration the pattern also looks slightly different: Cross-border merger and acquisitions (M&A) activity has been higher in the first years as consolidation of activities picked up but dropped again such that in 2006 more domestic rather than cross-border M&A deals were being completed. In terms of foreign activity, European banks have decided to locate some subsidiaries and branches in other countries, the latter of which can benefit from the fact that it is regulated according to the home country principle. Looking at the data the degree of penetration by foreign branches is very varied across countries: Generally speaking the smaller financial systems seem to have been more integrated into the European market in terms of the share of foreign branches were located in their markets. In the cases of Greece, Ireland, and Belgium these make up between 24% and 37% of their banks under supervision. In other smaller financial systems such as Luxembourg, Spain, and Portugal these still make up between 11% and 17% of total monetary financial institutions.

Conclusion

To summarize: European financial integration as well as financialization, inspired by the model of Anglo-Saxon hybrid and market-based financial systems, has been relatively strong if however varied across market segments. With the commoditization of lending activities and an increase in the availability of market information on borrowers the value of 'relationship' lending has declined and banks have had to search for new sources of comparative advantage. As a result, banking in the Euro Zone as well as outside of it has been changing. International capital mobility and the spread of a more shareholder-oriented way of organizing the economy and in particular financial relations have challenged the 'patient capital' institutions across the more coordinated market economies and, thus, also the bank-based financial systems supporting them.

Thus, there is clear evidence that the financial systems, as I have derived here for the years since 2000, have integrated bank-based and financial markets-based intermediation. Still banking in Europe is far from European. Progress in equity and bond markets has been much quicker, while credit market integration has been lagging somewhat – particularly where household and retail markets are concerned. On the asset side, financial market participants through financialization have increased their share of cross-border investment into securities whilst banks have started lending to a much larger extent to each other in the interbank market, thereby also increasing their liability side integration. This has allowed banks to leverage up relatively cheaply by borrowing from each other. Overall therefore the capital market and the interbank market have become more important channels of funding and investment also for banks. Progress has been more limited, where retail activities are concerned, as cross-border deposit-holdings and cross-border loans to non-banks have increased only marginally over the last years. Still, there is a measured if varied degree of integration in financial markets and the banking system in Europe – at the same time one cannot speak of a fully integrated market in banking, yet.

The pattern of integration and financialization described has subjected different financial markets to different degrees of competitive shocks. To what extent these shocks have been asymmetric and what this has triggered in terms of a regulatory and institutional response will be discussed in the next section.

4.3 Institutional change

To the extent that banks are the central actors in the bank-reliant financial systems of the Euro Zone, deepening financial integration and changes in the nature of banking can induce changes in institutions and regulation as well. Thus, in this account of regulatory change, as laid out in the model in section 4.1, I see regulatory interaction between different financial systems with varying stringency in various regulatory dimensions (see Chapter 3) as the key driver of institutional change. I argue, much like (Hardie & Howarth, 2009) that the increased financialization and the competitive pressures of integration have limited the provision of 'patient' capital, which has underpinned many European financial systems. The key change in the nature of banking and the way that it challenges the traditional configurations of the bank-based regulatory regimes – in particular of the 'relationship' finance as well as the 'stability-oriented' regimes – is captured by the argument made by Rajan in his infamous paper delivered to central bankers at Jackson Hole (2005, p.315-316). He firstly encapsulates the complementary configuration of patient capital and relationship-oriented banking as follows.

"In the 1950s and 1960s, banks dominated financial systems. Bank managers were paid a largely fixed salary. Given that regulation kept competition muted, there was no need for shareholders to offer managers strong performance incentives (and such incentives may even have been detrimental, as it would have tempted bank managers

to reach out for risk). The main check on bank managers making bad investment decisions was the bank's fragile capital structure (and possibly supervisors). If bank management displayed incompetence or knavery, depositors would get jittery and possibly run. The threat of this extreme penalty, coupled with the limited upside from salaries that were not buoyed by stock or options compensation, combined to make bankers extremely conservative. This served depositors well since their capital was safe, while shareholders, who enjoyed a steady rent because of the limited competition, were also happy. Of course, depositors and borrowers had little choice, so the whole system was very inefficient. [...]"

As the financial system develops and markets take on a stronger role, a system that he describes as de-regulated, this causes changes to incentives and the patience of capital:

"In the new, deregulated, competitive environment, investment managers cannot be provided the same staid incentives as bank managers of yore. Because they have to have the incentive to search for good investments, their compensation, their compensation has to be sensitive to investment returns, especially returns relative to their competitors. Furthermore, new investors are attracted by high returns. Dissatisfied investors can take their money elsewhere, but they do so with substantial inertia."

Clearly, the institutional underpinning of financial systems – both, the bank- and the market-based financial system – and the complementary regulatory regimes are being challenged by the changes that financial integration and financialization are inducing. How does this development in banking induce institutional change in regulation? As countries become more and more financially integrated, but are still domestically rooted enough such that the regulator will consider them 'national' or domestic banks, differences in the stringency of regulation relative to other countries will induce 'shocks to competitiveness'. In this case regulators will find themselves under political economy pressures to accommodate banks, which might lead to institutional change that reduces the regulatory differences between countries and thus works as a converging force. Such a dynamic can then lead to multiple regulatory downward adjustments across jurisdictions and the described 'race to the bottom' (proposition 1). However, I have also shown that instead countries in the presence of strong international standards can agree to cooperate and work towards a higher level of regulation altogether (proposition 2). The following section tests these predictions about the role of national 'regulatory' competitiveness considerations empirically.

4.3.1 The asymmetric impact of integration on national competitiveness

Firstly, I am interested in the symmetry of the impact of financial integration the Euro Zone. The Euro Zone and its different financial systems vary with respect to their relative openness as well as the point of departure in terms of regulatory stringency, which should lead to different institutional change predictions. To that extent I derive the degree of regulatory competitiveness and financial integration of each financial system to determine countries' relative position towards other jurisdictions. This allows me to make a prediction of the likely institutional change that the regulator will initiate given the interactions with the regulatory stringency of other jurisdictions. The logic of the trilemma, which sees a potential trade-off relationship between private interests in competitive banks and financial stability, on which the game-theoretical model of 4.1 is based, suggests that countries' optimal regulatory responses will be a function of

- *the level of regulation of other countries*;
- *the degree of financial integration between two financial systems*
- *potential differences in national regulatory preferences, which relate to the degree of profitability afforded to banks vs. stability*

To illustrate how asymmetric the Euro Zone countries are with respect to the above definition I plot two of these three dimensions graphically. Looking at these predictions empirically, it is instructive to look at the development of the main regulatory stringency instruments over time. The first time period for which we can make this comparison based on available data is between 1999/ 2000 and 2005/2006. This time period coincides with the existence of Basel I as the first international regime on banking regulation. The Basel I (as well as its successor Basel II) defines the amount of regulatory capital (CARs) a bank is to hold across all countries. Internationally-active banks were regulated to hold 4 percent of Tier 1 capital relative to risk-adjusted assets as well as 8 percent of Tier 1 plus Tier 2 capital relative to risk-adjusted assets. However, Basel leaves a substantial amount of freedom with respect to how national regulators define what counts as capital. There are ten dimensions along which this definition of regulatory capital can vary across countries along with the values of the respective countries in 1999/2000. Since this is arguably the most relevant area of variation in implementation of regulatory standards, particularly from the point of view of international competitiveness, we shall take this as a first test of the above predictions. To operationalize the first two variables of the game-theoretical model, I measure the following factors:

Level of capital stringency regulation, in relation to the countries' average as well as the degree of integration, measured by the relative share of foreign assets in total banking assets and liabilities (the two only differ marginally). For the definition of capital stringency institutions I again draw on the database by Barth, Caprio, and Levine (2006) (listed in addendum XXII in the Appendix).

Profitability of banks as measured by the return on assets, which importantly is a measure of profitability that does *not* include the reliance on leverage, since it is equal to the return on all of bank assets including borrowed funds (as opposed to the return on equity). The logic is that countries with very profitable banks will face less pressure to use regulatory means to push bank profitability.

Relative openness or integration, which I measure based on share of assets and liabilities on/ from foreign banks and jurisdictions.

The depiction below allows us to derive the macro-economic picture for the Euro Zone in 2000 as a suboptimal regulatory union, when it comes to being a 'level playing field': Due to regulatory differences, differences in profitability, and variation in the degree of openness, asymmetric competitive political economy shocks are likely to materialize over time, as financial integration proceeds and as European-level regulation increases competitive heat between banks.

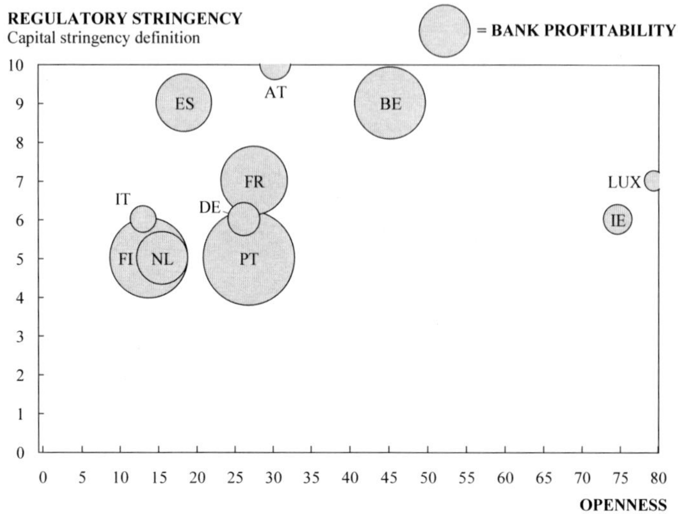

FIGURE 26: *Relative capital stringency, profitability and financial system openness in 2000*

Source: Author based on Bank for International Settlements data for openness and regulatory indices based on Barth, Caprio, and Levine (2006)

a Average for the Euro Zone weighted based on a countries' relative share of total banking assets

- On the East-West-dimension of the figure we see the *differences in relative openness* as well as the differences in profitability as reflected by the size of the bubbles: While banks in countries such as *Luxembourg and Ireland* as very small economies but strong and open financial systems are likely to come under increasing pressure in particular due to their relatively lower profitability, other financial systems such as Finland and Portugal are less likely to face such pressures due to their higher profitability and lower openness. Germany, Italy, the Netherlands, and France fall in-between and vary with their relative profitability.
- On the North-South-dimension we can see that *Spain, Austria, and Belgium* stand out due to their much *higher stringency of capital definition*, which might put them under pressure. But even here the picture is more heterogeneous: Spanish and Belgian regulators regulate their banks much more stringently but have a relatively profitable banking system to supervise, which therefore allows banks to fulfill these higher equity requirements more easily. Austria on the other side stands out as a much less profitable banking system as a whole with a sizable degree of openness of 30% measured by the share of foreign assets and liabilities of banks. On the other extreme again are Finland and Portugal as relatively lower regulated and very profitable financial systems, which could even afford to re-regulate banks more due to the relative competitiveness of their banks.

Based on the relative regulatory stringency and profitability we can classify the financial systems of Belgium, Austria, Spain, Luxembourg, and Ireland as subject to potential shocks to competitiveness. There is some variation amongst them in particular in the degree of openness, which as shown is a crucial driver of the strength, with which these pressures are likely to materialize. Hence, the next section will derive more robust estimators of this shock considering all relevant dimensions discussed here.

4.3.2 Institutional change in capital stringency definitions

To derive the actual competitive shock that is likely to derive from these regulatory differences we have to account for the actual financial linkages among the respective financial systems to get a sense of what the likely competitive exposures among banks of different jurisdictions are likely to be. As financial systems are not yet perfectly integrated, they find themselves exposed to some systems more than others. Also, by virtue of size, some financial systems are more significant as 'regulatory anchors' for other financial systems than others. To determine the relative regulatory competitiveness of a country, I combine values on its openness, its competitiveness position relative to others, and the financial exposures in an aggregate value, that provides all the information that the theoretical discussion touched upon.[86] For that the competitive distances vis-à-vis the other countries, $(k_j - k_i)$, are simply aggregated, weighted by the respective financial exposure, ε_{ij}, to that country, and then weighted with the openness score, λ_i, in order to generate a total score for each country (see addendum XXIII in the Appendix for values by country).

$$C_i = \lambda_i \cdot \sum_N (k_j - k_i) \cdot \varepsilon_{ij}$$

I calculate competitiveness factors k for each financial systems based on the distance in the *definition of capital stringency regulation* based on Barth, Caprio, and Levine (2006). This score then can be used as an indicator of the relative regulatory position of that country vis-à-vis all relevant countries in the sample. Moreover, since it measures the regulatory distance of a country's institutions to its relevant regulatory counterparts, it should also serve as a good predictor of the *direction of regulatory institutional change* in this country. The lower (higher) this score will be for a country, the more that country is exposed to countries that employ a laxer (stricter) definition of regulatory stringency or are more profitable, which might put its banks at a competitive dis-advantage (advantage), increasing the political economy pressures for institutional change. Moreover I calculate the *profitability of banks* and calculate the relative distance that countries have from Euro Zone average profitability to determine the degree to which Euro Zone integration after monetary union is going to exert adaptational pressures on banks in the Euro Zone to increase profitability and to reflect the banks' ability to generate bank capital from retained earnings.

---

[86] See Appendix for the data and specifics on the calculation of these values.

TABLE 19: *Relative shock to competitiveness and predicted institutional change in 2000 (shaded countries with stronger shocks to competitiveness)*

Country	*Stringency in capital definition* [a]	*Profitability/ ROA* [b]	*Predicted change in stringency*	*Actual change*	*Delta from prediction*
Austria	10	0.09%	-4.6	-4	0.6
Belgium	9	0.43%	-4.2	-6	-1.8
Spain	9	0.29%	-1.4	1	2.4
Luxembourg	7	0.04%	-1.0	0	1.0
Ireland	6	0.08%	-0.5	-3	-2.5
Italy	6	0.07%	-0.3	-1	-0.7
Germany	6	0.10%	0.1	1	0.9
France	7	0.4%	0.2	3	2.8
Netherlands	5	0.24%	0.8	0	-0.8
Finland	5	0.55%	1.1	-1	-2.1
Portugal	5	0.75%	3.9	4	0.1
Euro Zone avg.	*6.6* [b]	*0.22%* [b]			

a Calculated as differences relative to other countries weighted by their financial exposure to each other

b Calculated versus Euro Zone average with countries weighted by relative share of banking assets

Source: Author based on data from regulation indexes by Barth, Caprio, and Levine (2006) and capital and reserves data from the OECD (2011) "Bank Profitability" survey

To derive such an aggregate relative competitiveness value to explain institutional change in these countries I regress these two dimensions on the observed institutional change in capital stringency. This yields estimators of coefficients for each dimension that can then be used to translate the interaction between financial systems in terms of competitiveness into institutional change predictions, shown in column 'predicted change'. It is important to note that this procedure is of course statistically only indicative due to the very small sample size of countries included, but it should serve as a reasonably indicative measure of the relative role of competitiveness considerations in explaining institutional change in banking regulation and financial stability policy.

The figure below depicts the relative fit of these predictors with the actual change. We can see a relatively good match of these predictions and actual changes: Countries such as Austria that have been subject to relatively strong regulatory deviation and, thus, shocks to competitiveness have de-regulated more whilst countries such as Portugal, which have had relatively profitable banking systems and, thus no competitive shocks have re-regulated.

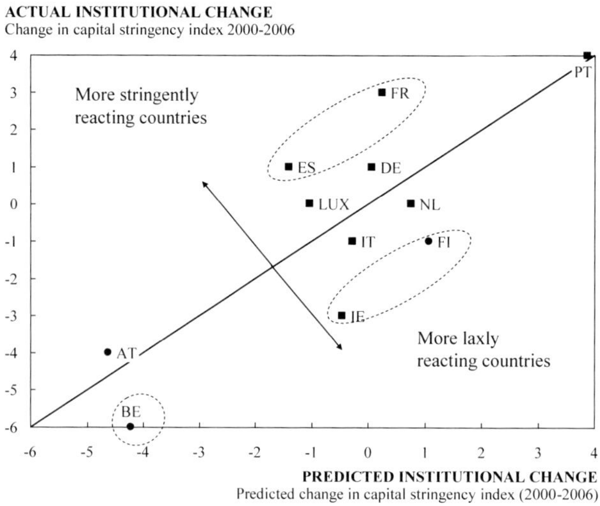

FIGURE 27: *Predicted and actual change in capital stringency in 2000*

Source: Author based on data from regulation indexes by Barth, Caprio, and Levine (2006) and capital and reserves data from the OECD (2011) "Bank Profitability" survey; the statistical fit between the model based on profitability and regulatory distance is reflected by an adjusted R^2 of .56 and two significant variables – these results still due to the small sample size should be treated with a caveat;

All in all, de-regulation is relatively balanced with re-regulation with four countries out of thirteen in total re-regulating and five countries lowering their standards with respect to capital stringency (see Appendix for all institutional change values). Taking the average of the institutional changes made, I find that countries have capital stringency definitions in the period from 2000 to 2006 are roughly the same at an average level of stringency of 7 (out of 10). As a third indication, the estimated function shows a negative constant of -.4, which implies that ceteris paribus even with no shock to competitiveness, countries will have lowered their definition standards somewhat. Thus, the pattern identified here is consistent with prediction 1, which stated that countries are likely to react to each others' relative levels of regulation – the more so the more open the financial system is.

Moreover, I find some evidence that regulatory standards have not been lowered across the board, which thus can be seen as consistent with prediction 2, which sees regulatory standards as mechanisms that can facilitate regulatory cooperation internationally. However, there is also evidence that on average capital stringency definitions in a period, in which Basel II was negotiated, have been lowered in response to competitiveness concerns. Thus, with respect to the question of the 'race to the bottom' or the 'race to the top' I find a differentiated pattern across the Euro Zone:

- There are some countries, notably the bank-based financial systems of Southern Europe with a stability-orientation, which have actually engaged in a *'race to the top'* by increasing regulatory standards. This was facilitated by the absence of a strong 'shock to competitiveness' in these financial systems, owing to relatively higher profitability of their banks and somewhat lower exposures to less regulated financial systems (than for instance Ireland or Belgium).

- There are other countries, notably Ireland and Belgium, which have reacted to the increasing exposure to other more profitable (Ireland) or less strictly regulated (Belgium) financial systems with more excessive capital stringency standards de-regulation consistent with the '*race to the bottom*'.

To appreciate this heterogeneity within the Euro Zone, which can be seen as the national regulatory preferences that drive this institutional change, I analyze the deviations from the pattern that the competitiveness story gives us. For convenience I plot the predictions and the actual institutional changes in the figure. Countries above the 45 degree line have reacted more stringently than predicted by their relative competitiveness score, whilst countries below the line have reacted more laxly. I apply some discretion in identifying in particular Ireland and Belgium, two bank-based and 'relationship'-finance financial systems, and as the most lax outliers and Spain and France, tow 'bank-based' and 'stability-oriented' financial systems, as the stricter countries. Interestingly we see that the countries that already have higher leverage ratios and lower capital adequacy levels, Belgium and Ireland, also were amongst the more aggressive de-regulators while Spain and France as 'stability-oriented' systems rely on more regulatory intervention. Portugal as the third 'stability-oriented' financial system also fits this pattern as it is the country re-regulating most strictly. Thus, it seems that there is some role of national preferences to the extent that countries in implementing national standards over time seem to fall prey to strong bank interests unless they have a more 'interventionist' regulatory regime such as the three financial systems of France, Spain, and Portugal. Finland also shows some downward deviation with respect to capital stringency regulation, however in the same period analyzed increased supervisory stringency, as capital levels in Finish banks went up substantially. Hence, the institutional change visible in the data here does not capture their trajectory adequately, which is why the change in capital stringency definition does not translate into economic outcomes.

The results are consistent with the notion that in implementing Basel regulation with some discretion, countries did indeed react to each others' regulatory stringency and depending on the strength of the competitiveness shock and national preferences were inclined to become laxer or stricter in their regulation. The usual caution that needs to be exercised with interpreting such results across a small, if however very relevant (given their combined economic weight), sample of countries of course remains. However, given that the intuition behind the observed pattern is very strong and in line with the theorizing, these results can be taken as a reasonably strong confirmation of the above predictions.

4.3.3 Institutional change in activities and conglomerate regulations

To expand the analysis to more regulatory dimensions I now turn to the other two areas of regulation, which were introduced in the previous chapter. I apply the logic of regulatory interaction due to competitiveness considerations to *conglomerate restrictiveness* - another important area of financial regulation towards banks, which shapes the degree to which conglomerates (such as under the universal bank or bankassurance model) can engage in financial activities, and to *activities*

The convergence of business models that accompanies this shift away from lending activities increasing the substitutability of products and, with the increased focus on yield, increases competition between banks across financial systems. From the perspective of the regulator this can have a strong impact on national bank competitiveness. Thus, we would expect the increase interactions that comes with financial integration between the different financial systems to lead to some institutional change and likely convergence, as banks adopt the universal banking business model of the European financial systems as well as the capital market orientation of the market-based systems. Again, I calculate the relative openness of the financial system, the exposures to other financial systems, and the regulatory distance in terms of conglomerate restrictiveness to determine the relative standing of countries towards each other. An application of the described approach will show, whether we the institutional change pattern in this regulatory areas is consistent with the regulatory competitiveness story that sees this as a reaction to integration pressures.

The figures below indicate that also in activities regulation and in particular in conglomerates restrictiveness countries have reacted to each other's relative regulatory stringency as the fit of the predicted and the actual regulatory changes is rather close. Importantly, in activities regulation on average there has been an increase in regulatory stringency, which is evidenced by the number of countries increasing regulatory stringency. In conglomerates regulation there is only a small a less significant decrease in regulation. Moreover, we can see a certain amount of convergence in both areas of regulation that is driven by two trends. Firstly, the most different financial system of the United States with its historically high stringency towards financial conglomerates and universal banking has leveled the playing field with the banks of the continent through its conscious move towards the universal banking system. Secondly, the European regulators – partially driven of course by conscious common regulatory efforts such as the Conglomerates Directive – have made efforts towards a more homogeneous level of regulation themselves.

The findings in the data as well as the real-world narrative seem consistent with the idea that countries indeed interact with each other. In activities regulation, due to the re-regulatory efforts of some continental European countries, I do not find a de-regulatory 'race to the bottom' but instead a regulatory convergence around a level of stringency that is somewhat higher than the level of the bank-based financial systems in 2000. At the same time it is still lower than the level of the more market-based financial systems and particularly the United States. In terms of deviations from the expected pattern in activities regulation I find that there is a particular deviation by the two 'self-regulatory' financial systems of the United Kingdom and Luxembourg. The United Kingdom, as a financial system with assumed regulatory preference for more laxity, actually de-regulated further from an already very low level of activity regulation and, thus, deviates very significantly from the pattern of a more converging regulatory change that the other countries exhibit. Luxembourg on the other hand has, coming from a similarly low base level of regulation, re-regulated more substantially putting it more in line with the other continental European financial systems. In conglomerates regulation no significant deviations from the competitiveness story can be made out.

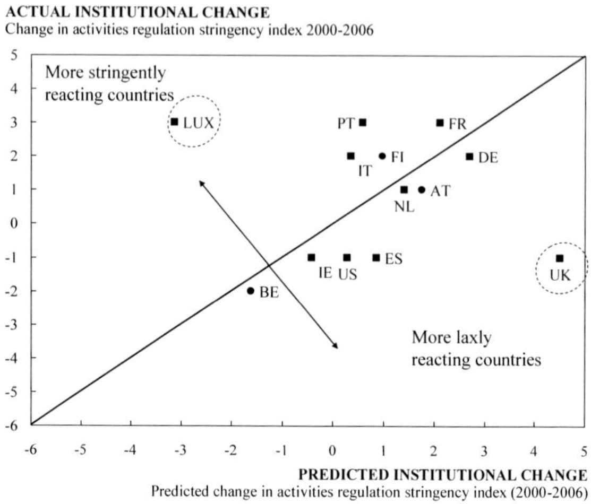

FIGURE 28: *Predicted and actual change in activities regulation stringency in 2000*

Source: Author based on data from regulation indexes by Barth, Caprio, and Levine (2006) and capital and reserves data from the OECD (2011) "Bank Profitability" survey; when excluding the extreme deviations of Luxembourg and the UK the model based on profitability and regulatory distance is yields an adjusted R^2 of .38 and a significant independent variable – these results still due to the small sample size should be treated with a caveat;

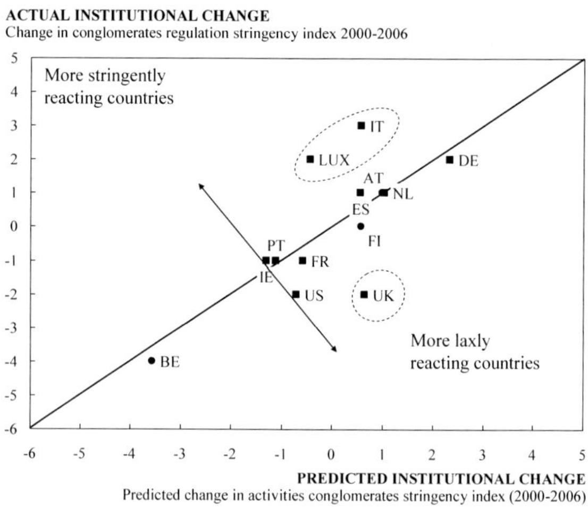

FIGURE 29: *Predicted and actual change in activities regulation stringency in 2000*

Source: Author based on data from regulation indexes by Barth, Caprio, and Levine (2006) and capital and reserves data from the OECD (2011) "Bank Profitability" survey; the statistical fit between the model based on profitability and regulatory distance is reflected by an adjusted R^2 of .53 and a highly significant independent variable – these results still due to the small sample size should be treated with a caveat;

4.3.4 Conclusion

I find that financial integration exerts political economy pressures that make competitiveness concerns a more salient regulatory concern. This amplifies the trade-offs along the trilemma, as private interests push for regulation to accommodate differences in national bank competitiveness through regulatory adjustments and institutional change. This has particularly been the case for the analyzed most recent period of financial integration, which has seem the mixing of the two formerly distinct archetypical bank- and market-based financial systems, which increased the substitutability of products between international universal banks.[88] My findings are balanced but more skeptical about the degree of actual regulatory cooperation due to the centrality of capital stringency regulation, where I find stronger divergence and in some cases a very strong lowering of standards over time due to competitiveness considerations (particularly in Ireland and Belgium). Also in activities and conglomerate restrictiveness the very important anchor country of UK followed by the United States exhibit de-regulatory trends, which resemble a race to the bottom-logic:

- Firstly, I find that *countries indeed interact and react to each others' regulatory institutions*. All three areas of regulation saw changes, which showed patterns that are consistent with strong international regulatory interaction based on competitiveness considerations. Of course, also the very negotiation of Basel I and II and now post-crisis also of Basel III is testament to the efforts towards cooperation due to the insight that financial stability externalities have increased to a level, where regulation within national confines no longer is a feasible alternative.
- Secondly, however, *the degree to which this regulatory cooperation has been* a real force for convergence *towards* a *higher level of regulation or instead been driven by a race-to-the-bottom logic differs by area of regulation*:
  - On the one hand there has been convergence and partial re-regulation mainly in the realms of *conglomerate and activity restrictions*. Countries have more or less converged around variants of the universal banking model, which allows some degree of financial conglomeration and engagement in lending as well as securities trading and real estate. For some countries, notably the UK and the United States, this represents a lowering of regulatory standards, as particularly the United States comes from a regulatory tradition with stricter activities regulation.
  - On the other hand there has been increasing divergence in the area of capital stringency definitions, which in some cases such as Ireland and Belgium has led to a very excessive de-regulation, consistent with a competitive laxity race. The table below summarizes this key finding in arguably the most central area of regulation for financial stability. Out of the countries that had a shock to competitiveness, as established here, only Spain 'leaned against the wind' in terms of requiring its banks to stick to a relatively strict definition of capital,

[88] Some analysts also find that there are implications for financial stability particularly for bank-based systems, since with the threat of dis-intermediation becoming more immiment, the ease of controlling financial stability through a limited number of financial intermediaries declines (R. G. Rajan & Zingales, 2002).

whilst all other countries accommodated the shock through some form of de-regulation in capital stringency. Given that Spain stands out as the least open and more profitable financial system out of the affected ones, this leaning against the wind was relatively easier than in the other affected countries. Thus, there is strong evidence that financial integration in the Euro Zone has led national regulators in the early 2000s to adopt a more accommodative regulatory stance, consistent with the trilemma, at the expense of financial stability considerations.

TABLE 20: *Regulatory reaction to shock to bank competitiveness*

		Regulatory reaction	
		Accommodate (institutional change as predicted)	*Leaning against the wind (institutional change stricter than predicted)*
Shock to competiti ve-ness	*None/ Weak*	Finland, Germany, Italy, Netherlands, Portugal	France
	Strong	Austria, Belgium, Ireland, Luxembourg	Spain

Source: Author

5
Committing to hawkishness? Time consistency problems in the interaction of banking supervision and monetary policy

"It is the highest impertinence and presumption, therefore, in kings and ministers to pretend to watch over the economy of private people, and to restrain their expense. They are themselves, always, and without any exception, the greatest spendthrifts in the society."

Adam Smith, The Wealth of Nations, 1776

"Had we tried to suppress the expansion of the subprime market, do you think that would have gone over very well with the Congress? When it looked as though we were dealing with a major increase in home ownership, which is of unquestioned value to society? Would we have been able to do that? I doubt it."

Alan Greenspan, Chairman of the Federal Reserve 1987-2006, CNBC-interview, 2011

In this chapter I want to expand the perspective of banking regulation in its dynamic context, looking at the interaction of monetary policy and banking supervision. Also, in this respect, as I have shown, the Euro Zone is truly 'sui generis'. It has a common currency and national banking regulation without very strong rules for the coordination of the two policy instruments. What this regulatory architecture of the Euro Zone fails to appreciate is the political *time consistency problem*, which the uncoordinated conduct of monetary policy and national banking regulation imposes on national supervisors. Good economics in an integrated monetary union requires supervisors *ex ante* to signal hawkishness; but *ex post,* when money is easy and the economy highly leveraged, democratic politics and bank lobby pressures can create insurmountable resistance. As regulators have to decide over regulatory policy throughout their national cycles of boom and bust, they will become subject to specific pressures that constrain their optimal actions, as the above quoted experience of Alan Greenspan in the lead up to the bubble of the housing bubble in the U.S. shows. With banking regulation as a national domain, such hawkish regulatory policy can easily become politically unviable. As a result, regulators will find it hard to muster the courage to break the leverage bubble in the face of strong domestic political resistance and will see leverage spiral out of control.

To solve potential problems of time inconsistency, institutions can be designed as a way of committing the regulator to a certain policy or regulatory paradigm (North & Weingast, 1989). This chapter analyzes in a comparative perspective how regulatory institutions have or have not been fit to respond to these dynamic challenges in different countries to learn more about the institutional trade-offs that regulators have to make. Particular focus rests on the demonstrated tension between commitment and flexibility (rules- vs. principles based supervision).

The argument developed is the following:

- Discretionary banking regulation, as under Basel II, suffers from *a time inconsistency problem*. A simple formal model shows that under discretion, that is without binding rules for the regulator, the regulator will find it hard to commit to a hawkish regulatory stance in the face of *private and political demands for increasing credit access*. The literature on leverage cycles and the political economy of credit access suggests a similar cyclical pattern, which implies that the costs of sticking to a pre-committed strategy of strict regulation will become too high at the point of decision, which again will lead to time inconsistent regulatory policy.
- Institutional responses to these time inconsistency problems can be conceptualized as consisting of *formal* and *informal constraints* on the regulator's policy choices. *Optimal institutional design* should reflect the factors specific to the national financial system and political and macro-economic environment that determine the trade-off between commitment and flexibility. Most importantly countries can install automatic rules-based stabilizers that require prompt corrective action by national regulators, when risks to financial stability are building up through for instance sharp increases in credit. However, very few Euro Zone countries have had these rules-based institutions place, thus, exposing the national regulators across the monetary union to asymmetric shocks to financial stability.
- *Empirical evidence* for the Euro Zone financial systems over the period from 2000 to 2007 confirms that *countries have indeed loosened their supervisory stringency in response to the asymmetric monetary temptations* (i.e., low real interest rates), which monetary union conferred upon them. Institutional indicators such as indicators of formal independence and legal accountability seem to have had very little restraining effects with the sole exception of actual limitations on the mandates of regulators in the form of stricter capital requirements rules (in the case of Spain). This suggests that the issue of time inconsistency of banking supervision is indeed a very relevant one and is all the more relevant, the less monetary policy and banking regulation are coordinated. Thus, the European model with national banking regulation and – for the Euro Zone countries – supranational monetary policy certainly hinders the national regulator's ability to commit to a hawkish policy stance in the face of tempting monetary conditions and the presence of private interests.

5.1 Rules, discretionary regulation, and supervisory commitment

This research, in line with the growing body of new political economy research , wants to endogenize the role of the government and the regulator. In doing so it needs to also account for the *dynamic* influences that enter the regulatory utility function, which was specified in the previous two chapters and is summarized by the trilemma. Political economy research in other policy areas has yielded more insights into the dynamics of economic policy-making, which have been framed with the concept of the *time consistency* of policy.

5.1.1 Defining time consistency problems

A policy can be defined as being time consistent, if the policy choice that was specified *ex ante* as optimal remains optimal *ex post* as well from the policy maker's point of view and will therefore still be pursued as intended at the point of decision (T Persson, 1987). Persson in a review of time consistency problems in other macro-economic contexts makes this instructive point very concisely and specifies the different dimensions that make time consistent policies a relevant policy problem (1987; p.2):

"Basically, the credibility problem arises for the following reason: Ex ante, before some choices have been made by the private sector (and maybe by another policymaker), an optimal policy induces some response of private behaviour. But ex post, after the choices have been made, the response to policy may be very different from the ex ante response, which makes the government's ex post constraints different from the ex ante constraints. Present some imperfection – an externality, a distortion, or a lack of policy instruments – which makes the ex ante optimal policy a 2nd best rather than a 1st best outcome, there is an ex post incentive to deviate from the ex ante optimal policy."

Banking regulation clearly runs the risk of being time inconsistent, since it suffers from all of the imperfections that Persson hints at: Most obviously, the pursuit of banking regulation's main objective of stability clearly has been shown to create many externalities. The effects of those externalities, specifically those on growth and bank competitiveness, raise the costs to what could - from a stability point of view – be considered an optimal policy. Even in the case when the ex ante formulated stability policy would take into account these externalities, a change in the relative costs to these externalities, which is beyond the control of the policy maker though, would make the policy suboptimal. Thus, time inconsistencies are very likely to occur in banking regulation.

Why does this time consistency of policy matter? The main reason is that the expectation towards policy induces other relevant actors such as private business (in this case banks and investors) and related policy makers (in this case mainly monetary policy makers) to make decisions on their course of actions, which are contingent on the likely policy pursued by the regulator: "*Forward-looking rational agents only believe a policy announcement that will be optimal to carry out ex post*" (T Persson, 1987; p.2). Thus, we have to show that indeed private actors as well as other policy actors do make relevant decisions based on their expectations towards the course of action the banking regulator has signaled to take. If we can show how these expectations matter for the optimality of policy, then the ability to conduct policy in a time consistent fashion is intimately related to the credibility of the decision-maker. Credibility of a sovereign policy maker though is always naturally limited, as Persson finds:

"If the government is able to make a binding precommitment to the ex ante optimal policy, the incentive to deviate ex post is immaterial. It is hard to think of situations where binding commitments can be enforced, however, because the government is by definition a sovereign decision maker. Therefore, those policies that would be optimal if binding commitments could be made, face a credibility problem because of the

incentive for ex post deviations. (...) Imposing credibility – in the sense of ex post optimality – adds an additional constraint to the government's policy problem, which in general implies welfare losses (in terms of the government objective function) relative to the ex ante optimal policy" (T Persson, 1987; p.2).

To resolve this credibility problem, independent institutions – amongst other things - have been suggested as a commitment device for policy makers (Barro & Gordon, 1983; K. Rogoff, 1985). The political economy work by North and Weingast (1989) have defined institutions in general to serve as commitment devices that ensure that time-varying discount rates of government do not lead to suboptimal policy-making by the sovereign:

"(...) while parties may have strong incentives to strike a bargain, their incentives after the fact are not always compatible with maintaining the agreement: compliance is always a problem. (...) Problems of compliance can be reduced or eliminated when the institutions are carefully chosen so as to match the anticipated incentive problems. (...) to succeed in this role, a constitution must arise from the bargaining context between the state and constituents such that its provisions carefully match the potential enforcement problems among the relevant parties. The constitution must be self-enforcing in the sense that the major parties have an incentive to abide by the bargain after its made" (North & B.R. Weingast, 1989; p.817).

Thus, the criteria for a solution are clearly specified: All actors in the game must be playing a dominant strategy such that the desired policy outcome is a Nash Equilibrium ex ante as well as ex post. Institutions can be employed to ensure that this is the case. It is in this sense that I analyze the design of the national and European level regulatory institutions.

5.1.2 Sources of time consistency problems in banking regulation

In order to systematically understand the way that time consistency problems arise and how they are dealt with, the following will now sketch out the specific way in which time consistency problems in banking regulation arise to depict how the strategic interaction between market participants and policy makers determines the outcomes that result from this. To understand the sources of time inconsistency in banking regulation we can first turn to the sources of such inconsistencies in monetary policy, which Goodhart describes as belonging to two categories: *"The case for central bank independence is based on two intellectual concepts. (...) The first is the 'no-trade-off' vertical longer-term Phillips curve. (...) The second is the concept of the political business cycle."* Thus, the inability of monetary policy to influence employment in the long-run as well as political interests in re-election that endanger the pursuit in the public interest of low inflation in the short-term are at odds and therefore make monetary policy potentially subject to time inconsistent behaviour. Two structurally similar sources of interests against financial stability can be identified for the case of banking regulation and will be discussed in turn.

Banks' interests

Firstly, banking regulators are subject to the *demand of private actors* such as banks that face shocks to their competitiveness and pose demands for laxer regulation. The variance of their demands over time comes from the change in the competitive environment as financial systems move through their *boom and bust cycles*, such cycles increasingly translate from markets to banks, as the latter are more invested in securities that are marked to market. Financial crises and the relative laxity of regulation preceding them are a recurring phenomenon these days just as excessive inflation preceding elections was in the 1970s. This recurring general pattern of financial bubbles and crises and the mania underlying them has been aptly described in the masterful work by Charles Kindleberger (2005; p.10):

"The feature of these manias are never identical and yet there is a similar pattern. The increase in prices of commodities or real estate or stocks is associated with euphoria; household wealth increases and so does spending. There is a sense of 'We never had it so good.' Then the asset prices peak, and then begin to decline. The implosion of a bubble has been associated with declines in the prices of commodities, stocks and real estate, and often these declines have been associated with a crash or a financial crisis. Some financial crises were preceded a rapid increase in the indebtedness of one or several groups of borrowers rather than by a rapid increase in the price of an asset or a security."

Financial instability is thus a recurring pattern that tends to have large macro-economic consequences, as it is often based on a general, widespread euphoria reflected in borrowers' decision-making. One of the key driving factors behind bubbles and manias is the growth of credit or, expressed in relation to the assets held, leverage (Kindleberger, 2005; p.10/ 55):

" (...) The cycle of manias and panics results from the pro-cyclical changes in the supply of credit; the credit supply increases relatively rapidly in good times, and then when economic growth slackens, the rate of growth of credit has often declined sharply. (...) During the economic expansions investors become increasingly optimistic and more eager to pursue profit opportunities that will pay off in the distant future while the lenders become less risk-averse. Rational exuberance morphs into irrational exuberance. (...) In the last hundred or so years the expansion of credit has been almost exclusively through the banks and the financial system; earlier, non-bank lenders expanded the supply of credit."

Thus, the build-up of leverage through excessive credit provision should be seen as one of the key drivers of manias, which exacerbate the cyclical nature of economic growth. This cyclical nature of credit and investment is closely related to the Minsky model, which argues that based on an exogenous positive shock to the macro-economy the outlooks and profit opportunities expand. Based on such optimism, the speculative share of finance increases and eventually busts as the economy slows again. Regulators will find it hard to spoil this optimism, since they will ultimately have to regulate this 'excessive leverage'. Anecdotal evidence from central bank governors illustrates this dynamic with the private sector. A former chairman of the Fed is being cited by Kindleberger (2005; p.80) in relation to this phenomenon as having been *"reluctant to take the 'punch bowl away from the party just as the party is getting going' because of the unfavorable public reactions."*

Political interests

Secondly, next to investors and borrowers, demands for leverage banking regulators are subject to the *demands of political actors* that want to use credit-fueled growth and booms to build their political support base and are therefore strongly opposed to hawkish policies that could reduce the growth dynamic. As an example of such policy, the governor of the Bank of Japan regulated Japanese banks in 1990 to limit lending to real estate loans, since the real estate market had been growing excessively in prices and leverage. The result of that policy was the bursting of the Japanese real estate bubble and with that a long period of recession and stagnation. This constitutes the first source of time inconsistency, since the costs for sticking to a hawkish policy stance through cycles are almost prohibitively high for most regulators. To illustrate this, it is instructive to see how Alan Greenspan commented with reference to the political game that even the independent Fed played along with in the lead up to the subprime market financial crisis of 2007/8 that saw credit and leverage spin out of control:

"The presumption that you could incrementally diffuse a bubble was a fantasy. Clearly, you cannot diffuse these things unless you hit them right on the head and break the economy - essentially, break the potential profitability that is engendering that sort of stuff. [Is there anything we could have done] to break the bubble? Yes, we could have. We could have basically clamped down on the American economy, generated a 10% unemployment rate and I will guarantee you we would not have had a housing boom, a stock market boom, or indeed a particularly good economy either" (CNBC, 2011).

These costs increase particularly, when the credit expansion takes place in a sector of the economy that provides benefits that are socially and politically valuable. As these benefits to society become perceived more widely by the public, the costs to clamping down on credit expansion become too large to bear for the regulator. As Rajan finds for the the case of the United States in the most recent financial crisis (2010; p.31): *"...eventually public support for housing credit was so widespread that few regulators, if any, dared oppose it."* Conceptually, thus one can think of credit towards political constituents or socially desirable objectives as the banking sector's ability to make side payments. As their own benefits increase through additional lending in a growing market segment, politicians receive side payments as they have a new lever to achieve higher levels of social utility at any given public budget. Politicians and bankers thus enter an alliance that comes at the cost of long-run stability. The strength of these interests combined makes it prohibitively costly for the regulator to stick to a hawkish regulatory policy stance. Credit has certain features that make it an attractive instrument of economic policy, as Rajan analyzes:

"Politicians love to have banks expand housing credit, for credit achieves many goals at the same time. It pushes up house prices, making households feel wealthier, and allows them to finance more consumption. It creates more profits and jobs in the financial sector as well as in real estate brokerage and housing construction. And everything is safe – as safe as houses – at least for a while. Easy credit has large, positive, immediate, and widely distributed benefits whereas the costs all lie in the future. It has a payoff structure that is precisely the one desired by politicians, which is why so many countries have succumbed to its lure."

This phenomenon becomes particularly relevant when one examines the dynamic that is implied by the above account: As politically induced credit becomes more widespread and drives up asset prices artificially, which as shown in the introduction was the case for certain Euro Zone countries with low real interest rates, the alliance for keeping credit high and supervisory action 'light-touch' becomes stronger and creates a real political barrier that becomes very difficult for regulators to cross. We can confirm this political economy hypothesis, looking again at a very instructive comment by the former Fed Chairman Greenspan, quoted also in the introduction of this chapter, regarding the Fed's ability to prevent excessive optimism in the subprime lending market from building up trough timely intervention:

"Had we tried to suppress the expansion of the subprime market, do you think that would have gone over very well with the Congress? When it looked as though we were dealing with a major increase in home ownership, which is of unquestioned value to society? Would we have been able to do that? I doubt it" (CNBC, 2011).

In a nutshell, capitalist financial systems inevitably produce manias, however, regulation plays an important role in mediating between mania and crisis. When it fails to engage in regulatory forbearance to prevent potential excesses from taking the financial system over the edge. This will be all the more the case, the larger the policy maker's role is in shaping economic outcomes, that is, the larger her discretion in formulating economic policy or regulation. In terms of the trilemma concept this implies that regulators under the increased discretion of the 'supervisory approach' will likely find it hard to commit to an overly stability-focused regulatory approach, when outside temptations (e.g., easing monetary conditions) impact dynamically and can be anticipated by private actors, who then incorporate this into their own strategy.

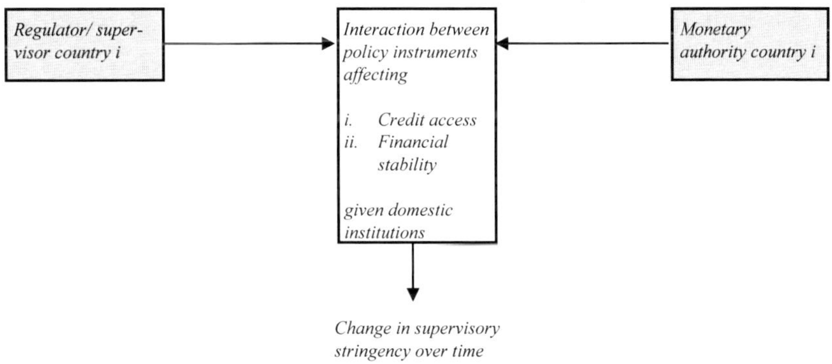

FIGURE 30: *Time inconsistent supervision of banks over time along the trilemma*

Source: Author

Regulatory discretion after Basel II

What is key to the commitment and time consistency problems that are assumed is the fundamental change that banking regulation and supervision underwent in recent years with financial globalization and the regulatory response that Basel II gave as a result. Basel II reacted to the increasing complexity and, as some argue, to the rising competition between financial centers by moving towards a more discretionary regulatory approach, in which the supervisory pillar took a more central role. Internal ratings methods took center-stage and would be supervised by regulatory authorities, which would focus their efforts mainly on the largest risks as well as the risk management techniques of banks. As a post-crisis IMF Staff Note reflecting on the nature of good supervision puts it:

"Supervision was (...) moving toward a greater recognition of banks' own methods to manage risks in meeting regulatory requirements. Basel II, in particular, was a landmark in its increased acceptance of banks' own internal models, spurred by advances in risk-modeling techniques. Thus, large and complex depository institutions with strong risk management were permitted greater use of their own methods to assess risks and accordingly determine the regulatory capital they needed to hold. What often is forgotten is that this ability was neither unrestricted nor permanent—Basel II also mainstreamed the three-pillar approach, articulating what was a very sound supervisory philosophy: that sound regulation (Pillar 1) had to be accompanied by strong supervision and risk management (Pillar 2) and complemented by strong market discipline (Pillar 3) to be effective" (Viñals, Fiechter, Kumhof, Laxton, & Muir, 2010, p.8).

Yet, the new emphasis, which in practice regulators laid on the supervision element and the internal assessment of required capital led to a new dynamic game of regulation and supervision, which is argued in the following to have made the time consistency problems more relevant and severe: Regulation and supervision now, with the added discretion of Basel II due to the numerous ways of reducing one's capital requirements, has to be credible to be effective: What is regulated or signaled at one point in time, has to be implemented when supervised at another point in time. The key to regulation now becomes the credibility of the supervisor and the way that this influences the banks' setting of its capital through its internal ratings.

Based on this observation, the following section formalizes the described nature of strategic interaction between the regulator and private actors. The game is assumed to consist of four stages including a chance move as depicted in the figure below. At the heart of the game is the observation that banking regulation and supervision really is a sequential and thus dynamic policy task. Regulators can set regulations and signal their regulatory stance at one point in time but ultimately work through the stringency of the supervision that they apply at a later point in time. These two policy stances can differ. Thus, regulation and supervision usually take place at separate times and under different circumstances, which is key to the results of this game. It is assumed that banking supervision is a 'discretionary' task. This has particularly become more relevant with the Basel II introduction of the 'supervisory approach', which has put supervision at the center of the regulatory practice and which – through many special regulations and exceptions – has allowed banks to keep much lower capital than the

8% capital adequacy requirements spelled out in the original agreements. The implication of these exceptions is that there is more leeway for banking supervisors to actually determine the amount of capital to be held under such a 'discretionary' regime. Thus, banking supervision as exercised at the point in time of supervision rather than regulation alone determines the actual level of capital held.

5.1.3 Banking supervision as a dynamic strategic interaction game

Specifying the game

How does this translate into a game-theoretical depiction of 'discretionary' regulation?[89] This game is dynamic and consists of two periods and a chance move by nature:

> **Stage 1:** The regulator can send a signal about her regulatory stringency in period 2 to banks to influence their expectations of the level of risk, in this case reflected by leverage held, they will be allowed to take.
>
> **Stage 2:** Then, nature (in the case of the Euro Zone for instance the ECB) determines a factor affecting the level of private interest, such as credit availability, in period 2, as indicated by the value of the parameter θ, which however is unknown to the regulator in period 1.
>
> **Stage 3:** At this stage banks then based on the observation of the true value of θ make up their minds about their expectations of leverage they will be allowed to hold, as denoted by L^e.
>
> **Stage 4:** Finally, after that but still in the same period, regulators observe the state of the private interest parameter θ and set actual regulatory stringency through capital adequacy to regulate leverage.

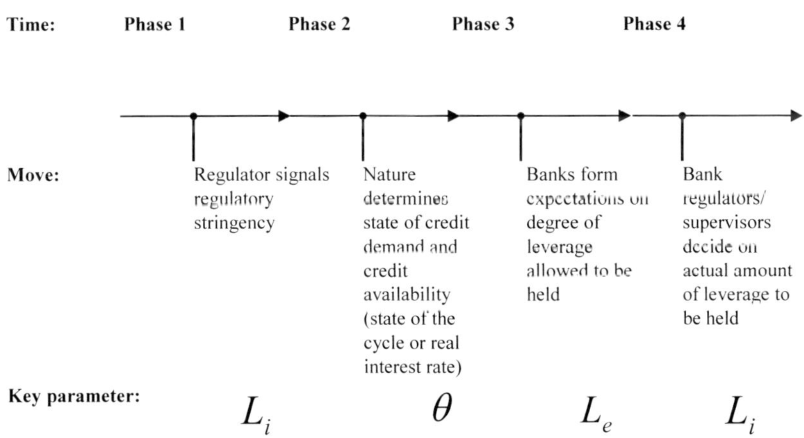

FIGURE 31: *Banking regulation and supervision as a dynamic commitment game*

[89] For a definitional paper on these issues in game theory see Klein & O'Flaherty (1993).

Whether or not the signal by the regulator in stage 1 will actually influence expectations of course depends on the ability to commit to such a time consistent policy stance. The conditions for that will be discussed later.

The game in extensive form looks as in the figure below. To specify this game more clearly we need to define a few key relationships. We shall assume the regulatory utility function based on the trilemma – that is one that needs to trade off the financial stability objective with another objective such as in this case credit availability. The disutility or cost function of the regulator therefore looks as follows (see Chapter 2 for a discussion and derivation of this function):

$$DisU_{regulatori} = \alpha_i L_i^2 + (1-\alpha_i)\varepsilon(P_i - P^e)^2 \qquad (5.1)$$

Actual private interest or credit availability is defined by the following equation:

$$P_i = \theta P^e + b(L_i - L^e) \qquad (5.2)$$

Here θ constitutes negative shocks to private interests, such as an asymmetric monetary policy shock or other factors affecting credit demand and availability, and is restricted to the range of values from >0 to 1. That is, actual private interests, that is credit demand/ availability P_i, deviates from expected private interest whenever $\theta <$ 1. The second term reflects the role that leverage, and with that regulation affecting levels of leverage (such as capital adequacy levels) has on this private interest in credit availability: As leverage goes beyond the level of leverage expected by banks already, credit availability is stimulated by an amount of b for each unit of L_i. Thus, the regulator is assumed to have a lever to stimulate bank lending with, which derives from being laxer on supervision and leverage enforcement than expected.

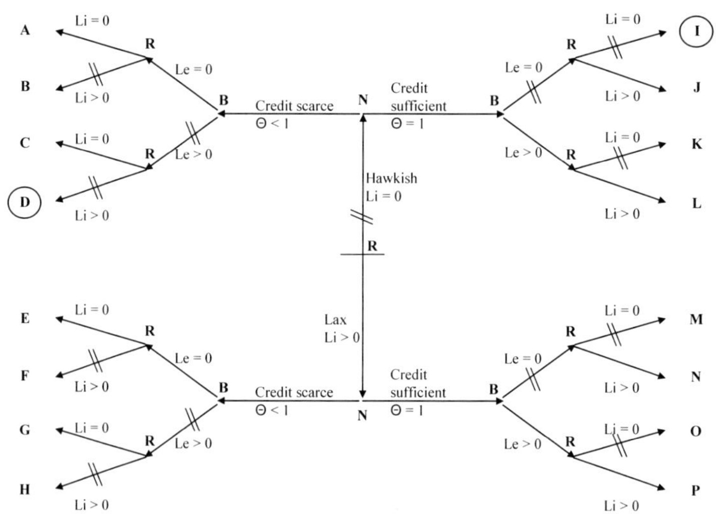

FIGURE 32: *Banking supervision as a dynamic commitment game with discretionary supervision*

The question that we have to answer with this game is whether or not the regulator can commit to a 'hawkish' policy that ensures financial stability across business cycles and varying levels credit scarcity. This strategy would imply that the regulator would play a strategy of ($L_i = 0, L_i = 0$), that she would announce and stick to a 'hawkish' policy of allowing no excess leverage above and beyond what is considered acceptable leverage. In terms of the above game this implies that the possible outcomes, contingent on bank expectations and credit scarcity, are A, C, I, and K, whereas the other outcomes (B, D, J, and L) cannot result. Yet, this simple commitment strategy is not time consistent, simply because the state of the economy that is unknown in stage one influences the best response of the supervisor when such a commitment has to be made, which leads to the following proposition:

Proposition 1: *Given that regulators have to trade off their financial stability objective with another objective (as in 5.1) that they care about ($\alpha < 1$) and that they can influence with the stringency of regulation/ supervision (as in 5.2), the following time consistency problem can be diagnosed: The optimal ex ante level of excess leverage and stringency of supervision is $L_i = 0$, yet, the optimal equilibrium ex post level of excess leverage is $L_i > 0$, when we assume that there can be negative shocks to credit availability (as with credit scarcity and $\theta < 1$ at times). Formally I propose that there are sequentially rational situations, when the disutility of pursuing this strategy is higher than other strategies, or formally the following inequality holds:*

$$DisU_{regulatori}(L_i = 0, L_i = 0) > DisU_{regulatori}(L = 0, L > 0) \qquad (5.3)$$

Solving the game

How do we solve this game to derive the possibility of a time consistent strategy for the regulator? As usual in dynamic games, we shall apply backwards induction and start with the action of the regulator in stage 4.

Stage 4: If we plug equation (5.2) into equation (5.1), we have the optimization problem that the regulator is faced with in this stage of the game:

$$DisU_{regulatori} = \alpha_i L_i^2 + (1-\alpha_i)\varepsilon\left[(\theta - 1)P^e + b(L_i - L^e)\right]^2 \qquad (5.4)$$

Minimizing this function by using the partial derivative with respect to P_i gives us the optimal stringency of supervision in this stage given all other parameters as follows:

$$L_i = \frac{(1-\alpha)\varepsilon b}{\alpha + (1-\alpha)b^2}\left[bL^e + (1-\theta)P^e\right] \qquad (5.5)$$

Hence, we can see that the level of stringency of capital regulation, L_i , depends on a few factors: Firstly and obviously, stringency of regulation varies with the relative preferences and costs attached to each policy objective. As α , i.e. the cost of instability and increasing leverage, goes up, the degree of leverage allowed for banks goes down. Secondly, whenever there is a shock to private interest from for instance relatively too tight monetary conditions, that is $\theta < 1$, ceteris paribus excess leverage will go up. Thirdly, if the economy is in a downturn, the higher the level of expected credit, P^e, the higher will be the excess leverage required to compensate for the lower leverage induced by the exogenous factor (e.g., ECB interest rate policy). Fourthly, ceteris paribus the higher the leverage expected, the higher the excess leverage that regulators will allow for. Lastly, as the benefit parameter *b*, that is the propensity of banks to turn excess leverage into credit, goes up, the total excess leverage required goes down, which is intuitive.

Stage 3: The next step will be for the rational bank to derive this expected behaviour by the regulator in stage 4 and to equate its own leverage expectations L_e with the optimal supervision policy by the regulator as specified in equation (5.5):

$$L^e = \frac{(1-\alpha)\varepsilon b}{\alpha + (1-\alpha)b^2}\left[bL^e + (1-\theta)P^e\right] = L_i \tag{5.6}$$

Re-arranging this term yields the optimal and only rational set of expectations that banks can hold in stage 3 regarding the likely stringency of supervision and resulting degree of permissible leverage for them to hold, which is:

$$L^e = \frac{(1-\alpha)\varepsilon b}{\alpha}\left[(1-\theta)P^e\right] \tag{5.7}$$

The key finding about this equation is that next to some key know parameters (the nature of preferences, the propensity of regulation to influence credit, and credit expectations) the expectations about banks crucially depend on the state of the economy θ.

Stage 2: What happens then in different states of the world, that is, different levels of the private interest for credit availability under discretionary supervision?

If the economy is in equilibrium on its *natural credit demand path*, that is $\theta = 1$, excess leverage in the economy will be zero, that is the above equation (5.7) becomes 0 as does equation (5.1). Hence, as borrowers have access to funds and banks are lending as expected, the regulator can stick to the regulated level of leverage and excess leverage beyond this remains zero and the regulator has no disutility:

$$DisU_{regulatori} = 0 \tag{5.8}$$

As the economy goes towards *boom* and credit becomes scarce, that is $\theta < 1$, equation (5.7) becomes positive (assuming of course that $\alpha > 0$, $b > 0$, and $P^e > 0$), which implies that some excess leverage is expected. This implies that it is never rational for banks to expect the regulator to stick to a strict stability policy, which would entail $L_e = 0$, in all states of the economy under a discretionary supervisory policy regime. In other words, the outcomes A and B in the extensive game can never be subgame perfect Nash equilibria, since they require the banks to hold an irrational belief given their knowledge of the regulator's utility function. Putting it intuitively: In the last stage, when the state of the exogenous shock is known, regulators will always want to stabilize credit availability by stimulating additional credit through a somewhat laxer supervisory policy. Anticipating this, banks will already expect higher leverage to be 'legitimate' under the discretionary regime. Thus, with perfect information about the regulator's inclinations and preferences as well as with knowledge of the state of the exogenous factor and monetary conditions, banks can anticipate this in their own regulatory strategy and leverage policy. Hence, we will see higher leverage expected and therefore the benefits from increasing leverage will be dissipated again, yet, the costs of instability remain for the regulator. The disutility for the regulator in the case of bust will be

$$DisU_{regulatori} = a\left[\frac{(1-a)\varepsilon b}{a}(1-\theta)P^e\right]^2 + b\left(\theta P^e - P^e\right)^2 \qquad (5.9)$$

The first term indicates the costs of having excess leverage, which rise with the known parameters and are positive as soon as θ <1, which is the case any time the private interest level is off the equilibrium or expected path. The second term indicates the positive costs from having credit availability below the equilibrium, which now – with bank expectations already equal to the amount of leverage made available by supervisors – can no longer help out of the slump. In essence, adaptive expectations dissipate the gains from such an excess leverage policy. Thus, higher leverage results under the discretionary supervisory regime due to rational expectations.

Stage 1: Going back to stage 1, what does this result imply for the regulator in terms of defining a time consistent policy stance? What we have shown is that with the possibility of a downturn, it is not *sequentially rational* for the regulator to play the strategy of ($L_i = 0, L_i = 0$) that we specified as a 'hawkish' strategy. This is because the regulator cannot stick to her announcement in all states of the world, when θ <1, since in those cases her disutility from sticking to the hawkish strategy is higher then the disutility for allowing some excess leverage. Hence, our proposition 7 could be shown to hold. Equation (5.7) applied to situations A and C shows that they are not possible outcomes, yet, they lie on the path of a hawkish strategy by the regulator. Hence, we can indeed identify a hawkish strategy of the regulator to be time inconsistent, contingent on course on the values of the parameters as specified in equation (5.7), which we will return to.

Of course we could specify alternative time consistent strategies that the regulator could stick to even under a discretionary supervisory regime. A time consistent strategy would be one that would make explicit the variation of the degree of stringency with the state of the economy: As such, a regulator could specify that she would pursue a zero-excess-leverage policy in all good states of the economy and would pursue a positive-excess-leverage policy in all bad states of the economy. Yet, one has to assume that a regulator would always assign some cost to announcing a non-hawkish policy, given that its mandate has a clear focus on preserving stability. Hence, this cost (which is not modeled here but intuitive) as well as the fact that all 'constructive ambiguity' about its likely course of action would clearly prevent them from pursuing such a policy, even if it were time consistent. Hence, we can dismiss any regulatory policy announcements that would entail the admission to a 'lax' regulatory style under certain conditions as non-feasible. Instead regulators can then only pursue a hawkish if however time inconsistent policy.

5.1.4 Conclusion: Discretionary versus rules-based supervision

We have seen that, ceteris paribus, the discretionary regime leads banks to anticipate higher levels of 'legitimate' excess leverage, which the regulator cannot credibly commit to avoiding. The result is socially suboptimal, since higher leverage and financial instability than desirable are the consequence. In the absence of a binding contract there is a suboptimal policy equilibrium, which private actors anticipate correctly.

What are ways out of this time inconsistency problem of discretionary supervision? The literature on time consistency problems in policy-making suggests two different types of responses (T Persson, 1987; Torsten Persson & Tabellini, 2002): Firstly, repeated games may add a reputational dimension to regulators' disutility function, which will then make the optimal outcome a possible equilibrium outcome. As private actors can observe past behaviour by the supervisors they can adjust their future beliefs and therefore 'punish' the supervisor for deviating from announcements. When the private sector adjusts strongly enough and supervisors care about the future (have a low discount rate) as well as about financial stability strongly enough, a more optimal outcome from a stability point of view can be created. The caveat of this solution to the time consistency problem is that such perfect information on the supervisor's actions in all supervised banks is very unlikely to prevail. It is more credible that the banks can know about the general utility function of the supervisor, but it is less easy to imagine that they will have knowledge of every supervisory policy decision made with different banks that are 'in trouble' and might have received laxer treatment.

However, the second theoretical alternative seems applicable: This option would be a rules-based regime, which would decide the supervisory stringency at stage 4 based on a clear rule rather than on a discretionary assessment of the optimal course of action. What would this rule entail? Naturally the regulator would optimize her disutility function (5.1) by setting $L_i = 0$ (the lower half of the decision tree in the figure below), which minimizes disutility. Hence, the optimal rule would prescribe a 'hawkish' strategy as follows: ($L_i = 0$, $L_i = 0$). Under such a rule naturally the bank would anticipate that the regulator would be unimpressed by any deviation of credit availability from the natural path and would have to set its expectations equal to the new rule, that is $L_e = 0$. From a public good and welfare point of view this regulator would clearly achieve higher levels of financial stability by minimizing excess leverage at every point in time regardless of the state of credit availability, as the below graph clearly shows in the outcomes A and I, which from a stability point of view are clearly more optimal (see figure below).

Rules-based supervision becomes more attractive the larger the costs of the theoretically derived time inconsistency problems are. We have seen that the size of the time consistency problem, that is the size of excess leverage in different states of the economy, is contingent on the following factors, as specified in equation (5.7):

$$L^e = \frac{(1-\alpha)\varepsilon b}{\alpha}\left[(1-\theta)P^e\right] \qquad (5.7)$$

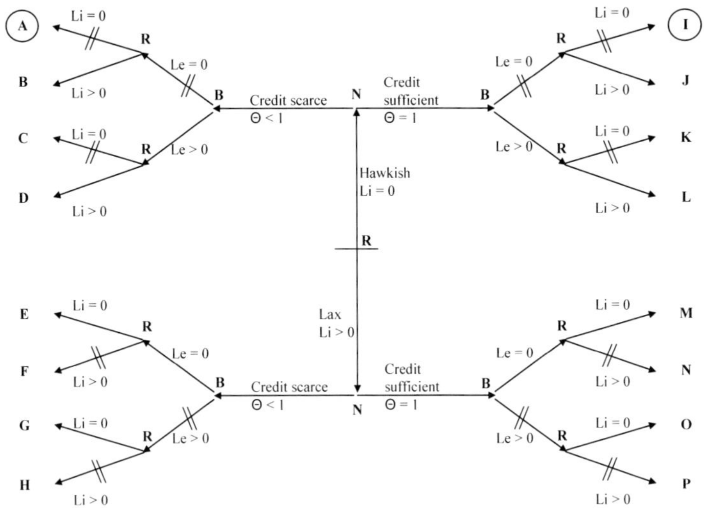

FIGURE 33: *Banking supervision as a dynamic commitment game with rules-based supervision*

Hence, time consistency problems bringing about higher excess leverage are more likely to result when certain factors in a country's financial system behave in such a way that the left-side term increases. This leads us to the next proposition, to be analyzed and verified empirically:

Proposition 2: *Banking supervisors will be less credible and able to commit to a 'hawkish' policy stance, when*

- α *is small, that is the perceived cost of having instability is small, which can derive from public interests in stability being weak or weakly organized*
- $(1-\alpha)$ *is large, that is the perceived cost of deviating from the expected level of credit availability is high, which can derive from private interests being strong or strongly organized and/ or private actors*
- *b is large, that is the propensity of excess leverage to be turned into credit is high, which could be seen as depending on the share of lending in bank assets*
- θ *is significantly smaller than 0, that is there is scarce credit due to high demand or low availability (e.g., because of monetary tightening)*
- P^e *is relatively high, that is the expected level of credit required to keep bank-dependent borrowers such as households and SMEs afloat is relatively high*

Based on this, we would expect to see more attempts to institutionalize a rules-based, credible supervisory regime in financial systems with these characteristics. Credible institutions could act as contracts between the supervisor and the banks, which would create shared expectations of a low-leverage policy in different states of credit scarcity.

This section has established theoretically why and when the time consistency and related credibility problem in banking supervision requires an institutional fix. Whether or not the time consistency problems materialize through higher systemic risks and excess leverage depends on the balance of political and economic factors, which we have identified:

- On the one hand are the temptation variables that tempt the regulator to be lax, which comprises the financial system and the economy's credit-reliance as well as exogenous policy factors such as monetary policy and its varying effect in an asymmetric monetary union with varying inflation rates such as the Euro Zone.
- On the other hand are the institutional factors such as the independence of the regulators, the clarity of the mandate, its accountability and resources.

The following sections will examine empirically to what extent these factors have been prevalent in the different countries and how the resulting balance that regulators struck has led to the differential build-up of systemic risks in the run-up to the 2007/8 financial crisis.

5.2 Asymmetric leverage temptations in a non-optimum currency area

5.2.1 Asymmetric ECB monetary policy effects on credit growth

To establish the particular cost of pursuing such a hawkish policy, we need to establish the degree of temptation and the nature of private interest that countries are exposed to in the time period under analysis. The derived results show that next to the features of the financial system, which have already been analyzed in previous chapters, there are certain exogenous factors relating to economic policy and cyclical credit reliance, which can affect the degree to which supervisory bodies are 'tempted' to regulate leverage more laxly. The main exogenous factor that shapes the degree of credit availability is the real interest rate, which by definition is composed of the nominal interest rate and the rate of inflation. In the context of a monetary union, the interest rate of course is set by the common central bank, while the rate of inflation is determined by other national idiosyncrasies such as the business cycle, growth, and wage-setting institutions. When a currency union does not fulfill the criteria of an optimal currency area perfectly, real interest rates can vary. Mundell specified his optimal currency area as an area, where the regions would be symmetrically affected by exogenous shocks and otherwise have a high mobility of the factors of production, namely labour and capital, to adjust to differences for instance in employment and productivity across the region (Mundell, 2007). Since the Euro Zone does not have full flexibility of labour, differences in inflation and output can persist across economies for some time, leaving the countries of the Euro Zone subjected to asymmetric monetary shocks of either too loose-fitting or too tight monetary policy. This phenomena of 'one size fits none' interest rates (Enderlein, 2005) therefore assigns a special role to banking regulation as an adjustment instrument to counter the otherwise excessive lending through targeted interventions and 'leaning against the wind' in case of excessively loose monetary policy effects.

To do so empirically, I establish the varying monetary conditions imposed by one central monetary policy in a non-optimum currency area such as the Euro Zone by calculating actual *average real interest rate levels* for each country, using the average rate of inflation across the different financial systems of the Euro Zone and the corresponding ECB nominal interest rates for the years from 2000 to 2006. The figure below shows the national credit growth and real interest rates for the Euro Zone countries. A look at the close correlation between confirms the importance of *real* interest rates in the monetary transmission mechanism, as theory would suggest as well as the asymmetry of the supervisory challenge across the Euro Zone. In some countries such as Germany with very high real interest rates and banks are facing have relatively lower credit demand, since lending is relatively unattractive at these rates. In other countries such as Portugal, Greece, Spain, and Ireland with lower real interest rates demand for credit is likely to be much higher, increasing the costs of maintaining a committed policy stance and a certain leverage ratio, since economic growth in those countries can very easily be stimulated by providing more credit at low real cost to borrowers. Interestingly Finland stands out somewhat with a relatively higher rate of credit growth given the high real interest rates it has faced. The price paid in this case of course is the risk to financial stability that goes along with extending excessive credit to the private sector, which can turn this growth into a bubble.

The extent to which institutional precautions and automatic regulatory stabilizers were in place to prevent this will be established in the next section.

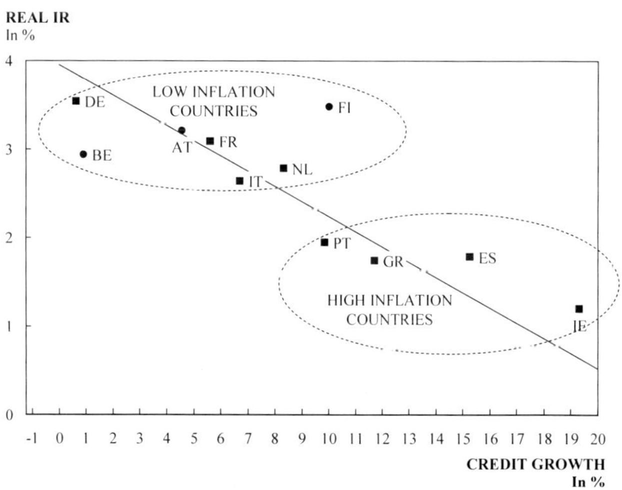

FIGURE 34: *Asymmetric monetary conditions in the Euro Zone 2000-2006*

Source: Author based on ECB data

5.2.2 The institutional fitness of Euro Zone supervisory bodies

As the previous analysis has shown, the most important factor in preventing excessive leverage in easy monetary times is the credibility of being independent enough from private and political interests to pursue such a rule in the face of resistance. It is this independence that lies behind good banking supervision, which an IMF publication on certain best practices fittingly defines as "learning to say No". This guide to the making of supervision identifies as the key to good supervision, which can be strengthened if *"society must stand with supervisors as they play their role as naysayers in times of exuberance"*. Such a supervisor then would be *"intrusive, skeptical, proactive, comprehensive, adaptive, and conclusive"* (Viñals, Fiechter, Kumhof, Laxton, & Muir, 2010, p.4). Analytically we can depict such an independent bank supervisor as a way of credibly signaling to the markets a higher α , that is a higher disutility attached to the creation of excess leverage due to a clearer mandate for financial stability and a clear willingness to stick to it.[90] Thus, credible institutions from a political economy perspective clearly are a key element in creating credible commitments (North & B.R. Weingast, 1989).

However, how does the regulator in practice establish such credibility in banking supervision? Based on my game-theoretical model, only *rules for supervisory action* can act as powerful commitment devices, even in the absence of full independence of the regulator. The practical political economy reasoning for such *rules* has been provided elsewhere by Borio (2010):

"The main advantage of rules is that, once in place, they do not require continuous justification or explicit decisions. If well structured, they can thus act as automatic stabilisers. They can also act as effective pre-commitment devices, relieving supervisors from what can be overwhelming political economy pressures not to take action: in the cross-sectional dimension, on fair competition grounds; in the time dimension, to keep enjoying an apparently endless boom. Moreover, the temptation to believe that "this time things are different" can be very powerful for everyone, including the authorities themselves (eg, Reinhardt and Rogoff (2009), Borio (2007a))."

Such credibility of rules is an important political economy component as it stiffens the backbone of the regulator to get involved in the face of political economy pressures to remain an uninvolved bystander.

Micro-prudential rules

The degree of micro-prudential credibility of supervisors can be broken down into two components: Firstly, the extent of supervisory powers relating to prompt corrective action (PCA) capabilities, that enable allowing regulators to enforce capital requirements more strictly; Secondly, the degree of forbearance or discretion that the supervisor is afforded in triggering these prompt corrective actions, with lower discretion increasing credibility. To measure these capabilities across countries I again

---

[90] Viñals et al. break down the required institutional components of such a credible supervisor along the two elements that enable prudent supervision: Firstly, such a supervisor must have the 'ability to act' and, secondly, the 'willingness to act' - an analytically useful distinction, which reflects in an intuitive way the findings of my model as well.

turn to the World Bank dataset on regulation and supervision (Barth et al., 2006), using the data from the 1999/2000 survey, since these institutional arrangements were in place for the time period analyzed (the later survey only took place in 2004/5 at the very end of the period analyzed).

For *prompt corrective action enforcement capabilities* I construct an index using the survey responses gathered across countries.[91] This index relates to the capabilities that regulators have to ensure that bank capital grows commensurate with bank lending, which goes to the core of the time inconsistency problems described. The index measures i) if failure to abide by a cease-desist type order can lead to automatic civil and penal sanctions on the directors and managers of a bank; ii) whether the supervisory authorities can order a bank's management to increase provisions to cover actual or potential losses; iii) whether the supervisory authorities can force a bank to change its internal organizational structure; whether the supervisory authorities can suspend the directors' decision to distribute iv) dividends, v) bonuses, vi) and management fees.

For *forbearance* I construct an index that assesses whether supervisors i) can forbear certain prudential regulations; ii) whether solvency deterioration below certain pre-established levels automatically lead to intervention; iii) whether infraction of any prudential regulation identified by a supervisor must immediately be reported; iv) whether there are mandatory actions in these cases.

Joining the two dimensions, we can now assess the Euro Zone countries' supervisory enforcement structure for its credibility. The below graph maps the countries in both dimensions. The assessment of the forbearance dimensions suggests that with the exception of Spain and Austria and to a lesser extent the Netherlands, Italy, and Greece, regulators in the Euro Zone still had substantial discretion over their supervisory enforcement decisions. With respect to PCA enforcement powers only Austria, and to a lesser extent Belgium, and Finland stand out as relatively powerful supervisors. All in all, we see a pattern of countries either relying on high prompt corrective action powers with some supervisory discretion in applying it, or on more limited correction powers but low supervisory discretion in applying it. Austria remains the one exception with very strong capabilities that are also enforced without much regulatory discretion. Germany on the other hand seems to have least enforcement capabilities along with very high discretion.

Thus, judging from this assessment it seems that with the exception of Austria the Euro Zone countries were institutionally not fit to withstand the temptation of easy monetary policy and credit-fueled growth, as supervisors were either not given all required corrective action powers or were given too much discretion in applying them, therefore subjecting them to high political economy pressures in a boom.

---

91 This index in this form is also used by Brewer III, Kaufman, and Wall (2008).

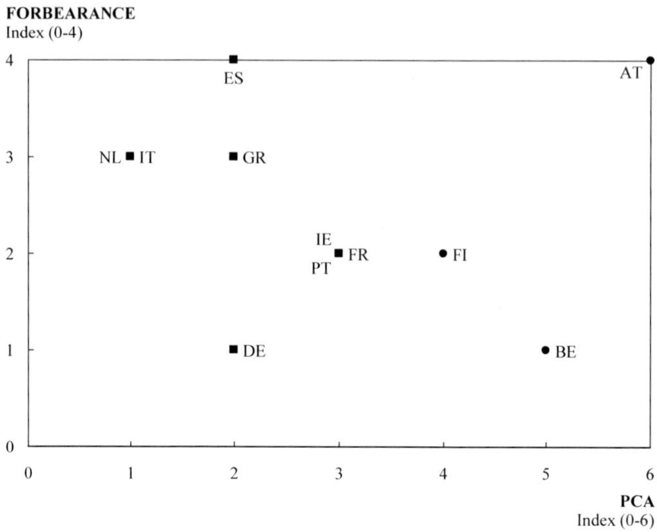

FIGURE 35: *Supervisory corrective action capabilities and discretion as of 1999/2000*

Source: Author based on data by Barth et al. (2006)

Macro-prudential rules

Beyond these relatively simple micro-prudential instruments related to enforcing capital adequacy or limiting the payout of dividends in distressed banks there are more sophisticated macro-prudential instruments, which can work in the same direction. The type of macro-prudential stabilizer required to support regulators in controlling leverage would either have to address credit growth (as for instance *loan-to-value limits* do) or would have to demand higher anti-cyclical capital charges (as *time-varying capital charges* or *dynamic provisioning* instruments do).[92] With respect to these specific instruments in the time period analyzed, only Spain introduced dynamic provisioning and therefore stands out as having a real rules-based macro-prudential instrument at hand whilst being subjected to a credit boom. The motivation for the introduction of dynamic provisioning is summarized by the Banco de España's director for financial stability as follows (Saurina, 2009):

"Banco de España, Spain's central bank and its banking supervisor, put dynamic - or statistical - provisions into place in July 2000, to cope with a sharp increase in credit risk on Spanish banks' balance sheets following a period of significant credit growth. Moral suasion had proved to be inadequate in inducing banks to become more conservative."

---

[92] For a discussion of these and more macro-prudential instruments see Bank for International Settlements (2010).

Since the introduction of this instrument has a substantial effect on credit growth and enhances the ability of the regulator to enforce capital adequacy with low discretion even in a boom, it should be added to the analysis of Spain's institutional arrangements. However, a more careful look is warranted, given that Spain has a bifurcated system of supervision, which assigns a different supervisory regime to the more regional public savings banks *cajas* than to the country-wide big banks. The *cajas*, originally established as regional financial institutions to help the poor, have been de-regulated, de-regionalized, and subjected to market forces in the course of the 1980s liberalization in 1988. However, the regional principle is still very active in the realm of supervision, where unlike other banks, the cajas supervised not only by the central bank, but also by the *comunidades autónomas*.[93] As such, in supervising the cajas the *comision de control* is voted into office by the local authorities. This supervisory commission composed of local administrators then also informs the Spanish central bank as supervisory authority and therefore disconnects caja banking supervision from the direct control of the Banco d'Espana. Thus, next to the presence in governing bodies, local politicians also have a supervisory channel of influence, which therefore limits the actual rules-based supervision of the central bank, as it inserts more regional discretion into the equation: Regional supervisors can adapt national standards of bank governance and management to the conditions in their region. I therefore decide to analyze the Spanish system as the bifurcated system that it is in the area of supervision.

The below table summarizes the findings once more, accounting now also for the use of macro-prudential instruments, in particular the strength of prompt corrective action capabilities by Spain for its big banks and the less stringent regime, which mainly applies to the cajas.

TABLE 21: *Institutional credibility of the supervisory authorities*

		Strength of micro- and macro-prudential prompt corrective action (PCA) capabilities?	
		Weak	*Strong*
Degree of discretion in applying PCA	*High*	Germany	Belgium, Finland, France, Ireland, Portugal
	Low	Italy, Netherlands, Spain (cajas)	Austria, Spain (big banks)

Source: Author

[93] For a concise but very comprehensive discussion of the politicized nature of the cajas in the 2000s see DB Research (2004).

5.2.3 Conclusion: Predictions regarding the build-up of leverage due to time inconsistent supervision

Based on the previous discussion I now want to generate predictions of which countries were most vulnerable to leverage buildup due to i) their reliance on credit and the temptations from easy monetary policy; ii) their institutional fitness, that is the corrective action capabilities and discretion afforded to supervisors. For that I join the two preceding sections' outcomes, the result of which is shown in the table below. The analysis suggests that in particular the high inflation countries with weak institutional credibility, that is Portugal, Ireland, and Spain, were at risk in the time period analyzed. Spain, as the previous section discussed, is split, since there were more stringent enforcement institutions in place on the national level, where the big banks are concerned, while on the regional level the Spanish savings banks cajas were subjected to a less stringent enforcement regime and are therefore also included in the high leverage corner of the matrix. For Austria, Belgium, Finland, France, Germany, Italy, and the Netherlands the macro-economic environment did not create such a strong temptation to leverage up, whilst for Spanish big banks the stricter dynamic provisioning regime is likely to prevent an uncontrolled spiraling of bank leverage. Therefore the application of the theoretical model would suggest particular leverage build-up for the countries in the bottom right corner of the matrix, whilst Austria would presumably be least affected. The next section will examine these predictions empirically.

TABLE 22: *Regulatory reaction to shock to credit availability*

		Institutional credibility, i.e. strong enforcement capabilities with low discretion?	
		Low	*High*
Shock to credit / credit reliance of economy	*Low (high real interest rates)*	Belgium, Finland, France, Germany, Italy, Netherlands	Austria
	High (low real interest rates)	Portugal, Ireland, Spain (cajas)	Spain (large banks)

Source: Author

5.3 Empirical analysis

To test the predictions made empirically, I will analyze the actual leverage build-up of the respective countries' banking systems, as measured by the relationship of assets to equity over time, against the tightness or looseness of the monetary regime, as measured by real interest rates prevalent in the same time period, which comprises the years between 2000 and 2006.[94] I will then further detail out the assumed causal processes through case studies of Ireland and Spain.

5.3.1 Bank leverage buildup across countries

The below graph shows the outcome of the analysis, depicting on the y-axis the monetary 'temptation', that is the average real interest rates under EMU by country (2000-06), as well as on the x-axis the change in the capital ratio in percentage points from 2000 to 2006. Moreover, the size of the bubble reflects the per annum credit growth rate to indicate to what extent the change in bank capitalization is driven by an expansion of credit. The first striking finding is the strong negative relationship that we can see between these two variables, which also proves to be statistically significant (of course to be treated with caution given the small sample size). This strong relationship between the relative fit of monetary policy and the change in leverage shows that credit growth in low inflation countries like Ireland, Spain, Portugal, and Greece indeed was not matched with a concomitant growth in bank capital, as indicated by the decrease in bank capitalization on the x-axis. Moreover, the only countries, which exhibit a real increase in bank capitalization are Germany, Austria, and Finland, all of which have relatively higher real interest rates and therefore less temptation to 'leverage up'.

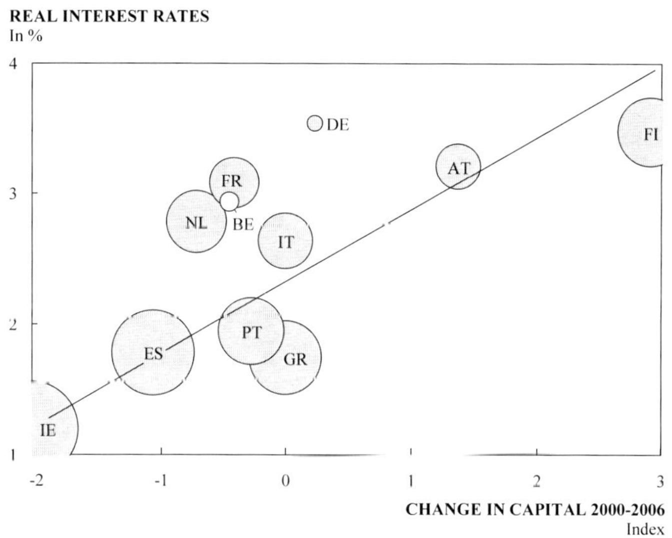

FIGURE 36: *Increase in credit volume and leverage due to monetary shock*

Source: Author based on ECB data

---

[94] This timeframe allows the use of comparable ECB data and also covers the onset of EMU until the beginning of the financial crisis and therefore is suitable to test the implication of national regulatory institutions in monetary union best.

Out of those three only Austria and Finland exhibit a significant increase in bank capitalization. In the case of Austria this confirms our prediction that strong credible regulatory institutions that rely on prompt corrective action will enable the supervisory authorities to be stricter in leverage supervision. In the case of Finland, the only market-based financial system in the Euro Zone sample here, this once more also shows the different dynamics that regulators and supervisors are subject to in different financial systems, as the credit reliance is much lower in a financial system with well-developed capital markets. The case of Finland moreover indicates, as evidenced by the size of the circle that even relatively stronger credit growth *can* go hand in hand with proportional or even disproportionally stronger capital growth. Finland in the time period analyzed experienced a similar credit expansion as Portugal or Greece with around 10% credit growth per annum, but still de-leveraged its banking system. This however then requires supervisory action to ensure that banks do not use a credit boom to expand their own leverage disproportionately, which failed to take place particularly in Ireland and Spain, but also in Portugal and Greece. Thirdly, a look at the other Euro Zone countries of the Netherlands, France, Belgium, and Italy shows that also in these cases the increase in credit throughout a benign period was not matched by a proportional growth in bank capital, since again bank leverage increased, if however more moderately by less than one percentage point.

The cases of Spain and Ireland as the most pronounced cases of leverage build-up over time in the Euro Zone are likely to provide the best insight into the drivers of time inconsistency in supervisory policy. I therefore want to analyze these two cases more in-depth to provide a more complete political economy narrative of time inconsistency problems in banking regulation, which can then serve to corroborate the causalities behind the correlations exposed in the preceding data analysis and ultimately to confirm the theoretical model developed in this chapter. The two countries also make a fair comparison, as they were the only countries in the Euro Zone subjected to shocks to bank competitiveness (see Chapter 4) and credit (monetary temptation), which therefore implies the trilemma was particularly pronounced in both countries, putting supervisory action at the risk of neglecting financial stability.

5.3.2 The case of Ireland

Credit reliance of the Irish economy 2000-2007/8

In response to the relatively loose-fitting monetary policy of the ECB, as reflected in the low average real interest rates, the Irish economy saw a strong economic expansion, which had its roots in expansionary fiscal policy and new access to foreign funding (Regling & Watson, 2010). While studies have shown that Ireland indeed experienced a genuine boom from 1994 to 2000 due to benign macro-economic conditions, sound economic policies as well as catching-up effects with its European neigbours, the following years saw a strong over-leveraging of the economy sustaining this momentum. Particularly drivers were a boom in investment in housing and commercial property, which again fed into positive wealth effects from rising property prices and increasing private consumption (P. R. Lane, 2010). In fact, credit was extremely attractive as real interest rates in the early 2000s even turned negative and then approached 2% towards 2006. With mortgage rates being largely variable in Ireland, this consistently expansionary economic environment fueled a 'plain vanilla' real estate boom and especially favoured household credit and small group of property developers. Importantly, the development of which moreover was well-documented by the Directorate General for Economic and Financial Affairs of the European Commission, which along with other observers repeatedly warned of the risks that accompanied the 300% rise in real house prices between 1994 and 2006 in analysis and comments (Malzubris, 2008).

The top figure below shows the expansion of credit and indicates very well how there was very little leveling off in the extension of credit from banks to households and firms in the transition from the boom in the late 1990s to the early 2000s under EMU. In fact, the annual growth rate of credit only decreased from 14% p.a. (1994-2000) to 10% (2000-2007/8) and therefore sustained a higher economic growth rate based on sustained leverage. Moreover, the below figure shows how bank lending increased (left scale) between 2000 and 2008 from around 49% of total bank assets to around 55%, whilst bank capital dropped in the same time period from around 6.5% of assets to around 3.5%. This very dramatic expansion of bank leverage to sustain growth of course could not have gone unnoticed by bank supervisors and therefore is consistent with the time inconsistency hypothesis advanced in this chapter.

Supervisory policy and bank leverage 2000-2007/8

In terms of the regulatory and supervisory reaction to this macro-economic environment, the post-financial crisis analysis by EU officials points to a general loosening of supervisory as well as a credit standards of domestic banks, which combined facilitated the boom through increasing bank leverage:

"[...] strongly risk-averse reactions by banks in Ireland and their supervisors would have been needed to help dampen a very risky boom-bust cycle. [...]The response of supervisors to the build-up of risks, despite a few praiseworthy initiatives that came late in the process, was not hands-on or pre-emptive. [...] Thus it is clear that, in various ways, official policies and bank governance failings seriously exacerbated Ireland's credit and property boom, and depleted its fiscal and banking buffers when the crisis struck." (Regling & Watson, 2010, p.6)

With respect to the supervisory motivations, which were behind this policy, the Regling-report moreover points to two sources: i) The lack of supervisory information due to lack of insight by the central bank; ii) the lack of political will and the challenge in overcoming the political resistance to a 'leaning against the wind'. Particularly the challenge of 'leaning against the wind' is striking, since it confirms the hypothesis that banking regulation in interaction with loose monetary conditions can lead to time consistent regulation:

"The response of supervisors to the build-up of risks, despite a few praiseworthy initiatives that came late in the process, was not hands-on or pre-emptive. To some degree, this was in tune with the times. The climate of regulation in advanced economies had swung towards reliance on market risk assessment. Domestically, moreover, there was a socio-political context in which it would have taken some courage to act more toughly in restraining bank credit. The weakness of supervision in Ireland contrasts sharply, however, with experience in those countries where

supervisors, faced with evident risks, acted to stem the tide." (Regling & Watson, 2010, p.6)

With respect to the decisive intervention by other supervisors, the report then cites Spain and Portugal, both of which had very different regimes (here labeled 'stability-oriented' regimes), which proved to be more resilient through stronger rules and consequent supervisory action in demanding higher capitalization for mortgage loans. In the Portuguese case, regulators even demanded that banks stretch out their cross-border funding maturities to avoid excessive short-term cross-border funding during a boom (Regling & Watson, 2010).

Clearly, the Irish experience shows that a boom with its origin in the general housing market makes decisive regulatory intervention particularly prohibitive, since a change in the availability of credit directly affects most voters and the perceived level of economic prosperity. This 'socio-political' environment, as the report phrases it, therefore creates this relatively insurmountable barrier, which even a very powerful supervisor as the Irish one finds hard to overcome. Thus, rather than the inability to identify bubbles, which often times central bankers identify as the chief reason not to expect regulatory 'leaning against the wind', it is the political economy challenge that is associated with decisive supervisory action to de-leverage the banking system and to reduce the credit availability to a highly credit-reliant economy.[95] The stronger reliance on 'principles-based' supervision rather than rules seems to have encouraged this lenient supervision in the Irish case as well, which therefore makes the outcome in terms of leverage and ensuing financial instability more devastating than in the Spanish case, as the following discussion will show.

5.3.3 The case of Spain

Credit reliance of the Spanish economy 2000-2007/8

Similar to the Irish economic development, Spain also experienced a property boom and bubble, the roots of which can be traced back to the early 2000s. As the left hand figure below shows, contrary to Ireland, credit growth was flat to negative in the 1990s (-2% p.a.) but then picked up strong momentum with monetary union (10% p.a.), which provided the macro-economic background against which lending became very affordable. Again much of the lending also took place in the construction sector (rising from ~11% of GDP to 16% of GDP) and particularly in the residential construction sector, which accounted for three quarters of the total construction sector expansion. Again the development of the Spanish housing bubble did not go unnoticed by observers. A report again by the Directorate General for Economic and Financial Affairs of the European Commission with the telling title "The Spanish housing market: Are we in for a soft landing?" already in 2006 discussed the drivers of the Spanish housing bubble as deriving from demography, disposable income, financial conditions and inflation with the latter being the most important driver of the four (Igal, 2006).

---

[95] A great illustration of the strong socio-political component of a housing bubble is provided in the narrative by journalist and former central banker David McWilliams, who already in 2005 described the property bubble in its economic, but also in its socio-political dimension, showing how an entire generation of the "Pope's Children" had built their wealth on credit.

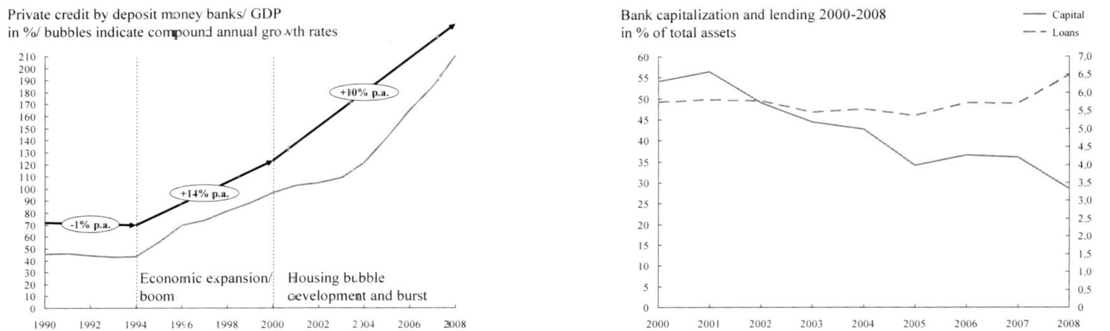

FIGURE 37: *Macro-economic development and credit reliance of the Irish economy*

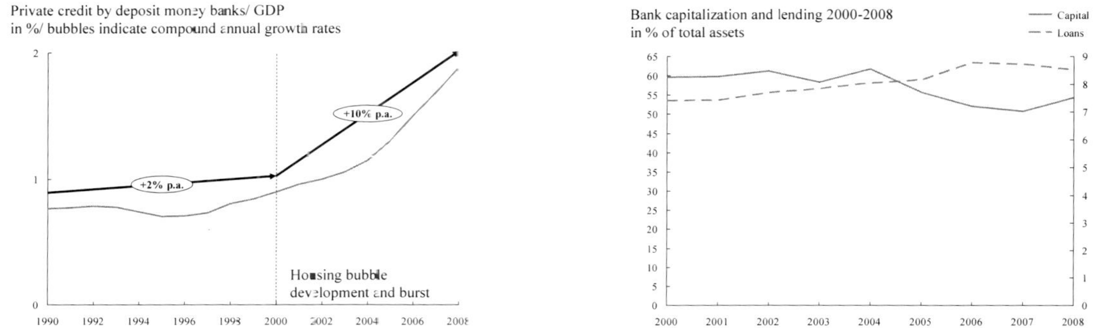

FIGURE 38: *Macro-economic development and credit reliance of the Spanish economy*
Source: Author based on ECB data

Again, the benign lending rates through monetary union fed into higher bank leverage, which however developed much more slowly and also was more modest in outcome than the Irish case. The graph below on the right hand side shows the development of bank lending to bank capital. Lending in the period between 2000 and 2006 expanded from 54% of total assets to 63%. Like in the Irish case bank capital contracted, however, with the marked difference that capital contracted much slower and more modestly from a level of 8.3% in 2000 to a still above Euro Zone average level of 7.2% in 2006.

Supervisory policy and bank leverage 2000-2007/8

The explanation for this differential development can be linked to the rules-based supervision regime, which the Bank of Spain had endorsed in the early 2000s, when supervisors had realized that moral suasion was insufficient to get banks to curb credit growth (Saurina, 2009). Instead supervisors implemented the macro-prudential instrument of dynamic provisioning measures, which charge a statistical provision on top of the expected loss provision in order to counter the somewhat understated calculation of loan risk in an upswing. This measure therefore directly counters the pro-cyclical risk and capital adequacy calculations, which banks tend to implement, since it demands anti-cyclical provisions on top. Since these provisions were based on clear rules and models provided by the Bank of Spain through regulation, no additional political or supervisory will was required in the implementation of these rules. Of course it should be mentioned that these dynamic provisioning rules were embedded in a general, more stringent framework of regulation towards banks by the Bank of Spain. As such, the Bank of Spain specified rules that increased the hurdles for commercial banks to set up "capital-lite" special vehicles for risky assets, invested in large and permanent teams of inspectors in major banks, and actively discouraged too innovative mortgage insurance programmes (Regling & Watson, 2010). This very different socio-political environment of course is likely a facilitating factor in enabling regulators and supervisors to pursue such a more 'stability-oriented' regime. To illustrate the gravity of these measures in terms of reducing bank profitability and competitiveness, Spanish central banker Saurina (2009) adds that the Spanish dynamic provisioning measures cost around 10% of banks' net operating income, which therefore makes them anything but a 'free lunch' for regulators to design.

In terms of the impact of this relatively stringent supervisory regime on bank leverage, outside observers such as the supervisory institutions belonging to the Financial Stability Board have credited Spanish supervisors with having averted higher leverage and financial instabilities (Financial Stability Board, 2011). As such, the peer reviewed report comments on the role of the supervisors very positively:

"The Spanish financial system weathered the initial brunt of the financial crisis relatively well compared to other advanced countries, primarily due to the Bank of Spain's strong regulatory stance and sound supervision, as well as an efficient, retail-oriented bank business model that is based on proximity to customers (as opposed to "originate-to-distribute"). Spanish banks entered the crisis with robust capital and strong counter-cyclical loan loss provisioning buffers. They were largely shielded from the subprime mortgage crisis due to low exposure to complex structured products as the Bank of Spain's regulations discouraged investments in such products and the

creation of off-balance structured investment vehicles and conduits." (Financial Stability Board, 2011, p.10)

Thus, the specific rules that created larger capital buffers turned out to be effective in preventing larger financial instabilities in the Spanish banking sector. Estimations have shown that EUR 19 billion of additional capital created through dynamic provisions helped the Spanish banks to absorb asset write-downs of EUR 47 billion throughout the crisis period between early 2008 to June 2010 (Financial Stability Board, 2011).

This very positive record and experience with rules-based supervision contrasts very sharply with the experience of the Spanish cajas, which were subject to a more discretionary supervisory regime and governance, which has already been described earlier. The strong political influence of regional politicians in supervising the cajas through the *comision de control* and governing bodies combined with the inability of the public savings banks to issue proper equity but instead to rely on debt issuance. The political influence led to higher lending to advance regional construction booms while the former restricted the growth of the capital base. Taken together this increased leverage and exposure to the Spanish housing boom much more than in the private sector with Spanish cajas having between 10% and 50% of their assets in real risky estate loans (Ysa, Giné, Esteve, & Sierra, 2010). Since the crisis the limitations of the cajas system of supervision and governance have been obviated and have triggered major reform efforts, which address many of the excessive discretionary powers of regional politicians in supervision and governance. Most relevant to the hypothesis of time inconsistency in banking regulation is the fact that these reforms are largely targeted at reducing the political discretion in supervision and governance through a reduction of maximum public voting rights from 50% to 40% and strengthening the role of expertise in the appointment of public officials to the boards (Financial Stability Board, 2011). Thus, the experience of the cajas' more discretionary supervision drives home the point that political interference in the interest of credit availability and growth as well as bank profitability is likely to reduce the concern for financial stability. This in turn makes the prudential and stringent supervision of banks potentially time inconsistent.

5.3.4 Conclusion

The preceding empirical analysis has shown that banking supervision throughout cycles of boom and bust can be time inconsistent, which through relaxed supervision and lower capital adequacy can lead to higher leverage and financial instability. This time inconsistency was shown

- Firstly, an aggregate level for the Euro Zone as a whole, as banking systems with stronger temptations to leverage due to lower real interest rates (and a high bank reliance) had a stronger decrease of bank equity to asset ratios than countries with relatively low real interest rates;
- Secondly, at a country level, using the Irish and Spanish experience in the lead-up to the financial crisis. Here it was shown that more discretionary supervisory regimes, such as the Irish one, had stronger and more sustained growth of bank leverage and went into the crisis more undercapitalized due to the strong exposures of banks to risky mortgage loans. Also it was shown that more rules-

based supervision as in Spain, whilst of course not preventing booms and busts from taking place, managed to reduce bank leverage in terms of growth and absolute level and through limited discretion eased the political burden on supervisors. In the case of the cajas, where supervisory discretion was larger, similar excesses and supervisory negligence can be attested as in the Irish case.

Thus, the Euro Zone's experience with national banking supervision in a monetary union very much bears out the time inconsistency hypothesis that I advance in this chapter. Above and beyond the factors illuminated here, the socio-political environment – for good and for ill – has been shown to matter in affecting supervisory stringency and stability outcomes. A 'light touch' philosophy of regulation as in Ireland along with vast participation in the housing market by large parts of the population proved to be a formidable barrier to stringent supervision, while a more 'stability-oriented' approach to regulation and supervision has been a great asset in the Bank of Spain's approach to supervision in a housing boom.

6

Conclusion

"Only a crisis—actual or perceived—produces real change. When that crisis occurs, the actions that are taken depend on the ideas that are lying around."

Milton Friedman

"The significant problems we face cannot be solved at the same level of thinking we were at when we created them."

Albert Einstein

Crises bring about changes not only in the institutional architecture of economic policy-making but also in the prevalent paradigms and ideas that drive policy-making to a substantial degree. For the Euro Zone countries the financial crisis of 2007/8 has obviated not only technical shortcomings in banking regulation, such as the neglect of the macro-prudential dimension of banking, but also the flaws of certain ideas behind the monetary union's financial stability architecture at large. As this work has shown, behind this regulatory architecture lies a fundamental failure to appreciate the political economy trade-offs that face democratic countries in global financial markets. Such choices boil down to the following simple but often under appreciated dilemma: What is good politics is not always good economics and vice versa. I find that this lack of consideration of economic *and* political incentives in the design of its institutional architecture is the ideational mistake that the Euro Zone's financial stability architecture has suffered from.

The delusion that sound economics would by its own virtue also be the policy of choice by politics has paved the way for the financial instabilities of the past that led to crisis. This runs counter to the experience of European integration, where the limitations of the politically agreeable have always formed the boundaries of the economically possible. However, as Barry Eichengreen (2007) showed elsewhere, *"the distinguishing feature of EMU is that it is a monetary union in the absence of political union"*. EMU therefore is truly 'sui generis' with important implications for banking regulation and financial stability policy. It is the tension between deepening *financial and economic* integration but remaining *political* fragmentation, which creates regulatory policy trade-offs, which national regulators to not always decide in favour of financial stability. The way that this lack of political will for integration has manifested in financial stability policy is through the institutional foundations: The conduct of monetary policy has been designed along the lines of a shared *economic interest*, which suggested supranational and independent monetary policy with a single clear objective of price stability; In the realm of banking regulation, regulation and supervision has remained a national policy domain with a complex and multi-dimensional policy objective subject to heavy *political and private interests*. This institutional asymmetry has provided the background for very asymmetric developments across the various countries, which have culminated in varying degrees of systemic crisis, bank failure, and output loss. As such, this research has illuminated the particular political economy workings of national regulators and central bankers in their conduct of regulatory financial stability policy within a monetary union. Thus, on a more normative policy level the key finding is that a functioning monetary union requires a sustainable regulatory architecture, which balances both – sound economics and credible politics.

In this section I want to i) briefly review the findings of this work, which were derived mainly from the analysis of European Monetary Union since its inception until the financial crisis 2007/8, before turning to ii) a discussion of the policyCh implications going forward for the Euro Zone; iii) I then also derive the implications for the study of political economy and varieties of financial systems before iv) concluding.

6.1 Summary of findings

My research has focused on how the conduct of financial stability policy and banking regulation varies depending on the underlying financial system structures and the varying role of banks. I have argued that next to financial stability, regulators have to consider other objectives such as domestic banks' competitiveness and their role in financing the economy at large, which therefore impact on the way that discretionary regulatory policy is executed. Because of *this multi-dimensional nature of financial stability policy* and the limited *instruments available* to address these multiple objectives, banking regulation is a very complex political that requires making tough political economy trade-offs. These trade-offs can create a real *trilemma* for the regulator in the short- and medium-term, particularly if discretion is 'excessive', that is when regulatory policy is not adequately supported by strong, rules-based macro-prudential instruments that allow some coordination with monetary policy. This trilemma argument has a *static* and *dynamic* dimension, the explanatory value of which I will now summarize and illustrate with reference to the Euro Zone countries.

Financial stability policy and banking regulation in its static, cross-sectional context

In analyzing the static differences in financial stability policy across countries I find that financial system differences, specifically the degree of bank-reliance and the nature of legal institutions, shape the nature of regulation and the degree of bank leverage in a substantial way. It is this bank-reliance and the relative strength of banks in the legal system in most continental European countries that explains the relatively high levels of leverage that were exposed by the financial crisis of 2007/8 in these countries' banks. As the table below shows once more, most financial systems in the Euro Zone have political economy interests in relatively high amounts of credit availability through banks. The historical prominence of *'relationship' finance* in the financial systems of Austria, Belgium, Germany, Italy, Netherlands, Ireland implies that financial stability policy has to be conducted in an environment, where banks have a strong role in providing finance and intertemporal risk-sharing to the economy through large universal banks.

TABLE 23: *Regulatory approaches to the trilemma across countries*

Regulatory dimension	*'Relationship'-finance*	*'Competitive self-correcting' finance*	*'Arm's length'-finance*
Financial stability	↑	*Market discipline/ lower moral hazard reduces salience of this objective*	Objectives managed with the instrument of regulatory stringency/ monetary policy
Credit availability	Objectives managed with the instrument of regulatory stringency/ monetary policy	↑	*Capital market presence reduces salience of this objective*
Competitiveness	↓ *'Patient capital' reduces salience of this objective*	Objectives managed with the instrument of regulatory stringency/ monetary policy ↓	Objectives managed with the instrument of regulatory stringency
Countries	*Credit-availability-oriented approach:* Austria, Belgium, Germany, Italy, Netherlands, Ireland *Stability-oriented approach:* Greece, Portugal, Spain, France	Luxembourg, United Kingdom	United States, Finland

Source: Author

As I have shown, the nature of the financial system tends to be somewhat 'sticky' and 'path-dependent', as historical institutionalists would put it, due to the presence of certain complementary configurations. As such, *'relationship' finance* regimes in bank-based financial systems have more strongly developed creditors and depositors rights, while lower shareholder rights and the institution of 'patient capital' reduce the salience of competitiveness considerations. In terms of outcomes the relationship finance countries share the observed high levels of leverage with the countries of the *'competitive self-regulatory' finance* – however for different reasons. Luxembourg and the United Kingdom as the exponents of 'competitive self-regulatory finance' have a hybrid financial system that emphasizes the role of highly competitive banks competitive banks. As such, good access to credit through is assured through banks and markets, whilst creditors and shareholders have strong institutionalized rights and the role of the regulator and government is more limited. Depositor rights and deposit insurance are less extensive to limit moral hazard. Instead strong market-side surveillance is emphasized in order to provide financial stability.

This contrasts with the *'arm's length' finance countries*, as which I classify the United States and, within the Euro Zone, Finland: These countries have a more market-based financial system, that relies less on banks for credit access but instead employs markets as institutional vehicles for corporate finance and risk-sharing. Shareholders and depositors are stronger here reflecting the focus on bank competitiveness and financial stability, while the salience of 'credit access' as a regulatory objective is clearly reduced due to the presence of deep and liquid capital markets. Regulators therefore have more leeway in using capital adequacy regulation for financial stability purposes only, which explains why these countries have lower levels of leverage and more capital – a result that I find to be very stable over time for both the United States and Finland in the time period analyzed. Also in this lower leverage bracket are the *'stability-oriented'* variations of the 'relationship' finance regime in Spain and Portugal, if however for different reasons. While these historically bank-based financial systems have been moving stronger towards capital-market financing due to reforms of their financial sectors in the 1980s and 1990s, which reduces the salience of the credit availability objectives, it is the stability-orientation and the stronger role of the regulator that have been shaping this regulatory approach. Institutionally this is reflected in the more extensive deposit insurance rights and the stronger role of shareholders, which balance the strong role of banks and help make these regimes more ‚stability-oriented'.

There are two special cases, namely France and Greece, which exhibit the same kind of institutional configurations as the other Mediterranean countries and are also traditionally bank-based. However, the two countries for different reasons are not quite configured according to the same complementary logic and therefore can be considered the 'most different' cases in the above classification: Greece in comparison with the other Euro Zone countries analyzed is not as developed of a financial system and banking system but is likely somewhat more bank-dependent than the data actually reveals. Moreover its financial stakeholder rights are also relatively less developed, which again make a classification somewhat less robust. France on the other hand is harder to classify due to its very dynamic development and institutional change, which has been occupying political economy researchers in the last years. As such, France went from being a model case of the coordinated market economy with high reliance on bank finance according to the 'relationship'-finance logic to becoming a more and more liberal market economy with a much stronger role for shareholders and capital markets, which also shifted beliefs and reduced cross-shareholdings in a significant way.[96] France therefore resembles the United Kingdom in many ways as it has developed a more hybrid financial system with stronger shareholder rights, but it also has a somewhat more 'interventionist' culture in regulation that makes it more stability-oriented and less laissez faire: All in all it has a less complementary configuration and will be an interesting subject of study for future research.

Financial stability policy and banking regulation in a dynamic context

This static configuration though in the course of financial integration and the evolving divergence of real interest rates under monetary union has become subjected to exogenous shocks and institutional change. To the extent that regulators are subject to national private interests and political economy pressures, they are prone to making trade-offs that are suboptimal from a financial stability and economic welfare point of

[96] For a study of the patterns of change in coordinated market economies and the variation in institutional change see Culpepper (2005, 2011). For a more holistic view on the change in varieties of capitalism see V. A. Schmidt (2000).

view – the more so when their institutional environment fails to insulate them sufficiently from such political economy pressures.

As summarized in the below table, I show that in its dynamic context the financial system and in particular the banking sector becomes subject to exogenous shocks to competitiveness and credit availability, which affect the conduct of financial stability policy and banking regulation through the assumed regulatory objective function. Firstly, the *national variation in implementation of international and European-level regulatory standards* at the same time has laid the foundations for an 'unlevel playing field', causing national regulators to react to each other's regulatory stringency. *Relative competitiveness and regulatory stringency* patterns during the time of Basel II negotiations and EU-internal regulatory reforms explains the way that countries implemented Basel standards and the changed their capital definition stringency across the Euro Zone.

TABLE 24: *Exogenous shocks in the time period 2000-2007*

		Monetary shock/ reliance on credit availability	
		Weak/ Low	*Strong/ High*
Shock to bank competi-tiveness	*Weak*	Finland, France, Germany, Italy, Netherlands	Portugal
	Strong	Austria, Belgium, Luxembourg,	Ireland, Spain

Source: Author

In particular the strong lowering of standards in capital stringency definition in Austria, Belgium, and Ireland can be explained through their relative openness and stricter regulation (AT and BE) and lower profitability (AT and IE) at the time. Luxembourg kept an intermediate level of stringency whilst Spain stands out as an exception to the pattern, as it re-regulated. This can be partially explained with the higher profitability of the Spanish banks but also with the relative stability-orientation of the regulatory regime, which I demonstrated in other regulatory areas as well.

Secondly, *asymmetric monetary shocks and differences in credit reliance* explain the variation in supervisory stringency over time. The *resulting shocks to credit and economic output* put high political economy pressures on regulators, who in the absence of rules-based regulators instruments have found it hard to commit to a hawkish policy stance. This is true in particular for Portugal, Ireland, and Spain (as well as Greece), where low real interest rates have caused a credit and property boom, which creates a formidable political economy hindrance to hawkish regulatory action. This is where macro-prudential instruments come in as an important regulatory innovation to 'stiffen the spine' of the regulator by acting as automatic stabilizers. I find that rules rather than additional regulatory powers or formal organizational matters are key to ensuring stability-oriented regulation. The comparison between Spain and Ireland, both of which had been subjected to simultaneous shocks to competitiveness and easy money, illustrates this: Ireland has had the formally most independent and powerful regulator in the form of a 'mega central bank', but yet has shown the strongest de-regulation and escalation in bank leverage through a lending boom. Spain, on the other hand, also as an independent central bank regulator but with more modest freedom in terms of accountability through control by the Ministry of Finance, had implemented dynamic provisioning as an instrument and could at least limit the damage, even though the regionally and politically controlled cajas went on a more extensive lending spree regardless. Other countries such as Germany, France or Austria, where regulators were not put to the test in this way through loose monetary conditions, did not see such escalations in credit growth and therefore had different leverage and thus financial stability risks going into the crisis. In Finland, as the only real market-based financial system, banks even decreased their leverage despite high credit growth due to even stronger capital growth, which again is consistent with bank-reliance as a strong predictor or regulatory stringency.

Financial stability outcomes in the Euro Zone

Even though my research aims to explain regulatory behaviour rather than stability outcomes, the prior findings do lend themselves to a very brief analysis of the latter as well. This research has inquired into the differences in capital adequacy levels in banks as a driver of leverage and financial instability: The static analysis has yielded insights into which financial systems tend to regulate for higher and lower leverage; the dynamic analysis has yielded two regulatory sources of rising leverage, namely the relaxation of capital definitions in response to shocks to competitiveness as well as the relaxation of supervision and enforcement in response to attractive monetary conditions.

The below figure at least provides an indication that the increase in leverage through reductions in the quality of capital held (Southward movements along the y-axis) as well as increases in leverage through higher asset to equity ratios (Westward movements along the x-axis) seem to coincide with a more systemic breakout and higher costs of the financial crisis. Specifically the cases of Ireland and Belgium, both of which de-regulated substantially in the time period analyzed, have been subjected to the strongest breakout of the crisis and find themselves in the South-Western space of the figure. More conservative regulators in Portugal, Spain, and France with their 'stability-oriented' regimes have been able to avoid systemic banking crises at first. Spain of course needs to be analyzed as a bifurcated supervisory regime and banking system, as it was not the large banks under the exclusive supervision of the Bank of Spain Spain's but instead the cajas with a strong element of regional supervision, which later on brought on a more systemic crisis due to the laxer supervision of their leverage and real estate market exposures. The case of Austria is particularly interesting as it reveals the power of non-discretionary regulation and supervision. Despite a strong lowering of capital definitions, Austria managed to have much lower costs of the financial crisis at ~9% of GDP than Belgium or Ireland due to its relatively rigid enforcement rules, which demand immediate and corrective action, when capital adequacy is violated. This, of course along with a less volatile macro-economic environment and no housing boom, seems to have limited the financial instabilities in Austria relative to other de-regulating countries.

FIGURE 39: *Regulatory and supervisory choices and financial stability outcomes*

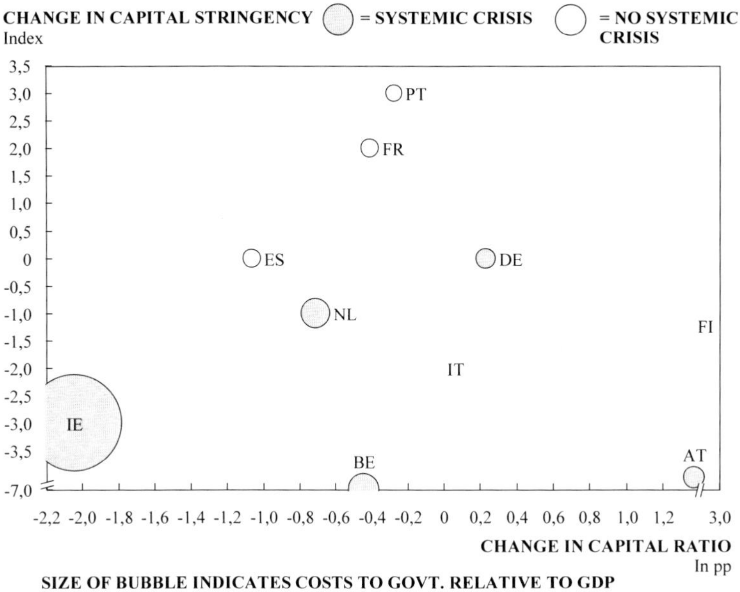

Source: Author based on data by Laeven and Valencia (2010); data for Finland and Italy not available

6.2 Theoretical implications

My approach to the study of financial stability policy and the findings for the countries analyzed have certain implications for the research fields of comparative political economy and comparative financial system analysis. Specifically I set out to create a more comprehensive theoretical framework drawing on existing literature, which would allow the researcher to understand the political economy of banking regulation from a more encompassing perspective. In deriving *cross-sectional regulatory preferences*, establishing the way that regulators interact with each other on the *international level*, and showing how the *practice of supervision over time* can be subject to exogenous shocks and time inconsistencies I have made certain observations that can inform future research in this field. I would like to summarize the most important three implications: i) The interaction of national banking regulation with supranational monetary policy, which creates deeply political trade-offs; ii) The relevance of financial system structures and bank reliance in comparative political economy; iii) The important distinction between 'talking the talk', that is coordinating on regulation internationally, and 'walking the walk', that is implementing the agreed standards stringently in the national context.

The interaction of financial stability policy/ banking regulation with monetary policy and the architecture of a monetary union

The multi-dimensional objective function of banking regulators already makes the conduct of financial stability policy a more political undertaking that is coined by hard trade-offs and thus requires more attention by political economy researchers. However, as I have shown for the Euro Zone, in the context of monetary union this national instrument that largely belongs to the realm of 'quiet politics' can become a very tempting lever for government to pursue its domestic economic objectives. As countries have surrendered the instrument of monetary policy and hence are only left with banking regulation, the conduct of regulation is much more loaded with multiple policy objectives. The resulting regulatory outcomes with their very real distributional implications therefore provide real insights into the politics and complementarities that informs the regulatory decision-making process. Yet, the specific study of banking regulation in the context of monetary union has thus far not generated much attention among scholars, who have instead focused on the global arena and the degree of international coordination or Europeanization of this policy area instead. However, the study of countries in a monetary union is particularly relevant from a political economy perspective. This study of banking regulation in the context of a monetary union therefore is still a very innovative and even unique approach that I find worth expanding on, since it yields valuable insight into the real trade-offs in this policy field and the variance of how these trade-offs are resolved: Thus, as countries face the dynamics of strong financial integration and asymmetric monetary conditions in a monetary union, the researcher has a very rich set of different institutional contexts and related political economy trade-offs that lend themselves to analysis. Since monetary unions tend to be financially more integrated with each other they therefore yield insights that can be useful for generalization about the likely impact of further financial integration on the conduct of financial stability policy.

Moreover I believe that the actual conclusions about the degree of integration and the tensions between the technocratic conduct of monetary policy and the slightly more politicized conduct of regulation can yield valuable insights into the actual workings of economic policy in EMU. Much in line with scholars of the varieties-of-capitalism literature I find that this *interaction* of different economic policies with each other is crucial to understanding political motivations and economic outcomes. For instance, if one did not analyze Spain's regulatory policy in its interaction with the, in this case, loose monetary policy of ECB, one would be led to conclude that Spain's regulators had a preference for lax regulation. Instead, when considering the exogenous monetary shock, it is clear that the Spanish regulators at least were stricter than most other countries such as for instance Ireland that were subjected to the same kind of shocks. Thus, to generate real insights about economic policy motivations one needs control for exogenous adaptational pressures and the interactions of various policy fields with each other.

The relevance of bank reliance and the financial system for comparative political economy analysis

This research has detailed out the relevance of the financial system configuration and in particular the degree of bank reliance for the conduct of financial stability policy across countries. This emphasis builds on the body of literature that has analyzed the systemic complementarities across countries, integrating insights from the comparative financial systems, law and finance, and varieties of capitalism literature. However, in integrating these insights into a coherent account of how the role of banks and markets differs, it is an innovation that might prove useful for further research, as it yields distinct regulatory regimes that address the three political economy objectives of stability, bank competitiveness, and credit access in different complementary ways.

In conceptualizing my financial system classification, which on the one dimension looks at the relative influence of financial stakeholders through legal institutions and on the other dimensions identifies the relative reliance on markets vs. banks, I found that these bodies of theory thus far are very disjoined. Even though the law and finance literature, the comparative financial systems literature and the varieties of capitalism literature all implicitly or explicitly share some dichotomy of bank- and market-based economies, their classifications rest on somewhat different elements of the system such as either the legal tradition, the nature of intermediation and risk-sharing, or the provision of 'patient capital'. As I have shown, these elements together really can be seen as complementary solutions to the trilemma, as every economic system needs to bring into equilibrium the interests of the financial stakeholders and the needs of the economy. I think that this classification can be useful for further comparative research on banking regulation, since it appreciates the variation in preferences that countries assign to these objectives by virtue of their path dependent financial systems. As such, this classification goes beyond the works by other political economy scholars, who have worked out more 'universal' claims about the regulatory dilemma between competitiveness and stability as decisive dimensions without introducing the nature of the financial system as an explicit explanatory variable. These accounts in my opinion do not lend themselves very well to comparative political economy analysis since they do not appreciate the variations in how financial systems ensure credit supply, risk-sharing as well as the differences in the role of banks. Only by establishing these differences in the nature of the financial system more holistically, it can be shown how the financial system structure shapes the relative salience of certain objectives and has real implications for economic outcomes such as bank leverage and credit supply as well as political outcomes such as the cooperation on regulation internationally and the stringency of international standard implementation.

The difference between 'talking the talk' and 'walking the walk' in implementing international regulatory standards and supervision over time

Much theoretical debate has centered around the question of whether we have observed a tendency for re-regulation or a competitive race for laxity in financial regulation in the last two decades, focusing in particular on the role of the Basel negotiations and international capital adequacy standards. Whilst these analyses have yielded interesting insights into the role of expert networks and international policy coordination, many scholars have been taking the harmonization outcomes such as the minimum level of capital required for banks for granted. The conclusions therefore have often been that re-regulation and a 'race to the top' have resulted and that, when faced with crisis, countries get together at the international level and coordinate in the form of new regulatory regimes and harmonized standards.

While my findings are consistent with the idea that regulatory paradigms and international regimes usually only change *radically* in the face of crisis, I also find that in times when regulatory policy is a non-salient policy field of 'quiet politics' (in Culpepper's sense, 2011) there are important patterns of standard implementation and issues of time inconsistency that lead to deviation from intended courses of action that have gone largely unnoticed in the literature. These deviations however are very significant and, hence, when accounted for might lead scholars to very different conclusions about the strength of international coordination and the actual extent of re-regulation. Hence my findings suggest that political economists that want to analyze whether regulatory bodies are also going to 'walk the walk' of harmonizing standards can complement their analysis of political processes and discourses of international coordination with two things:

- Firstly, analysts need to incorporate more *economic analysis of actual regulatory outcomes of regulation* with real relevance for financial stability. As such, this analysis here has shown that despite of Basel harmonization efforts the actual holdings of real and 'hard' equity capital in relation to assets still varies significantly across countries and, as the crisis has shown, can not be explained by variations in risk exposure.[97] Instead negotiated solutions often reflect the underlying interests and financial system configurations of the various countries participating in Basel.
- Secondly, political economy analysts should focus more attention on the *actual implementation record* as well as the *nature of enforcement over time* to judge the actual significance of international coordination efforts. The more quantitative look at the development of regulatory institutions such as capital stringency over time suggests that countries' implementation records differ very much from the cooperative rhetoric that accompanies the agreement of harmonized standards. Moreover the analysis of changes in actual capital held over time suggest that regulators and banks can use the significant amount of discretion afforded to them in defining risk exposures and enforcing capital adequacy levels in ways that actually lead to significant deviations from the jointly agreed standard.

There are certain challenges associated with the measurement of institutional change and the sample sizes that can be generated for comparable sets of countries. However I think that it is the *combination* of a thorough understanding of the political economy processes and the quantifiable regulatory and economic outcomes, which will make for even more relevant political economy theorizing in the field of banking regulation and financial stability policy.

6.3 Policy implications: The Euro Zone as an optimal regulatory union?

What does it mean for policy? A few years after the breakout of large scale financial instability, the need for macro-prudential instruments and other technical requirements

[97] This finding is shared for instance by economic analysis by for instance Brewer III, Kaufman, and Wall (2008) but has largely gone unnoticed in the political economy literature to date.

of better financial stability policymaking is already on the agenda of the G20 and the Euro Zone.[98] Hence, rather than rehearsing the important insights gained in the technical realm, I want to focus on the bigger political economy implications. What is required to put the two back into balance is a new set of rules and institutions as part of a new regulatory architecture. The findings suggest that the Euro Zone might have to complement monetary union with regulatory union and move from discretionary to rules-based supervision.

Policy choices: The dilemma behind the trilemma

The argument developed in my research in essence boils down to the basic tension between the domestic political requirements of the nation state and the economic dynamics of an integrating financial market.[99] My work has shown that in an integrating monetary union good regulation would require of the regulator to go against certain national demands and interests by 'leaning against the wind' and conducting 'good technocratic' policy from a financial stability point of view. While the trend in Basel II's 'supervisory approach' was towards more regulatory discretion, the crisis has shown that this discretion is very asymmetric and usually only works in the direction of more regulatory laxity. However, regarding the enforcement of these rules, the job of taking away the punch bowl, just as the party gets going, will still not be popular with national regulators. To complement its monetary union, the Euro Zone could move towards regulatory union as well. This requires countries to surrender more regulatory and supervisory sovereignty to new European-level institutions such as the European Banking Authority and the European Systemic Risk Board. With the right enforcement capabilities these institutions can then ensure that rules, once agreed, are actually and equally enforced in the face of domestic challenge. This will stiffen the spine of national regulators in the next boom.

Policy options: Integrating into a regulatory union?

So what can policy do about it? Taking the trilemma facing national regulators seriously, requires thinking beyond national regulation and looking for global or, in the case of the Euro Zone, European governance formats, which reduce the national demands, which in the case of financial stability and banking regulation lobby for easier credit and more competitive national banking. Thus, in banking regulation the policymaker can either ignore such popular opinion or subject *itself* to more integration. One basic resolution, intensely debated with the introduction of more European level regulator capacities, is the Europeanization of financial stability regulation through some form of 'regulatory union'. Since my findings have pointed out the limitations of the Euro Zone model of *national* banking regulation in an integrating monetary union, I would like to establish the policy implications by

---

98 For an overview and a survey of the current practice amongst central banks see Bank for International Settlements (2010).

99 In this sense, national financial stability policy in an integrating market is another case of what Dani Rodrik has coined the "fundamental political trilemma of the world economy". Rodrik makes the argument that "We want economic integration to help boost living standards. We want democratic politics so that public policy decisions are made by those that are directly affected by them (or their representatives). And we want self-determination, which comes with the nation-state. […] we cannot have all three things simultaneously. The political trilemma of the global economy is that the nation-state system, democratic politics, and full economic integration are mutually incompatible. We can have at most two out of the three" (Rodrik, 2002).

focusing on the prerequisites for a *European* governance of banking regulation and financial stability. Thus, in the following I suggest a political economy account of an optimal regulatory union, which I define as a centralized regulatory regime, which applies one relatively uniform standard of regulatory stringency across all participating member countries.[100] I propose a *political economy* account, which differs from a purely economic account (as the equivalent theory of optimal currency areas by Robert Mundell), since *political considerations* such as the competitiveness of national banks and the required degree of credit access of specific constituents are considered in defining optimality. This account builds on the developed utility function and trade-offs hypothesized in this chapter to derive the most critical conditions required for a regulatory union. In its consideration of political interests, domestic institutions and the role of financial systems this account explicitly goes beyond the adjustment of to shocks through mobile economic factors and acknowledges the national and ultimately political nature of regulation.

Policy pre-requisites: Reflections on a regulatory union

To establish the prerequisites for such an optimal regulatory union, I build on the well-established model of the optimum currency area by Mundell. In his original formulation Mundell specified an optimal currency area as an area, where the regions are affected symmetrically by exogenous shocks and otherwise have a high mobility of the factors of production, namely labour and capital, to adjust to differences for instance in employment and productivity across the region (Mundell, 2007). In such a case countries could then surrender the instrument of monetary policy for purposes of a common currency. This logic of 1) understanding the extent to which countries are affected by exogenous shocks symmetrically, and 2) analyzing the extent to which countries have other natural adjustment factors at their disposal, which alleviate the need to react with an asymmetric policy instrument, shall serve as the blueprint for this political economy account of optimal regulatory unions as well. Moreover, from a political economy perspective we have to account for 3) the variation in regulatory preferences with respect to the different objectives along the trilemma. A deviation from average regulatory preferences increases a country's costs of entering a 'regulatory union', as this increases the likelihood that this country will not get the preferred degree of stringency in regulation.[101]

A political economy account reflects both political and economic considerations: Economic logic suggests that the degree of financial integration and capital mobility as well as the symmetry of exposure to exogenous shocks and financial structure are important factors in determining the optimality of a regulatory union; Political and

---

100 The model of regulatory union that I have in mind is a consciously stylized one, which essentially reflects the institutional equivalent of the European Central Bank on a regulatory level. Such a regulatory body would, analogous to setting uniform interest rates, determine a uniform regulatory stringency standard across the entire Euro Zone with no national regulatory discretion. I employ such a rigid definition of a regulatory union, since integration of the regulatory function at the European level ultimately boils down to unifying regulatory standards and 'leveling the playing field'. This is not to say that there aren't regulatory union concepts that are more flexible than the one assumed here – but for the purpose of the analysis of this concept it is worth examining the stylized solution rather than a hybrid form.

101 Here I build on the most comprehensive and suitable model in relation to a regulatory context, which has been developed by Dell'Ariccia and Marquez (2003). Their model suggests that the degree of symmetry in preferences determines the cost-benefit calculation of countries deciding to form a centralized regime or to stick to an independent regime. For a summary of its findings see the discussion in section 4.1.

varieties-of-capitalism logic also suggests that policy preferences can differ across countries and therefore need to be harmonized to some degree as well, if one size is to fit all. Thus, in order for a uniform regulatory standard to meet the national regulatory objectives, the Euro Zone countries within such a regulatory union need to

- Hold relatively *symmetric preferences* for financial stability;
- Be *relatively symmetric in terms of exposure to exogenous shocks* to stability, competitiveness, and credit access;

Alternatively it will have to retain the *structural or regulatory adjustment capacities*, which allow them to adjust to the remaining unexpected asymmetric shocks (for example through having capital market access in case of a national credit crunch).

To the extent that the Euro Zone can achieve either the second and third elements perfectly, they can of course serve as substitutes for each other, that is, in the absence of any asymmetry of shocks to the financial system no further adjustment capacities on the national level would be needed. Since these factors are unlikely to be attained, both of the criteria will likely have to be in place for a regulatory union to work. The most obvious ways to achieve this for the Euro Zone would be through the following two structural prerequisites:

- A relatively *homogenous financial and institutional structure* to converge regulatory preferences, which entails
  - A *more homogeneous and diversified financial system structure* with stronger capital markets that allow for the diversification of credit access away from banks
  - Either *more homogeneous levels of competitiveness* or *truly European banking* with pan-European banks providing substitutable services and the ability to let banks fail, which would reduce the role of domestic competitiveness considerations in the conduct of regulation
- A *more symmetric monetary union* that reduces the asymmetry of exogenous shocks to credit access and stability.

Such a regulatory union could then be regulated with a relatively uniform standard of regulatory stringency, appropriate for the pursuit of financial stability in the union's countries and would only in infrequent situations of asymmetric shocks allow adjustment through substitution of credit access either by foreign banks or capital markets.

6.4 Outlook

In conclusion, having focused my analysis on a neutral and theoretically informed analysis of the conduct of financial stability policy in the past, I would like to finish with a slightly more normative and practically informed look into the future, evaluating the chances of the Euro Zone to overcome its deficiencies in the area of financial stability policy. After having studied the strength of the forces of political and economic interests in this policy field for the last two years, I maintain that ignoring the political economy incentives behind institutional structures is not only politically not viable but also likely to produce economically suboptimal policy outcomes in the long run. Thus, the question is: To what extent does the Euro Zone fulfill the *political economy* criteria for being a regulatory union?

After my preceding analysis of the years from 2000 to 2008 and the resulting financial instabilities it should come at no surprise that I am skeptical regarding the optimality of the Euro Zone as a regulatory union. Differences in financial system structure and an asymmetric real interest rate have put the instrument of national regulation under strong political economy pressures to adapt to asymmetric shocks to bank competitiveness and credit availability. Whilst financial structures are converging somewhat, as Chapter 4, there are still some marked differences in the degree of bank reliance and the relative profitability and competitiveness of banks in the Euro Zone. The fact that many aspects of banking still remain domestic will likely keep these considerations relevant for some more time.[102] Thus, whilst policy efforts moving the Euro Zone's financial systems in this direction will likely converge market structures further, in the meantime we will likely see further political economy pressures on national banking regulation that are likely to lead to trade-offs with the pursuit of financial stability. To date, the financial crisis has not triggered real structural changes to financial systems, which would have led to a real integration of banking and all banking related policy matters to the European level. Ultimately, as long as the ECB remains a central bank without 'lender of last resort' capabilities and without a European-level finance ministry to back it up from a fiscal point of view, there will be no European-level regulatory integration. The crisis has shown that at the end of the day, when the national balance sheet has to bear the losses incurred by its national banks, authority runs along national lines. Therefore it is likely to too early to demand full regulatory integration, since the political economy preconditions are not yet met. This is not that surprising, considering that the U.S. took about a century in going from the creation of a national banking charter towards an integrated banking market (Veron, 2011).

On the other hand, as I have shown as well, the costs of national regulation within monetary union can be substantial, raising the following more nuanced question: Short of a regulatory union and full integration of banking policy into the European-level financial stability architecture, what can be done to enhance financial stability? My analysis suggests that even with diverging regulatory preferences, three measures can be taken to enhance regulation and financial stability in the Euro Zone and beyond.

Firstly and most obviously, *international capital adequacy standards*, that is Basel regulations, need to be more stringent with respect to capital adequacy regulation and target *actual leverage* levels of banks. My work and related research have shown that domestic political economy considerations have led domestic regulators to negotiate standards, which make too many exceptions through arbitrary risk-weights and which favoured the universal banking model, excessive securitization, and excessive financing of sovereign debt, and the creative definition of equity capital. As a result,

---

[102] For a similar point of the continued link between national regulation and banking but a slightly different policy recommendation with a view to more integration see Veron (2011). Veron finds that a common banking regulatory policy is a "a necessary condition for the survival of the monetary union".

leverage ratios still varied widely and persistently across countries. The financial crisis has evidenced the plain fact that the equity cushions calculated according to such sophisticated methodologies were simply too low and thus not suitable for inspiring confidence.[103]

Secondly, the conduct of banking supervision can be enhanced through *binding rules that limit the amount of discretion for banking supervisors,* in particular in realms, where political economy pressures are high and are likely to tempt them to be too lax. Differential implementation of the standards have opened the doors for regulatory arbitrage and the infamous race to the bottom. The interplay of internal rating mechanisms and discretionary supervision has moreover tempted regulators to deviate from agreed capital stringency standards. Because regulatory and supervisory decisions can have strong distributional implications and thus can be subjected to too many influences, rules are likely to produce better expectations and beliefs in the credibility of a financial stability regime. [104] Countries should surrender more regulatory and supervisory sovereignty to new European-level institutions such as the European Banking Authority and the European Systemic Risk Board. With the right enforcement capabilities these institutions can then ensure that rules, once agreed, are actually and equally enforced in the face of domestic challenge.

Thirdly, regulators and politicians need to tackle the *structural problems of moral hazard* that affect all large leveraged financial institutions that are allowed to engage in risky business activities. Banks in the presence of deposit insurance are subject to strong problems of moral hazard. I have shown that there are different complementary constellations across different countries that rely on different degrees of regulatory intervention and market discipline, respectively. However, in all different regulatory regimes ranging from the most market-reliance ones (such as the UK) to the most interventionist (such as arguably France or Spain) there have been bank failures and systemic crises. Hence, there is ample evidence that neither reliance on market disciplining forces nor regulatory forbearance alone are likely to deal with the incentive problems of banks. Whilst regulatory reforms are already under way, limitations on bank size and potentially bank risk taking are required to re-establish market discipline that needs to complement regulatory efforts.

In the last area of regulatory reform, we can again see that despite the converging forces of financial integration, variations in financial system configurations still matter for policy-making. The conclusions of expert advisory groups set up in response to the financial crisis seem to re-affirm this point, re-establishing the regulatory traditions of the respective financial systems, which de-regulation seemed to have removed. In the United States Dodd-Frank re-introduced a stricter separation of investment banking and lending activities by establishing the (watered down) Volcker rule, which limits proprietary trading activities by banks. In the United Kingdom the Vickers-

---

103 With Basel III being negotiated against the background of a sovereign debt crisis, there is a real chance that the anxiety over yet another credit crunch will lead regulators to phase higher capital requirements over too long of a time period and will limit leverage ratios at too low levels, thus sowing the seeds of the next phase of financial instability.

104 In this realm the EU has already made some progress as it has put in place European-level institutions in all three financial sectors (in the case of banking the European Banking Authority), which focus on the implementation of rules into national law and practice and are thus limiting the discretion national supervisors.

Commission has introduced the idea of 'ring-fencing' banks speculative activities in the areas of wholesale and investment banking from their retail banking activities. In the higher bank-dependent continent such strong measures have still been absent.

Combined these measures will at least alleviate the political economy pressures on regulators. As Euro Zone countries move more towards variants of shareholder capitalism, higher equity stakes provided by shareholders along with increased market side surveillance are required. Additional limitations on bank size could reduce the likely degree of regulatory capture by virtue of the size of the balance sheet. Moreover, the reversion to a reliance on rules is likely to benefit regulators by limiting their and have stronger shareholder rights, which are however balanced temptations and the political economy pressures to accompany it.

No matter what shape the European financial system will take in the future, financial stability can only result from a re-adjusted and more balanced interplay of economic *and* political incentives. The moral hazard inherent in banking requires a clear role for regulators and unforgiving regulatory boundaries, while the complexities involved in managing risks efficiently leave a clear role for the market and the free enterprise system. This leaves me to rephrase Milton Friedman's famous quote of Clemenceau in the following way: Money is far too serious a matter to be left to *either* bankers or central bankers alone.

Appendix

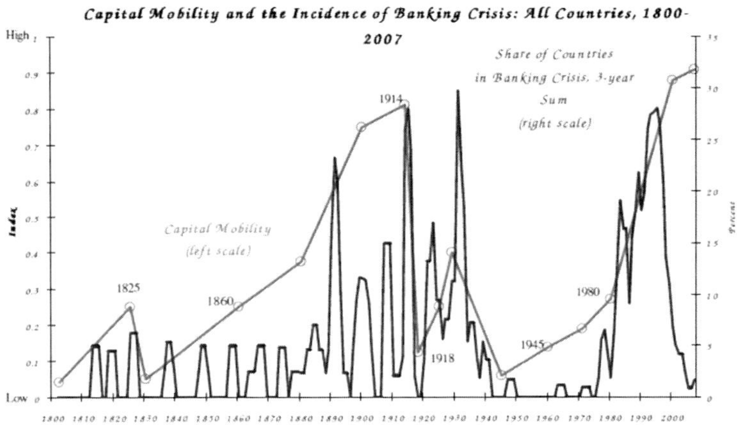

ADDENDUM I: *Incidence of Banking Crises and Rise of Capital Mobility*

Source: Reinhart & Rogoff (2009)

ADDENDUM II: *Banking Crises in European Economies and Their Costs*

Country and Episode	*Description*	*Costs*
Finland 1991 - 94	Savings banking sector badly affected; Government took control of 3 banks that together accounted for 31% of total system deposits	Recap. costs amounted to 11% of GDP
Spain 1977 - 85	1978 - 83: 24 institutions were rescued; 4 were liquidated, 4 were merged and 20 small/medium sized banks (Rumasa Group) were nationalized. In total, 52 out of 110 banks were experiencing solvency problems, representing 20% of total banking system deposits	Estimated losses of banks were equivalent to ~ 16.8% of GNP
Sweden 1991 - 94	Nordbanken and Gota Bank insolvent, accounting for 21.6% of total banking system assets. Sparbanken Foresta intervened, accounting for 24% of total banking system assets. Overall, 5 of 6 largest banks, accounting for over 70% of banking system assets experienced difficulties	Cost of recapitalization amounted to 4% of GDP
Norway 1987 - 93	Central Bank provided special loans to 6 banks, suffering from post-oil recession of 1985 - 86 and from problem real-estate loans; state took control of 3 largest banks (equivalent to 85% of banking system assets, whose loan losses had wiped out capital), partly through a Government Bank Investment Fund (Nkr 5 billion) and the state-backed Bank Insurance Fund had to increase capital to Nkr 11 billion	Recapitalization costs amounted to 8% of GDP

Source: Gerard Caprio, The World Bank "Episodes of Systemic and Borderline Financial Crises", (2003)

ADDENDUM III: *National banking regulators and their financial stability mandates*

Country	*Financial stability mandatesw of national regulatory institution*
Austria	"The main tasks of the OeNB center on contributing to a stability-oriented monetary policy within the Eurosystem, ***safeguarding financial stability in Austria*** and supplying the general public and the business community in Austria with high-quality, i.e. counterfeit-proof, cash. ***"Security, stability and trust"*** encapsulates the guiding principles the Oesterreichische Nationalbank has been committed to in serving Austria and Europe alike."
Belgium	"Apart from monetary stability, maintenance of an ***efficient, high-quality financial system*** is a key objective for any modern central bank." "The challenge lies in ensuring that market forces operate to the full while preventing major disruption of the financial system, which ***would jeopardise all sectors of the economy***."
Finland	"The Bank of Finland's statutory task is to act with a view to maintaining and developing ***stable, reliable and efficient financial and payment systems*** in Finland. The Bank of Finland aims to identify risks to financial stability and contribute to the prevention of financial crises. As a means of achieving these objectives, the central bank conducts refinancing and payment operations, analyses threats to financial stability, including system weaknesses, and participates in systems development. The Bank of Finland cooperates closely with other supervisory and regulatory authorities. Safeguarding the stability of the financial system – ***macroprudential supervision – is thus a shared responsibility***."
France	"The Commission's mission is to ***protect depositors*** as well as to act as watchdog over the French banking and financial system ***to ensure its profitability and financial stability***."
Germany	"…***secure a financially sound banking industry*** and, ultimately, the ***stability of the financial system***." "Its primary objective is to ensure the ***proper functioning, stability and integrity of the German financial system***. Bank customers, insurance policyholders and investors ought to be able to trust the financial system."
Greece	"The Department for the Supervision of Credit and Financial Institutions of the Bank of Greece is responsible for the prudential supervision of credit and financial institutions, with a view to ***ensuring the smooth operation and stability of the Greek financial system***."
Ireland	"The Bank's mandate for financial stability is derived from that of the Eurosystem, which has a clear mandate to ***contribute to financial stability in the Euro Area***. This provides the basis for the Bank's responsibility for financial stability in Ireland and in the Eurosystem. The Bank's responsibility to contribute to the overall stability of the financial system also involves: – stability of the monetary system. The Bank will monitor this as part of its Eurosystem monetary policy function. It will act daily in the markets and deal with day-to-day fluctuations in liquidity; – financial system infrastructure, in particular the payments system.

	The Bank must ensure the smooth operation of the payments system; – overview of the financial system as a whole. The Bank is uniquely placed to do this. Through its involvement in the payments system it may be the first to spot potential problems. The Bank will be able to advise on the implications for financial stability of developments in the domestic and international markets and payments systems and can assess the impact on monetary conditions of events in the financial sector; – undertaking official financial operations in exceptional circumstances in order to limit the risk of problems affecting particular institutions spreading to other parts of the financial system; and – increasing the ***efficiency and effectiveness of the financial sector*** by promoting improvements in its infrastructure.“
Italy	“The Bank of Italy supervises banks and other financial intermediaries having regard to the ***sound and prudent management*** of the persons subject to supervision, to the ***overall stability, efficiency and competitiveness of the financial system and to compliance with provisions concerning credit***.”
Luxembourg	“The CSSF's prudential supervision of companies of the financial sector aims at the following: – ***promoting a considered and prudent business policy*** in compliance with the regulatory requirements – ***protecting the financial stability*** of the supervised companies and of the financial sector as a whole – supervising the quality of the organisation and internal control systems – strengthening the quality of risk management.”
Netherlands	“De Nederlandsche Bank (DNB) works for a reliable ***financial system*** in which institutions meet their obligations.”
Portugal	“Banco de Portugal is responsible for the prudential and market conduct supervision of credit institutions, financial companies and payment institutions with a view to ***ensuring the stability, efficiency and soundness of the financial system, as well as the compliance with rules of conduct and transparency requirements towards bank customers, thereby ensuring the safety of deposits and depositors, and the protection of consumer interests***.”
Spain	“The objective of these functions, which must always be conducted in co-ordination with the Eurosystem, is to ***guarantee secure and efficient financial and payment system***s. ***Financial stability, defined as when monetary and financial systems operate smoothly and efficiently***, assumes that credit institutions distribute the funds received from savers to those customers requesting funds and that bank services are provided to clients normally.”
United Kingdom	“A stable financial system is a key ingredient for a healthy and successful economy. ***People need to have confidence that the system is safe and stable, and functions properly to provide critical services to the wider economy. It is important that problems in particular areas do not lead to disruption across the financial system***.

United Kingdom (cont'd)	The Bank has a statutory objective to ***"contribute to protecting and enhancing the stability of the financial systems of the United Kingdom"***. The Bank does this through its risk assessment and risk reduction work, market intelligence functions, payments systems oversight, banking and market operations, including, in exceptional circumstances by acting as lender of last resort, and resolution work to deal with distressed banks."
United States	"Today, the Federal Reserve's duties fall into four general areas: – conducting the nation's monetary policy by influencing the monetary and credit conditions in the economy in pursuit of maximum employment, stable prices, and moderate long-term interest rates – ***supervising and regulating banking institutions to ensure the safety and soundness of the nation's banking and financial system and to protect the credit rights of consumers*** – ***maintaining the stability of the financial system and containing systemic risk that may arise in financial markets*** – providing financial services to depository institutions, the U.S. government, and foreign official institutions, including playing a major role in operating the nation's payments system"

Source: Author based on national central banks and regulators (accessed March 1st, 2010)

ADDENDUM IV: *Accountability and legal liability of banking regulators in 1999/2000*

Country	*Regulatory Institution*	*Accountable to Parliament?*	*Legally liable?*
Austria	Ministry of Finance	Yes	Yes
Belgium	Banking and Finance Commission	No, to Minister of Finance and Minister of Economic Affairs	Yes
Finland	Financial Supervision Authority	Yes	Yes
France	Commission Bancaire, Banque de France	Yes	Yes
Germany	Federal Banking Supervisory Office	No, to Ministry of Finance	No
Greece	Bank of Greece	Yes	Yes; though no cases so far.
Ireland	Central Bank of Ireland	Not reported	No
Italy	Bank of Italy	No, To the administrative courts	Yes
Luxembourg	Banque Central de Luxembourg/ CSSF	No, to the Minister of Finance	The Executive Board of Directors are liable in case legal actions are taken against the CSSF
Netherlands	De Nederlandsche Bank	Nobody	No
Portugal	Banco de Portugal	No, to depositors	No
Spain	Banco de Espana	No, all administrative decisions of the Banco de Espana can be appealed before the Ministry of Finance (except regulations which are to be appealed before the Courts)	Yes
United Kingdom	Financial Services Authority	No, her Majesty's Treasury	No; unless he or she acted in bad faith
United States	OCC, FDIC, FED, State Governments	No, to Department of Treasury	No

Source: Author based on World Bank data as reproduced in Barth, Caprio, & Levine (2006)

ADDENDUM V: *Regulatory instruments and regulatory objectives (● = primary use of instrument; ○ = secondary (unintended) effects of instrument)*

Type	*Regulatory Instruments*	*Financial stability*	*Profitable and competitive banking system*	*Efficient access to credit*
Activity Restrictions	Asset restrictions	●	○	○
	Restrictions on geogr. reach	○	●	●
	Restrictions on products	●	○	○
	Investment requirements	○	○	●
Com-petition	Antitrust/ competition policy	○	●	●
	Entry restrictions	●	●	○
Con-duct	Conduct of business rules	○	●	●
	Conflict of interest rules	○	●	○
Operatio-nal Requir.	Capital adequacy standards	●	○	○
	Liquidity requirements	●	○	○
	Investment requirements	○	○	●
Interest margin	Interest rate ceilings on deposits	●	○	●
	Interest rate ceilings on loans	○	○	●
Deposits	Deposit insurance	●	○	
Dis-closure	Disclosure requirements	●	○	

Source: Author; part of the instruments adapted from Allen & Herring (2001)

ADDENDUM VI: *Macro-prudential instruments and regulatory objectives (● = primary use of instrument; ○ = secondary (unintended) effects of instrument)*

Type	*Regulatory Instruments*	*Financial stability (micro-/ macro-)*	*Profitable and competitive banking system*	*Efficient access to credit*
Capital adequacy	Time-varying capital requirements	●	○	○
	Higher quality of capital	●	○	○
	Prompt corrective action for capital	●	○	○
	Contingent capital	●	○	○
Liquidity	Debt maturity/ asset liquidity reg.	●	○	○
	FX lending restrictions	●	○	○
Interconnectedness	Concentration limits	●	●	●
	Systemic capital surcharges	●	○	○
	Subsidiarisation	●	○	○

Source: Author based on input from Bank for International Settlements (2010) and Hanson, Kashyap, and Stein (2010)

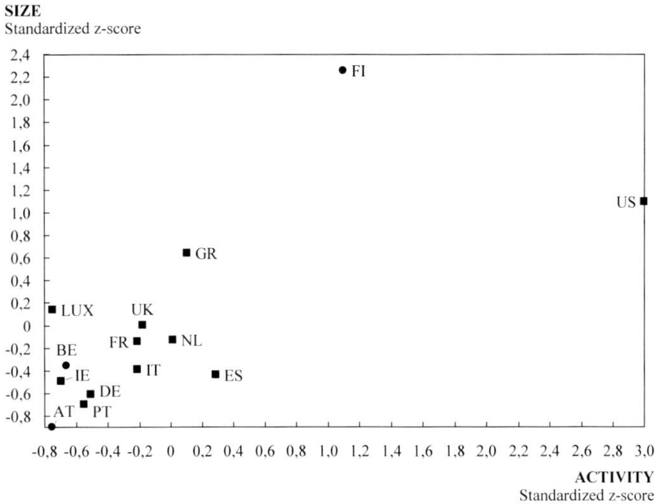

ADDENDUM IX: *Asset and maturity transformation and risk-sharing across financial systems (higher values indicate higher reliance on capital markets relative bank intermediation)*

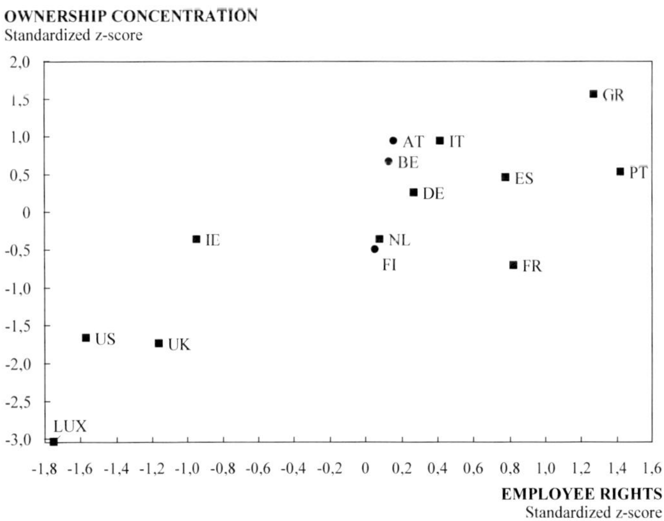

ADDENDUM X: *Corporate governance across financial systems (higher values indicate higher role for insider-based governance by stakeholders and banks or 'Hausbanken' vs. outsider-based governance)*

Source: Author based on data from Levine (2000) and OECD; To ensure comparability of the different variables, a standardization procedure was performed

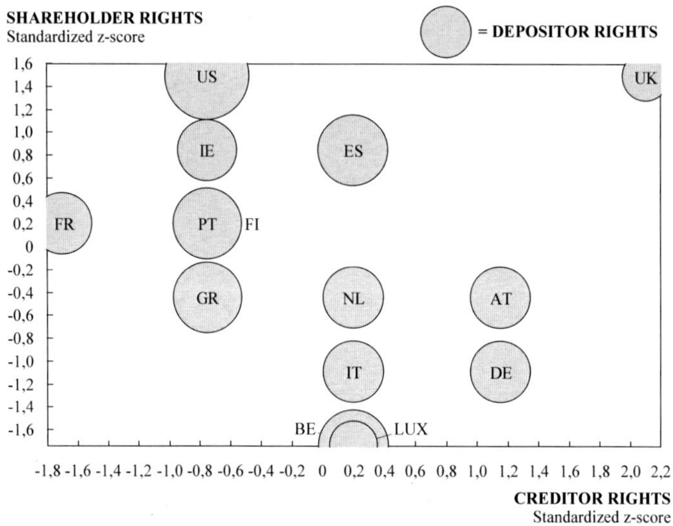

ADDENDUM XI: *Legal institutions across financial systems (higher values indicate higher role for shareholders and creditors, respectively)*

Source: Author based on data from La Porta, Lopez-de-Silanes, Shleifer, and Vishny (1998)

ADDENDUM XII: *Correlation matrix of financial sub-system variables*

Correlations

		Bank-Market-Activity	*Bank-Market-Size*	*Employee rights*	*Ownership concentration*
Bank-Market-Activity	*Correlations according to Pearson*	1	,702**	-,269	-,247
	Significance (2-sided)		,005	,353	,395
	N	14	14	14	14
Bank-Market-Size	*Correlations according to Pearson*	,702**	1	-,233	-,308
	Significance (2-sided)	,005		,423	,284
	N	14	14	14	14
Employee rights	*Correlations according to Pearson*	-,269	-,233	1	,822**
	Significance (2-sided)	,353	,423		,000
	N	14	14	14	14
Ownership concentration	*Correlations according to Pearson*	-,247	-,308	,822**	1
	Significance (2-sided)	,395	,284	,000	
	N	14	14	14	14

**. The correlation is significant at the 0,01 (2-sided) level

Source: Author

ADDENDUM XIII: *Screeplot for financial system clustering*

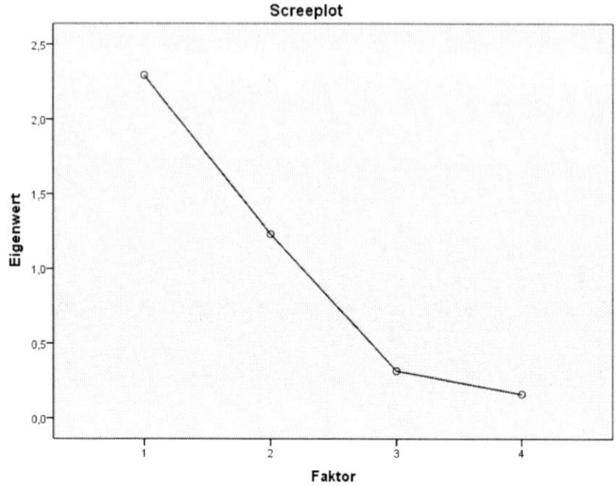

ADDENDUM XIV: *Results of the financial system clustering analysis*

KMO- and Bartlett-Test		
Kaiser-Meyer-Olkin-score		, 531
Bartlett-Test for sphericity	Approximate Chi-Square	21,114
	df	6
	Significance after Bartlett	,002

	Cluster centres of the final solution		
		Cluster	
	Bank-based	*Hybrid*	*Market-based*
Bank-Market-Size	-,3495606837	,0712000075	1,6766034112
Ownership concentr.	,3905833559	-2,3883644402	-1,0846605358
Bank-Market-Activity	-,3167520742	-,4630756432	2,0468360142
Employee rights	,4422809576	-1,4555535422	-,7558512459

	ANOVA					
	Cluster		*Deviations*			
	Average of squares	*df*	*Average of squares*	*df*	*F*	*Sig.*
Bank-Market-Size	3,427	2	,207	11	16,554	,000
Ownership concentr.	7,313	2	,541	11	13,507	,001
Bank-Market-Activity	4,906	2	,290	11	16,923	,000
Employee rights	3,668	2	,515	11	7,124	,010

Source: Author

ADDENDUM XV: *Legal institutions index composition methodology*

	Shareholder rights	*Creditor rights*	*Depositor rights*
Logic	Higher values denote stronger shareholder say	Higher values denote stronger creditor protection	Higher value denote stronger depositor protection
Range of values	0-6	0-4	0-6
Dimensions covered by the index (one point added to the index for each)	1. Proxy voting by mail possible 2. Shareholders not required to deposit shares prior to the General Shareholders'. Meeting 3. Cumulative voting or proportional representation of minorities in the board of directors is allowed 4. Oppressed minorities mechanism is in place 5. Minimum % of share capital that entitles a shareholder to call for an Extraordinary Shareholders'. Meeting is less than or equal to 10 % (the sample median) 6. Shareholders have preemptive rights that can only be waved by a shareholders vote	1. Creditors' consent or minimum dividends to file for reorganization 2. Secured creditors are able to gain possession of their security once the reorganization petition has been approved (no automatic stay) 3. Secured creditors are ranked first in the distribution of the proceeds that result from the disposition of the assets of a bankrupt firm 4. The debtor does not retain the administration of its property pending the resolution of the reorganization	1. Deposit insurance is explicit (vs. implicit) 2. Foreign currencies covered by deposit insurance regime 3. Inter-bank deposits covered 4. No co-insurance, that is no sharing of costs in case of failure with the depositor, is required 5. Payment in case of bank failure is per deposit and not per depositor 6. There is a permanently funded fund for the deposit insurance
Data source	La Porta, Lopez-de-Silanes, Shleifer, and Vishny (1998)		Demirgüç-Kunt, Karacaovali, and Laeven (2001)

Source: Author

ADDENDUM XVI: *Correlation matrix of financial sub-system variables*

		Creditor rights	Depositor rights	Shareholder rights
Correlation	*Creditor rights*	1,000	-,484	-,111
	Depositor rights	-,484	1,000	,321
	Shareholder rights	-,111	,321	1,000
Significance (1-sided)	*Creditor rights*		,040	,353
	Depositor rights	,040		,132
	Shareholder rights	,353	,132	

ADDENDUM XVII: *Screeplot of the legal institution clustering*

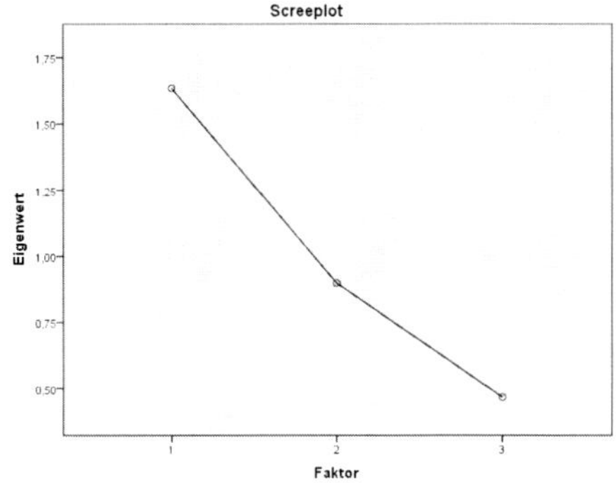

ADDENDUM XVIII: *Results of the legal institutions clustering analysis*

KMO- and Bartlett-Test		
Kaiser-Meyer-Olkin-score		,519
Bartlett-Test for sphericity	*Approximate Chi-Square*	4,217
	df	3
	Significance after Bartlett	,239

Cluster centres of the final solution			
	Cluster		
	1	*2*	*3*
Creditor rights	,521094165913	2,107032931733	-,747656846744
Depositor rights	-,421677068563	-1,405590228544	,562236091417
Shareholder rights	-1,092963922436	1,490405348776	,475510277943

ANOVA						
	Cluster		*Fehler*			
	Mittel der Quadrate	*df*	*Mittel der Quadrate*	*df*	*F*	*Sig.*
Creditor rights	4,991	2	,274	11	18,189	,000
Depositor rights	2,628	2	,704	11	3,732	,058
Shareholder rights	5,378	2	,368	11	14,599	,001

Source: Author

ADDENDUM XIX: *Correlation matrix of financial sub-system and legal institution variables*

		Correlation matrix						
		Bank-Market-Activity	*Bank-Market-Size*	*Employee rights*	*Ownership concentration*	*Creditor rights*	*Depositor rights*	*Shareholder rights*
Correlation	*Bank-Market-Activity*	1,000	,702	-,269	-,247	-,304	,772	,536
	Bank-Market-Size	,702	1,000	-,233	-,308	-,351	,412	,239
	Employee rights	-,269	-,233	1,000	,822	-,277	,142	-,171
	Ownership concentration	-,247	-,308	,822	1,000	-,062	,228	-,208
	Creditor rights	-,304	-,351	-,277	-,062	1,000	-,484	-,111
	Depositor rights	,772	,412	,142	,228	-,484	1,000	,321
	Shareholder rights	,536	,239	-,171	-,208	-,111	,321	1,000
Significance (1-sided)	*Bank-Market-Activity*		,003	,176	,197	,145	,001	,024
	Bank-Market-Size	,003		,212	,142	,109	,071	,205
	Employee rights	,176	,212		,000	,169	,314	,279
	Ownership concentration	,197	,142	,000		,416	,217	,238
	Creditor rights	,145	,109	,169	,416		,040	,353
	Depositor rights	,001	,071	,314	,217	,040		,132
	Shareholder rights	,024	,205	,279	,238	,353	,132	

Source: Author

ADDENDUM XX: *Screeplot of the final financial systems clustering*

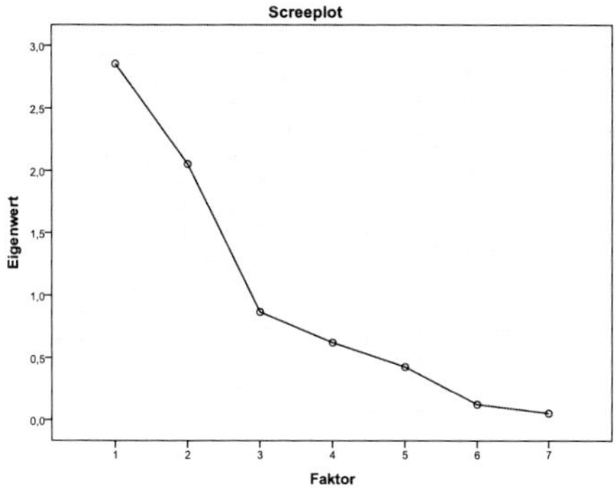

ADDENDUM XXI: *Results of the final financial systems clustering*

KMO- and Bartlett-Test		
Kaiser-Meyer-Olkin-score		,477
Bartlett-Test for sphericity	*Approximate Chi-Square*	46,579
	df	21
	Significance after Bartlett	,001

Cluster centres of the final solution

	Cluster			
	Relationship	*Competitive 'self-regulatory'*	*Arm's length*	*'Stability'-oriented*
Creditor rights	,362500289330	1,155469672241	-,747656846744	-,747656846744
Depositor rights	-,257691541900	-1,405590228544	1,546149251398	,316257801422
Shareholder rights	-,662402377234	-,124200445731	,844563030973	,198720713170
Bank-Market-Activity	-,467686696189	-,463075643222	2,046836014253	-,090350141233
Bank-Market-Size	-,477653130973	,071200007529	1,676603411271	-,157422012941
Employee rights	,020156033227	-1,455553542288	-,755851245995	1,075468344302
Ownership concentration	,344839359328	-2,388364440245	-1,084660535846	,459199350942

	ANOVA					
	Cluster		*Deviations*			
	Average of squares	*df*	*Average of squares*	*df*	*F*	*Sig.*
Creditor rights	2,271	3	,619	10	3,670	,051
Depositor rights	3,177	3	,347	10	9,158	,003
Shareholder rights	1,344	3	1,078	10	1,247	,344
Bank-Market-Activity	3,384	3	,285	10	11,887	,001
Bank-Market-Size	2,367	3	,203	10	11,652	,001
Employee rights	3,336	3	,299	10	11,154	,002
Ownership concentration	4,886	3	,592	10	8,247	,005

Source: Author

ADDENDUM XXII: *Regulatory stringency definition*

	Capital stringency index
Logic	Higher values denote stricter definition of what regulators acknowledge as counting towards regulatory capital
Range of values	0-10
Dimensions covered by the index (one point added to the index for each)	1. Initial disbursements or subsequent injections of capital only with cash and government securities. 2. Initial disbursements of capital not to be done with borrowed funds. 3. Sources of funds used as capital verified by regulator/ supervisor. 4. Minimum ratio varies in line with Basel guidelines. 5. Minimum ratio varies as a function of market risk. 6. Minimum ratio varies as a function of bank's risk. 7. Unrealized foreign exchange losses are deducted. 8. Unrealized securities portfolio losses are deducted. 9. Market value of loan losses not realized in accounting books are deducted. 10. Less than 50% of revaluation gains are allowed to count.
Data source	Barth et al. (2006)

ADDENDUM XXIII: *Banking regulatory institutions for the Euro Zone countries, the United Kingdom, and the United States*

Financial system	*Country*	*Weight within grouping*	*Activities restrictions*	*Delta from weighted average*	*Financial conglom. restrictions*	*Delta from weighted average*	*Capital stringency*	*Delta from weighted average*	*Supervisory stringency/ CAR levels*[a]	*Delta from weighted average*
'Relationship'-finance-regime	*Austria*	2.0%	4	-1.9	5	-1.6	10	3.2	4.7%	-1.6%
	Belgium	2.9%	7	1.1	8	1.4	9	2.2	3.8%	-2.6%
	Germany	18.6%	3	-2.9	4	-2.6	6	-0.8	4.1%	-2.3%
	Ireland	2.1%	6	0.1	7	0.4	6	-0.8	6.6%	0.2%
	Italy	7.3%	7	1.1	5	-1.6	6	-0.8	6.8%	0.5%
	Netherlands	6.7%	4	-1.9	4	-2.6	5	-1.8	3.8%	-2.5%
'Competitive self-regulatory'-regime	*United Kingdom*	7.5%	4	-1.9	7	0.4	7	0.2	5.1%	-1.2%
	Luxembourg	2.3%	4	-1.9	6	-0.6	7	0.2	3.6%	-2.8%
'Arm's-length' finance	*United States*	31.4%	9	3.1	9	2.4	7	0.2	9.1%	2.7%
	Finland	0.6%	5	-0.9	4	-2.6	5	-1.8	10.8%	4.5%
'Interventionist' regime	*France*	12.7%	4	-1.9	7	0.4	7	0.2	4.6%	-1.7%
	Greece	0.0%	7	1.1	6	-0.6	4	-2.8	N/A	N/A
	Portugal	0.8%	6	0.1	8	1.4	5	-1.8	11.8%	5.5%
	Spain	4.9%	6	0.1	5	-1.6	9	2.2	8.3%	1.9%

Source: Author based on data from regulation indexes by Barth, Caprio, and Levine (2006) and capital and reserves data from the OECD (2011) "Bank Profitability" survey

a Capital adequacy here measured as real equity (Tier 1 capital; no regulatory definition) as a share of total assets in 2000

Three steps are required to calculate the regulatory competitiveness score based on the data below to reflect the actual variation in regulatory interactions and decision processes across countries:

Firstly, the respective *financial openness* for each financial system is presented to capture the extent to which a country's regulator is likely to be pre-occupied with comparing her own country's regulatory stringency with other countries. The theory predicts that with increasing financial openness such considerations will start to play a more important role.

Secondly, a table of *financial relationships* between the same countries shows the scale and respective weight of financial exchanges between two financial systems and, thus, the degree to which the banks are likely to compete with each other as well. For this purpose I draw on data from the Bank of International Settlements, capturing the financial liabilities of a country towards another country in the years 2000 on a borrower basis. These values are expressed relative to the total financial liabilities of a country to reflect the relative importance that the financial exposures take for the country's financial system.

Thirdly, a table shows the *regulatory distance* between different countries, which reflects the difference in the respective regulatory stringency between financial systems. This table contains the difference between these countries in the regulatory stringency indexes of the respective regulatory institutions Barth, by Caprio, and Levine (2006) and is calculated from the point of view of the country in the y-column.

ADDENDUM XXIV: *Development of regulatory institutions 1999/2000 – 2005/2006*

	Capital restrictiveness		*Bank activity restrictiveness*		*Conglomerate restrictiveness*	
Country	*1999/2000*	*2005/2006*	*1999/2000*	*2005/2006*	*1999/2000*	*2005/2006*
Austria	10	6	4	5	5	6
Belgium	9	2	7	5	8	4
Finland	5	4	5	7	4	4
France	7	9	4	7	7	6
Germany	6	6	3	5	4	6
Greece	4	4	7	6	6	6
Ireland	6	3	6	5	7	6
Italy	6	4	7	9	5	8
Luxembourg	7	6	4	7	6	8
Netherlands	5	4	4	5	4	5
Portugal	5	8	6	9	8	7
Spain	9	9	6	5	5	6
Average (Euro Zone)	6.6 (6.6)	5.5 (5.4)	5.4 (5.3)	6.1 (6.3)	6.1 (5.8)	6 (6)
United Kingdom	7	6	4	3	7	5
United States	7	6	9	8	9	7

Source: Author based on indexes and data by Barth, Caprio, & Levine (2006)

Bibliography

Acemoglu, D. (2009). Lessons for Economics. *Critical Review*, *21*(2-3), 187-194.

Acharya, V. V. (2009). A theory of systemic risk and design of prudential bank regulation. *Journal of Financial Stability*, *5*(3), 224-255.

Acharya, V. V., & Richardson, M. (2009). Causes of the Financial Crisis. *Critical Review*, *21*(2-3), 195-210.

Acharya, V. V., Pedersen, L., Philippon, T., & Richardson, M. (2010). Measuring systemic risk. *NYU Vlab Website*. Retrieved from http://vlab.stern.nyu.edu/welcome/risk

Admati, A. R., DeMarzo, P. M., Hellwig, M., & Pfleiderer, P. (2010). Fallacies, irrelevant facts, and myths in the discussion of capital regulation: Why bank equity is not expensive. *Policy*. Max Planck Inst. for Research on Collective Goods. Retrieved from http://www.nber.org/public_html/confer/2011/CFs11/Admati.pdf

Adrian, T., & Brunnermeier, M. K. (2008). CoVaR.

Aiyar, S. (2011). How did the crisis in international funding markets affect bank lending? Balance sheet evidence from the UK. *Bank of England Working Paper No . 424*, 1-31.

Aizenman, J., & Pinto, B. (2005). *Managing Economic Volatility and Crises - A Practicioner's Guide*. Cambridge: Cambridge University Press.

Alexander, P. (2011). How lower bank capital requirements could boost the economy. *The Banker*, p. 2.

Allen, F., & Gale, D. (2001). Comparative financial systems: a survey. *Center for Financial Institutions Working Papers*, (April). Wharton School Center for Financial Institutions, University of Pennsylvania. Retrieved from http://ideas.repec.org/p/wop/pennin/01-15.html

Allen, F., & Herring, R. (2001). Banking regulation versus securities market regulation. *The Wharton School University of Pennsylvania - Prepared for the Asian Development Bank Institute/Wharton Financial Institutions Center Conference on Financial Regulation, Securities Markets versus Banks, and Crisis Prevention held July 26-27, 2001*. Retrieved from http://escal.free.fr/docs/finance/bankingregulation.pdf

Alt, J. E., & Shepsle, K. A. (1990). *Perspectives on Positive Political Economy*. Cambridge: Cambridge University Press.

Assenmacher-Wesche, K., & Gerlach, S. (2008). Ensuring financial stability: financial structure and the impact of monetary policy on asset prices. *Working Paper*. Retrieved from http://papers.ssrn.com/sol3/papers.cfm?abstract_id=1114053

Authers, J. (2010). *The fearful rise of markets*. Upper Saddle River, New Jersey: Financial Times Press.

Bacher, J., Pöge, A., & Wenzig, K. (2010). *Clusteranalyse* (3rd ed.). München: Oldenbourg Verlag.

Bagehot, W. (1897). *Lombard Street: A Description of the Money Market*. London: Scribner's.

Baily, M. N., Litan, R. E., & Johnson, M. S. (2008). The Origins of the Financial Crisis. *Business and Policy at Brookings*, (November).

Bank for International Settlements. (2006). *Core Principles for Effective Banking Supervision. Bank for International Settlements*.

Bank for International Settlements. (2010). Macroprudential instruments and frameworks : A stocktaking of issues and experiences. *Report submitted by the Committee on the Global Financial System*, (38).

Bank of England. (2009). The Role of Macroprudential Policy. *Discussion Paper*.

Barro, R., & Gordon, D. (1983). A positive theory of monetary policy in a natural rate model. *The Journal of Political Economy*, *91*(4), 589-610.

Barth, J. R., Caprio, G., & Levine, R. (2006). *Rethinking Banking Regulation: Till Angels Govern*. Cambridge: Cambridge University Press.

Barth, J. R., Caprio, G., & Levine, R. (2008). Bank Regulations Are Changing: For Better or Worse ?

Basinger, S. J., Brook, S., & Hallerberg, M. (2004). Remodeling the Competition for Capital : How Domestic Politics Erases the Race to the Bottom. *American Political Science Review*, *98*(2), 261-276.

Bebchuk, L., & Spamann, H. (2009). Regulating bankers' pay. *Georgetown Law Journal, Vol. 98, No. 2,*. Retrieved from http://papers.ssrn.com/sol3/papers.cfm?abstract_id=1410072

Beck, T. (2008). Bank competition and financial stability: friends or foes? *G20 Seminar on Competition in the Financial Sector in Bali, February 2008*, (February). Retrieved from http://papers.ssrn.com/sol3/papers.cfm?abstract_id=1152483

Beltratti, A. (2009). Why Did Some Banks Perform Better during the Credit Crisis ? A Cross-Country Study of the Impact of Governance and Regulation Why Did Some Banks Perform Better during the Impact of Governance and Regulation. *Money*.

Bernanke, B. S., & Gertler, M. (2000). Monetary policy and asset price volatility. *NBER working paper*.

Bernanke, B., & Blinder, A. S. (1992). The Federal Funds Rate and the Channels of Monetary Transnission. *American Economic Review*, *82*(4), 901-921. Retrieved from http://www.nber.org/papers/w3487

Bernhard, W., Broz, J. L., & Clark, W. R. (2002). The Political Economy of Monetary Institutions. *International Organization*, *56*(4), 693-723.

Bhide, A. (2008). An Accident Waiting to Happen. *Critical Review, 21*(2-3), 211-247.

Bhide, A. (2009). An Accident Waiting to Happen. *Critical Review, 21*(2-3), 211-247.

Bordo, M. D., Eichengreen, B., Klingebiel, D., & Soleadad Martinez-Peria, M. (2001). Is the Crisis Problem Growing More Severe? *Economic Policy, 32*, 51-82.

Borio, C. (2010). Implementing a macroprudential framework: Blending boldness and realism. *Bank for International Settlements*, (July). Retrieved from http://www.bepress.com/cas/vol6/iss1/art1/

Borio, C., & Lowe, P. (2002). Asset prices , financial and monetary stability : exploring the nexus. *BIS Working Papers*, (114).

Borio, C., & Zhu, H. (2009). Capital Regulation , Risk-taking and Monetary Policy: A Missing Link in the Transmission Mechanism? *BIS Working Papers*.

Boyd, J., & Chang, C. (1998). Moral hazard under commercial and universal banking. *Journal of Money, Credit and Banking, 30*(3). Retrieved from http://www.jstor.org/stable/10.2307/2601249

Braithwaite, T., & Jenkins, P. (2011, September 12). JPMorgan chief says bank rules "anti-US." *Financial Times*.

Brewer III, E., Kaufman, G. G., & Wall, L. D. (2008). Bank Capital Ratios Across Countries: Why Do They Vary? *Journal of Financial Services Research, 34*(2-3), 177-201.

Brownlees, C. T., & Engle, R. F. (2010). Volatility, Correlation and Tails for Systemic Risk Measurement. *NYU Stern School of Business Vlab*. Retrieved from http://vlab.stern.nyu.edu/welcome/risk

Brunnermeier, M. K. (2009). Deciphering the liquidity and credit crunch 2007-2008. *Journal of Economic Perspectives, 23*(1), 77-100.

Brunnermeier, M. K., Crockett, A., & Goodhart, C. (2009). The Fundamental Principles of Financial Regulation. *Geneva Reports on the World Economy 11*.

Buiter, W. H. (2007). Lessons from the 2007 financial crisis*. *Paper submitted to the UK Treasury Select Committee*, (November).

CEBS. (2002). *Charter of the Comitiee of European Banking Supervisors*. Retrieved from http://ec.europa.eu/internal_market/bank/ebc/index_en.htm

CNBC. (2011). *"House of Cards" Documentary*.

Calomiris, C. W. (1995). Universal Banking and the Financing of Industrial Development. *World Bank Working Paper 1533*.

Carmassi, J., Gros, D., & Micossi, S. (2009). The Global Financial Crisis: Causes and Cures*. *JCMS: Journal of Common, 47*(5), 977-996.

Caruana, J. (2010). Macroprudential policy : working towards a new consensus. *Remarks at the high-level meeting on "The Emerging Framework for Financial Regulation and Monetary Policy" jointly organised by the BIS's Financial Stability Institute and the IMF Institute*, 1-6.

Casserley, D., Härle, P., & Macdonald, J. (2009). *Should commercial and investment banking be separated?*

Chadha, J. S., & Holly, S. (2011). New Instruments of Monetary Policy. *University of Kent School of Economics Discussion Papers*, (January).

Chandler, A. D. J. (1994). *Scale and Scope* (1st ed.). Cambridge, MA: Harvard University Press.

Chant, J., Lai, A., Illing, M., & Daniel, F. (2003). *Essays on Financial Stability.*

Čihák, M. (2006). Central Banks and Financial Stability: A Survey of Financial Stability Reports. *Paper prepared for a seminar on current developments in monetary and financial law, October 23-27, Washington D.C.*

Cioffi, J. W., & Höpner, M. (2006). The Political Paradox of Finance Capitalism: Interests, Preferences, and Center-Left Party Politics in Corporate Governance Reform. *Politics & Society*, *34*(4), 463-502.

Clarke, T., & Chanlat, J.-F. (Eds.). (2009). *European Corporate Governance: Readings and perspectives*. Abingdon: Routledge.

Copelovitch, M., & Singer, D. A. (2008). Financial Regulation, Monetary Policy, and Inflation in the Industrialized World. *The Journal of Politics*, *70*(3), 663-680.

Crockett, A. (2001). Why is financial stability a goal of public policy? *Handbook of Monetary and Fiscal Policy*, 7-36.

Culpepper, P. D. (2005). Coordinated Financial Systems since 1990. *Journal of Political Economy*, *57*(January), 173-199.

Culpepper, P. D. (2011). *Quiet Politics and Business Power: Corporate Control in Europe and Japan*. Cambridge: Cambridge University Press.

DB Research. (2004). Spain's cajas: deregulated, but not depoliticised.

Davies, H. (2004). Integrated Regulation in the United Kingdom. In J. Carmichael, A. Fleming, & D. Llewellyn (Eds.), *Aligning Financial Supervisory Structures with Country Needs* (pp. 237-255). Washington D.C.: World Bank Institute.

Davies, H. (2010a). Is Regulation Really for Sale? *Project Syndicate*, (December 20th).

Davies, H. (2010b). *Banking on the future: The fall and rise of central banking*. Princeton: Princeton University Press.

Davies, H., & Green, D. (2008). *Global Financial Regulaton*. Cambridge: Polity Press.

De Larosière, J., Balcerowicz, L., Issing, O., Masera, R., McCarthy, C., Nyberg, L., Pérez, J., et al. (2008). Report of the high-level group on financial supervision in the EU. *Brussels: European Commission.*

De la Dehesa, G. (2009). Should the ESCB be the Leading Euro Area Supervisor. *Briefing Paper for the ECON Committee, March (Brussels: European Parliament).*

Deeg, R. (1999). *Finance Capital Unveiled.* Ann Arbor, MI: The University of Michigan Press.

Deeg, R. (2005). Change from Within: German and Italian Finance in the 1990s. In W. Streeck & K. Thelen (Eds.), *Beyond Continuity: Institutional Change in Advanced Political Economies* (1st ed., pp. 169-202). Oxford: Oxford University Press.

Dell'Ariccia, G., & Marquez, R. (2006). Competition among regulators and credit market integration. *Journal of Financial Economics*, *79*(2), 401–430. Elsevier. Retrieved from http://linkinghub.elsevier.com/retrieve/pii/S0304405X05001376

Demirgüç-Kunt, A., Karacaovali, B., & Laeven, L. (2001). Deposit Insurance around the World: A Comprehensive Database. *Policy Research Working Paper, Washington, DC: World Bank.*

Dewatripont, M., & Tirole, J. (1999). *The Prudential Regulation of Banks* (2nd ed.). Cambridge, MA: MIT Press.

Diamond, D. W. (1984). Financial Intermediation and Delegated Monitoring. *Review of Economic Studies*, *51*(3), 393-414.

Diamond, D. W., & Rajan, R. (2009). The credit crisis: Conjectures about causes and remedies. *American Economic Review*, (December).

Economist. (2009). The long climb - A special report on the world economy. *October*, 1-18.

Eichengreen, B, El-Erian, M., Fraga, A., & Ito, T. (2011). Rethinking central banking. *Committee on International Economic Policy and Reform, September.*

Eichengreen, Barry. (2007). Sui generis EMU. *Revision of a paper prepared for the European Commission's workshop "EMU@10: Achievements and Challenges," 27 November 2007.* (pp. 1-43). Retrieved from http://www.nber.org/papers/w13740

Eichengreen, Barry. (2008). *Globalizing Capital* (2nd ed.). Princeton: Princeton University Press.

Eichengreen, Barry, & Rourke, K. H. O. (2009). A Tale of Two Depressions. *Advisor Perspectives.* Retrieved from http://economicforumonline.org/_source/downloads/ataleoftwodepressions.pdf

Eijffinger, S. C. W., & de Haan, J. (1996). The Political Economy of Central-Bank Independence. *Special Papers in International Economics (Princeton University)*, (19).

Elsas, R., & Krahnen, J. P. (2004). Universal Banks and Relationships with Firms. In J. P. Krahnen & R. H. Schmidt (Eds.), *The German Financial System* (pp. 197-232). Oxford: Oxford University Press.

Enderlein, H. (2004). *Nationale Wirtschaftspolitik in der europäischen Währungsunion* (Vol. 49). Frankfurt/ New York: Campus Verlag.

Enderlein, H. (2005). One size fits none. *Central Banking Journal*, 24-28.

Enriques, L., & Volpin, P. (2009). Corporate Governance Reforms in Continental Europe. In T. Clarke & J.-F. Chanlat (Eds.), *European Corporate Governance: Readings and Perspectives* (pp. 253-270). Abingdon: Routledge.

Epstein, G. A. (2005). *Financialization and the World Economy*. Northampton, MA: Edward Elgar Publishing Ltd.

European Central Bank. (2006). *The European Central Bank - History, Role and Functions. Main*. Frankfurt.

European Commission. (2005). Indicators of Financial Integration in the Euro Area. *Report*.

European Commission. (2009a). Economic Crisis in Europe : Causes , Consequences and Responses. *European Economy*, *7*.

European Commission. (2009b). *Proposal for regulation of the European Parliament and of the Council on Community macro prudential oversight of the financial system and establishing a European Systemic Risk Board*. Brussels.

European Commission Internal Market and Services. (2005). Financial Integration Monitor - 2005 - Background Document. *Working Paper*.

Federal Reserve. (2011). *The Federal Reserve System Purposes & Functions* (Vol. 2, p. 146).

Ferguson, R. W. (2002). Should Financial Stability Be An Explicit Central Bank Objective ? *Challenges to Central Banking from Globalized Financial Systems - Conference at the IMF in Washington, D.C., September 16–17, 2002*.

Financial Stability Board. (2011). Peer Review of Spain. *Review Report*, (January).

Fischer, S. (1977). Long-Term Contracts, Rational Expectations, and the Optimal Money Supply Rule. *Journal of Political Economy*, *85*(1), 191. doi:10.1086/260551

Fleming, J. M. (1962). Domestic Financial Policies under Fixed and Floating Exchange Rates. *IMF Staff Papers*, *9*, 369-379.

Fonseca, A. R. (2006). How bank capital buffers vary across countries . The influence of cost of deposits , market power and bank regulation How bank capital buffers vary across countries . The influence of cost of deposits , market power and bank regulation. *Business*.

Frach, L. (2007). *Finanzaufsicht in Deutschland und Großbritannien* (VS Verlag .). Wiesbaden.

Frankel, J. A., & Rockett, K. E. (1988). Macroeconomic Policy Coordination When Policymakers Do Not Agree on the True Model. *The American Economic Review*, *78*(3), 318-340.

Frankfurter Allgemeine Zeitung. (2011, April 12). Finance Watch - Interessenverband als Gegenpol zur Finanzlobby. *Frankfurter Allgemeine Zeitung*. Frankfurt.

Freixas, X., & Rochet, J.-C. (2008). *The Microeconomics of Banking* (2nd ed.). Cambridge, MA: MIT Press.

Frenkel, M., & Rudolf, M. (2010). *Die Auswirkungen der Einführung einer Leverage Ratio als zusätzliche Beschränkung der Geschäftstätigkeiten von Banken* (pp. 1-105). Retrieved from http://posterous.com/getfile/files.posterous.com/temp-2011-10-10/mpDakieqGDyltovAjysoJycerhIrhIqpHbHEyCsFHkdHulAHHdIDJphGnFqt/100503_Gutachten.pdf

Friedman, J. (2009). A Crisis of Politics, Not Economics. *Critical Review*, *21*(2-3), 127-183.

Friedman, M., & Schwartz, A. J. (1963). *A Monetary History of the United States 1867-1960. 1963*. Cambridge, MA: National Bureau of Economic Research.

Gale, D., & Allen, F. (2001a). *Comparing Financial Systems*. Cambridge, MA: MIT Press.

Gale, D., & Allen, F. (2001b). *Comparing Financial Systems*. Cambridge, MA: MIT Press.

Garcia Herrero, A., & del Rio, P. (2005). Central Banks as Monetary Authorities and Financial Stability. In Donato Masciandaro (Ed.), *Handbook of Central Banking and Financial Supervision in Europe2* (pp. 3-24). Northampton, MA: Edward Elgar Publishing Ltd.

Geanakoplos, J. (2010a). Solving the Present Crisis and Managing the Leverage Cycle. *Economic Policy*, (August), 101-131.

Geanakoplos, J. (2010b). Solving the Present Crisis and Managing the Leverage Cycle. *FRBNY Economic Policy Review*, (August), 101-131.

Geanakoplos, J. (2010c). The leverage cycle. *NBER Working Paper*, 1-66.

Gilpin, R. (2001). *Global Political Economy: Understanding the International Economic Order*. Princeton: Princeton University Press.

Global capital markets : Entering a new era. (2009)., (September).

Goodhart, CAE. (2010). The changing role of central banks. *BIS Conference Papers*, 1-35. Retrieved from http://papers.ssrn.com/sol3/papers.cfm?abstract_id=1717776

Goodhart, Charles, & Schoenmaker, D. (1995). Institutional separation between supervisory and monetary agencies. In Charles Goodhart (Ed.), *Oxford Economic Papers*. London: Macmillan.

Goyer, M. (2009). Varieties of Institutional Investors and National Models of Capitalism: The Tranformation of Corporate Governance in France and Germany. In T. Clarke & J.-F. Chanlat (Eds.), *European Corporate Governance: Readings and Perspectives* (pp. 233-252). Abingdon: Routledge.

Guiso, L., Jappelli, T., Padula, M., & Pagano, M. (2004). Financial Market Integration and Economic Growth in the EU. *Paper presented at the 39th Panel Meeting of Economic Policy*, (April).

Hakenes, H., & Schnabel, I. (2006). Bank Size and Risk-Taking under Basel II †. *Supervision*, *49*(88).

Hall, Peter A. (1993). *The Political Power of Economic Ideas: Keynesianism Across Nations*. Princeton: Princeton University Press.

Hall, Peter A, & Soskice, D. (2001). *Varieties of Capitalism: The Institutional Foundations of Comparative Advantage*. (Peter A. Hall & D. Soskice, Eds.) (1st ed.). Oxford: Oxford University Press.

Hall, P.A., & Soskice, D. (2001). An introduction to varieties of capitalism. *Oxford University Press, Oxford*, 1–69.

Hancke, B., Rhodes, M., & Thatcher, M. (2007). Introduction: Beyond Varieties of Capitalism. In B. Hancke, M. Rhodes, & M. Thatcher (Eds.), *Beyond Varieties of Capitalism* (1st ed., pp. 3-38). Oxford: Oxford University Press.

Hanson, S., Kashyap, A., & Stein, J. (2010). A Macroprudential Approach to Financial Regulation. *Paper Prepared for the Journal of Economic Perspectives*, *July*.

Hardie, I., & Howarth, D. (2009). Die Krise but not La Crise ? The Financial Crisis and the Transformation of German and French Banking Systems. *JCMS: Journal of Common Market Studies*, *47*(5), 1017–1039. John Wiley & Sons. Retrieved from http://www3.interscience.wiley.com/journal/122655202/abstract

Hartmann, P., Maddaloni, A., & Manganelli, S. (2003). The euro area financial structure: Structure, integration, and policy initiatives. *European Central Bank Working Paper 230*.

Helleiner, E. (1994). *States and the Re-Emergence of Global Finance*. Ithaca, N.Y.: Cornell University Press.

Helleiner, E., & Pagliari, S. (2010). Crisis and the Reform of International Financial Regulation. In E. Helleiner, S. Pagliari, & H. Zimmermann (Eds.), *Global Finance in Crisis* (pp. 1-18). New York: Routledge.

Hellmann, T., Murdock, K., & Stiglitz, J. E. (1997). Financial restraint: toward a new paradigm. In M. Aoki, H.-K. Kim, & M. Okuno-Fujiwara (Eds.), *The Role of*

Government in East Asian Economic Development (pp. 163-207). Oxford: Clardendon Press.

Hellwig, Martin. (2008). Systemic risk in the financial sector: an analysis of the subprime-mortgage financial crisis. *Reprints of the Max Planck Institute for Research on Collective Goods, 2008/43.*

Hellwig, Martin, & Staub, M. (1996). Panel Discussion - Statements and Comments Capital Requirements for Market Risks Based on Inhouse Models - Aspects of Quality Assessment. *Journal of Economics*, *132*, 755-775.

Herring, R. J. (2007). The Rocky Road to Implementation of Basel II in the United States. *Atlantic Economic Journal*, *35*(4), 411-429. doi:10.1007/s11293-007-9094-6

Hnatkovska, V. (2005). Basics of Volatility (Technical Appendix). In J. Aizenman & B. Pinto (Eds.), *Managing Economic Volatility and Crises - A Practicioner's Guide* (pp. 521-565). Cambridge: Cambridge University Press.

Hodson, D., & Mabbett, D. (2009). UK Economic Policy and the Global Financial Crisis : Paradigm Lost ?*, *47*(5), 1041-1061.

House of Commons Treasury Committee. (2009). *Banking Crisis: regulation and supervision - Fourteenth Report of Session 2008–09 (Report, together with formal minutes, oral and written evidence). House of Commons Treasury Committee.*

House of Lords Economic Affairs Committee. (2009). *Second Report on Banking Supervision and Regulation.*

Howells, P., & Bain, K. (2008). *The Economics of Money, Banking, and Finance* (4th ed.). Essex: Person Education Limited.

Hönighaus, R. (2010). EU verzweifelt an Finanzindustrie - Parlamentarier fordern Gegenstimmen zur Bankenlobby. *Financial Times Deutschland*. Brussels.

Höpner, M., & Krempel, L. (2004). The Politics of the German Company Network. *Change*, *8*(4), 339-356.

Igal, J. Y. (2006). Country in Focus: The Spanish housing market: are we in for a soft landing? *Ecfin Country Focus*, *3*(1).

Ioannidou, V. P. (2005). Does monetary policy affect the central bank ' s role in bank supervision ? *Journal of Financial Intermediation*, *14*, 58-85.

Issing, Otmar. (2003). Monetary and financial stability: Is there a trade-off? *BIS Papers*, *18*, 16–23.

Iversen, T. (1998). Wage bargaining, central bank independence, and the real effects of money. *International Organization*, *52*(03), 469–504. Cambridge Univ Press.

Iversen, Torben. (2005). *Capitalism, Democracy, and Welfare* (1st ed.). Cambridge: Cambridge University Press.

Jackson, J. K. (2009). The Financial Crisis : Impact on and Response by The European Union. *CRS Report for Congress*, *7-5700*.

Jappelli, T., & Pagano, M. (2008). Financial market integration under EMU. *CSEF Working Paper No. 197*, (April). European Commission. Directorate-General for Economic and Financial Affairs. Retrieved from http://papers.ssrn.com/sol3/ papers.cfm?abstract_id =1344670

Kapstein, Ethan B. (1994). *Governing the Global Economy*. Cambridge, MA: Harvard University Press.

Kapstein, E.B. (1989). Resolving the regulator's dilemma. *International Organization*, *43*(02), 323–347. Cambridge Univ Press. Retrieved from http://journals.cambridge.org/abstract_S0020818300032938

Kapstein, Ethan B. (1992). Between power and purpose: central bankers and the politics of regulatory convergence. *International Organization*, *46*(1), 265-287.

Kashyap, A. K., & Stein, J. C. (2002). *The role of banks in monetary policy: A survey with implications for the European monetary union. Economic Perspectives* (pp. 2-18).

Kashyap, A., & Stein, J. C. (1994). The impact of monetary policy on bank balance sheets. *NBER Working Papers 4821*.

Kentaro, T. (2003). A Regulator ' s Dilemma and Two-level Games : Japan in the Politics of International Banking Regulation. *Social Science Japan Journal*, *6*(2), 221-240.

Keohane, Robert O, & Nye, J. (1977). *Power and Interdependence: World Politics in Transition*. New York: Little, Brown and Company.

Keohane, R.O., & Nye, J. S. (1997). Interdependence in World Politics. In G. T. Crane & A. Amawi (Eds.), *The Theoretical evolution of international political economy: a reader*. New York: Oxford University Press.

Kindleberger, C. P., & Aliber, R. Z. (2005). *Manias, panics, and crashes* (5th ed.). New York: Palgrave Macmillan.

Klein, D. B., & O'Flaherty, B. (1993). Commitment and Time Consistency: A Game-Theoretic Discussion. *Working Paper*. Retrieved from http://papers.ssrn.com/ sol3/papers.cfm?abstract_id=485214

Krahnen, J. P., & Elsas, R. (2002). Collateral, relationship lending, and financial distress: An empirical study on financial contracting. *Goethe-Universität Frankfurt Working Paper*.

Krahnen, J. P., & Schmidt, R. H. (2004). *The German Financial System*. Oxford: Oxford University Press.

Kroszner, R. S., & Strahan, P. E. (2001). Obstacles to Optimal Policy: The Interplay of Politics and Economics in Shaping Bank Supervision and Regulation Reforms. In F. S. Mishkin (Ed.), *Prudential Supervision - What Works and What Doesn't* (pp. 233-273). Chicago: Chicago University Press.

La Porta, R., Lopez-de-Silanes, F., Shleifer, A., & Vishny, R. W. (1998). Law and Finance. *Journal of Political Economy*, *116*, 1113-1155.

Labaton, S. (1999). Congress passes wide-ranging bill easing bank laws. *The New York Times*. New York. Retrieved from http://www.nytimes.com/1999/11/05/business/congress-passes-wide-ranging-bill-easing-bank-laws.html

Lake, D. A. (2006). International Political Economy: A Maturing Discipline. In Barry R. Weingast & D. A. Wittman (Eds.), *Oxford Handbook on Political Economy* (1st ed., pp. 757-777). Oxford: Oxford University Press.

Lane, C. (2009). Changes in Corporate Governance of German Corporations: Convergence to the Anglo-American Model? In T. Clarke & J.-F. Chanlet (Eds.), *European Corporate Governance: Readings and Perspectives* (pp. 157-173). Abingdon: Routledge.

Lane, P. R. (2010). The Irish Crisis. *IIIS Discussion Paper No. 356*.

Levine, R. (2000). Bank-Based or Market-Based Financial Systems : Which is Better ?

Levine, R. (2010). The governance of financial regulation: reform lessons from the recent crisis. *International Review of Finance*, (329). Retrieved from http://onlinelibrary.wiley.com/doi/10.1111/j.1468-2443.2011.01133.x/full

Llewellyn, D. T. (2004). Institutional Structure of Financial Regulation and Supervision. In D. T. Llewellyn, A. Fleming, & J. Carmichael (Eds.), *Aligning Financial Supervisory Structures with Country Needs* (pp. 17-92). Washington D.C.: World Bank Institute.

Llewellyn, D. T. (2005). Integrated Agencies and the Role of the Central Banks. In Donato Masciandaro (Ed.), *Handbook of Central Banking and Financial Supervision in Europe* (pp. 109-140). Northampton, MA: Edward Elgar Publishing Ltd.

Lucas, Robert E., Jr. Sargent, T. J. (1980). *Rational Expectations and Econometric Pratice.* (University.). Minneapolis, MN.

Lütz, S. (2002). *Der Staat und die Globalisierung von Finanzmärkten*. Frankfurt/ New York: Campus Verlag. Retrieved from http://www.mpifg.de/pu/mpifg_book/mpifg_bd_43.pdf

Lutz, S. (2003). Convergence within National Diversity : A Comparative Perspective on the Regulatory State in Finance. *MPIfG Discussion Paper*, (07).

Macey, J. R. (1993). The Inevitability of Universal Banking. *Faculty Scholarship Series. Paper 1654.*

Maclennan, D., Muellbauer, J., & Stephens, M. (1998). Asymmetries in housing and financial market institutions and EMU. *Oxford Review of Economic Policy*, *14*(3), 54-80. doi:10.1093/oxrep/14.3.54

Malzubris, J. (2008). *Country in Focus: Ireland's housing market: bubble trouble.*

Masciandaro, D. (2007). Divide et impera: Financial supervision unification and central bank fragmentation effect. *European Journal of Political Economy*, *23*(2), 285-315.

Masciandaro, D, Quintyn, M., & Taylor, M. (2008). Inside and outside the central bank: Independence and accountability in financial supervision Trends and determinants. *European Journal of Political Economy*, *24*(4), 833-848. Elsevier B.V.

Masciandaro, Donato. (2004). Central Banks or Single Financial Authorities? A Political Economy Approach. *SSRN Electronic Journal*, 2-61. doi:10.2139/ssrn.493522

Masciandaro, Donato. (2005). Central Banks and Single Financial Authorities: Economics, Politics, and Law. In Donato Masciandaro (Ed.), *Handbook of Central Banking and Financial Supervision in Europe* (pp. 67-108). Northampton, MA: Edward Elgar Publishing Ltd.

Matutes, C., & Vives, X. (2000). Imperfect competition , risk taking , and regulation in banking. *European Economic Review*, *44*, 1-34.

McKinsey & Company. (2008). *London: Wining in a Changing World: Review of the Competitiveness of London's Financial Centre*. London.

McKinsey Global Insitute. (2010). *Debt and deleveraging : The global credit bubble and its economic consequences*.

Merrouche, O., & Nier, E. (2010). What Caused the Global Financial Crisis ?– Evidence on the Drivers of Financial Imbalances 1999-2007 ¤. *IMF Working Papers*.

Merton, R., & Bodie, Z. (2005). Design of Financial Systems: Towards a Synthesis of Function and Structure. *Journal of Investment Management*, (May 2002), 1-44.

Mian, A., Sufi, A., & Trebbi, F. (2011). The Political Economy of the Subprime Mortgage Credit Expansion, (February).

Mishkin, F. S. (2001). Prudential Supervision: Why Is It Important and What Are the Issues? In F. S. Mishkin (Ed.), *Prudential Supervision - What Works and What Doesn't* (pp. 1-30). Chicago: Chicago University Press.

Morin, F. (2009). A Transformation in the French Model of Shareholding and Management. In T. Clarke & J.-F. Chanlat (Eds.), *European Corporate Governance: Readings and Perspectives2* (pp. 110-123). Oxford: Routledge.

Mosley, L. (2003). *Global Capital and National Governments*. Cambridge: University of Cambridge Press.

Mosley, L., & Singer, D. A. (2009). The Global Financial Crisis: Lessons and Opportunities for International Political Economy. *International Interactions*, *35*(4), 420–429. Routledge. Retrieved from http://www.informaworld.com/index/917056978.pdf

Mundell, R. A. (1962). Capital Mobility and Stabilization Policy under Fixed and Flexible Exchange Rates. *Canadian Journal of Economic and Political Science*, *29*, 475-485.

Mundell, R. A. (2007). A Theory of Optimum Currency Areas. *The American Economic Review*, *51*(4), 657-665.

Murdock, K. C., Stiglitz, J. E., & Hellmann, T. F. (2000). Moral Hazard in Banking, and Prudential Regulation: Are Capital Requirements Enough? *The American Economic Review*, *90*(1), 147-165.

Nier, E. W. (2009). Financial Stability Frameworks and the Role of Central Banks: Lessons from the Crisis. *IMF Working Papers*, *09/70*.

Noia, C. D., & Giorgio, G. D. (1999). Should Banking Supervision and Monetary Policy Tasks Be Given to Different Agencies? *International Finance*, *2*(3), 361–378.

North, D. C., & Weingast, B. R. (1989). Constitutions and commitment: the evolution of institutions governing public choice in seventeenth-century England. *The journal of economic history*, *49*(04), 803–832. Cambridge Univ Press. Retrieved from http://journals.cambridge.org/abstract_S0022050700009451

Olson, M. (1965). *The logic of collective action: public goods and the theory of groups*. Cambridge, MA: Harvard University Press.

Oosterloo, S., & de Haan, J. (2005). The Role of Central Banks in Fostering Financial Stability. In Donato Masciandaro (Ed.), *Handbook of Central Banking and Financial Supervision in Europe* (pp. 25-66). Northampton, MA: Edward Elgar Publishing Ltd.

Orphanides, A. (2007). Taylor Rules. *Federal Reserve Board Finance and Economics Discussion Series*, (18).

O'Reilly, L. (2004). The New Structure of Financial Regulation in Ireland. In J. Carmichael, A. Fleming, & D. Llewellyn (Eds.), *Aligning Financial Supervisory Structures with Country Needs* (pp. 129-147). Washington D.C.: World Bank Institute.

Padoa-Schippoa, T. (2002). Central Banks and Financial Stability: Exploring a Land In-Between. In V. Gaspar, P. Hartmann, & O. Sleijpen (Eds.), *The Transformation of the European Financial System* (pp. 269-328). Frankfurt: European Central Bank.

Pagano, M. (2001). The political economy of finance. *Oxford Review of Economic Policy*, *17*(4), 502–519. Oxford Univ Press. Retrieved from http://oxrep.oxfordjournals.org/content/17/4/502.short

Pagano, M., & Volpin, P. (2001). The political economy of finance. *Paper prepared for the Oxford Review of Economic Policy*.

Peltzman, S. (1993). George Stigler's Contribution to the Economic Analysis of Regulation. *The Journal of Political Economy*, *101*(5), 818–832. JSTOR. Retrieved from http://www.jstor.org/stable/10.2307/2138597

Perez, S. (1998). Systemic Explanations, Divergent Outcomes: The Politics of FinancialLiberalization in France and Spain. *International Studies Quarterly*, *42*(4), 755-784. Retrieved from http://onlinelibrary.wiley.com/doi/10.1111/0020-8833.00105/abstract

Perotti, E., & von Thadden, E.-L. (2003). The political economy of bank and market dominance. *ECGI Working Paper Series in Finance*, *23*(September).

Persson, T. (1987). Credibility of macroeconomic policy: An introduction and a broad survey. *Rochester Center for Economic Research, Working Paper No. 107*, (107). Retrieved from http://swepub.kb.se/bib/swepub:oai:DiVA.org:su-41573?tab2 =abs&amp ;language =en

Persson, Torsten, & Tabellini, G. (2002). *Political Economics: Explaining Economic Policy* (1st ed.). Cambridge, MA: MIT Press.

Phelps, E. S., & Taylor, J. B. (1977). Stabilizing Powers of Monetary Policy under Rational Expectations. *Journal of Political Economy*, *85*(1), 163. doi:10.1086/260550

Pinho, P. (2009). Determinants of Portuguese Bank's Provisioning Policies: Discretionary Behavior of Generic and Specific Allowances. *Journal of Money, Investment and Banking*, *10*(10).

Plümper, T., Troeger, V. E., & Winner, H. (2009). Why is There No Race to the Bottom in Capital Taxation? *International Studies Quarterly*, *53*(3), 761–786.

Posner, E. (2009). *The Origins of Europe's New Stock Markets*. Harvard University Press.

Posner, E. (2010). European Approach to Financial Regulation. In E. Helleiner, S. Pagliari, & H. Zimmermann (Eds.), *Global Finance in Crisis2* (pp. 108-120). New York: Routledge.

Prati, A., & Schinasi, G. J. (1999). Financial stability in European economic and monetary union. *Princeton Studies in International Finance*, (86).

Quaglia, L. (2007). Committee Governance in the Financial Sector in the European Union. *Sussix European Institute Working Paper*, *96*.

Quaglia, L. (2008). *Central Banking Governance in the European Union - A Comparative Analysis*. London: Routledge.

Quaglia, L. (2009). The'British Plan'as a Pace-Setter: The Europeanization of Banking Rescue Plans in the EU?*. *JCMS: Journal of Common Market Studies*, *47*(5), 1063-1083.

Quaglia, L. (2010). *Governing Financial Services in the European Union: Banking, Securities, and Post-Trading* (1st ed., p. 196). New York: Routledge.

Rajan, R. (2001). Financial Systems, Industrial Structure, and Growth. *Oxford Review of Economic Policy*, *17*(4), 467-482. doi:10.1093/oxrep/17.4.467

Rajan, R. (2010). *Fault Lines*. Princeton: Princeton University Press.

Rajan, R. G. (1998). Do we still need commercial banks?

Rajan, R. G. (2005). Has Financial Development Made the World Riskier? *NBER working paper 11728, November*.

Rajan, R. G., & Zingales, L. (2002). Banks and Markets: The Changing Character of European Finance. In V. Gaspar, P. Hartmann, & O. Sleijpen (Eds.), *The Transformation of the European Financial System2* (pp. 123-184). Frankfurt: European Central Bank.

Rajan, R., & Zingales, L. (2003). *Savings Capitalism from the Capitalists: Unleashing the Power of Financial Markets to Create Wealth and Spread Opportunity*. New York: Crown Business.

Rajan, R., Zingales, L., & Economic, N. B. O. (2000). The great reversals: The politics of financial development in the 20th century. *Development*, (July 2000). Retrieved from http://papers.ssrn.com/sol3/Delivery.cfm/nber_w8178.pdf?abstractid=264433&mirid=1

Regling, K., & Watson, M. (2010). A Preliminary Report on The Sources of Ireland 's Banking Crisis, 1-49.

Reinhart, C. M., & Rogoff, K. S. (2009). *This Time is Different*. Princeton: Princeton University Press.

Rogoff, K. (1985). The optimal degree of commitment to an intermediate monetary target. *The Quarterly Journal of Economics, (November).*

Rosenbluth, F., & Schaap, R. (2003). The domestic politics of banking regulation. *International Organization*, *57*(2), 307-336.

Ross, S. A., Westerfield, R. W., & Jaffe, J. F. (2002). *Corporate Finance* (6th ed.). McGraw Hill.

Saurina, J. (2009). Dynamic Provisioning - The Experience of Spain. *Crisis Response - Public Policy for the Private Sector*, (July).

Scharpf, F. W. (1997). *Games Real Actors Play: Actor-Centered Institutionalism in Policy Research*. Boulder, Colo.: Westview Press.

Schinasi, G. J. (2004). Defining financial stability. *IMF Working Papers*, *14/187*.

Schmidt, R. H. (1999). Differences between financial systems in European countries: consequences for EMU. *Paper prepared for the Conference on "The Monetary Transmission Process", organised by the Deutsche Bundesbank, in Frankfurt/M., March 26./27. 1999.* Univ., Fachbereich Wirtschaftswiss. Retrieved from http://www.wiwi.uni-frankfurt.de/schwerpunkte/finance/wp/550.pdf

Schmidt, R. H., & Tyrell, M. (2001). Pension Systems and Financial Systems in Europe: A Comparison from the Point of View of Complementarity. *University of Frankfurt Working Paper Series: Finance & Accounting*, (65a). Retrieved from http://en.scientificcommons.org/1011213

Schmidt, R. H., & Tyrell, M. (2003). What constitutes a financial system in general and the German financial system in particular. *University of Frankfurt Working Paper Series: Finance & AccountingWorking Paper Series*, (111).

Schmidt, V. A. (2000). Still Three Models of Capitalism? The Dynamics of Economic Adjustment in Britain, Germany, and France. In S. Lütz & R. Czada (Eds.), *Die Politische Konstitution von Märkten* (pp. 38-72). Wiesbaden: Westdeutscher Verlag.

Schoenmaker, D., & Goodhart, C. (1992). Institutional Separation between Supervisory and Monetary Agencies. *FMG Special Papers*.

Schoenmaker, D., & Oosterloo, S. (2008). Financial Supervision in Europe: A Proposal for a New Architecture. *Building the Financial Foundations of the Euro-Experiences and Challenges, London: Routledge* (pp. 337–354). Retrieved from http://staff.feweb.vu.nl/dschoenmaker/Chapter 15 Financial Supervision final version Jan 31.pdf

Schüler, M. (2003a). Incentive Problems in Banking Supervision-The European Case. *ZEW Discussion Paper*, (03-62).

Schüler, M. (2003b). How Do Banking Supervisors Deal with Europe-wide Systemic Risk? *ZEW Discussion Paper*, (03-03).

Simmons, B. A. (2001). The International Politics of Harmonization: The Case of Capital Market Regulation. *International Organization*, *55*(3), 589-620. doi:10.1162/00208180152507560

Simmons, B. A., Dobbin, F., & Garrett, G. (2007). The Global Diffusion of Public Policies: Social Construction, Coercion, Competition or Learning? *Annual Review of Sociology*, (33), 449-472.

Singer, D. A. (2004). Capital Rules: The Domestic Politics of International Regulatory Harmonization. *International Organization*, *58*(3), 531-65.

Singer, D. A. (2007). *Regulating Capital - Setting Standards for the International Financial System*. New York: Cornell University Press.

Singer, D. A. (2010). The US regulatory response. In E. Helleiner, S. Pagliari, & H. Zimmermann (Eds.), *Global Finance in Crisis* (pp. 93-107). New York: Routledge.

Sinn, H. W. (2004). The new systems competition. *Perspektiven der Wirtschaftspolitik*, *5*(1), 23–38.WileyOnlineLibrary.Retrieved from http://onlinelibrary.wiley.com/doi/10.1111/j.1468-2516.2004.00125.x/abstract

Sinn, H.-W. (2010). *Kasino Kapitalismus - Wie es zur Finanzkrise kam, und was jetzt zu tun ist* (1st ed.). Berlin: Ullstein Verlag.

Stigler, G. J. (1962). What Can Regulators Regulate? The Case of Electricity. *Journal of Law and Economics*, *5*, 1-16.

Stiglitz, J. E. (2000). *Economics of the Public Sector* (3rd ed.). W. W. Norton & Company.

Stolz, S. (2002). Banking Supervision in Integrated Financial Markets: Implications for the EU. *CESifo Working Paper no. 812*.

Strange, S. (1988). *States and Markets* (1st ed.). London: Pinter.

Streeck, W. (2003). Taking uncertainty seriously: complementarity as a moving target. *The Transformation of the European Financial System - Proceedings of OeNB Worksjops*, (1). Retrieved from http://www.nationalbank.at/de/img/workshop_no1_1__tcm14-8224.pdf#page=101

Streeck, W., & Thelen, K. (2009). Institutional Change in Advanced Political Economies. In B. Hancke (Ed.), *Debating Varieties of Capitalism - A Reader* (pp. 95-134). Oxford: Oxford University Press.

Tagesspiegel. (2010, August). Die Ohnmächtigen im Europaparlament. *Tagesspiegel*. Berlin.

Taylor, J. B. (2008). The Financial Crisis and the Policy Responses : An Empirical Analysis of What Went Wrong. *Bank of Canada - Festschrift in Honour of David Dodge*, (November), 1-18.

Tinbergen, J. (1952). *On the theory of economic policy*. Amsterdam: North Holland.

Verdier, D. (2001). Capital Mobility and the Origins of Stock Markets. *International Organization*, 327-356.

Veron, N. (2011). *Euro area banks must be freed from national capitals* (pp. 1-2).

Vitols, S. (2004). Changes in Germany's Bank-Based Financial System: A Varieties of Capitalism Perspective.

Vives, X. (2001). Restructuring Financial Regulation in the European Monetary Union. *Journal of Financial Services Research*, 57-82.

Viñals, J., Fiechter, J., Kumhof, M., Laxton, D., & Muir, D. (2010). The Making of Good Supervision: Learning to Say "No." *IMF Staff Position Note;* Retrieved from http://www.iadb.org/intal/intalcdi/integ/integ1B.asp?sub_base=TESAURO&az=1&desc=FONDOMONETARIOINTERNACIONAL,FMI&orden=anioD&desc_tipo=and&origen=A

Wallison, P. J. (2009). Cause and Effect: Government Policies and the Financial Crisis. *Critical Review*, *21*(2-3), 365-399.

Walsh, C. E. (2003). *Monetary Theory and Policy* (2nd ed., pp. 1-40). Massachussetts: MIT Press.

Walter, A., & Sen, G. (2009). *Analyzing the Global Political Economy* (1st ed.). Princeton: Princeton University Press.

Ware, D. (1996). Basic Principles of Banking Supervision. *Handbooks in Central Banking (Bank of England)*, (7).

Weingast, Barry R., & Wittman, D. A. (2006). The Reach of Political Economy. In Barry R. Weingast & D. A. Wittman (Eds.), *The Oxford Handbook of Political Economy* (1st ed., pp. 3-25). Oxford: Oxford University Press.

White, L. J. (2009). The Credit-Rating Agencies and the Subprime-Debacle. *Critical Review*, *21*(2-3), 389-399.

Ysa, T., Giné, M., Esteve, M., & Sierra, V. (2010). The effects of the crisis on the Spanish banking system: Do Spanish cajas need a corporate governance makeover? *Working Paper*.

Zimmermann, Herbert. (2010). British and German approaches to financial regulation. In E. Helleiner, S. Pagliari, & H. Zimmermann (Eds.), *Global Finance in Crisis* (pp. 121-136). New York: Routledge.

MIX
Papier aus verantwortungsvollen Quellen
Paper from responsible sources
FSC® C105338

Printed by Books on Demand, Germany